From **SCHOOL PROGRAM** to **SCHOOL PLANT**

A Discussion of Problems
of Planning School Buildings

JOHN H. HERRICK
Head, School Plant Division,
Bureau of Educational Research,
Ohio State University

RALPH D. McLEARY
Superintendent of Schools,
Jackson, Michigan

WILFRED F. CLAPP
Assistant Superintendent,
School Organization and Plant,
Michigan Department of Public Instruction

WALTER F. BOGNER
Architect, Cambridge, Mass., and
Professor of Architecture, Harvard University

Henry Holt and Company · New York

23584–0116

Printed in the United States of America

To Mabel, Isabelle,

Dorothy, and Edith

PREFACE

THE Secretary of the Board of the Commissioners of the Common Schools of Connecticut, in his first annual report (1838–1839), spoke of the schoolhousing problem in these words:

> In the whole field of school improvement there is no more pressing need of immediate action than here. I present with much hesitation, the result of my examinations as to several hundred schoolhouses in different parts of the State. I will say, generally, that the location of the schoolhouse, instead of being retired, shaded, healthy, attractive, is in some cases decidedly unhealthy, exposed freely to the sun and storm, and in nearly all, on one or more public streets, where the passing of objects, the noise and the dust, are a perpetual annoyance to teacher and scholar,—that no play-ground is afforded for the scholar except the highway,—that the size is too small for even the *average* attendance of the scholars,—that not one in a hundred has any other provision for a constant supply of that indispensible element of health and life, pure air, except the rents and crevices which time and wanton mischief have made; that the seats and desks are not, in a majority of cases, adapted to children of different sizes and ages, but on the other hand are calculated to induce physical deformity, and ill-health, and not in a few instances (I state this on the authority of physicians who were professionally acquainted with the cases,) have actually resulted in this—and that in the mode of warming rooms, sufficient regard is not had either to the comfort and health of the scholar, or to economy.[1]

1. Quoted in Barnard, Henry, *School Architecture; or Contributions to the Improvement of Schoolhouses in the United States,* Cincinnati: H. W. Derby & Co., 1854, pp. 16–17.

The same kinds of problems confront us today, even though school-houses have been greatly improved. Many sites are too small, many buildings poorly located and inadequately equipped for today's needs. Over-crowding is serious and increasing. Many buildings are unsanitary or are otherwise hazardous to the pupils and others who use them. Instruction and other phases of the school program are often seriously restricted by inappropriate buildings.

These are conditions which will be expensive for the taxpayers of America to correct. But we cannot afford not to correct them. An educated citizenry is essential to the survival and improvement of our democratic institutions and to our economic well-being as well. More and better schoolhousing is only one, but an important one, of the required elements in the development of more effective public education.

It is clear to all who know the present situation that there must be a vast amount of schoolhouse construction for some years to come. Since the building facilities often shape the school program, the manner in which this problem is met today will determine to a significant degree the education of thousands of children well into the twenty-first century. It behooves us, therefore, to do the job well and with an eye to the needs of the future.

The current schoolhousing problems cannot be solved by boards of education, or superintendents of schools, or architects, or school-plant specialists alone. There are no magic fountains from which will flow the needed foresight and ingenuity, let alone the money, to do the job that is necessary. Effective solution of the problem requires clear understanding and intelligent participation by laymen, architects, and professional educators alike—by teachers and custodians and school cooks and the man in the street as well as by superintendents of schools and members of boards of education.

No one publication can serve the needs of so diverse a group. In writing the present volume, the authors have had in mind graduate students in educational administration, practicing school administrators, and school-plant consultants as the principal readers. They aim to give these persons a basic understanding of the goals to be achieved and of the problems to be employed in planning, an appreciation of the role that architects and other designers play, and a basis upon which they can reach decisions and give approvals as required.

For the architect and other designers, or prospective practioners in these fields, the major purpose is to clarify their role in the larger educational setting. An effort is made to strengthen the case for thorough educational planning and at the same time to support excellent practices in architecture and design.

It is hoped that the book will be of practical value to both the educational administrator and the designer in their respective fields, but it is not intended as a "do-it-yourself" manual to help either one, or the layman, to do the work of an experienced professional outside his own field. Rather, it should awaken in all an increased awareness of the need for professional guidance and competent assistance in the various specialized aspects of school-plant planning.

In preparing this book, the authors have drawn from their experiences such materials as seem to them most likely to be useful in understanding the scope and complexity of the problems involved. The text points occasionally to examples of the wrong approach to the building of schools and begins with a statement on the consequences of hasty planning. The unfortunate cases referred to occur in a multitude of variations in an untold number of cities and towns. This may be partly because the building of a school is a new experience to many persons who carry responsibilities in the planning process. With the pressure to provide adequate housing for the pupils of a growing population and rapidly developing new communities, the danger of hasty action and inadequate planning increases. To prevent mistakes, to avoid pitfalls, and primarily to offer guidance through all the steps that lead from the formulation of the school program to the completion of the school plant, this book was written.

JANUARY 15, 1956   THE AUTHORS

CONTENTS

PART TWO

The School Plant and Its Features

PART ONE

The Processes of Planning School Plants

CHAPTER 1

AN OVERVIEW OF MAJOR PROCESSES

Major Steps in a Building Program
Role of the Superintendent of Schools
Role of the Board of Education
Role of Specialists
Role of Other Persons
Administrative and Advisory Relationships

HASTY PLANNING

THE board of education of a small community realized a few years ago that a school construction program of some kind was necessary. The elementary school building was 75 years old, the high school on the same site was built in the 1920's, and both buildings were becoming crowded. After being discussed in several board meetings, a bond issue was submitted to the electorate for a new high school building on a new site. The voters rejected the proposal.

Construction prices were high, and the board of education considered them a significant factor in the failure at the polls. It decided, therefore, to wait for a more favorable time, and no action was taken for several years. When the overcrowding became serious, a quick survey was made by an educational consultant, and the board decided to remodel the high school building and expand the existing elementary school facilities. An architect was also employed, and machinery was set in motion to analyze the school program in detail and to develop from this analysis suggestions as to the design of the new construction and the remodeling. The intention was that these suggestions would make the new and remodeled facilities more appropriate for the type of school program desired.

After a few quick exploratory conferences with the superintendent and educational consultant, the architect prepared preliminary drawings for the elementary school addition which he submitted to the board of education, even though the educational planning program had barely begun. The educational consultant was given no opportunity to examine the drawings before he met with the board and the architect to consider them. The drawings provided small classrooms with no work counters, science centers, reading corners, or other special facilities. The rooms were so arranged that they could not be remodeled later at reasonable cost to correct these deficiencies.

During the board meeting the educational consultant pointed out the major deficiencies of the plans as he saw them and suggested certain changes that could be made with a minimum loss of drafting time. His suggestions were accepted, and the board instructed the architect to modify the drawings. The following morning, several board members became concerned about the delay necessitated by the revision of the plans. A special meeting was called before noon, the action of the preceding evening was rescinded, the preliminary drawings were approved as originally submitted, and the architect was instructed to proceed with working drawings and specifications. The addition was constructed accordingly.

This hasty procedure unfortunately is not unusual. While the details vary, many boards of education make a tardy decision to build, employ an architect, and have him prepare drawings and specifications without benefit of adequate study of the educational program. They then approve his quickly developed plans and proceed with the construction. If a building that is educationally satisfactory results, it is by chance. Too frequently, a building is constructed which is satisfactory for the educational program of a generation ago but which is neither adequate for today's program nor readily adaptable to changes in the future. The price of this superficial planning is inadequate educational opportunities for the community's children for the next half century or more.

The causes for such haste are many and varied. Often there is a failure to anticipate needs sufficiently far in advance to permit proper planning. No one takes the responsibility for periodic study of trends in enrollments and for estimating the enrollments of even a few years ahead. A second, and more basic, cause is that the superintendent of schools and members of the board of education have had little or no experience in a school-building program and fail to realize the length of time required to study school-building needs and the time needed for adequate educational and architectural planning before construction actually starts. This was the primary cause of difficulty in the community cited above.

Major Steps in a Building Program

THE total process by which a school building is planned and constructed can be broken down into many specific steps, beginning with the initial study of need and ending with the formal acceptance of the completed structure by the board of education. Normally, two to five or more years may elapse between these two steps, depending upon the size and complexity of the problem, the availability of the necessary specialized assistance, and other factors.

For purposes here the entire process is summarized under four headings. First is the survey of the over-all needs of the school system followed by the educational planning, the architectural planning, and the construction phases for each building. These steps are not wholly separate and sequential, but overlap. However, for clarification, each is expanded briefly at this point and then explained more fully in later chapters.

SURVEY OF NEEDS

A school-plant survey is a study of the over-all building needs of a school district. It seeks answers to such questions as the following:

1. What should be done with existing buildings? Which, if any, should be abandoned for school use, and what should be done with those that are abandoned? What grades should be assigned to those that are retained?

2. In existing buildings which are kept in service, what major improvements should be made? Which buildings should be enlarged, and what facilities should be added?

3. If existing buildings are to be replaced, where should the new buildings be located and how large should they be?

4. Should any new schools be established at new locations, now or at some future date? If so, where and for what grades? How large should they be?

In answering these questions, the survey staff must analyze the school program, both instructional and otherwise, to determine the types of facilities needed. It is necessary to estimate the future enrollments in order to have a basis for determining the size and number of buildings required. Existing buildings must be carefully appraised to judge how they can be used most advantageously. The outcome of the survey is a general plan for future construction and other school-plant improvements, usually with suggestions as to means of financing the program.

EDUCATIONAL PLANNING

After the survey has been completed and the board of education has decided what level of building (high school, elementary, etc.) to erect, an intensive detailed study should be conducted to ascertain precisely what facilities are needed. The mere statement of the number of pupils to be housed in the new structure is not sufficient. The numbers of classrooms and other types of space required depend in part upon the number of pupils and in part upon the nature of the school program. For example, the statement that 300 pupils are to be housed in a new elementary school building does not tell whether a cafeteria, a music room, or a crafts shop is needed, or even how many classrooms are essential. In addition to determining the types and numbers of rooms and spaces required, it is necessary to know the numbers of people and kinds of activities to be performed in each type of room, the kinds and quantities of materials and equipment a room should contain, and where it should be located in respect to other parts of the building and grounds. Answers to such questions as these come from a detailed analysis of the types of activity to be carried on in each type of room, that is, from a careful study of the entire school program.

This type of study is generally called educational planning.[1] It follows the survey and the board's decision to proceed with construction. Unlike the survey, which encompasses all school buildings in the school district, educational planning is done separately for each new building or addition and for each major remodeling project.

ARCHITECTURAL PLANNING

Once the educational planning for a specific building project has been finished, the architect can proceed to design the building and to develop the drawings and specifications necessary for bidding and construction. His first job is to create a plan that will provide the educational facilities which have been specified as a result of the preceding educational planning activities. In other words, his first responsibility is to design the environment for the desired educational program. If he is to do this adequately, each set of plans must be tailor-made; "ready-to-wear" blueprints will not fit. They are apt to bind and pinch the program at critical spots.

Another responsibility of the architect is to fit the building to the site

[1] The term "educational planning" obviously has meaning beyond the school-plant planning field. Also, there is educational planning done as a part of the building survey, as discussed in a later chapter. In this volume, however, the term is used to refer to a specific step in the planning procedure and not in its broader sense.

in such a way as to achieve the proper interrelationship of the outdoor facilities with those inside the building, as well as to promote economy in the erection and operation of the building. Considerations of natural lighting and ventilation also enter into the planning of the site as well as into the design of the structure itself.

The achievement of a successful design may require the preparation of many sets of preliminary drawings over a period of several months. This is the most creative phase of the architect's work and cannot be hurried if a product of high quality is to be achieved.

Once the basic design has been established and the preliminary plans approved by the board of education, the architect develops the detailed drawings and specifications required for securing bids from contractors. These same documents are used by contractors during construction, supplemented by drawings of details and other precise instructions furnished by the architect as needed.

CONSTRUCTION

The erection of the building is the fourth and final step in the four-stage process. The construction proceeds in accordance with the architect's drawings and specifications and preferably under his supervision.

In securing a satisfactory school building, a considerable span of time—possibly several years—will elapse from the first realization of need to the completion of construction. For this reason, and to avoid the dangers of hasty decisions, early study and effective progression in planning are a must.

Role of the Superintendent of Schools

THE success of a given school district in conducting adequate studies and planning in the securing of a new building depends in large measure upon the realization by certain individuals and groups of their duties and responsibilities in this field. Of these persons, the superintendent of schools [2] occupies the key position.

According to the best practice of school administration, the superintendent of schools is the chief executive of the board of education and the sole executive directly responsible to the board. As such, he must be responsible for anticipating needs, arranging for necessary studies, and

[2] The term "superintendent of schools" is used in this discussion to include assistant superintendents, business managers, or other subordinates responsible to the superintendent for certain aspects of administration.

making appropriate recommendations in the school-plant field as in other aspects of school operation.

Certain existing exceptions are recognized, though not endorsed by the authors. In some school systems, more than one executive is responsible to the board of education. In such cases some other official might have the role here assigned to the superintendent. In other situations the responsibility for planning school buildings is vested in an official or board other than those responsible for the regular operation of the schools. This situation is regrettable since those who plan the building in large measure determine the program.

Whatever the local variations may be, the superintendent of schools and his staff must assume the leadership and either arrange for proper planning within the school organization or seek by all legitimate means to persuade other responsible officials or agencies to do so.

IN ANTICIPATING NEEDS

A primary responsibility of the superintendent and other administrative staff members is to study and plan continuously for the future. This is true for all aspects of the school program. Regarding the school plant, the administration should maintain records of up-to-date information about enrollment trends; about probable future enrollments, housing, industrial, and other developments likely to affect school needs; and about the status of existing buildings in terms of safety, sanitary conditions, adequacy for the needs of the desired program, and margin of capacity in relation to anticipated enrollments.

The maintenance and periodic review of such records will assist the administration to foresee building needs before a crisis occurs, and thus to forestall hasty planning and construction. Such habitual foresightedness is the best possible insurance against inadequate planning.

IN CONDUCTING THE BUILDING SURVEY

At appropriate times the superintendent of schools should either initiate a school-building survey to be made by his own staff or arrange to have an outside agency make one. He should advise the board of education of the need for systematic study and furnish suitable recommendations for obtaining it. These should include suggestions concerning the employment or assignment of personnel necessary for the purpose.

During the conduct of the survey the superintendent might assume the major responsibility for making the study, possibly with some advisory assistance from outside. Or, the major responsibility might rest upon some outside agency or group. If the latter is the case, the superintendent is responsible for furnishing needed information. Much of this is statistical in nature and can readily be provided from his files. More difficult to supply, and often of more significance, is information regarding school policies and school program, present and anticipated.

In furnishing the survey staff with information, the superintendent of schools must strive to avoid all personal bias. Likewise, he should refrain from making recommendations until the survey staff has reached tentative decisions and wishes to check its thinking with him. It makes little sense to employ a staff to conduct an impartial study and then seek to persuade it to endorse a predetermined plan of action.

Upon completion of the survey, the superintendent and his staff have two responsibilities. The first is to make whatever recommendations and arrangements may be necessary to secure the proper study and analysis of the report by the school staff, the board of education, other official bodies concerned, and the community at large. The second is to make, after careful analysis, recommendations concerning adoption, modification, or rejection of each proposal in the report. This is equivalent to saying that the superintendent, after suitable study of the survey staff's proposals, presents to the board of education his recommendations for adoption of a comprehensive school-building program. Upon approval of the program, he should take appropriate measures to implement it.

IN EDUCATIONAL PLANNING

One of the first steps in implementing the program developed by the survey is to arrange the necessary educational planning. This may be done largely by the school staff or with the assistance of an outside educational consultant. The local school staff should be involved, and pupils and parents might also participate in the process. However it is to be done, the superintendent should advise the board of education of the need for educational planning, suggest the necessary arrangements, and seek whatever board approvals might be required.

During the process of educational planning the need for decisions concerning the future school program is even greater than during the survey. Many of the decisions made at this time will be fixed by the brick and mortar of the new structure. This imposes upon the superintendent a major leadership responsibility in program planning. He must bring together the persons and groups to be involved, co-ordinate their efforts, and present to the proper bodies for consideration and final decision the various issues and proposals for change.

As the educational planning progresses, a set of written educational specifications for the new building should be produced to be presented by the superintendent to the board of education, with appropriate recommendations. Upon approval by the board of education, these educational specifications should be transmitted by the superintendent to the architect.

IN SELECTING SITES

If a new site is to be acquired, the superintendent bears the responsibility for planning the procedure and presenting appropriate recommendations to the board of education. Definite criteria should be adopted, and all proposed sites should be analyzed in terms of the standards established. Test borings, geological studies, topographical surveys, real estate appraisals, architectural analyses, or other technical services may be required in studying a prospective site. The services of an educational consultant and architect may be needed in establishing the criteria or in appraising a particular property. The superintendent must arrange for the services of these specialists as needed and secure proper approvals and clearances from the board of education.

When a site has been selected, it is the superintendent who makes the appropriate recommendation to the board of education and upon approval proceeds with the measures necessary to acquire the property.

IN ARCHITECTURAL PLANNING

As the architect becomes involved in planning the building, many questions will arise that were not fully answered by the educational specifications. The superintendent of schools must furnish the answers or make arrangements for others to do so. If an educational consultant aided in preparing the specifications, the superintendent should arrange for him to answer or assist in supplying answers to the architect.

The architect from time to time will submit preliminary drawings for criticism. The superintendent or one of his staff should review these drawings and arrange to secure the criticisms of the educational consultant, school staff committees, and others involved in the preparation of the educational specifications. When the preliminary drawings have reached the proper stage, the superintendent should submit them to the educational consultant for checking, and then recommend to the board of education that they be approved and that the architect be instructed to proceed with working drawings and specifications.

During the remainder of the architectural planning there should be further, though possibly fewer, occasions for the architect to refer questions to the superintendent. When the final drawings and specifications are received, they should be carefully checked by the staff and the educational consultant. Then, with the superintendent's recommendation for approval, they are ready for the consideration of the board of education.

IN CONSTRUCTING THE BUILDING

The typical and best practice is for the architect to analyze the bids, make recommendations concerning the awarding of contracts, supervise the work of the contractors, and handle the incidental business affairs. If this is followed, the superintendent's office is relieved of considerable detail work. If the analysis of bids or the supervision of construction is handled by the school staff, as it is in some cases, many duties and responsibilities discussed in this book as coming under the architect's supervision would fall upon the superintendent and his staff. If the architect supervises the construction, which is the better practice, the superintendent must receive from him and transmit to the board of education all necessary change orders, requests for payments to contractors, reports of progress, and the like.

IN SELECTING FURNISHINGS

Practices with respect to the selection of equipment and furnishings for a new building vary greatly. The architect usually specifies the fixed equipment, such as laboratory desks, but the furniture, draperies, and other nonfixed items are often selected by the school staff under the leadership of the superintendent. The educational consultant is often involved in the process.

The most satisfactory method involves the consultation of the architect, the educational consultant, and the school staff. Whatever the procedure, it is the responsibility of the superintendent of schools to see that necessary decisions are made concerning these items and that orders are placed in ample time to permit delivery when needed.

IN ACCEPTING AND OPENING THE BUILDING

Upon completion of construction there is normally a careful inspection of the building before it is formally accepted by the board of education. The superintendent should arrange with the architect for such inspection, and upon completion should make appropriate recommendations to the board of education.

Before the new building is occupied, it is essential to instruct the staff with respect to its use. Operating employees must be taught the proper care and use of any new type of equipment, and the teachers who have not had close contact with the planning should be told of the anticipated use of various building features. The arrangements for these various instructional meetings also rest with the superintendent.

SUMMARY OF SUPERINTENDENT'S ROLE

This account of the duties of the superintendent may be appalling to one who has never been through a building program, but, even so, many details are omitted. The job is a large one, and the superintendent or someone on his staff must devote a great deal of time to it if the maximum of success is to be achieved.

This description is based squarely on the concept that the superintendent of schools is the chief executive of the board. It assumes that all requests, reports, and recommendations flow through him to the board and that he is responsible for implementing the board's decisions. It assumes also that the board looks to him for analysis and recommendation concerning any major proposal or request that comes to it. This does not mean that the architect, the educational consultant, or others do not speak directly to the board. On the contrary, they may have extended conferences at certain times with the board. The superintendent, however, would arrange the necessary details for the conferences, and would be the person with whom to talk later regarding interpretation or implementation of the conclusions reached.

Role of the Board of Education

WHILE the board of education is closer to the ultimate source of authority (the people) than is the superintendent, the superintendent's role has been discussed first because it clarifies much of what might be said about the role of the board.

IN GENERAL

The major premise of the authors is that the board of education is the legislative and policy-forming group and the superintendent of schools the chief executive officer. In terms of this widely held concept, the major responsibilities of the board of education with respect to school operations in general are:

1. To formulate and adopt general policies for the operation of the schools.

2. To select a competent superintendent and hold him accountable for the proper execution of the board's policies.

3. To furnish the superintendent of schools with the necessary staff, buildings, equipment, and funds to put the board's policies into effect.

4. To evaluate the effectiveness with which the board's policies are being carried out in the operation of the school system.

The responsibility for formulating policies rests with the board. This does not mean that the superintendent plays no role in this sphere. Obviously, he should frequently suggest policies to the board, challenge existing policies, participate in the discussion of matters of policy, and otherwise assist the board in arriving at sound decisions. Also, he and his staff should be free to establish certain operating policies for carrying out the total job entrusted to them by the board of education.

Similarly the board of education may suggest for the consideration of the superintendent certain procedures and raise questions regarding the effectiveness of his ways of doing things. In the final analysis, however, he should be free to select his own methods of implementing board policies and should be held responsible for producing the desired results.

This division of duties between the board of education and the superintendent will relieve the board of many petty details and leave it free, as it should be, to give maximum attention to the larger and more important issues involved.

IN A BUILDING PROGRAM

Viewed in the light of the above statements, the major functions of the board of education in relation to a building program are to:

1. Be alert to probable future building needs and call upon the superintendent for pertinent data.

2. Grant the necessary authorization and provide the necessary funds to permit progress at the various stages of the building program as outlined above. This includes the employment of educational consultants, architects, and other specialists as required.

3. Act with reasonable promptness and decisiveness upon various questions of educational policy raised during the progress of the survey or the planning of a building.

4. Act upon the survey recommendations and thereby officially establish a long-range building program.

5. Approve the educational specifications for each building project within the total building program.
6. Approve the necessary sites and provide for the acquisition of them.
7. Approve the preliminary plans and, later, the working drawings and specifications prepared by the architect.
8. Authorize the requesting of bids and award construction contracts.
9. Approve change orders and authorize necessary payments during the construction.
10. Formally accept the completed structure.

Some boards of education appoint a special building committee to handle many details. This procedure is quite inconsistent with the principles set forth above, because such a committee often does detailed work which should be left to the superintendent. Further, it is quite likely that the other members will be denied the opportunity to have full knowledge as a basis for action upon such building problems as do come before the entire board. Finally, it tends to divert the attention of board members from the major issues and to bring their efforts to focus on minor details.

Role of Specialists

PASSING reference has been made to various specialists who might be involved in planning and constructing a new school building. These include educational consultants, architects, engineers (acoustical, electrical, mechanical, structural, etc.), geologists, realtors, and others. All might not be concerned with any one project, and only the first three are employed with sufficient frequency to justify further attention here.

EDUCATIONAL CONSULTANTS

The educational consultant is a type of specialist used increasingly in planning school buildings. His role is to advise the superintendent and the board of education with respect to the educational aspects of the building program. While he has much specialized knowledge about school buildings, he has no responsibility for the architectural and engineering aspects of planning except to appraise their effect upon the school program.

The educational consultant may play a major role in making a school-building survey. He may be given complete responsibility for conducting the survey with a staff of his own choosing. In other cases, he may serve as an adviser to some local person or group responsible for the survey. In the latter case, he would assist in planning the study and setting up the proper procedures and would help in interpreting the findings and formulating the recommendations.

He may have a similar role in the educational planning of a specific building. He may be completely responsible or serve only as an adviser. His work involves meetings with the school staff, and possibly others, to plan the school program and decide what building facilities are required to house it. It involves, also, the preparation of written educational specifications for the guidance of the architect, conferences with the architect with respect to the latter's plans as they develop, and checking the architect's completed plans to ensure that they provide the necessary educational features.

At the time of selection of the site, the educational consultant might advise on establishing suitable criteria and selection procedures. He might also assist in appraising a proposed site in terms of its suitability for a school. Finally, he might aid in the selection of suitable equipment and furnishings for the new building.

Since the educational consultant is a relative newcomer in the field, many superintendents, boards of education, and architects fail to consider the use of his services. The services of the educational consultant are essentially different from those of the architect and can be of great value both to the school authorities and to the architect in securing a better school building.

ARCHITECTS AND ENGINEERS

Essentially, the job of the architect is to design the facilities needed for the educational program, to prepare the documents necessary for bidding and construction, and to supervise construction. The building and grounds must be pleasing in appearance, easy and safe to operate, and economical to construct and maintain. During construction the architect oversees the job to make certain that the board of education receives the quality called for in the drawings and specifications.

During the planning stage the architect calls upon many specialists to assist him. These are engineers, for the most part, and they may be members of his own organization or outside persons. These specialists are used in designing the site improvements and planting; the structural aspects of the building; the lighting, heating, ventilating, and plumbing systems; the sanitary system; the acoustics; and possibly several other special features. The architect should be, and usually is, responsible for co-ordinating the work of these various specialists.

In addition to designing the building, the architect may be consulted on technical matters in the survey of an existing building, and usually should be consulted in the selection of a site before a final decision is made.

Role of Other Persons

For the most part, the role of other persons and groups requires no extensive discussion here, but will be treated at appropriate places in later chapters. The principal groups to be considered are the school staff, pupils, and the citizens of the community in general.

Teachers and other members of the school staff must work from day to day with the building facilities provided. They have a rich background from which to propose features which would help them to do their work more easily and effectively. The professional staff members also can make significant contributions to planning the educational program which is an essential part of both the survey and the educational planning of a new building. For these reasons, school employees frequently serve on committees to assist in the planning of new buildings, and at times they are members of survey committees.

Pupils have seldom participated in building studies, but they probably could make important contributions and at the same time further their own education. They have contributed effectively in other planning projects. Their evaluations of existing buildings might reveal strengths and weaknesses not apparent to adults. In like fashion, their suggestions with respect to a new building might result in improvements that would otherwise be overlooked.

Groups of citizens are frequently called upon to assist in conducting a school-building survey, and at times to make the survey with the advice of an educational consultant. Citizens also serve on many groups responsible for the planning of new school buildings or for the curriculum studies that precede the planning of buildings.

Administrative and Advisory Relationships

The selection and recruitment of the persons to participate in the various phases of planning a school building are of crucial importance, but it is equally essential that the relationships among these various persons and groups be clearly defined and understood by all. The discussion up to this point has implied clearly a key role for the superintendent of schools and suggested certain relationships between him and other participants and between those participants and the board of education.

The justification for the school-building survey rests upon the proposition that the chances of error, and especially of major error, will be greatly reduced by a comprehensive study of the total school-plant needs of the community as far into the future as the available data and known survey techniques will permit.

General Nature of the Survey

ALL surveys, by definition, are characterized by comprehensiveness. A well-designed survey includes careful scrutiny and analysis of all the pertinent facts, but it ordinarily does not stress the examination and appraisal of the minutiae of the subject or the preparation of extremely detailed recommendations. Thus a survey of school-plant needs is designed to develop in broad outline a comprehensive plan for future school-plant improvements in a given school district or other geographical area and to recommend the next steps toward realization of this plan. For example, a proposal that a new elementary school building be erected for a certain number of pupils would be appropriate in a survey report, but a detailed description of the facilities to be provided in the new building would not belong in such a study. This more detailed description, which is an essential basis for good architectural planning, is properly developed after the school-building survey has been completed and the pertinent survey recommendations adopted by the appropriate governing agency.

The complete school-plant survey procedure, reduced to its simplest terms, consists of three steps: (1) determining the total school-plant needs; (2) appraising the existing school-plant facilities in relation to these needs; and (3) formulating proposals to close the gap between needs and existing facilities. The collection and analysis of the necessary statistics and other information and the formulating of sound recommendations involve the use of many detailed procedures of more or less technical nature. Each of these detailed procedures is discussed at some length in later chapters. The discussion here is limited to a more general description of the survey.

For purposes of this general description, the survey will be viewed as the collecting and organizing of information around four basic questions, each of which is stated and briefly discussed in the paragraphs that follow.

QUESTION 1. *What are the total school plant needs of the district now and in the foreseeable future?*

This question must be answered in both quantitative and qualitative terms. On the quantitative side, it is necessary to know how many pupils will have to be housed and how much schoolhousing they will require.

This involves the rather technical and difficult processes of predicting future enrollments. While this job can never be done with complete assurance that the predictions are correct, careful studies can produce useful forecasts, and in most cases considerable accuracy can be achieved for the years immediately ahead.

The qualitative aspect of this question has reference to the nature of the school program, broadly defined. It is necessary to know what is to be taught, the general manner of teaching, and the desired size of class. Basic information is required about school lunches, health services, and other noninstructional aspects of the program offered to pupils. Since most school buildings are used by older groups as well as children, it is necessary to seek information about the adult education program and community use of the school plant. In other words, the survey must include examination of the full range of activities for which the school plant will be used, and a determination from this list of the general nature of the physical facilities required.

The analysis of the quantitative and qualitative aspects of the school-plant needs should be carried to the point where it is possible to list the numbers, types, and capacities of facilities that are required.

QUESTION 2. *To what extent are existing school-plant facilities adequate in relation to these needs?*

The answering of this question is essentially a matter of comparing what is available with what is needed and of deriving from the results a list of additional facilities required. It is necessary to determine whether there are enough classrooms at the right places and to judge whether the classrooms and other facilities are reasonably adequate for the type of school program desired. In appraising an existing facility, attention is also given to matters of health and safety and to the economic aspects of its continued use.

QUESTION 3. *What financial resources are available for a program of school plant improvements?*

Many school districts operate under constitutional or statutory restrictions upon the amount of money available for major capital improvements. Even when this is not the practice, it cannot be assumed that there are no limitations on the amount of money that will be provided by the community. The extent to which financial considerations will be a factor in determining the survey recommendations will vary with such factors as the nature of the financial arrangements and the urgency of the school-plant needs. These obviously will not be the same in all places.

QUESTION 4. *In the light of the answers to the foregoing questions, what school-plant improvements should be recommended?*

In the reply to this question lies the whole purpose of the survey. It is necessary that definite recommendations be made concerning the future use or abandonment of each existing facility, the remodeling or expansion of each existing site and building, the acquisition of new sites and of new buildings, and in some cases the timing or priorities to be observed in making the improvements.

Essential Characteristics of a Good Survey

TEN criteria for judging a survey are suggested at this point, three of them primarily dealing with the processes involved and the remainder concerned more with the nature of the recommendations resulting from the study. These criteria are discussed here as points of view for the evaluation of a completed survey project. The implications for planning the survey process and the ways in which these criteria affect the selection of the personnel to make the survey will be considered in subsequent chapters.

The three criteria related primarily to the survey processes itself are:

1. The study should be conducted and reported as an impartial overview of the needs of the entire school district.
2. The procedures used in the collection and analysis of data should be technically sound and accurately used.
3. The survey should be so conducted and reported as to be relatively easy to keep up to date.

The remaining criteria which are more closely related to the nature of the recommendations resulting from the survey are:

4. The recommendations should be of such nature that the resulting physical plant most effectively facilitates the desired school program.
5. The recommendations should provide adequate capacity for housing the anticipated future enrollments.
6. The recommendations should take into account any existing or projected plans for the future development of the community and region.
7. The recommendations should include or be based on a stated long-range plan, as well as plans for the immediate future, and should provide a reasonable degree of flexibility to meet unforeseen changes in the future.

8. The recommendations should be of such nature as to provide the most value to the community for each dollar spent.

9. The recommendations should be straightforward and unequivocal and clearly supported by the data.

10. The recommendations should propose improvements which have a reasonable chance of acceptance without sacrificing principles of good planning.

These criteria are neither mutually exclusive nor all inclusive in nature, nor are they to be considered as absolutes. As a group they characterize the better surveys and they provide a good basis for planning a survey report.

Each of the criteria is repeated and explained on the pages that follow.

CRITERION 1. *The study should be conducted and reported as an impartial overview of the needs of the entire school district.*

Frequently a certain section of a school district or a certain segment of the population will, without sufficient regard to other needs, bring pressure upon the superintendent and board of education to make improvements of concern to them. They may, for example, seek a new school building in their neighborhood, or a new and larger gymnasium for interscholastic athletics, and never inquire about other building needs. At other times, the school authorities may become so engrossed in a proposed solution to one building problem that they lose sight of another. An excellent example of the latter is the city, mentioned early in this chapter, that was so intent upon erecting a new high school building that the elementary school needs were overlooked. The staff of a building survey will not ignore the wishes of these groups, but will view them only as possible solutions to be studied and analyzed along with other hypotheses developed during the survey. If it is to be of the most value, the survey must give equal and impartial consideration to the needs of all parts of the school district and all aspects of the school program.

A particular hazard to be avoided is the uncritical acceptance of the status quo or of points of view commonly held in the community. Frequently, local people, including the school authorities, fail to see the possibilities of meeting some of their problems by such means as changing the boundaries of attendance districts or converting existing buildings to new uses, or they have set minds with respect to the future usefulness of an existing building. If the survey is to be of maximum value, the maintenance of the status quo must be only one of the many solutions to be considered in arriving at the recommendations.

Sometimes a survey staff will find that an earlier survey has been made by some other person or agency and that a copy of the earlier report is made available. If the new survey is to be of maximum value, it is essential that an independent approach be made. This does not imply that the earlier study was inadequate, but, if the old recommendations are accepted without question as still valid, the usefulness of the new study may be destroyed or significantly limited. The primary value of the earlier report would seem to be as an aid to the new survey staff in checking its thinking and in detecting possible blind spots or errors of emphasis in its work. As such, the old report would be most useful in the closing stages of the new study and might well be ignored until that time. Earlier reference to the old report might be used to secure factual data needed to check certain trends or to fill gaps in the information available to the new staff from other sources.

Another aspect of this first criterion is that the survey report itself must be written to reflect the comprehensive and impartial approach here advocated. The readers of the report, whoever they may be, should be helped to see the larger problems in place of the minor details or the concerns of certain groups and to observe the objective and impartial logic leading to the survey recommendations. If the readers should find the report to be otherwise—if they should find it to be a rationalization of predetermined conclusions or an evasion of significant facts or problems—they may well reject it. Or worse, they might use the report and its shortcomings as ammunition in a factional dispute in the community, and this to the detriment of the children.

The first criterion may be summarized by stating that the good survey is one that is conducted and reported with: (a) equal attention to the needs of all parts of the school system and all aspects of the school program; (b) major attention to the larger problems rather than to those of minor nature which the local school authorities can readily handle; and (c) deliberate and unfaltering suspension of judgment as to solutions until all the evidence is in and all reasonable hypotheses have been analyzed.

CRITERION 2. *The procedures used in the collection and analysis of data should be technically sound and accurately used.*

Technical competence in this field includes knowledge of and ability to use the specialized techniques involved, but of more importance is sound judgment in the selection and application of these techniques and the interpretation of the findings. The job is by no means a routine, mechanical one.

Some of these technical procedures are relatively simple and easy to employ, while others are quite difficult and complicated. An example of the former is the taking of a preschool census. The estimating of future enrollments and the calculation of the capacity of a high school building are illustrations of more technical aspects of the study. The latter two obviously require greater technical competence than conducting a census, but even the simplest procedures require a high degree of thoroughness and accuracy. Preschool census reports are almost notoriously inaccurate, map work is often carelessly done, and many errors appear in such obviously unchanging statistics as the enrollments of preceding years.

A survey report based upon inaccurate data, faulty handling of data, or inappropriate technical procedures may be worse than no survey at all because of the false sense of security it may create.

CRITERION 3. *The survey should be so conducted and reported as to be relatively easy to keep up to date.*

Since no survey report can be a permanent guide to a board of education in its building program, there is frequent need for reviewing or bringing up to date an earlier study. In a large school system there is almost certain to be a need for rechecking some of the recommendations before they are put into operation several years later. These needs for reopening and extending a survey report make it necessary for the original work to be done so that revision is relatively easy.

The most important single suggestion for making it easy to bring a survey up to date is that the exact source and precise nature of all statistical data be recorded. This need can be well illustrated by reference to enrollment data. A typical survey report would give enrollments in recent years and some estimates for the future. A person seeking to extend these tables would ask immediately such questions as these:

1. Are the original figures given as of a certain date each year, and, if so, what date?
2. Do the original figures indicate membership at a given date, average membership, average daily attendance, or cumulative enrollment to a given date?
3. Do the original figures include nonresident pupils?
4. Do the original figures include ungraded pupils, children in special classes, or postgraduates?

Appropriate footnotes or explanations in the text would answer these questions, and exact citation of sources would open to the later investigator another means of identifying and defining the original data. Further, it should be a fixed rule that the source of data in every table should be noted and that every map should be properly identified and precisely dated.

A second suggestion for making a report easy to revise is that it contain a reasonably adequate record of how the various data were actually derived. For example, a statement in the original report of the estimated capacity of a high school building would be of more value to the future surveyor if he could know the process by which the capacity was originally determined.

A third suggestion, which should be obvious but clearly needs to be made, is that the original report be organized according to a logical outline. The later investigator should be able to locate all essential information on a given point with reasonable effort. If the reporting of the data in the original report is not logical, there is the danger that the later investigator will overlook certain essential information as he studies a particular problem. There are, of course, certain limitations in the most logical outline, and cross references in the text are helpful in overcoming them.

Finally, it is suggested that a file of work materials be maintained that is so organized as to be helpful to any other investigator seeking to bring the study up to date. Extensive use of this device, or the filing of supplementary technical reports with the superintendent of schools or board of education, would, of course, make possible the omission of many details from the published survey report.

These suggestions with regard to keeping a survey current are not meant to imply that a school system should make one survey and then forever after keep revising it. Such continuous study is desirable, but there would seem to be merit in conducting a completely fresh study from time to time.

CRITERION 4. *The recommendations should be of such nature that the resulting physical plant most effectively facilitates the desired school program.*

The school plant is a teaching aid, as is a library book or a piece of science apparatus. All teaching aids, including the school plant, have value to the schools only insofar as they serve the instructional purposes at hand. Thus the nature of the desired instructional program should determine the type of physical plant to be provided. This is the most important principle in the whole school-plant planning field.

Since the programs of today's schools are not limited to the instruction of children, this principle must be broadened to encompass all aspects of the school program. If public recreation activities are to be conducted on school grounds or in school buildings, to cite but one example, the school plant facilities must be planned accordingly.

School programs are not static. Their changing character is repeatedly brought to the attention of those who must try day after day to teach in antiquated structures designed for educational programs of 1875 or 1900. The seeming inevitability of educational change requires that school plants be designed with major focus on the emerging program of the schools rather than the current one and that ample provision be made for the adaptation of the plant to changes as yet unsuspected.

The most effective survey is possible only when related to local school and community planning for the future. As a basis for the survey, many policy decisions are required regarding the scope of the program, the desired vertical organization, the optimum size of school, transportation and other auxiliary services, and many other related problems. If these decisions are made too quickly, they may or may not provide a sufficiently sound foundation for the work of the survey staff. An effective survey is much more likely if it is but one phase of a continuing program of planning at the local level, rather than an isolated and passing effort.

CRITERION 5. *The recommendations should provide adequate capacity for housing the anticipated future enrollment.*

If adequate capacity is not provided, the school program is certain to suffer. The usual first step toward a restricted program is the conversion of various nonclassroom spaces to classroom use, thus eliminating or curtailing the activities for which these spaces were originally designed. At times these converted spaces do not lend themselves to the new use, as, for example, when a stage is pressed into service as a classroom. A later step which usually curtails the school program is the use of short sessions with two or more groups of pupils using the same classroom each day.

A survey which satisfies Criterion 5 will include of necessity some estimate of future enrollments. Since such estimates cannot be wholly accurate, the survey recommendations should permit reasonable future adjustments in the capacity of the plant.

CRITERION 6. *The recommendations should take into account any existing or projected plans for the future development of the community and region.*

The nature and extent of the survey staff's concern for the plans of other community agencies will depend upon many local factors. In some cases the staff will go to these agencies only to secure such data as they may have or to seek their opinions as to the course of future developments. In other situations it will find official plans well developed, and possibly officially adopted or partially executed, and will shape its school-plant proposals accordingly. It may, however, find certain parts of these official plans contrary to the best interests of the schools and will recommend modifications. Where official plans are meager, the survey staff may want to develop its report in such manner as to strengthen the case for more planning in the community as a whole.

The school survey staff may find significant uncertainties in the plans of other agencies. It may discover, for example, that a major street relocation is being considered or that a significant change in zoning is under study. These various possibilities should be studied and their implications for the school plant analyzed. The survey recommendations must then, if possible, provide enough flexibility to permit future adjustment as required by the changes in community plans that actually develop.

While the survey in the recommendations phase will be concerned with physical facilities such as streets, playgrounds, and school buildings, effective community planning is essentially program planning. The schools and other agencies should jointly consider the needs of the community and the role of the municipality, the schools, the churches, scouting groups, and other public and private institutions in meeting these needs. Only by such cooperation can the most satisfactory physical facilities be achieved.

CRITERION 7. *The recommendations should include or be based on a stated long-range plan, as well as plans for the immediate future, and should provide a reasonable degree of flexibility to meet unforeseen changes in the future.*

This criterion is implied in the discussion of the preceding criteria, but it is of such importance that it merits separate mention. All too often an immediate problem will be solved in ways that will prove embarrassing at some future date. While it is impossible to foresee the future with certainty, it is possible to reduce the errors by careful long-range planning. The plans for immediate improvements may have to be compromises because of financial or other limitations, but they should be of such nature that they will not prevent the ultimate realization of the long-range goals.

One of the very tangible values of long-range planning is that it often makes possible the acquisition of needed sites while land is still vacant and reasonable in price. If needed sites are not purchased early, the result is likely to be the ultimate acquisition of a site which is too small, poorly located, or unduly expensive to develop.

CRITERION 8. *The recommendations should be of such nature as to provide the most value to the community for each dollar spent.*

Any official responsible for the expenditure of public funds has an inescapable obligation to be economical. This does not necessarily mean that taxes should be reduced, but rather that the goods and services desired by the public should be secured at the lowest cost consistent with the desired quality. Saving money in ways which impair the effectiveness of the school program is not economy. The superintendent of schools and the board of education have the responsibility of using the public's money wisely, and the survey staff must share this responsibility with them.

CRITERION 9. *The recommendations should be straightforward and unequivocal and clearly supported by the data.*

A common purpose for a school-plant survey is to secure the considered judgment of a competent individual or group concerning the course of action to be taken. This does not mean that the board of education will or should accept all of the recommendations of the survey, but it does require that the members of the survey staff state clearly what they think should be done and why. A survey which ends in vague recommendations poorly supported, or unnecessary alternative recommendations which pass the problems back to the board of education, may be worse than none.

There are occasions, of course, when the survey staff will be forced to make alternative recommendations or to delay completion of the report until certain local decisions have been made or the outcome of certain pending events is known. In such cases, if alternative recommendations are included in the report, the reasons for each should be clearly stated, and the conditions under which the survey staff would choose each alternative should be set forth.

While this criterion calls for specific recommendations, it does not imply that the survey staff should be dogmatic. Rather, the approach should be one of stating clearly what the survey staff believes the course of action should be and the reasons for its beliefs. The major alternatives considered and rejected should be explained, and the reasons for the rejections stated. This approach will give the local school authorities the full benefit of the thinking of the survey staff, and still enable these authorities to exercise their own judgment intelligently.

> **CRITERION 10.** *The recommendations should propose improvements which have a reasonable chance of acceptance without sacrificing principles of good planning.*

The fundamental purpose of a survey is to improve education; no improvement will follow a recommendation which is rejected by the community or which is beyond the power of the community to provide. At the same time, any competent survey staff will have certain principles which it will not, and should not, sacrifice.

The development of a long-range, and somewhat idealistic, plan as the first step is one solution to this problem. There should not be, and usually need not be, any yielding on major principles at this point. In the development of the recommendations for immediate improvements certain compromises may be necessary because of financial or other limitations. These should, of course, be of such nature as not to obstruct the ultimate realization of the long-range plan.

The obstacles which arise and require compromise may be inescapable. A case in point is the legal limits which some states impose upon the power of boards of education to raise funds for school-building purposes. In other instances the obstacles may be more apparent than real, or may be of such character that they can be removed. Some of the advice given to the survey staff by local people regarding public opposition to certain measures is of this latter type. In one case, for example, the survey staff concluded that a new high school building was required, and proposed that it be erected on a new and ample site at the edge of the city. Many local people insisted that the city council would never provide money to build on this site, and urged that the new building be placed on the existing small site in a downtown location. The survey staff did not accept this advice. After several years of public debate and several elections the larger site was approved. The high school pupils of this city for generations will benefit from the fact that the survey staff did not accept at face value the statements of certain local groups that the new site would never be approved.

The survey staff in facing such a problem must rely heavily upon the confidence which exists or which it can engender in its competence and in the sincerity and good judgment of the local school authorities. A clear, logical presentation, free of bias, is essential. The basic facts must stand out clearly, and the reasoning from these facts to the conclusions and recommendations must be clear and sound. Simple, matter-of-fact presentation is required rather than partisan pleading or rationalization. The statement and explanation of the various rejected solutions is also helpful in promoting thoughtful consideration by the public.

Use of the Survey Findings

THE typical school-plant survey culminates in a written report. Such reports are usually quite detailed and include many tables, charts and maps. The detailed survey report comprises an orderly presentation of the essential data, explanations of the processes employed in analyzing and interpreting the information, explanations of the significance of the various findings, and statements and explanations of the recommendations.

THE SURVEY REPORT

Such a report is invaluable to the school authorities responsible for the decisions concerning the acceptance or rejection of the recommendations and useful to those civic leaders who wish to examine the complete report. For most people, however, a less detailed presentation is needed. In some surveys two reports are prepared—one a complete report for the school authorities and a limited number of laymen and the other a digest or illustrated booklet summarizing the major findings and recommendations for wider distribution. Still another plan is to submit a single brief report for general use and accompany it with a few copies of various technical reports for use by the school authorities.

Upon receipt of the survey report, whatever its form, the board of education might well take it under advisement and defer action pending detailed study by the board itself and by the community. The board should by official action refer the report for study to any planning commission or other official body interested in the problem. Beyond that it should arrange for the widest possible discussion of the recommendations at public meetings, in the press, and on the air.

One of the most effective ways of promoting public understanding of the school-plant problem is to have many citizens involved in the survey process. However, even when this is done, there will be need for systematic presentation to the whole community. Even if no major effort is required to secure approval of the necessary financing, wide public understanding of all major school problems is essential to the long-term welfare of public education, and the opportunity afforded by a building survey should not be overlooked.

NEWS STORIES

Whether or not citizens actively participate in the survey, the public should be kept informed of major developments during the study. News stories in the papers or over the air can keep the public aware of the progress being made and help develop a readiness for proper consideration of the report when it is available. These progress reports can be limited to the announcement of certain happenings or can reveal selected survey findings. With respect to the latter, the public reporting of findings and conclusions during the progress of the survey must be so handled as to leave the survey staff completely uncommitted to any particular recommendation and must avoid the creation of any public hopes or expectations which might be shattered by the final report. It would be perfectly safe, for example, and quite proper, to publicize the findings of a preschool census or to give the results of the enrollment projection studies, since these would be quite unlikely to be changed later in the study. An early report on the evaluation of an existing building, however, might be so worded as to lead to an expectation of the building's replacement, but the survey staff in the final analysis might have to conclude that it would have to continue in use. Early publicity of this sort might seriously hamper, rather than facilitate, the effective public study of the final report and the actual launching of the program of school plant improvements.

OFFICIAL ADOPTION AND EXECUTION

After a suitable period of time for public discussion, study, and report by other agencies, and study by the school authorities, the board of education should take official action adopting, modifying, or rejecting the recommendations of the survey. Any major modifications should be made only with full understanding of the implications. It is quite likely that the modifications have already been considered by the survey staff, and the board might well seek its advice before actually approving any major alteration.

If the carrying out of any major recommendation is delayed for a long period, it is advisable that it be rechecked immediately prior to execution. This is important because no survey staff can anticipate all of the changes that might occur which would affect the school-plant needs of the community. The relocation of a major highway, a major change in zoning, and the development of a new subdivision or housing project are but a few illustrations of changes which might not have been foreseen at the time of the survey and which might require modification of the building program originally proposed in the survey report.

PERIODIC REVIEW

Finally, it cannot be said too emphatically that definite plans should be made at the end of the survey project for keeping it up to date in the future. In some situations, a periodic restudy would suffice; in others, especially in large cities, provision should be made for a continuing survey. As a minimum, the plans for keeping the survey current should include:

1. Annual review of the enrollment projections, including study of birth rates, school holding power, promotion policies, enrollments in nonpublic schools, industrial and zoning changes, and other factors which will affect the number of children enrolled.

2. Annual evaluation of existing buildings in respect to health, safety, and adequacy for the desired school program.

3. Sufficiently frequent major restudy to avoid the need for hasty decisions in a crisis.

CHAPTER 3

THE BUILDING SURVEY:

ANALYSIS OF NEEDS

Determining the School Program
Analyzing the School Program to Determine School-Plant Needs
Estimating Future Enrollments to Determine School-Plant Needs

———————

IT WAS stated in the preceding chapter that any school building survey must include at least the following three steps: (1) determining the quantity and quality of school-plant facilities that will be needed in the foreseeable future; (2) assessing the adequacy of existing facilities to meet these needs; and (3) formulating recommendations for closing any gap between existing facilities and the anticipated needs. Considerations of cost and financial resources are also usually included, although some surveys, particularly if more concerned with long-range than immediate plans, may not require any sharp focus on the financial aspects.

In this chapter the techniques or procedures used in the first of these three steps, that is, in determining the school-plant needs, will be examined. The discussion is organized around the following three topics:

1. Determining the school program.
2. Analyzing the school program to determine school-plant needs.
3. Estimating future enrollments to determine school-plant needs.

Determining the School Program

THE fundamental tenet in all school-plant work is that the physical facilities should be designed to promote the desired school program. Application of this principle at the time of a school-plant survey requires that the study be designed to include careful analysis of the school program in order

35

to ascertain the necessary physical facilities. The resulting list of facilities then becomes a basis for evaluating the existing school plant and for formulating recommendations for improved facilities.

Before the school-plant survey staff can analyze the school program, the nature of the program must be determined by the proper local school authorities, preferably by official action of the board of education. The program should be based upon extensive study, and it is to be expected that its formulation would require concerted effort over a longer period of time than would be needed for the school-plant study. Indeed, there should be more or less continuous study of the school program in any school system. The ideal situation from the standpoint of a school-plant survey staff is to have at its disposal a recently completed study of the school program or a continuous study of such nature that seasoned decisions can be made available with reasonable promptness to the building survey staff.

Such an ideal situation seldom exists. On the contrary, all too often a building survey is undertaken with little or no preliminary program planning and with a deadline date that makes it impossible to include in the survey more than a hasty and possibly superficial consideration of what the school program ought to be. The building survey staff members have no magic wand with power to remedy this situation. However, they cannot shrug their shoulders and say that the lack of proper program planning is no concern of theirs.

NATURE OF PROGRAM STUDY

While it is not the object of this volume to describe in detail how to plan the school program of a community, such planning must so often be done in part in a building survey that a few general suggestions will be made. First, a few essential characteristics of such a study will be presented, and then brief consideration will be given to major factors which should be analyzed in deciding upon the school program in a given community.

The characteristics which are suggested are three in number. First, the study should be comprehensive enough to cover all aspects of the school's program. It should not be limited to regular classes for children, but should encompass every activity using the school plant, regardless of age or other characteristics of the participants and regardless of whether sponsored by the board of education or by others. Secondly, the study should be oriented toward the future, with a reasonable degree of imagination and idealism. The physical facilities based on the survey results will remain in use for many decades, probably a half century or more in the case of a well-planned new building, and it would be a mistake to be too provincial or unduly timid in the basic program planning at this stage. It is clearly implicit in these first two characteristics that the program planners must look far beyond the walls of the school building or the fence around the playground and view the school as a vital and changing force in the community as a whole. It should be clear, also, that such planning is properly a community-wide job in which the school system should be only one of several cooperating agencies. The third characteristic suggested is that the study include adequate attention both to the underlying purposes and philosophy of the schools and to the specifics of the program. School-building planners and survey workers are helped but little by broad philosophical statements alone; they must know also the nature of the program built upon the philosophy. The philosophical aspects of the study are essential first steps for the program planners and provide useful background in helping the school-plant workers to understand the proposed specific program elements, particularly with respect to possible future changes.

BASES FOR SCHOOL PROGRAM

The scope, content, methods, and other attributes of the total school program rest in the final analysis upon three foundations—(1) the purpose of the school in society; (2) the nature of the learner and the learning process; and (3) the character of the community in which the school functions. Any adequate study of a school program must attend to these factors.

Role of the School in Society

The American people today realize that a school system is an instrument which they can use for providing the kind of society or way of life they desire. Schools can be used to support, nourish, and improve democracy or to undergird and uphold an authoritarian way of life. The former is the clear choice of all but a mere handful of Americans. This being the case, those who plan school programs must constantly ask themselves what groups of people must be reached and what types of behavior must be engendered in these people. Can the goal be achieved if only children from 6 to 18 years of age are in school, or must the school program encompass a much larger segment of the population over a longer period of time? Can the goal be attained if the school program is limited to imparting the basic knowledges and skills of the traditional three R's, or must it be broadened to include certain other knowledges, skills, habits, understandings, and attitudes? Answers to these and a host of related questions must be found as one basis for planning the school program.

Nature of Learners

The second major ingredient in the planning process is understanding of the nature of the learner and the learning process. Do children become better citizens, for example, by learning facts about American history and government or by participating in properly directed student councils and other group activities, or what combination of these and other activities will be most effective in producing the desired results? Can arithmetic be taught best by drill and recitation, by having children engage in a variety of properly guided and interesting activities involving the use of arithmetic, or by some combination of these and other teaching procedures? Answers to these and many similar questions are necessary in developing sound methods in the schools, and these answers must be based upon understanding of the learner rather than upon adherence to past practices.

Nature of Local Community

The extent to which the nature of the local community will affect the school program depends upon the purposes of the schools. Since it is generally accepted in American society that the schools should assist people to become more effective participants in all kinds of community activities, it is reasonable to expect that a comprehensive study of the school program will embrace the gathering and analysis of considerable information about the local community and its people. Included might be studies of such topics as mobility and age of population, needs and opportunities for young people, what happens to young people after leaving school at graduation or before, recreational interests and facilities, and extent of employment of mothers and facilities for care of their children.

DEPTH OF STUDY

Such is the general nature of the problem of planning the school program. If the most appropriate physical facilities are to be provided, this program planning must be done thoroughly. To accomplish this, adequate time and competent personnel are essential. If such planning has not preceded the building survey, the extent to which it is done then will depend upon several factors. If the building survey is primarily concerned with the development of a long-range program, or if the community for some other reason cannot or is not likely to undertake major school-plant changes in the near future, the program planning can be less detailed. If, on the other hand, major changes are to be made soon, detailed program planning should start at once, both to serve the needs of the survey and to permit the more detailed building planning which comes after the survey and before the architectural work on a specific building project. The absolute minimum of program planning that should be done in connection with a survey would be one or two meetings of selected school personnel to answer the basic questions to which the survey staff must have answers.

Analyzing the School Program to Determine School-Plant Needs

WHATEVER the nature of the previous program planning, the building survey staff must make a detailed program analysis to provide a foundation for its evaluation of existing buildings and its recommendations for new construction or other improvements. Pertinent written documents must be studied, policy decisions noted, and questions regarding the program listed for later discussion. Among the documents to be so examined would be the reports of any previous studies of the school program, curriculum bulletins of various kinds, official statements of board policy, superintendent's annual reports, and any other materials describing any aspect of the school program. Since the survey staff's need for such information is not always fully recognized, persistent questioning is often necessary to gain access to all helpful sources of information.

After the available written materials have been studied, one or more conferences should be held with representatives of the school staff and possibly others. In these meetings the survey staff should seek answers to questions arising from the analysis of written materials and raise additional questions to fill gaps in the needed information. Where little or no advance program planning has been done, these conferences must be the sole or main source of program information for the survey staff, and thus might be of somewhat different character or longer duration. Throughout these conferences the survey staff members have the responsibility of raising questions about the local decisions, pointing out alternatives, describing and explaining pertinent trends in education, supplying relevant facts about practices and points of view elsewhere, and in other ways helping the local school authorities to make better decisions regarding their own future school program.

PRESENT POLICIES

As a result of these conferences and the study of the pertinent documents, the survey staff will have a statement of rather specific program policies upon which to base later parts of the survey. These policies will deal with a host of topics including such matters as courses of study, size of class, size of school, and noninstructional services to be provided. Approval of all or some of these policies by the board of education would be advisable in some cases, while in others approval by the superintendent would suffice. If adequate approval is not secured, the risk is increased that the staff's recommendations will be upset by an unexpected change of policy or because the wrong policies were assumed in making the recommendations.

POSSIBILITY OF CHANGE

In making its analysis of the school program the survey staff will find it helpful to look at each aspect of the program in terms of possible future changes. It might, for example, seek to ascertain for each aspect of the program such information as the following: (1) present practice; (2) changes that would be made promptly if building facilities were available; (3) changes that are quite certain to be made but which depend upon more than building improvements; and (4) possible changes that are more distant and less certain to be desired or achieved. A device such as the chart below might prove helpful in summarizing this information. A few sample entries have been made to indicate how the chart might be used.

Aspect of program	Present practice	Immediate future if building facilities are available	Desired as soon as building and other conditions permit	More distant and uncertain; may never be provided
Nursery schools	No	No	No	Perhaps
Kindergartens	No	Yes, at each elementary center	—	—
Average class size in elementary school	37	30	25	—
Elementary school lunchrooms	No	No	Yes, for about 40% of the enrollment	—

Partial Suggested Chart for Analyzing School Program

The use of some such classifications will prove very helpful to the survey staff in its later work. In evaluating existing buildings the staff will give major attention to the facilities for those aspects of the program desired in the immediate future and will not rate a building low for lack of facilities that may be needed in the more distant future. Using the hypothetical data in the chart, for example, the survey staff would be critical of an elementary school building with no kindergarten facilities but would ignore the lack of nursery school quarters. The classification would also prove useful at the time of formulating the survey recommendations. Again using the same hypothetical data, the survey staff would try to formulate its recommendations to provide kindergarten facilities in each elementary school building and would set aside space for lunchrooms or try to provide for easy addition of lunchroom space later. No particular attention would be given to the nursery school except to avoid creating any unnecessary obstacles to the later provision of the necessary quarters.

CHECK LIST OF PROGRAM QUESTIONS

The specific aspects of the program which need to be examined in some such manner are many and varied. Because of the great variations in school programs and the differences in the scope and purposes of building surveys, each survey staff must prepare its own list. The following questions are designed to suggest items for inclusion without being either restrictive or exhaustive:

1. General policies
   a. What is the optimum enrollment of an elementary school? A secondary school? What is the maximum size beyond which no new elementary school should go? Secondary school?
   b. What is the maximum distance an elementary school pupil should normally be required to walk to school? A secondary school pupil?
   c. What is the maximum time an elementary school pupil should normally be on a school bus for any one trip? A secondary school pupil?
2. Scope of program
   a. What ages or grades are now served?
   b. Will there be any downward extension to include kindergarten or nursery school pupils?
   c. Will the program be extended upward to include additional grades, junior college pupils, or adult classes?

  d. What does or will the program include with respect to
night schools, summer schools, camping, public library,
public recreation, and community center activities for
children or adults, regardless of sponsorship or source of
financial support?

3. Vertical organization

  a. What types of schools (elementary, junior high, etc.) are
now in existence and which grades are included in each?

  b. Is there any firm policy with respect to the pattern of
vertical organization, or is the survey staff free to recommend the plan which it considers best under the circumstances?

4. Elementary schools

  a. What subjects or areas of learning will normally be
handled in the regular classrooms?

  b. To what extent is the activity or experience approach to
learning used, or what different types of individual or
group activity will take place in the regular classrooms?

  c. What instructional activities for normal children will require special classrooms (e.g., gymnasiums, libraries, arts
and crafts rooms, music rooms)?

  d. What daily schedule will be followed, particularly of
those activities which are departmentalized and require
some changes of room?

  e. What is the desired average classroom size? The maximum size?

  f. What nonclassroom instructional activities are included,
such as assemblies, student councils, dramatics, outside
play, etc., and how are they scheduled?

  g. What administrative and supervisory staff, including
secretarial personnel, will be provided?

  h. What will be the nature and extent of the health service
program?

  i. What will be the nature and extent of the child study
and guidance programs?

  j. Will noon lunches or other food be served? If so, to how
many and according to what schedule?

  k. What special provision is made for atypical school children? Types of special classes? Class size? Nature of
special class activities?

5. Secondary schools[1]
   a. Which grades are included?
   b. Which subjects are required and which are elective in each grade?
   c. On the average, what percent of the pupils in each grade take each elective subject, and what percents can reasonably be expected in the future?
   d. What is the desired average class size in each subject? Maximum size?
   e. What will be the nature of the homeroom program (schedule, activities, size of group)?
   f. What will be the nature of the extra-class instructional activities, including assemblies, clubs, student government, intramural sports, interschool athletics, etc? Names of groups? Nature of activities? Size of groups? Schedule?
   g. What is the weekly schedule of classes?
   h. In each subject what are the various kinds of class activities which influence space requirements?
   i. What provision will be made for atypical children? Types of special classes? Class size? Nature of special class activities?
   j. What will be the normal number of teaching periods for teachers in each subject area? What use will be made of a teacher's classroom during his nonteaching periods?
   k. What administrative and supervisory staff, including secretarial personnel, will be provided?
   l. What will be the nature and extent of the health service program?
   m. What will be the nature and extent of the guidance and counseling program?
   n. What noon lunches or other food will be served, to how many pupils, and according to what schedule?
6. Other aspects of program
   a. What will be the summer school program? Which buildings? Subjects? Enrollments? Size of classes?
   b. What week-end or vacation activities will be offered? Nature of activities? Schedule? Size of groups?

[1] Make separate analysis for each type of secondary school (junior high, senior high, junior college, etc.).

  c. Will outdoor education and camping be provided? If so, to what pupils, in what sized groups, and according to what schedule?

  d. Will public library service be provided in school buildings? If so, in which buildings? Nature and extent of program in each building?

  e. Will public recreation activities be conducted on school grounds or in school buildings? If so, what will be the nature of the activities? Size of groups? Schedule?

  f. What will be the adult education program? Which buildings? Subjects? Size of groups? Schedule?

  g. What other community activities will make use of school buildings or grounds? Nature? Frequency? Number of people in each type of activity?

7. System-wide services

  a. What central office personnel must be housed, including administrators, supervisors, clerical and secretarial workers, buildings and grounds workers, and others?

  b. What central facilities are needed for staff meetings, committee meetings, and group work?

  c. What central professional library services, health clinics, psychological and adjustment services, and other centralized services will be provided?

  d. What will be the nature and extent of central warehousing and repair services?

  e. What transportation of pupils will be provided and what will this require in the way of garage and repair services?

LIST OF NEEDED FACILITIES

When properly recorded and analyzed the answers to these questions will enable the survey staff to prepare a list of the types of facilities required in each kind of school. Since certain multiple-use spaces may be appropriate, the list at this stage may not be conclusive as to each specific type of room needed. For example, the list may not specify that separate auditorium, gymnasium, and lunchroom spaces should be provided in each elementary building regardless of size or other conditions, but it should indicate clearly that each building should have available suitable space for assembly, physical education, and lunchroom use if these are required by the program.

Number of Elementary School Classrooms

To some extent the list can and should give quantitative information for determining the number or capacity of rooms of each type necessary for any given number of pupils. At the elementary school level, for example, the list should specify one regular classroom for each given number of pupils, one assembly space for a certain minimum percent of the enrollment of each building, one full-time indoor physical education teaching space for each given number of classrooms, etc. This information can then be used later in determining not only how many classrooms are required at each school, but also what combinations of other rooms are feasible. For example, if the physical education program necessitates one full-time teaching space for each 18 classrooms, it is obvious that a combination auditorium-gymnasium would not be appropriate in an 18-classroom building, since any assembly activity would be at the expense of physical education. However, with this physical education load, such a combination room could be used in a 12 classroom building, insofar as the scheduling is concerned.

Number of Secondary School Classrooms

Determining the number of teaching stations to house a secondary school program is much more difficult. This is true because the number varies not only with the total enrollment but with the number of periods per week in each subject and in the total weekly schedule, the subject enrollments, policies concerning class size, and other policies of the individual school or school system. Essentially what is needed is some index, table, or other device that will indicate how many teaching stations are needed for each subject area for a given number of pupils in total enrollment. Various ways of doing this have been and can be derived, but whatever the method, it is essential that the calculations be based on the educational program and operating policies which the school in question would be likely to follow if the necessary plant facilities were available. No one set of indexes or tables will suffice for all schools.

One approach which has been found useful, regardless of the degree of departmentalization, is to calculate an index for each subject area or group of subject areas in the program of the school in question. These indexes express the number of pupils in the total enrollment in a given grade or grades for which one teaching station will serve. For example, an index of 450 for industrial arts means that for each 450 pupils in total enrollment (not industrial arts enrollment) there will be required one industrial arts teaching station.

The formula for calculating the index for any subject area is as follows: [2]

$$\text{Index} = \frac{CS \times TP \times TE}{SE \times SP}, \text{ in which}$$

cs is the average class size desired for the subject or subjects for which the index is being calculated.

TP is the total number of periods per week that the average teaching station can be used in the subject or subjects for which the index is being calculated. This is the total number of periods in the weekly schedule adjusted to allow for: (*1*) nonuse of room during lunch; (*2*) nonavailability of room if a teacher is permitted to use his room during nonteaching periods; and (*3*) the impossibility of 100-percent utilization because the number of periods per week for each group of pupils does not divide evenly into the total number of periods in the weekly schedule.

TE is the total enrollment in the grade or grades for which the index is being calculated.

SE is the enrollment in the subject or subjects for which the index is being calculated.

SP is the number of periods of instruction per week in the subject or subjects for which the index is being calculated.

By way of illustration, the following is the calculation of the index for chemistry and physics in a hypothetical three-year high school of 1200 pupils. Numerically stated the various factors are:

cs—the average class size is 25 pupils.

TP—the weekly schedule is 30 periods. Since chemistry and physics meet 7 periods per week, only 28 of the 30 periods can be used. *TP* is, therefore, given a value of 28.[3]

[2] This approach is an adaptation of the formula developed by Conrad for determining the capacity of a secondary school building. See Conrad, Marion J., *A Manual for Determining the Operating Capacity of Secondary School Buildings.* Columbus: Bureau of Educational Research, Ohio State University, 1954. For related techniques see also Anderson, Homer W., *A Method for Determining the Housing Requirements of Junior High School Programs.* University of Iowa, Studies in Education, Vol. 3, No. 3. Iowa City: University of Iowa, 1926; and Packer, Paul C., *Housing of High School Programs.* Contributions to Education, No. 159. New York: Teachers College, Columbia University, 1924.

[3] It is at this point that allowance is made for the impossibility of scheduling all rooms for 100-percent utilization. Anderson and Packer, cited in the preceding footnote, and others would make further correction for this factor. For more extensive discussion of this point, see pp. 117–120.

TE—the total enrollment in all three grades is 1200.

SE—the total course enrollment in these two subjects is 125.

SP—each class in these subjects meets 7 periods per week.

The index for chemistry and physics, then, is:

$$\frac{25 \times 28 \times 1200}{125 \times 7}, \text{ or } 960.$$

The index of 960 in this example means that for every 960 pupils in grades 10 through 12 there is need for one teaching station for chemistry and physics. Obviously, this index would be changed by any modification of the average class size, the number of periods each teaching station can be used per week, the number of periods per week in each class, or the percent of pupils enrolling in these subjects. Thus, the index reflects the operating policies of the individual school, and is not a generalization based on average practices in a number of schools or someone's notion of an ideal or practical program.

Final List of Facilities Needed

At the conclusion of its analysis of the program, the survey staff should prepare a detailed list of the facilities needed in the near future in each type of school. These lists would provide one basis for evaluating existing buildings and later be used for preparing recommendations for remodeling and new construction. The lists prepared at this time would include both quantitative and qualitative information. With respect to the former, the list should mention each type of facility required and indicate the basis for determining the number needed in a building of any given size. With respect to lunchrooms, assembly rooms, and similar spaces, the list should indicate how to determine their size or capacity in a school of any given size and kind. On the qualitative side, these lists should note the essential features of each type of room, insofar as these would need to be listed to prevent overlooking them later in the survey.

The following partial lists, which are purely hypothetical and in no sense recommended standards, reveal further the nature of the lists proposed:

Elementary Schools

1. One kindergarten room for each 50 pupils (two groups of 25 each). Separate entrance. Separate toilets.
2. One classroom for each 25 pupils in grades 1 and 2. Room toilets, sink, library corner, science center, and construction

area in room. Movable equipment including wardrobes.
Suitable for projected audio-visual aids.

3. Assembly space adequate for at least 60 percent of the enrollment at one time, preferably separate from gymnasium.
Desirable to have gymnasium or other space available for
occasional large gatherings.

Secondary Schools

1. One regular classroom for each 60 pupils in grades 10
through 12. Minimum of 800 square feet. Suitable for projected audio-visual aids. Movable seating and other equipment.

2. One chemistry and physics room for each 960 pupils in
grades 10 through 12. Room suitable for all chemistry and
and physics activities—study, recitation, discussion, group
work, laboratory work, use of projected audio-visual aids,
etc. Demonstration table and pupil laboratory tables with
water, gas, and electricity. Separate storage and preparation
room.

In addition to these general lists for each type of building there might
be need for special lists for certain buildings, for the central administrative
quarters, or for other particular aspects of the complete plant. The number
and nature of these special lists will, of course, vary considerably from one
survey to another, depending upon the local school program and the scope
and depth of the particular survey.

The specific suggestions which have been made with respect to analyzing
the school program and preparing lists of needed facilities are not followed
by all survey workers, and they need not be. The essential thing is not that
any one procedure be followed, but that each survey staff set up and use an
orderly procedure for determining the school-plant facilities needed to
house the desired school program. It is essential, also, that this analysis be
made in such a manner that the results can be used to evaluate existing
buildings, to plan changes in existing buildings, and to determine in a
general way the facilities to be provided in any new construction that is
recommended.

Estimating Future Enrollments
to Determine School-Plant Needs

A CONSIDERABLE degree of uncertainty is inevitable in any estimate
of future enrollment. This is true because no one can foresee the many
factors which will affect the number of children in school in the future.

Even in a community of relatively stable population, there are such unpredictable factors as changes in birth rates, in policies regarding age of admission to school and promotion from grade to grade, in the power of the school to hold children until graduation, and in the percentage of children attending nonpublic schools. In other communities, and to some extent in all, the future school enrollments will reflect the course of such events as industrial growth and decline, decentralization of industry, and shifting of population to urban areas or from cities to suburbs. These in turn are dependent upon a host of other forces which cannot be fully anticipated.

These many uncertainties do not justify carelessness or evasion of the problem but should lead the survey worker to be wary and always seeking improved procedures. There are occasional school-plant surveys where this aspect is not very critical, but in most cases the recommendations will depend in considerable measure upon what the future enrollment is expected to be, either within broad limits or rather more precisely. With all the possibilities of error, the use of a carefully developed forecast based upon the best available data and techniques is superior to any alternative such as unsupported guessing, assuming a static enrollment, or assuming that recent trends will continue indefinitely.

In general, the estimates for only a few years hence are more accurate than those for the more distant future. Such short-term estimates can be based on known numbers of preschool children or known birth data, and the other relevent factors can be better foreseen. It would seem advisable in most school systems for the local school authorities to keep an up-to-date file of basic information and annually to make their own estimates for the next five or six years. The information thus procured would be useful in anticipating problems sufficiently early to allow time for adequate school-plant planning, which is so often lacking. Also, the information would be extremely useful in planning other aspects of school operation.

No one method of estimating is likely to be equally appropriate in all surveys. This is true for several reasons. In the first place, each variation of technique involves different assumptions as to trends, and some of these assumptions will not be defensible in certain communities. The survey worker must be fully aware of the assumptions underlying any techniques he employs and must constantly check their appropriateness in the school system under study. Secondly, the techniques chosen should depend in part upon the degree of refinement required for the particular survey in question. In certain studies of long-range character, for example, the estimates can be much more approximate than where a new building is to be planned immediately, and a different technique of estimating will be appropriate. Also, it is unfortunately true that the method of estimating must often be selected or adapted in terms of the data which are available to the survey staff.

THE SURVIVAL TECHNIQUE

The survival technique, with many variations, is in common use.[4] Basically, this involves two steps: (1) determining the rates of survival from grade to grade in the past; and (2) estimating future enrollments grade by grade by applying the survival rates thus determined. For example, if the rate of survival from grade 1 to grade 2 has been 95 percent in the recent past, it is assumed that the same rate will continue to prevail in the future, and the second-grade estimates each year will be 95 percent of the first grade the year before. Other grades are estimated in like fashion. Kindergarten or first-grade enrollment estimates are based upon rates of survival from birth five or six years earlier or upon preschool census data.

Securing Birth Data

In estimating kindergarten or first-grade enrollments from birth data, it is necessary to determine accurately how many children were born alive each year for the past 10 to 15 years to mothers living in the school district. The total number of live births occurring in the district is not the proper figure, since it may include many children born in local hospitals to nonresident mothers, or it may omit many babies born to resident mothers who go outside the district for maternity care. A trend toward increasing use of hospital facilities for childbirth accentuates the defects of total live births as a basic figure, since it tends to cause more mothers to leave their district of residence for maternity care.

Even where the birth data are presumably classified according to residence of mothers, some wariness on the part of the survey staff is in order. Errors of classification in such data are common. For example, the classification may be on the basis of post office address, ignoring the fact that post office district lines frequently do not coincide with the boundaries of municipal corporations or school districts. Even where the classification is accurate, the birth statistics may be reported by health districts that do not coincide with the school districts.

[4] For a discussion of other techniques see Strevell, Wallace H., "Techniques of Estimating Future Enrollments," *American School Board Journal*, 124:35–38, March, 1952. Also Larson, Knute G., and Strevell, Wallace H., "How Reliable Are Enrollment Forecasts?" *School Executive*, 71:65–68, February, 1952.

With proper birth data at hand, the next step is to determine the relationship of the number of births each year to enrollments in the lowest public school grade five or six years later. The relationship to kindergarten enrollment five years later can be used if the percentage of eligible children who actually enroll in kindergarten does not change substantially from year to year. Where such fluctuations do occur, the birth data should be related to first-grade enrollment six years later. Since kindergarten enrollment is not compulsory, there is often a gradual increase in the percentage of eligible children who attend kindergarten, but the reader can readily adapt the proposed procedure to include this grade when the circumstances warrant it. When the kindergarten is omitted, reasonable estimates of the kindergarten enrollment can be made later from the estimates made for the first grade. This is done by studying the relationship of kindergarten enrollments and first-grade enrollments in recent years and then making the kindergarten estimates in terms of any trends observed in this relationship.

Determining Survival Rate from Birth to First Grade

For a projection from birth to grade 1, the first step is to divide the first-grade enrollment each year (using the same date each year) by the number of resident live births six years earlier. The quotient is expressed as a percent of survival from birth to first grade. This is done for several years back, say for 10 years, and a weighted average computed. The annual figures are then carefully scrutinized, trends and shifts in pattern observed, and explanations sought by recalling events which might affect the survival rates. Fluctuations from year to year are normal and reflect changes in such factors as the impact of migration, the enrollment of resident pupils in schools outside the district, the enrollment of non-resident pupils in the local schools, the percentage of local children electing to attend nonpublic schools in preference to public schools, the policy with respect to age of admission to the first grade, and the policy with respect to promotion to the second grade. Where no reasonable explanation can be found, the fluctuations may indicate faulty birth data, incorrect first-grade enrollment data, or errors in calculation.

The reasonableness of the average rate of survival from birth to first grade also needs examination. Let us assume, for example, that the average mortality from birth to age six in a certain community is 5 percent. The average rate of survival from birth to first grade in this case should be 95 percent. If the calculated average is more, an explanation should be sought in such factors as net gain from migration, acceptance of nonresident pupils, enlargement of the school district with no corresponding adjustment of birth data, or failure of the birth data to fit precisely the geographical area covered by the school district. Defective enrollment or birth data and errors of calculation are other possible explanations to be examined. If the weighted average in this hypothetical case is below 95 percent, an explanation should be sought in such factors as net loss from migration, loss of children to nonpublic schools or to schools outside the district, changes in district boundaries with no corresponding adjustments in birth data, failure of the birth data to fit precisely the geographical area of the school district, failure of many 6-year-olds to enroll in school, defective enrollment or birth data, and errors in calculation.

When an acceptable rate of survival from birth to first grade has been achieved, it is necessary to decide whether it can be used without change in estimating future first grades. An adjustment in the survival rate will be required if it seems likely that the net effect of migration will change, that the nonpublic schools will take more or fewer pupils, or that transfers to or from other public schools will be materially different. Some temporary adjustment may also be required because of an anticipated change of policy in respect to age of admission. Only sound judgment based upon careful analysis of all available evidence can determine what adjustment, if any, to make in the survival rate.

Estimating First-Grade Enrollment from Birth Data

Having decided upon a rate of survival from birth to first grade that is appropriate to use for the future, the next step is to estimate the first-grade enrollments for the next six years by applying the survival rate to the number of births for each of the past six years. This is the limit of estimates for first-grade enrollments using known birth data.

If this procedure is used to make first-grade estimates beyond six years into the future, it is necessary first to estimate the number of births each year for several years in the future. This is done by multiplying an estimated total population each year by an estimated birth rate, which is expressed in number of births per thousand people. Population estimates for future years can often be secured from utility companies, official planning agencies, or chambers of commerce. Clues can also be obtained from analysis of data in official census reports. Birth rates can be expected to change somewhat gradually in normal times, but the magnitude and direction of change are impossible to foretell. The writings of students of population problems, health officials, and local official planning agencies are possible sources of clues on this point.

Any estimates of total population obtained for this purpose must be carefully scrutinized. Some will be based on cautious and realistic interpretations of the available evidence, while others will be designed primarily for boosting civic pride or attracting business or industry to the community. They may or may not apply reasonably well to the exact territory included in the school district. It is sometimes possible to check such estimates in a rough way by seeking to determine how many additional dwelling units can be provided on the residential land available and how many people there would have to be per dwelling unit to reach the predicted total population.

Estimating First-Grade Enrollment from Census Data

An alternative procedure for estimating first-grade enrollments is to use preschool census data in place of birth figures. All children below school age are listed and classified according to year of anticipated enrollment in the first grade. As when birth data are used, the raw figures cannot be used directly. Adjustments may be required for mortality (probably only in the youngest group) and for enrollment in other schools. These various adjustments can be most easily made if a preschool census has been taken regularly over a period of years and the pattern of survival from one age group to the next is known. Even then, however, the possibility of changes in these survival rates in the future must be examined.

The use of preschool census data introduces another source of error that must be guarded against. The common experience with such data has been that the count is increasingly incomplete as the age level decreases. In other words, the census discloses a smaller percent of the 4-year-olds than it does of the 5-year-olds, a smaller percent of the 3-year-olds than the 4's, etc. This requires that the enumerators make certain that a report of every dwelling unit is received and that every child is counted. Questions must be put by enumerators in such a way that the respondent clearly understands that all children, not just those in school or those expected to be enrolled in public schools, are to be reported.

If a preschool census is to be taken, it would be well to set up a master file of dwelling units with a separate card for each unit and to plan the census field work each year to include each card. Land-use maps prepared by official planning groups, aerial photographs, or a field canvass, separately or in combination, would be helpful in developing the original file. Beyond that point, the file should be kept up to date by regular checking of permits for new construction, remodeling, and demolition of structures. If such a file is continuously revised, it would be well to make a count of numbers of units at a regular time each year, so that trends can later be determined. The count should be made at the time of the school census each year, and should be made according to the same geographical units used in classifying the census data. This would make it possible to study trends in the number of children per dwelling unit in different parts of the school district, and, if desired, to do this separately for different age or grade groups. Such data would prove to be invaluable in later planning.

Estimates of Enrollment Above Grade 1

Beyond the first grade the percent of survival from each grade to the next is calculated year by year for the past 5 to 10 years and a weighted average determined. For each grade the annual rates should be examined for trends or shifts of pattern and explanations sought for any unusual fluctuations. The average, too, should be checked as to reasonableness. With a relatively stable population and no greater amount of retardation, the survival rates will be reasonably close to 100 percent throughout the period of compulsory school attendance and will then fall to lower levels. Relatively high rates will be observed at those points where large numbers of nonpublic school pupils or nonresident pupils transfer to the local public school system. High rates at other grade levels reflect net gains from migration or extensions of the boundaries of the school district.

After checking the survival rates, the averages may have to be adjusted to allow for anticipated changes in the net effect of migration, in the percent of children going to other schools, and in the number of pupils accepted from outside the school district, or in the policies in regard to promotion. If secondary school estimates are made for any appreciable length of time into the future, there may also need to be some upward adjustment for improved holding power. In spite of the impressive gains in holding power in recent years, there is still much room for improvement. School policies with respect to curriculum, student activities, transportation, fees and hidden costs, and other aspects of the program will have a bearing on how many young people remain in high school until graduation.

The adjusted survival rates are used to project the enrollments grade by grade and year by year into the future. The rate of survival from first to second grade is applied in turn to each year's estimate for grade 1, and by this process the second-grade estimates are derived. The same procedure is then used to convert second-grade estimates into third-grade estimates, and so on grade by grade until estimates have been completed for all grades.

The table on page 56 shows the survival technique using hypothetical birth data chosen to illustrate the factors discussed above. Unfortunately, the actual data in most instances are not so easy to interpret because they reflect simultaneously the effects of a complexity of unmeasured and often unidentified forces. The table should, however, help to clarify the procedures used.

Example Using Birth Data

In the table the survival from birth to first grade fluctuates from 80 to 89 percent, with only one year going above 85 percent. In the year where the 89 percent appears (1949–50), the rates of survival throughout the school system seem to be higher than in other years. This is due to a sharp influx of new families with the opening of a new factory. The weighted average percent of survival from birth to first grade is 83.5. Omitting the one high figure (89 percent) reduces this to 82.9 percent, which is not a significant change. Health department records in this community indicate that about 5 percent of the live births do not survive till school age. Analysis of public and nonpublic school enrollment figures for the 10-year period reveals that the nonpublic schools have taken an average of 17 percent of the first-grade children. The original group reduced successively by 5 percent and 17 percent leaves 78.85 percent remaining. Allowance for 5-percent nonpromotion in grade 1 increases this 78.85 percent to 82.8 percent (78.85 × 1.05), which is about the same as the averages above. Examination of the evidence suggests no other major gain or loss from migration or change in district boundaries which would have affected the percent of survival. These several percents (83.5, 82.9, and 82.8) hover around 83, and 83 percent may be used as an approximate survival rate to date.

The next step is to determine whether this average can be used for estimating the future. No evidence is found indicating any early change in school district boundaries, in the percent going to nonpublic schools, or in other factors that might affect the rate of survival from birth to grade 1. Therefore, the first-grade enrollments for the next six years, which appear below the broken line, are derived by multiplying each annual birth total in turn by .83. For example, the estimate of 168 for 1958–59 is 83 percent of the 202 births in 1952.

The table shows rates of survival from first to second grade that average

Hypothetical Enrollment Projection Table

Enrollment and percent of survival in each succeeding grade

Births Year	Births Number	School year	Grade 1 Number	Grade 1 % sur.	Grade 2 Number	Grade 2 % sur.	Grade 3 Number	Grade 3 % sur.	Grade 4 Number	Grade 4 % sur.	Grade 5 Number	Grade 5 % sur.	Grade 6 Number	Grade 6 % sur.	Grade 7 Number	Grade 7 % sur.	Grade 8 Number	Grade 8 % sur.	Grade 9 Number	Grade 9 % sur.	Grade 10 Number	Grade 10 % sur.	Grade 11 Number	Grade 11 % sur.	Grade 12 Number	Grade 12 % sur.
1939	109	1945–46	87	80	81	93	84	98	85	97	88	99	89	97	88	99	87	99	108	123	91	84	76	83	65	89
1940	115	1946–47	97	84	83	95	82	101	84	100	87	102	87	99	90	101	89	101	110	126	92	85	77	85	68	89
1941	111	1947–48	91	82	90	93	82	99	80	98	84	100	84	97	87	100	90	100	110	124	95	86	75	82	68	88
1942	144	1948–49	120	83	86	94	90	100	81	99	78	98	80	95	83	99	86	99	113	126	96	87	80	84	65	87
1943	143	1949–50	127	89	111	101	89	103	94	104	85	105	82	105	83	104	86	104	110	128	102	90	84	87	73	91
1944	133	1950–51	113	85	122	96	120	99	89	100	94	100	81	95	83	101	85	102	110	128	95	86	88	86	74	88
1945	132	1951–52	108	82	107	95	120	98	119	99	90	101	92	98	79	98	82	99	105	124	94	85	79	83	78	89
1946	169	1952–53	140	83	100	93	108	101	118	98	119	100	89	99	91	99	80	101	103	125	90	86	79	84	71	90
1947	197	1953–54	165	84	132	94	101	101	105	97	120	102	115	97	90	101	91	100	101	126	87	84	74	82	70	89
1948	186	1954–55	154	83	158	96	132	100	100	99	106	101	117	98	113	98	91	101	113	124	87	86	73	84	66	89
1949	189	1955–56	157	83	146	95	158	100	131	99	101	101	104	98	117	100	114	101	115	126	97	86	73	84	65	89
1950	186	1956–57	154	83	149	95	146	100	156	99	132	101	99	98	104	100	118	101	144	126	98	86	81	84	65	89
1951	197	1957–58	164	83	146	95	149	100	145	99	158	101	129	98	99	100	105	101	149	126	124	86	83	84	72	89
1952	202	1958–59	168	83	156	95	146	100	148	99	146	101	155	98	129	100	100	101	132	126	128	86	104	84	74	89
1953	200	1959–60	166	83	160	95	156	100	145	99	149	101	143	98	155	100	130	101	126	126	114	86	108	84	93	89
1954	208	1960–61	173	83	158	95	160	100	154	99	146	101	146	98	143	100	157	101	164	126	108	86	96	84	96	89

NOTES: 1. All data are hypothetical.
2. Figures above the broken line represent actual enrollments; those below, estimates.

95 percent, and other averages in the first eight grades hover around 100 percent. The relatively low survival to grade 2 reflects the higher incidence of nonpromotion in grade 1. The average survival of 126 percent from grade 8 to 9 reflects the transfer of pupils from the eight-year parochial elementary school to the public high school, the enrollment of nonresident pupils from a neighboring district that operates no high school, and some loss of pupils who drop out of school completely. The percents of survival in the higher grades reflects the lack of holding power when attendance is no longer compulsory.

The method of projecting above grade 1 can be shown best by an example. The second-grade enrollment of 146 in 1955–56 is 95 percent of the first grade enrollment of 154 the preceding year. All other projections above the first grade are made in the same manner.

Variation Using Census Data

If preschool census data were used instead of birth data to predict the first grade, the table would be very similar. The two columns for birth data would be omitted, and an additional column would be inserted at the left for each preschool age group. Thus, there would be columns for ages "under 1," "1 to 1.9," etc., up to school age. Or, the column headings might be "−6," "−5," etc., indicating the number of years before admission to the first grade. The calculations in these preschool age columns would be made in the same manner as explained above for grades above the first grade.

A variation in the survival technique is to use groups of ages or grades rather than single ages or grades for estimating. For example, the enrollment in the first six grades might be based upon the entire preschool group, or grades 7 through 9 might be estimated by the rate of survival from grades 4 through 6. If the pattern of vertical organization is fixed in advance and cannot be changed by the survey recommendations, such grouping is satisfactory. If, however, the survey workers are free to recommend changes in the grades to be housed in a given type of school, the estimates must be by single grades to permit the survey staff to try out different groupings of grades as recommendations are developed.

Nonresident Pupils

The enrollment of large numbers of nonresident pupils frequently complicates the use of the survival technique. If these numbers change frequently, or if the nonresident territory has not been or may not be constant in extent, it would be preferable to exclude the nonresident pupils completely from the data, to estimate the resident enrollment separately, and then to make special allowance at the end for the nonresident pupils.

Enrollments in Nonpublic Schools

Enrollment in nonpublic schools is another frequent complicating factor. Information should be secured relative to enrollment of district residents in such schools over a period of years, and trends observed. Information should also be secured about plans of these schools for enlarging the number of children enrolled. In some cases, it will be safe to assume that the nonpublic schools will take a certain percent of the total enrollment; in others, the number of children in such schools, rather than the percent, should be held constant. In some situations, it may be well to combine the data, make a single projection for all schools, and then split the estimated totals into public and nonpublic school enrollments. The latter is especially desirable when the nonpublic schools are used to capacity or when a major expansion of their facilities is in prospect.

The Migration Factor

The third and most baffling factor that complicates the use of the survival technique is the migration of families into and out of the district, especially where rapid gain of population is involved. In a very rapidly growing suburb, for example, the first grade may have averaged four or five times the number of 1-year-olds five years earlier, or 400 to 500 percent of the number of births six years before. Similar, though lower, inflated survival rates would be found at all grade levels. If these survival rates are used for estimating the future, it is automatically assumed that the net effect of migration will remain at the same high level. This assumption may prove to be false, either because vacant building lots are no longer available or because economic or other factors retard the flow of new families into the district. The survey staff can make adjustments in the survival rates to reflect its judgment as to the future pattern of migration, but it can never be very certain of the soundness of its judgment.

The rapidly growing suburb usually attracts younger couples with a relatively high number of children of preschool and school age and with a relatively high number of females of child-bearing age. This results in rather sharp increases in school enrollment. Unless migration provides a constant replenishment of the supply of young couples, the enrollment will drop as the years go by, possibly to as little as one third or one fourth of the number of school children per family. If the influx of new families is rapid, the enrollment will crest earlier and higher than would be true with a slower rate of in-migration. Later peaks might occur as a result of a second influx of younger families, because of the conversion of single houses to multifamily dwellings, or because of the coming of people of a different socio-economic background.

The Rapidly Growing Community

In districts of this sort, the use of the survival technique with no adjustment of rates will produce estimates that are unsound because they assume essentially no change in the net effect of migration and other factors. These estimates may be useful as one reference point, but cannot be the sole basis for recommendations. Other similar points of reference may be obtained by adjusting the survival rates downward to squeeze out all or part of the effect of migration, or by increasing the rates to allow for accelerated growth. Again, the estimates may be helpful in understanding the problem as a whole, but cannot be dependable as a basis for many of the recommendations that must be made in the survey. Estimates for the next five or six years are particularly useful in this type of community, with the expectation that the building program will have to be adjusted from year to year as new insights into the future are revealed.

Sound planning in the rapidly growing district requires particularly the development of a long-range plan. It is helpful here to make some estimate of the ultimate number of dwelling units that can be developed under probable zoning regulations and with probable lot sizes, and then to estimate roughly how many pupils these dwelling units would produce. Maintenance of a file of dwelling units and census data over a period of years, as suggested earlier, will provide ratios of pupils per dwelling unit that will be very useful at this point. These estimates will be crude, but they will give clues that will prove useful in thinking about such problems as the pattern of vertical organization and the future number of schools of each type. Such an analysis in one suburban community, for example, made it perfectly clear that continued expansion of the existing secondary school building was inadvisable. Rather, it was obvious that the future would require not two secondary schools as contemplated, but possibly six to eight.

District Boundary Changes

A final complication that is often encountered is a change in district boundaries which has substantially affected the calculated survival rates for recent years. Where this has occurred only once or twice, adjustments in the rates can be made by omitting certain years from the averages. In other instances, detailed figures can be secured as to the number of children gained or lost in each grade, and the survival rates can be recalculated as though no change in boundary had occurred. Where no such treatment is possible, a preschool census is almost essential, and survival rates have to be assumed or estimated on the basis of the meager data available.

ESTIMATES BY ATTENDANCE AREAS

A question which often arises is how to make enrollment estimates by attendance districts or other parts of a school district. This is exceedingly difficult unless the subdistricts are very large. All of the uncertainties of estimating for the entire district become more serious in the small area, and the necessary breakdown of the basic data is frequently difficult or impossible to secure. The ebb and flow of school population which characterizes a whole city is also observed in the subdistricts and is more difficult to cope with in the smaller area. A change from residential to other use might affect greatly the school population of a single attendance area and yet be hardly noticeable in the school district as a whole. Also, changes in the character of the housing can result in marked changes in enrollment in a small area. There are usually but few children in a large apartment building. Next in order, perhaps, are the garden-type apartments and small single houses, followed in turn by larger singles, duplexes, and other multifamily houses, and tenements. The small single homes may supply a heavy enrollment in the kindergarten and primary grades but not beyond. Many neighborhoods gradually change from good residential areas to slums and tenements, accompanied by marked gains in enrollment. Others hold more firmly to their original character and fluctuate in enrollment as older generations are replaced by new. Urban redevelopment of substandard areas may increase or decrease the population of school age. Changes in the nationality or religious composition of the population may also occur with resulting changes in the number of children and in the enrollment in nonpublic schools. The erection of enlarged parochial or private school facilities may substantially affect the number of pupils which the public schools must house.

Because of these many uncertainties, it seems quite necessary in most surveys to accept the impossibility of making estimates by attendance districts and to be satisfied with generalized information based on counts of vacant lots and similar information. Under these circumstances the survey recommendations must allow for considerable flexibility in capacity in each part of the school district. Several ways of providing this flexibility are suggested in Chapter 5.

It should be obvious at this point that the survey worker makes many judgments that can cause his enrollment estimates to go higher or lower. If only one set of estimates is made, each choice should be the one leading to the lower estimate. This will tend to prevent overbuilding, which results in an irretrievable loss, and leaves the door open to later correction of errors by enlarging the buildings if sites are adequate and buildings are expansible. The best course in most instances would seem to be to prepare one set of estimates which is conservative and a second set of opposite character. The recommendations could then be tested as to their appropriateness for any enrollment level within the range of the two sets of estimates.

CHAPTER 4

THE BUILDING SURVEY:

ANALYSIS OF RESOURCES

Evaluating Existing School-Plant Facilities
Appraising the Site Situation
Analyzing the Financial Resources

THE preceding chapter has discussed the ways of determining quantitatively and qualitatively what school-plant facilities are needed to house the educational program of the community being surveyed. Before recommendations can be formulated, it is necessary now to determine what existing and potential resources are available for meeting these needs. This involves: (1) an evaluation of existing facilities to determine the extent to which they can be used to satisfy the established needs; (2) an appraisal of existing and potential sites; and (3) a determination of the financial resources available. This chapter is addressed to these three problems.

Evaluating Existing School-Plant Facilities

THE school plant of any community represents a major investment of public funds, and it behooves all concerned to make the most effective use of existing facilities worthy of continued use. This requires that the building survey staff acquire detailed knowledge of all existing facilities. This can be done in part by securing written reports, drawings, and other documents from local school authorities and in part by actual inspection of the facilities by the survey staff.

GENERAL NATURE OF THE APPRAISAL

Whatever the sources of information, the survey staff members need to appraise each building or other facility in terms of such questions as the following:

1. Is the facility suitable for continued school use or should it be retired from such service? If the latter, how urgent is the need for retirement?
2. If it is not to be continued in school service, what disposition should be made of it?
3. If it is to continue in service, what is the most appropriate school use for it, what improvements are needed to make it satisfactory, and what is its capacity?

The decision in regard to abandonment or continued use hinges on many factors, including location in relation to place of need, capacity in relation to need, physical condition and resulting costs of operation and maintenance, conditions affecting the health and safety of the occupants, adequacy for the desired school program, and the cost of any changes required to correct existing deficiencies. There is a high correlation between age and these deficiencies, but age alone is no indication that a building should be abandoned or retained.

If a building is to be abandoned for regular school use, consideration should be given first to the suitability for other school purposes. It might, for example, be remodeled for use as central offices, warehouse, or maintenance shops, or for some aspect of adult education or community service. If it cannot be put to any such school use, thought should be given to possible uses for other public purposes before a decision is made to sell the property.

The decision to continue any building or site as a part of the school plant must be based upon its reasonable conformity to the following criteria:

1. The facility is likely to be needed at the place where located.
2. The facility is reasonably safe and healthful or can be made so without undue expense.
3. The facility has, or can economically be provided with, all necessary features to promote the desired school program.
4. The building can be put into good condition and operated and maintained at reasonable cost.

In its evaluation of existing facilities, the survey staff must have criteria such as these in mind, and apply them to every piece of school property. Office buildings, warehouses and shops, garages, detached athletic fields, unused buildings, and vacant land, along with buildings currently used for regular classes, should all be included. Final decisions with respect to a facility cannot be made at the time of inspection, since the information from all other parts of the survey must be considered before recommendations can be established. Therefore, at the time of inspection, attention should be focused upon the various possible uses of each facility, upon its advantages and disadvantages for each such use, and upon the possibility and approximate cost of the necessary alterations or additions. In other words, the survey staff at this time must set up all reasonable hypotheses with respect to the future of each facility and collect such evidence as possible regarding the soundness of each hypothesis. Normally, it can be expected that at least one re-examination of most buildings will be required before recommendations are fixed.

SCORE CARDS

The evaluation process, then, consists essentially of two aspects— (1) the formulation of hypotheses regarding the future use of each facility, and (2) the orderly collection of pertinent information. Numerous score cards have been published for the latter purpose. While there is considerable variation in these score cards, they have much in common. They all provide for the systematic checking of each building according to a detailed list of questions or criteria, and all are accompanied by or include a statement of the criteria or standards to be used. Also, most of them provide for numerical scores, usually on the basis of 1,000 points for a perfect building. A score is given on each of several hundred specific items, and these scores are added to get the total score. The items are frequently grouped into major categories, and subscores are obtained for each category. Provision is often made for converting numerical scores into descriptive ratings such as "excellent," "good," etc.

Advantages of Score Cards

The use of score cards of this kind has two advantages. For the inexperienced survey worker, whether he be a professional educator or a layman, the score card provides a guide for the orderly and systematic inspection of a building and the recording of observations. This purpose is best served when the numerical scores are accompanied by adequate notes concerning the conditions upon which they are based. Many score cards do not provide adequately for the recording of such observations. A second advantage of a device of this kind is that it provides a means of making rough comparisons among the buildings of a given school system or among several school systems. These comparisons within the school system can be one basis for establishing the priorities in a large building program, although other factors should also be considered.

Weaknesses of Score Cards

The weaknesses of score cards are several. First of all, most of the score cards are such that two or more persons evaluating a given building will not arrive at the same total score or part scores. Two persons using the same set of criteria will have different impressions of the degree to which a given building feature meets these standards and will give different scores, even though they see and are aware of the same physical conditions. One score card seeks to minimize this flaw by starting with a perfect score on each item and having the observer deduct a stipulated number of penalty points for each observed shortcoming in a list printed in the score card booklet.[1]

A similar weakness is that any one observer looking at the same building on two different occasions is likely to assign quite different scores. It is difficult, if not impossible, to avoid letting the scores on many items be influenced by the good or bad impression made by some one feature of the building, by the cordiality of the staff, or by some other irrelevant factor. This shortcoming, too, is partially offset by the penalty scoring approach.

A more basic objection to the score card is that the total score, which is obtained by adding scores on individual items, loses much of its meaning by the process of adding items which are not of like character. Adding a score on fire alarms to one on accessibility of site and one on size of classrooms hardly produces a meaningful total, except in a very general way. The process of adding the scores on individual items to get a total score is somewhat analogous to the adding of blood pressure, temperature, pulse rate, respiration rate, and white corpuscle count to arrive at a total health score for an individual. A common device for meeting this objection is to provide for part scores, such as, for example, a part score on school site. These are expressed in some numerical fashion, and in the McLeary score card are the basis for a profile chart. Fewer dissimilar items are combined in the part scores than in the total scores, but the basic flaw remains.

In some surveys a critical score has been used for determining whether to retain or abandon a building. For example, a score of 400 to 500 has been established as the point below which a building should not be considered for continued use. This practice breaks down under critical examination because it is not the low score per se that should be used to

[1] McLeary, Ralph D., *Guide for Evaluating School Buildings.* Cambridge, Mass.: New England School Development Council, 1952.

determine whether to abandon a building. A very old structure, for example, might have a score of 450 because of its small site, physical deterioration, unsafe condition, poor fenestration, inefficient use of space resulting from poor design, excessive cost of heating because of the high ceilings and useless hall space, lack of many needed types of rooms, and similar defects not easy to correct. Another building, only a few years old, on a good site, and of good quality throughout, might have the same low score of 450 largely because of the lack of many needed facilities, such as administrative offices, clinic, assembly space, gymnasium, and lunchroom. These facilities could easily be added, and in fact their construction might have been postponed because of shortage of funds at the time of original construction. It is obvious that the two scores of 450 do not indicate the same quality of building and do not suggest the same recommendations in the survey report.

These comments regarding score cards seem to add up to something like this. An experienced survey worker can make an adequate evaluation of a building without the use of a score card, and in fact might be only wasting time using such a device. The score card does, however, provide a useful guide to the orderly inspection of a building by inexperienced observers, and it provides a means of making very rough comparisons of one building with another. The use of a score card is not to be deplored if its limitations are recognized and the scores interpreted and used accordingly.

BASES OF EVALUATION

Regardless of whether or not score cards are used in the evaluation of existing buildings, information must be sought and organized systematically around such basic questions as the following for each building:

1. Is the building properly located?
2. Are the building and site safe and healthful?
3. Are the facilities adequate for the desired program?
4. Is the building adequate as to capacity?

Information on these several questions can be recorded and summarized in various ways. An outline or check list can be prepared for each building with spaces for recording some of the information, or a large chart can be used to record information on several buildings. The specific items to be included in such a document will depend in part upon the desired program of the particular school system. The discussion in the preceding chapter of the analysis of the school program will suggest many items to be included.

Location of Building

In judging the location of a school building, attention must be given to the convenience and safety of pupils in traveling to and from school. Travel distances should be reasonable and the routes of travel should be as free as possible of hazards of all kinds. Consideration should also be given to the attractiveness and wholesomeness of the neighborhood in which the school is located and to trends in neighborhood development.[2]

Health and Safety

The evaluation of building and site in terms of health and safety can be exceedingly detailed, but a more limited consideration would be appropriate in a general building survey. Specific suggestions of items to be included can be gleaned from later parts of this volume [3] and from an abundance of other school-plant literature. Assistance in most communities could also be secured from local safety officials. Whatever list of specifics is developed, it would seem that the following should be covered:

1. *Fire safety*—type of construction with respect to combustibility and spread of fire; barriers against the spread of fire and gases; type, location, and condition of heating plant, including fire safeguards in the boiler room or furnace room and places of fuel and ash storage; condition of electrical wiring; location and protection of hazardous areas such as shops; fire alarms and fire-fighting equipment, including types, location, number, and recency of service of fire extinguishers; location, number, marking, and condition of regular exits, with particular attention to the accessibility and safety of use in emergency; location and condition of fire escapes, if required, with particular attention to accessibility and ease and safety of use; and storage practices as related to fire hazards.

2. *Structural adequacy*—condition of foundations; evidences of recent cracking, leaning, or bulging of walls; rigidity of floors, especially of ones supported by wood; condition of stairways, especially of the treads; and condition of copings, cornices, parapets, and other portions of the building which might deteriorate and cause injury by falling on someone below.

3. *Sanitary facilities*—locations of and sanitary conditions in toilet rooms; adequacy and accessibility of handwashing facilities,

[2] See Chapter 12 for further discussion of site criteria.   [3] See Chapters 20–22.

including hot and cold water, soap, and towels; location, type, and cleanliness of drinking fountains; and purity of water.

4. *Heating and ventilating facilities*—performance in providing suitable thermal conditions and proper ventilation, including control of odors originating within the building.

5. *Housekeeping*—cleanliness of building; freedom of building and site from unsightly storage, particularly of garbage, ashes, and refuse; and control of rodents and vermin, especially in food storage and preparation areas.

6. *Visual environment*—amount and control of natural light, including location, size, and shielding of windows; adequacy and control of artificial lighting, including control and shielding of fixtures; and control of brightness range through use of proper finishes on room surfaces and equipment.

7. *Auditory conditions*—ease of hearing in all rooms and especially assembly rooms; adequacy of control of noise level through arrangement or construction of the plant.

8. *Site conditions*—arrangement of buildings, drives, playgrounds, and other site facilities; type and condition of playground surfacing and equipment; other hazards.

9. *Safety of access*—hazards encountered in traveling to and from school.

10. *Miscellaneous*—slipperiness of floors and stair treads; projections into corridors and stairways; electrical shock hazards; and safety devices on water heaters and boilers.

In checking health and safety conditions, defects will have to be listed. It is important, however, to note also the possible ways of remedying these defects, since the survey recommendations should seek to improve health and safety conditions. Many aspects of health and safety can be checked by the experienced survey worker or by local school officials. However, there will be cases when more expert knowledge is required, and a competent engineer or architect should be consulted. The safe course is to consult the technical expert in any case of serious doubt.

Adequacy for Desired Program

No check list can be presented here for appraising a building in terms of its adequacy for the desired program. A different list will have to be prepared for each survey and, as a matter of fact, for each type of school in a given school system. The list for an elementary school, for example, will not be the same as for a high school, and a building housing an extensive adult education program will need different facilities than one not so used. An indication of the types of items to include in such check lists can be gained from the discussion in Chapter 3 under the heading "Check List of Program Questions."

For a given survey the check lists to be used in this part of the evaluation of the existing buildings should be prepared on the basis of the analysis of the program discussed in the preceding chapter. The check lists should cover every major aspect of the program both inside and outside the building, whether a part of the regular school day or not. They should bring out the needs not only of the program of the present, but also of the program as it is expected to develop in the near future.

A helpful device in checking a building for program adequacy is to have prepared in advance of inspection a report showing such things as size of site, size and use of each room, number eating at school and capacity of lunchroom, and similar information which the analysis of program reveals to be necessary. Architectural drawings or sketches are also useful documents which can save many return trips to check items missed on the first inspection.

As a building is checked for program adequacy, possible ways of correcting deficiencies should be noted, and thought should be given to possible conversion of the building to some other use to which it might be better adapted.

Size of Building

Closely related to the matter of program adequacy are the questions of optimum size and maximum size of school. In the process of program determination discussed in the preceding chapter, decisions should be made with respect to these points. At the time of evaluating an existing building its actual size should be noted and compared with the desired size previously established.

Calculation of Capacity

The checking of the capacity of an existing building is not something that can be done at the time of field inspection, although certain essential information may be obtained at that time. The field work will be most productive if there is secured in advance complete information regarding number of rooms, arrangement of building (floor plans), class schedule, size of class, etc. Then, at the time of field inspection, doubtful items can be checked and gaps filled. Particularly important at this time is the checking of each room to see whether it is suitable for inclusion in computing capacity and what alternative uses might be appropriate. With this type of checking, the actual calculations can then be made upon return to the office, and the field notes will make it possible to adjust the computed capacities as different proposals for the use of certain rooms are considered.

Elementary Schools. The capacity of a given building depends upon the nature of the program to be housed within it, as well as upon the number and size of its rooms and spaces. An elementary school building, for example, would have a different capacity with an average of 30 pupils per room than with 25. Also, the capacity of an elementary school building would be reduced if the program required that certain rooms be set aside for music, art, or other special use. During the development of the survey recommendations alternative uses of certain buildings may be examined, and a separate capacity calculation will be required for each alternative use.

In the typical elementary school the capacity calculation is rather simple. The total number of classrooms is determined. Rooms which are judged to be unsatisfactory for classrooms are then deducted. Also, any rooms which are needed for special classrooms or are to be converted to any other use are deducted. The remaining number of regular classrooms is then multiplied by the desired average class size to determine the building capacity. If a platoon system (which the authors do not endorse) is in operation, the special classrooms as well as the regular classrooms would be in full-time use, and the total number of regular and special classrooms would be multiplied by the average class size to determine the capacity of the building.

The kindergarten or nursery school may operate with fewer pupils per group and possibly more groups per day or week than in the higher grades. For this reason, these rooms might be considered separately in the calculations of capacity and their capacities reported separately.

Secondary Schools.[4] If the principle is accepted that the building should fit rather than determine the program, the effective capacity of a secondary school building for a specific program is the number of pupils that can be properly accommodated in the subject area where overcrowding would first

[4] The discussion of this topic is based largely on Conrad, Marion J., *A Technique for Determining the Operating Capacity of Secondary School Buildings.* Doctor's thesis. Columbus: Ohio State University, 1952. For a shorter and more readily available source, see Conrad, Marion J., *A Manual for Determining the Operating Capacity of Secondary School Buildings.* Columbus: The Bureau of Educational Research, Ohio State University, 1954.

occur. If the science rooms, for example, are adequate for a total enrollment of only 300 and all other facilities could accommodate a school of 1,000, the effective capacity of the building is only 300 for that particular program. The capacity, of course, can be increased by changing the program, erecting additional science rooms, or converting existing space to provide additional science rooms. The fact remains, however, that the capacity of the building as it stands for the program desired is only 300.

To determine the capacity of a building in the light of this concept, use is made of the indexes explained in Chapter 3.[5] The index for each subject is multiplied by the number of teaching stations of each type available. This will give the total enrollment for which the facilities in each area are adequate. If one area is quite low, as is usually the case, some upward adjustment may be possible by shifting excess teaching stations in another subject area to the subject area where a shortage exists. For example, if the regular classrooms would accommodate a total school of 1,200 pupils and business education only 700, some regular classrooms might be assigned to business education to bring the two more nearly into balance.

In addition to teaching stations, there are other facilities which are necessary and must be considered. Among these are offices, assembly rooms, lunchrooms, libraries, rest rooms, storage rooms, shower and dressing rooms, and corridor lockers. If any of these is not adequate for the capacity otherwise calculated, some adjustment is required. If new construction is not used to remedy the defect, some existing space must be converted. This may result in a reduction in the number of teaching stations in one or more subject areas, and the capacities in these areas would have to be reduced accordingly.

Percentage of Utilization [6]

Building surveys frequently involve the calculation of percentages of utilization, especially at the secondary school level. Two types are usually identified—room utilization and pupil-station utilization. The former has reference to the extent to which all the teaching stations are in use throughout the week; the latter focuses attention on the degree of use of individual seats or other work stations for pupils. If a room for English is occupied by a class 27 periods out of a 30 period week, its room utilization is 90 percent (27 ÷ 30). If it is designed for classes of 30, it can accommo-

[5] See pages 45–47.
[6] For detailed discussion of utilization see Morphet, Edgar L., The Meas-urement and Interpretation of School Building Utilization. New York: Teachers College, Columbia University, 1927.

date 900 pupil-periods (30 × 30). If the average class during the 27 periods of use is only 20, the room actually accommodates only 540 pupil-periods (27 × 20). Thus, its pupil-station utilization is only 60 percent (540 ÷ 900). In reporting utilization data, rooms are usually classified into regular or academic classrooms and special classrooms. The former are those rooms with relatively little special equipment, which can be used for several different subjects, such as English, foreign language, mathematics, and social studies. The special classrooms are those with more highly specialized equipment, such as those for science, industrial arts, and home economics.

Figures on the percentage of room and pupil-station utilization give a general impression of the degree of overcrowding and may permit certain comparisons with other buildings. Their usefulness, however, is limited by lack of agreement as to what constitutes an acceptable degree of utilization. Also, when rooms are grouped in these calculations, particularly special classrooms, significant variations in utilization may be concealed. There may be serious overcrowding in one type of special classroom and very little use of another type, both hidden beneath a normal percentage of utilization for all special classrooms.

The indexes described in the preceding chapter are more precise and useful tools than the percents of utilization. They fix attention upon the particular subject areas of limited capacity, while subjects are grouped in the usual utilization figures. The indexes show the shortages and excesses of capacity in terms of number of pupils, while the percents of utilization are not so precise. The indexes show not only *what* but *how much* adjustment in capacity is needed in each subject area; the percents of utilization do not. Finally, the indexes once derived have a variety of uses, whereas percents of utilization do not. They can be used for computing the capacity of existing buildings, for analyzing capacities with various alternative uses, for planning alterations or additions, or for determining the room and space requirements of a new building.

Appraising the Site Situation

MENTION has already been made of the evaluation of school sites in terms of safety, program adequacy, and location. This appraisal of the present situation is important, but it alone will not suffice. Before the survey staff reaches the point of fixing recommendations, it must also in many cases give consideration to possible new locations for new buildings or new locations for existing schools. Since new locations must be judged in part by their relationship to sites which are to continue in use, it is necessary that the locations of all schools, existing or proposed, be considered together. Thus, at this point, the analysis of present facilities and the formulation of recommendations are quite inseparable.

NEEDED TOOLS

Proper study of school locations requires detailed knowledge of the school district which can be obtained only by actual field inspection. The survey staff must traverse the territory with sufficient frequency to become familiar with its principal features such as the layout of streets, the principal obstructions or hazards to children going to and from school, and the nature and extent of residential construction and other improvements.

In addition to the information gained by field inspection, there are many types of maps or other documents that will prove useful. As a minimum there should be at hand a map or maps showing the locations of existing school buildings and unused school sites and indicating the approximate place of residence of each pupil. These can be prepared with relative ease from the school records. Attendance officers, bus drivers, and others who are thoroughly familiar with the school district can be very helpful in their preparation. These same maps should also indicate the boundaries of the existing attendance districts. It is helpful to have them so mounted that possible changes in boundaries can be shown by string or other movable devices during the period of study. It will also be helpful to have maps or aerial photographs showing the locations of houses and other buildings and of vacant land. If there is an effective zoning ordinance, a map of the zoning is an aid in studying the potential enrollment growth and in selecting school sites. Traffic flow maps are useful, and in hilly country a topographical map is valuable.

The availability of maps and aerial photographs varies greatly from place to place, and considerable search is often required to locate them. A good city, regional, or state planning office can usually supply most of what is needed. Chambers of commerce and public utilities companies may be able to furnish certain items or to suggest sources.

Many cities or larger regions have developed extensive plans with the aid of professional planning agencies. These plans deal with future zoning, street locations, public transportation, parks, and other aspects of community life. If any such study has been made, the survey staff should become familiar with the report and with any steps taken toward its implementation or modification.

DESIRABLE SITE CHARACTERISTICS

Before extensive work is done on the site problem, it is essential that the survey staff reach some decision as to what constitutes a satisfactory site. The criteria used may grow in part out of policies established by the local school authorities, but there are also some standards that are applicable in any school system. Such criteria are discussed in Chapter 12, and need not be repeated here. The point to be emphasized now is that the survey recommendations should reflect a considerable effort to have all schools located on sites that meet suitable standards of excellence.

In its consideration of new school locations, the survey staff must give some thought to the matter of cost. Although the price of the land usually represents only a small fraction of the total cost of the completed building, it is frequently a point of dispute and public criticism. Unless the price is exorbitant, suitability of location, adequacy of size, and other factors related to the effectiveness of the school program should be given far more weight than the dollar cost. A good building on a poor site actually represents a considerable waste of public funds because of the restrictions it places on the development of a suitable school program. It is important in making comparisons to include any unusual expenses for grading, retaining walls, removal of rock or other obstructions, special footings or piling, and other extra expenses occasioned by the physical features of the site. Similarly, the availability of public water, sewers, gas, and electricity should be considered, and the cost of any necessary special installations should be included in the total site cost.

Often, in order to avoid an expenditure for a new site, it is proposed that some existing public land be used. This is quite appropriate if the land is properly located and otherwise suitable for school use, and if its use for school purposes will not rob the community of some other needed facility. Increasing population and changing patterns of community living require increasing space for public recreation and other activities which should not be overlooked by the school survey staff. This is not meant to deny the wisdom of joint use of land by the schools and other public agencies, if the attractiveness of the cooperative approach does not result in overlooking any inadequacies of the site for school and the other purposes in mind.

OTHER CONSIDERATIONS

Before the actual process of site selection is undertaken, consideration must also be given to policies in regard to optimum or maximum size of school, desired vertical organization, or other local policies that would affect the number of schools and hence the number and location of sites. Since these policies are dealt with at some length in the next chapter, they need not be further discussed at this point. They are, however, of great importance and must not be neglected by the survey staff as it approaches the site problem.

SITE SELECTION PROCESS

Armed with the necessary maps and other tools and being thoroughly familiar with the site criteria and the local policies related to the site problem, the survey staff is ready to begin the search for sites worthy of detailed study. Field visitation, aerial reconnaisance, and study of maps and aerial photographs are useful approaches at this stage. The search should start at the place where the requirements of centrality and accessibility are best satisfied, and then move outward as necessary to find promising sites.

The sites which are chosen as most promising should be subjected to thorough analysis and comparison. There can be no mathematical calculation to determine which of the several sites is best, but a better judgment will be made if there is a systematic point-by-point comparison in terms of some list of desired site characteristics such as those discussed in Chapter 12. In judging the various sites with respect to adequacy of size, it is well to make tentative layouts unless the size is quite large. Templates should be cut to scale to represent the building and the various play and service areas and should then be placed on the site drawing in various relationships to one another. This will test the site's ability to accommodate all of the facilities in proper arrangement.

Analyzing the Financial Resources

THE proper procedure in planning a program of school-plant improvements is to determine first of all what improvements are needed. This is done by analyzing the school program and projecting the school enrollments to determine needs, and by evaluating the existing facilities to determine how well they satisfy the needs. The recommendations are then formulated to close the gap, and the cost of the recommended improvements is estimated. This determines the amount of money that is to be raised.

Public enterprises, like those of the private individual or family, are seldom planned in this idealistic manner with an expectation of full realization. Rather, the expenditures have to be fitted to real or seeming limitations on the amount of money available. This attention to limitations is especially necessary in planning improvements for the immediate future, but may be quite superficial when long-range plans are under consideration. In some cases the establishment of priorities and the spreading of plant expenditures over a period of years can be employed to ease the impact on limited resources.

AVAILABLE FUNDS

The nature of the financial limitations that must be considered in a building survey varies considerably from place to place. In many states there are legal limitations on the amount of debt or the tax rate. Some of these restrictions are fairly easy to modify, while others are so difficult to change that they can be considered as fixed so far as the survey staff's work is concerned. Where legal restrictions do not exist, there may be some limitations imposed by the board of education or by some other body having control over funds for school capital outlay. These limitations will have all degrees of immunity to argument and public pressure.

With such a variety of conditions, there can be no one approach suitable in all building surveys. If there are definite legal limitations, the survey staff should analyze the pertinent legal documents and calculate the available funds accordingly. If the restrictions are more flexible, the survey staff can only assay by their judgment what the practical limits are.

FINANCIAL COMPARISONS

The financial sections of building survey reports frequently present data with respect to the ability and effort of the school district to support its schools. These data may or may not have a bearing on the recommendations presented, but they are usually desired by the board of education and other readers of the survey report. Whatever other values they may have, they do help to create the climate of opinion in which the survey recommendations are considered, and legitimately so.

The data on ability and effort are frequently presented to show two aspects: (1) trends in the school district over a period of years, and (2) comparisons with other similar school districts.

Ability to Finance Schools

In assessing the ability of a school district to finance education, there is no one universally accepted index of ability. The tax valuation per pupil is often used, especially where building funds come largely from taxes on property. This breaks down when comparisons are made with places where the ratios of assessments to true values are not the same, or when the local ratios have changed during the period in question. Where funds for school-plant improvements come largely from other kinds of taxes, property tax valuations decrease in significance. Other indexes that have been used include total income tax payments, average income per family, volume of wholesale or retail sales, value of manufactured products, and value of farm products.

The places used for comparison of ability should be reasonably similar in size and general characteristics, and none of the bases used for selection should in itself be an index of ability. Comparisons of highly industrialized cities with cities in predominantly agricultural areas or with strictly residential cities would have less meaning than comparisons within a more homogeneous group. All districts included in comparisons on a per pupil basis should also provide education for the same span of grades unless appropriate adjustments of the data can be made.

Effort to Support Schools

Measures of effort frequently used include tax rates, expenditures per pupil for school purposes, and extent of approval of school finance measures submitted to the voters. Tax rates, like valuations, vary with assessment practices, and need to be adjusted for any wide differences in assessment ratios. This difficulty can be offset by using tax per capita, unless there are wide variations in the percentage of the total tax paid by corporations rather than by individuals. Expenditures per pupil can include current costs, all school costs, or only those for capital outlay. If capital outlays are included, a relatively long period of years must be included because expenditures for new school plants fluctuate considerably from year to year within a given school district. The support of schools may be reflected in the amounts of bond issues and tax levies approved by the voters or by records of the votes for and against specific school issues on the ballot.

In choosing school districts for comparisons of effort to support schools, the selection should be limited to places of reasonably similar ability. Also, all of the districts should operate the same span of school grades. Similarity in other respects is not so important as in the case of comparisons of ability.

In some cases, there may be considerable local interest in comparisons with near-by school districts or with other districts that would not conform to the established criteria. Such comparisons are not objectionable if made separately and properly identified. Statement of the reasons for their inclusion would also seem to be appropriate.

CHAPTER 5

THE BUILDING SURVEY:

FORMULATING RECOMMENDATIONS

Facts Needed in Formulating Recommendations
Procedures in Developing Recommendations
Criteria for Testing Recommendations

Preceding chapters have described the general nature of the survey approach to the development of a comprehensive building program and have proposed and explained certain procedures by which the essential facts are brought to light and organized for use. When the steps up to this point have been completed, the survey workers will be saturated with facts about the problem, and they will have some hypotheses as to the solution. In fact, the staff may be fairly sure that it has the right solution in mind. However, it must not actually have decided upon a solution, nor must it assume that all of the possible solutions have yet come to mind. Keeping an open mind until all the necessary facts are in and studied is an essential attribute of any competent survey worker, whether he be a specialist or a person who does but one survey in his lifetime.

Facts Needed in Formulating Recommendations

THE facts which the survey staff will have when it reaches the point of preparing recommendations will be many and detailed. Chief among them will be the following:

  1. With respect to the types of facilities needed to house the
      school program.

      a. A list of the types of facilities which will be needed in
          the immediate future for housing the program that is

quite certain to be provided in the community under study.

b. A list of the types of facilities which are likely to be needed to house activities which may be added to the program at a later date.

c. As much information as is available regarding current or proposed developments in the community which may affect the program of the schools in such a manner as to influence the type of physical facilities required.

2. With respect to the quantitative aspects of school plant needs.

a. Estimates of future school enrollments by age or grade levels, together with an understanding of the probable direction and possible range of error in the estimates.

b. Similar information about other quantitative aspects of the total need, such as requirements for public meeting spaces.

c. As much information as is available regarding the probable future geographical distribution of the total load.

d. As much information as is available regarding current or proposed developments in the community which might affect the number of pupils enrolled or other quantitative aspects of the total need.

3. With respect to the present facilities.

a. For each facility that is being or reasonably might be used for some part of the program, detailed information as to existing health and safety conditions, suitability for the desired program, possible alternative uses, capacity in relation to probable needed capacity, suitability of location, relative cost of operation and maintenance, and feasibility and cost of alterations or additions to make the facility more usable in the program.

b. Information regarding other existing or proposed facilities in the community which might reasonably be used in ways which would reduce the total plant needs of the schools.

c. Information regarding any current or proposed developments in the community which would materially alter the availability, suitability, or capacity of any existing facility which might be used to house any part of the total program.

4. With respect to site locations.
    a. Thorough knowledge of the geographical features, existing or proposed streets and other improvements, and other physical features.
    b. Knowledge of local policies regarding travel distances for pupils.
    c. Knowledge of potential sites which might be used for new schools or for relocating existing schools.
5. With respect to finances.
    a. Specific knowledge about any limitations which must be considered in developing a building program for the community.
    b. Information regarding any current or proposed development which might materially affect the amount of money available.
    c. Knowledge of approximate costs of the various types of improvements which might be recommended.

Procedures in Developing Recommendations

THE task of the survey staff at this point is to develop a solution that squares with these facts and conforms to other criteria discussed later in this chapter. The solution will consist of two kinds of recommendations. First, and of major importance, are those that indicate the over-all pattern of schools throughout the district. Essentially these recommendations have to do with the locations of schools, the approximate boundaries of their attendance areas, and the grades and numbers of pupils to be housed in each. The second type of recommendation concerns the specific improvements to be made in each building.

Since the task of formulating recommendations is essentially creative in nature, it does not lend itself to prescription or formula. The skilled survey worker will have developed certain ways of working with data which have been found to be effective in formulating sound recommendations. While he may use the same general approach in all surveys, he will find that some modifications are necessary to fit the particular conditions of each new study. Modifications of procedure will most often be necessitated by lack of certain needed data in the desired form, by the possession of additional data not usually available, or by variations in the desired degree of refinement of the recommendations or of their projection into the future.

ESSENTIAL CHARACTERISTICS

Whatever procedures are used in developing the recommendations, there are three essential factors: (1) the developing of appropriate hypotheses as to the proper solutions; (2) the critical analysis of every hypothesis; and (3) the exercise of sound judgment in making the final decision. A fertile imagination is essential in bringing to light every promising hypothesis as to the proper recommendation to be made at each point of decision. This imagination must be unfettered by loyalty to the status quo in the local community; must be completely unrestrained by any local pressures, real or anticipated; and must be nourished by extensive knowledge of how similar school-plant problems have been solved elsewhere. The essential power of critical analysis requires a strict avoidance of prejudgment, honest and thorough application of suitable criteria, and thorough exploration of the implications and interrelationships of each hypothetical solution. Sincere humility and honest self-criticism will serve the survey workers well at this point. However careful the preceding analysis has been, there comes a time when judgment must be exercised in the choice of the final recommendations. The development and analysis of various hypotheses narrow the field and provide the essential knowledge about each possible course of action, but do not lead automatically and unerringly to a proper solution.

FOUR SUGGESTED STEPS

Without denying what has been said with respect to the variability and individuality of the procedures by which the survey recommendations are derived, one approach will be described. This will reveal further the problems involved and serve as a possible starting point in the development of other approaches. The procedure now proposed consists of four basic steps, as follows:

1. Preparation of a summary of the essential facts and conditions ascertained in the earlier portions of the survey.
2. Preparation of a list of criteria to be used in testing tentative recommendations.
3. Development of a long-range plan which is consistent with the local facts and conditions and which meets the established criteria.
4. Development of recommendations for more immediate execution, which are consistent with the local facts and conditions, which meet the established criteria, and which are in harmony with the long-range plan.

Summary of Essential Facts

The nature of the summary of essential facts and conditions was indicated early in this chapter and attention was called to the importance of completing this phase of the work before reaching any decision as to the solution of the problem. A suggested procedure with respect to Step 1 is that the rough draft of the report up to the point of recommendations be written at this time. This will provide the review necessary to prepare the summary of essential facts, and at the same time will tend to keep the text, as well as the summary, free of bias in favor of some one set of recommendations. All essential facts should be developed in the text and stated in the summary without regard to the recommendations which they might imply, and the wording must be neutral.

Establishing Criteria

The detailed criteria which might be set up in Step 2 will depend upon the point of view of the survey staff and others involved in a given study, but there should be general agreement on the major criteria. Be that as it may, any difference of opinion as to the list of criteria does not invalidate the procedure of using some such list in the manner suggested. For purposes of illustration here, the following criteria will be used:

1. The recommendations should provide facilities which are safe and healthful for all who use them.
2. The recommendations should provide facilities which will foster the development of all aspects of the desired program of the schools.
3. The recommendations should provide adequate capacity in all types of facilities when needed and where needed throughout the school district.
4. The recommendations should take into account the applicable portions of any community plan which has been developed.
5. The recommendations should avoid any discrimination in favor of or against any segment of the population or section of the school district.
6. The recommendations should provide all needed facilities at reasonable cost and within such financial limitations as must be observed.

These criteria overlap and duplicate to some extent the criteria stated in

Chapter 2 for judging the quality of the total survey. In the present chapter, however, the development is more detailed and is pointed specifically to the problems encountered by the survey staff in formulating and testing the survey recommendations.

Establishing a Long-range Plan

The development of the long-range plan (Step 3) involves decisions as to the future pattern of vertical organization, the use or disposition of each existing building, and the probable new schools to be established. The plan must be consistent with known facts about the present and future and sufficiently flexible to permit adaptation to meet future developments which can be foreseen as possibilities but not predicted as certainties. At the same time, this long-range plan must be such that it can be achieved by a reasonable transition from the plan which is recommended for the immediate future. This latter requirement implies clearly that the long-range plan cannot be completed without partial development of the recommendations for the immediate future—in other words, that Steps 3 and 4 must be carried out somewhat simultaneously. However, an effort should be made constantly to find a proper long-range plan and to fix this before all the details of the more immediate plans are finally established.

In the development of the long-range plan, all of the major alternatives must be isolated for analysis. Some of these will be fairly obvious, while others will come to mind less readily. All survey workers, and especially those who are inexperienced, must be constantly on guard lest the prevailing pattern in the community blind them to other possibilities and lest they be satisfied to examine only the one or two most obvious alternatives. Imaginative and thoughtful use of the criteria in both Steps 3 and 4 will often suggest solutions which might otherwise escape notice, especially if close attention is directed to ways of overcoming the defects and difficulties revealed by such analysis. The reading of other school-plant survey reports and other literature on school buildings may suggest other tentative solutions for analysis.

In the final testing of the long-range plan selected for recommendation, it may be helpful to compare it in some detail with the principal alternative plans. These comparisons should be strictly in terms of the established criteria. The summarizing of these comparisons in the written report might help the survey staff to clarify its thinking and later would permit readers of the completed report to make better judgments with respect to the survey proposals.

Short-range Proposals

In the development of the recommendations for the immediate future (Step 4), the problems are essentially the same as in Step 3, except that the proposals must be fitted more closely to the facts relative to enrollments, capacities and other attributes of existing buildings, and financial resources. At the same time, these immediate recommendations must be such that they do not obstruct, and preferably lead toward, the achievement of the long-range plan.

The completion of Step 4 should result in specific recommendations with respect to each existing or proposed building. For an existing building, the recommendation might be that it continue in its present use without alteration; that it be improved by remodeling, renovation, site expansion or improvement, or enlargement; that its use or attendance area be changed; that it be temporarily withdrawn from use; that it be replaced by a new building; or that it be abandoned for school use and sold. For a new building, the recommendations should indicate the approximate location, the capacity and grades to be housed there, the approximate attendance area, and the major types of facilities to be included.

In the course of formulating these recommendations, the major alternative recommendations should be carefully analyzed in terms of the established criteria. This comparative analysis building by building often requires repeated re-examination of the proposals with respect to the other buildings in the school system and of the long-range plan. Something less than the best solution for a given existing building may be necessary to get the best over-all set of recommendations for the entire school district for the immediate future or the best long-range plan.

The completion of Steps 3 and 4 will require judgments as to the feasibility of remodeling or enlarging certain buildings and at least approximate estimates of cost. The experienced survey worker will be able to make many of these judgments, but the services of a competent engineer or architect should be sought, except when the problems are quite simple. If this is not done, the survey recommendations may be upset by later detection of errors of judgment which should have been found during the survey.

ALTERNATIVE RECOMMENDATIONS

Frequently in the formulation of recommendations the survey staff may consider the inclusion in its report of alternative proposals on a given point or of a recommendation that a decision be made at some future date. There may be occasions when such lack of definiteness in the recommendations is justified, but the survey staff must be on guard lest one of these courses of action is followed to evade making a decision on a difficult point. Alternative recommendations on a given point may be of equal merit when considered in isolation, but their seeming equality may diminish sharply or vanish completely as attention is shifted from the particular issue at hand to the pattern of recommendations for the entire school district or to the long-range plan. There are many instances where a clear choice among alternative plans for one building is necessary in order to permit definite and appropriate recommendations with regard to other buildings in the school system. As a general rule, one of the courses of action should be chosen and presented as the recommendation of the survey staff, and the alternative or alternatives should be discussed in the accompanying text in a manner that reveals the principal arguments for each and the reasons for the final choice.

DEFERRED DECISIONS

A recommendation for a deferred decision on some point may seem necessary in certain instances. This is especially true where there is some pending major decision in the community which must be made before the course of action of the schools can be clearly charted. Such pending decisions might concern such public affairs as a transfer of territory from one school district to another, a slum clearance project, or a major street relocation program, or they might involve such private activities as the construction, removal, or location of a major industrial or housing project. In some of these instances the date of decision will be known in advance, and it may be advisable to postpone the completion of the entire survey until that time. In other cases, the extent of the delay may be so uncertain or so great that it will be advisable to complete the survey report with some of the recommendations left open.

If it should be decided that the survey must be completed with certain questions left open for later decision, the written report should make clear the reasons for lack of a clear-cut recommendation. If possible, it would be well also to indicate the general nature of the alternative recommendations that might be made and the conditions under which each would be appropriate. This handling of such cases might help the survey staff in its analysis and also make it easier for the school authorities to choose the proper course of action when the required facts do become available. In some cases, the future may be so uncertain that it would be advisable to have the survey reopened and completed by the original survey staff when the necessary facts become known.

Criteria for Testing Recommendations

ALTHOUGH there may be general acceptance of the suggested procedure and the proposed criteria for testing the recommendations, there will undoubtedly be less agreement on the details of application. In spite of this, each of the proposed criteria will be further discussed and possible applications pointed out. This will illustrate further the proposed procedure and develop more fully the meaning of the criteria.

In considering the several criteria, it must be kept in mind that they are closely interrelated and must be used accordingly. For example, Criterion 1 (health and safety) might be completely satisfied by removal of an existing hazard, but this might be done in such a way as to impair the educational usefulness of the building (Criterion 2), to reduce the capacity below the needed level (Criterion 3), to deprive one school of a facility provided in other buildings (Criterion 5), or to result in an unreasonable cost for the improvement achieved (Criterion 6).

> **CRITERION 1.** *The recommendations should provide facilities which are safe and healthful for all who use them.*

The importance of this criterion has been stressed earlier and it is no doubt generally accepted. Attention has also been given in the preceding chapter to the principal aspects of the school plant which need especially to be examined with respect to health and safety. The evaluation of existing buildings, which is an essential part of the survey preceding the formulation of recommendations, should have resulted in a list of specific hazards in each building. The recommendations should be checked against this list to see that suitable corrections are proposed, unless, of course, the building is to be abandoned at an early date. Many of the unsafe conditions in a school building are not due to a poorly designed original structure, but rather to improper maintenance or operation. For example, fire doors on boiler rooms may be properly designed and installed but kept blocked open, or fire escape doors may be kept locked. In such cases a recommendation with respect to the maintenance and operation of the plant would be in order. If periodic inspection or other suitable procedures for the detection and reporting of hazards are not in use, they might well be recommended in the survey report.

In determining the pattern of attendance districts, effort should be made to minimize the hazards encountered by pupils in traveling to and from school. Since it is beyond the power of the survey staff, or of the school authorities in most instances, to remove or relocate these hazards, the survey recommendations must often be altered in the interest of greater safety. Where it can properly be done, the boundaries of the attendance districts should coincide with the lines of hazard, rather than to have these lines cross the attendance districts. Since the number of potential school locations is usually limited and areas too small to support a school are often surrounded by hazards, the ideal solution from the standpoint of safety is seldom attainable.

CRITERION 2. *The recommendations should provide facilities which will foster the development of all aspects of the desired program of the schools.*

By the time the survey staff is ready to formulate recommendations, it should have available the results of a study of the total program of the schools and probable future changes in it. Over and beyond those activities traditionally associated with schools, this study will have considered such aspects as health and guidance services, lunchroom services, and other auxiliary services for children. Activities conducted for children in school buildings or on school grounds during vacation periods will also have been studied, as will also all types of activities for the adults of the community.

Check List of Facilities

As a result of these studies the survey staff should have a list of the school plant facilities needed to permit the full realization of the desired program of today and the immediate future and a similar list to meet program changes in the more distant future. These lists ought to take due account of other public facilities in the community which can satisfactorily be used for part of the school program.

The principal task in the application of this criterion at this stage in the survey is the checking of the tentative recommendations against these lists. All of the facilities needed in the immediate future should be provided in the recommendations for immediate execution. The facilities which will be needed to meet some anticipated program change in the more distant future might be available in some existing building, but might require later remodeling or new construction. The long-range plan should be checked to see that these facilities can be provided when needed; the recommendations for immediate improvements should be checked to see that they at least do not set up any obstacles to the later achievement of these more distant goals. The checking suggested here might well be done by the use of some such device as the accompanying work sheet.

Suggested Work Sheet for Checking Adequacy
of Facilities Proposed in
Tentative Recommendations

Needed Facility	Buildings			
	Adams	Brown	Davis	Quincy
Immediate Future				
Kindergarten	X	X	O	X
Lunchroom	X	S	X	N
Health Suite	S	X	X	X
~~				
Scout Room	X	X	X	O
More Distant Future				
Nursery School Quarters	L	L	D	L
Community Little Theater	L	N	N	N

Explanation of Symbols
  X—*Reasonably adequate provision made by recommendations.*
  S—*Some provisions made by recommendations; best that can be recommended now.*
  O—*No provision in recommendations; although needed now, no reasonable way found to provide.*
  N—*Not provided in recommendations; not needed in this building.*
  L—*Not provided in recommendations; can be added later as needed.*
  D—*Not provided and difficult to add later as needed; no obstacles created by present recommendations.*

This work sheet, which is filled in with purely hypothetical information, would reveal to the survey staff such information as the following:

  1. The tentative recommendations will provide the Adams

building with all facilities now needed, although the health suite is not as good as desired. Facilities needed in the more distant future can be added as required.

2. The Brown building will have all needed facilities, although the lunchroom will not be wholly satisfactory.

3. The tentative recommendations make no provision in the Davis building for a kindergarten, and no suitable way can be found to remedy this defect within this pattern of recommendations. The later addition of a nursery school would be difficult, but the recommendations create no obstacles not now existing.

4. The Quincy building will have all needed facilities except the scout room, for which no provision can be made. The lunchroom and little theater are not needed at this building.

The defects revealed by the use of such a check sheet might be removed by some other pattern of recommendations. For example, changing from an eight-year to a six-year elementary school might release space for some of the facilities that could not otherwise be provided. This shift might, of course, introduce other objectionable features, which would have to be considered in the final judgment as to the proper pattern of recommendations. All the check sheet can do is to help bring out into the open the strengths and weaknesses of each set of tentative recommendations.

Missing Facilities

Very frequently the set of recommendations finally chosen as most satisfactory will leave certain buildings with some missing or substandard facilities. These should not be ignored or concealed in the report, but should be pointed out and the reasons explained.

Balance of Facilities

A recurring and troublesome problem in applying Criterion 2 is to avoid an improper balance among the facilities provided for the different parts of the total program. The relative emphasis upon various aspects of the program is a matter of opinion, but the survey staff should at least indicate some of the dangers of imbalance and attempt to provide facilities for a better rounded program. The building of a large and elaborate interscholastic athletic plant at the expense of adequate classrooms is one example of the type of distortion to be avoided. Another common error is the provision of more adequate facilities for high school pupils than for younger pupils.

Size of School

Adequate attention to Criterion 2 requires not only the presence of certain facilities, but also their availability in a proper setting. This means sites in pleasant environments and buildings of attractive appearance and suitable size.

No standards as to the optimum number of pupils in a school have been established by objective means, but it is generally believed that a school which is too large or too small can impair the effectiveness of the educational program. Therefore, some policies about school size must be agreed upon, applied, and reported in a school-plant survey. A helpful approach to the problem may be to consider the factors that tend to produce better education as the school increases in size, and also those that are generally less conducive to quality with a larger enrollment. Theoretically, there is a size at which these two sets of opposing factors are best in balance, and it is at this point that the optimum size is found. This idea is represented in simplified form in Figure 2, with the optimum size represented by the

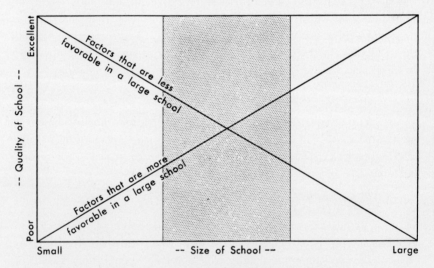

Figure 2. Relationship of Size and Quality of School.

point of crossing of the two lines. Obviously the relationship is not so precise as suggested by the two perfectly straight lines, nor can the point of crossing be so neatly located. The shaded area suggests that there is a range of size within which a reasonable quality of program can be provided. The determination of the point of crossing and the width of the shaded area are matters of judgment to be based upon thoughtful analysis of the factors involved.

Among the favorable factors which tend to be more prevalent in schools of larger enrollment are the following:

1. Greater variety of courses offered with more frequency and regularity and with greater adaptation of content and methods to the varying abilities of different groups of pupils.

2. More extensive and balanced programs of pupil activities (interscholastic athletics, intramural athletics, hobby clubs, literary groups, musical organizations, student councils, etc.).

3. More adequate provision of lunchrooms, health examinations, counseling, psychological assistance, and other special services.

4. Greater success, with some exceptions, in recruiting and holding qualified teachers and in providing the educational leadership necessary to keep them growing professionally.

5. More adequate provision at reasonable cost of necessary building facilities and equipment of certain types.

The failure of the very large school to achieve a high quality of education seems to be related causally to the following:

1. The increased difficulty of administration, with the accompanying tendency of the principal to neglect his functions as a leader because of preoccupation with operating the machinery.

2. The increased difficulty of unified staff planning and attack upon problems that should be of school-wide concern, i.e., the greater tendency for each teacher or department to operate independently rather than as part of a school-wide team.

3. The increased tensions and fatigue of teachers in a large school with more activity and noise, more formalization of operating procedures, and more conflicting demands upon their time and energy.

4. The increased difficulty of focusing effective attention upon the problems and needs of the individual pupil, especially in schools where the instruction of a given child is the responsibility of a number of different teachers during the same semester or year.

5. The less favorable psychological reaction of the pupil to the school situation, including the awe, or even fright, and the tensions of the young child in a very large school, and

the misbehavior of the older child whose identity is lost
in the mob.

Sound as these considerations may be in a theoretical sense, the survey staff must have some numerical expression of the size of a school which will be the goal in the school district under study. Thoughtful consideration of such factors as those listed is helpful, or even necessary, but does not automatically produce the desired answer. Judgment, and preferably group judgment, is required. The decision in the end is one for the local school authorities to make.

It is probably of interest in this connection that among school-plant planners there is considerable agreement on two classrooms per grade as the optimum in an elementary school, with one as the minimum and three as the maximum. However, there are some who would reject the whole concept of grade organization, and many who would favor small school buildings with only a few classrooms each. At the secondary school level there is much less agreement, with the upper limit ranging from 1,000 to 1,500 pupils. Many would say that 600 to 800 is the optimum at the secondary school level.

Controlling School Size. In setting up the recommendations, there may be considerable difficulty in holding the sizes of certain schools to the desired maximum, or of being reasonably certain that future growth will not require enlargement beyond that point. One solution to this difficulty is the planning of two or more schools on a single large site, either in completely separate buildings or in a single structure so designed as to provide a considerable or even complete independence of operation within the buildings and on the playgrounds. This solution can result in substantial economy in the costs of site purchase, site improvement, construction of facilities that can be jointly used (such as the heating plant), and maintenance and operation of buildings and grounds. A variation of this solution is the development of numerous small units on a single large site, especially where the instructional program is not highly departmentalized. These units may be from one to four classrooms each. This may permit the utilization of more economical construction techniques, depending upon building codes, zoning requirements, and other local factors.

Another device for offsetting the evils of a very large school, especially at the secondary school level, is to break the whole into smaller subgroups, or "houses" as they are sometimes called, with each subgroup administered separately but under the general leadership of the principal of the whole school. This organization would not preclude the joint use of such special facilities as the auditorium and lunchroom, or even others, but in general the plan will operate most effectively with a building arrangement that provides some degree of physical isolation of each subgroup. At best, this plan is a partial antidote to the evils of extreme size, and the provision of additional schools in separate buildings is the preferable solution.

Another solution at the elementary school level is to provide a number of small units throughout the attendance district. These units are usually of two or four rooms and most often house the younger children. Sites are usually relatively small, and the buildings are self-contained and reasonably automatic in operation. As the pupils grow older, they transfer to the larger center with a bigger site and the more specialized facilities needed for older children. This solution is applicable only where the program is relatively free of departmentalized instruction requiring a variety of special classrooms.

Additions to Buildings. A pitfall to be avoided in making recommendations is the erecting of a series of small additions to an existing building because of financial limitations. If the enrollment is growing, this process can eventually result in an excessively large building because there will never be enough money at one time to start a new building. It might be preferable in the long run to accept large classes or substandard facilities for a few years until funds can be accumulated to start a new building, and thus to checkmate the drift toward a single building larger than is educationally desirable. The survey staff needs to be particularly alert to this danger in a suburban community which still transports its pupils to one building and has not yet realized that it is becoming or is about to become so densely settled that numerous schools should be provided so that most pupils may be within walking distance of the one they attend.

A solution which is preferable to repeated small additions to the existing building in such a situation is the establishment of a new center on a new site properly located with respect to the long-range plan. This new center might be started with a simple building containing only a few classrooms, or even only one, provided the initial construction is undertaken within a comprehensive plan for the later development of the entire site.

Vertical Organization

There are many possible schemes of vertical organization. Among the most common are the 8–4, which provides eight-year elementary schools and four-year high schools, and the 6–3–3, with the three-year junior high coming between a six-year elementary school and a three-year senior high school. Other plans in use include the 7–5 and the 6–4–4, the latter including the junior college. A kindergarten may or may not be added to the elementary school under any of these plans.

In some school systems, there will be a rather firm policy in favor of some one pattern of vertical organization. This policy may have come from the program planning done as part of the building survey, or it may have another origin. In other school systems, there will be a willingness to accept whatever pattern seems best in the light of the survey findings. If the latter is the case, major attention in the comparison of the various tentative recommendations must be given to the relative quality of the educational facilities that can be provided under different plans. This should be the most important single factor in the choice of the pattern, although financial limitations or other considerations may force some yielding on this point.

This approach to vertical organization is based on the assumption that there is no one pattern that will provide the best educational program in all communities. The major determinants of the quality of the educational program are the nature of the educational leadership, the competence of the teaching staff, the adequacy of the educational supplies, and the character of the physical plant. The first three of these are independent of the pattern of vertical organization. If any one type of vertical organization will make possible a physical plant with superior teaching potential and with reasonable conformity to the other criteria, it should be adopted.

Administrative Offices

One final problem should be mentioned in connection with Criterion 2, since it is often overlooked. This is the need for suitable space for housing the central administration. Facilities needed include office space for the superintendent and other personnel, a meeting room for the board of education, and possibly warehouse and shop space as well as storage for buses and other motor vehicles. In deciding upon a location for the central administration, the primary concern should be the effect upon the educational program. Frequently, if not usually, this requires housing these functions apart from any school building.

In finding a solution to this problem, the survey staff has several alternatives to consider. Central administrative quarters can be rented, or they can be provided in a building or buildings erected or purchased by the school district for the purpose. In some cases, a school building no longer required for other school purposes can be converted at reasonable cost to very satisfactory administrative space. In other cases, it will be possible to isolate one wing of a school building for use by the central administration. The degree to which this solution will be satisfactory will depend upon how completely it can be isolated from the portion of the building used by the school, and how well the children can be protected from the traffic and noise incidental to the operation of the administrative center. Such separation may be easier to provide in a new building than in any existing one. With modern transportation, and particularly the extensive use of private automobiles, there is no need for the central administration of the school system to be in the heart of the business district.

> **CRITERION 3.** *The recommendations should provide adequate capacity in all types of facilities when needed and where needed throughout the school district.*

The use of this criterion in the development of the survey recommendations depends upon the availability of reasonably reliable estimates of future enrollment and accurate figures with respect to the capacities of existing buildings. In the case of the former, although it is quite impossible to have precise enrollment estimates by attendance areas or other small districts, the survey staff should have some clues as to the range within which the enrollment in a given area might reasonably be expected to fluctuate. With respect to capacity, it is necessary to know not only the capacity of each building with its present facilities and educational program, but also the effect upon capacity of any proposed building alterations or modifications of the program. The manner in which capacity figures and district-wide enrollment estimates are developed has been discussed in earlier chapters.

The survey staff will need, at the time of drafting recommendations, a considerable amount of other information. The most useful items which might be used are:

1. Tables showing trends in school enrollment, population of school age or total population, and social composition of the population by school attendance areas, census tracts, or other subdivisions of the school district.

2. Maps showing the residence locations of pupils and possibly of preschool children.

3. Information in map or table form showing the numbers of dwelling units and types and ages of housing, preferably by areas smaller than the school district.

4. Maps or aerial photographs showing the existing topography and land use, the areas available for future home construction, the locations of existing school buildings both within the school district and in surrounding territory which might conceivably become a part of the school district at some

future date, and the locations of transportation routes and other features related to the selection of locations for schools.

5. Information in map or other form regarding zoning, proposed street relocations, or other similar community plans.

As pointed out earlier, the survey staff even when armed with all these tools usually cannot make any very precise estimate of future enrollment for the attendance area of one school or for any other small portion of the school district. At best, these types of information provide clues to help in deciding the best course of action to propose in the light of the available evidence. This seemingly inevitable uncertainty with respect to future enrollment forces the survey staff to be satisfied with something less than a sure answer and to devise various means of hedging against the uncertainties of the future. The ideal survey recommendations in this respect will permit upward or downward adjustment in the capacity of each type of school in each part of the school district. This ideal is hard to attain, but much progress toward it can be achieved by certain devices.

Expansible Capacity

The possibility of upward adjustment of capacity is the easier to build into the survey recommendations. Future additions can be made to most existing buildings, although sometimes at great cost, existing buildings can be replaced at some future date by new buildings of larger size and more economical design, and new buildings can be planned for future enlargement as needed. The possibility that some existing or new building may become too large should be considered and should be guarded against by procuring new sites for possible new school centers in the future or sites large enough to accommodate more than one school building at a single location. If no vacant land is available at the time of the survey, the purchase of the additional land for this purpose might well wait until the need for it is clear, but the purchase of vacant land can be justified with less certainty that it will be needed. In general, vacant land adjacent to an existing site should be recommended for purchase unless there are clear reasons to the contrary.

Hedges Against Declining Enrollment

While it is more difficult to hedge against a future decline in enrollment, there are several techniques available. It frequently happens that old buildings exist in an area which needs additional capacity in the years immediately ahead, but which may lose population later. In cases of this kind, new buildings can be so located that they will be properly spaced if some or all of the older buildings are eliminated in the future. In these instances, no addition should be proposed for any existing building which would not be needed in the future in event of a substantial enrollment loss.

A few cities have designed new buildings with a permanent core of facilities that are likely to be needed for the lifetime of the building. The total capacity is then regulated by bringing in or taking away portable classroom units attached at predetermined places to a corridor of the permanent building. Similar to this is the plan of erecting a number of small house-like units on a large site. Units of this type are usually of one to four classrooms each. If properly designed, these can be removed and used elsewhere in the school system, or sold or rented for other uses when no longer needed for school purposes at the original location. Some cities also make use of prefabricated or demountable buildings that can be moved from one place to another. Older wooden buildings of this type were quite unsatisfactory, but new buildings of more satisfactory materials are available and can be erected at reasonable cost and provided with automatic heating plants, good ventilating equipment, sanitary facilities, good lighting, and other properties of good classrooms in permanent construction. These units are quite satisfactory if placed near a permanent building on an adequate site, and teachers seem to prize the freedom they provide from the distractions in the main building.

Although most old school buildings have relatively little value for any other purpose, it is possible to design a new structure with future conversion to some other use clearly in mind. The small units just described can be converted to residential or other nonschool use. In one midwestern city an elementary school building in an area that is rapidly shifting to commercial and light industrial activities was so designed to make it quite easy and inexpensive to convert to warehouse or light manufacturing use. Units of a few classrooms for the younger pupils could be designed for later conversion to apartments, if permitted by zoning regulations.

In the application of Criterion 3, attention should be given to the possibility of securing a more satisfactory distribution of capacity by the conversion of a school building, now or in the future, to some new school use. This is not an endorsement of the all-too-frequent practice of handing down an outmoded high school building to the elementary school. A conversion of the type suggested can be justified only when Criterion 2 can also be satisfied, that is, when truly suitable, and not just barely acceptable, educational facilities will result at all levels. The chances of successful conversion in the future can be enhanced by proper design of new buildings. This conversion of buildings to new school uses may be accomplished without change in the pattern of vertical organization or it may require the adoption of a new pattern. In the latter event, much more is at stake than the solution of the problem in this one section of the school district.

Shifting Attendance District Boundaries

An inexpensive, and seemingly obvious, method of adjusting enrollments to capacities is often overlooked, namely the shifting of attendance district boundary lines. The changing of the boundaries often meets opposition based on tradition, but such objections can seldom justify the expense of new construction while existing buildings are poorly utilized. The case for this solution, except as a temporary expedient, is weakened if the changes divide some neighborhood or community with a considerable degree of sociological unity or force pupils to face adverse conditions in getting to and from school. Once this type of adjustment is started there may be a succession of changes throughout the school district or a large segment of it in order to solve the problem in a single building.

The Rapidly Growing Area

Especially difficult problems are faced by the survey staff in a rapidly growing residential suburb in a metropolitan area. Such communities frequently have large amounts of vacant land suitable for residential use. The timing and extent of growth, however, cannot be ascertained, since they depend largely upon factors outside the school district in question. Frequently, these communities still think of themselves as rural or suburban and find it difficult to envision a future with a large number of school buildings to which most pupils can walk instead of being transported to a single building.

In a situation of this kind, a long-range plan is the most important outcome of the survey. It should be conceived in terms of the maximum future enrollment that seems possible, with necessary school locations spotted throughout the district, with the sites large enough to accommodate more than one building, if necessary, and with locations suitable for future pupils to walk to and from school.

The question frequently arises in rapidly growing communities, and occasionally in other places, as to the relative advisability of starting a new school center or transporting pupils to some existing building. Unless the population is sparse, transportation should be considered only a temporary solution. The primary aim of this proposal is not to avoid the cost of transportation, but rather to provide the neighborhood in which the children live with a school which can serve as a rallying point for many activities conducive to wholesome neighborhood life.

District Reorganization

In the development of survey recommendations the survey staff must frequently be concerned with the possibility of the addition or loss of territory by school district reorganization. The degree of probability of such change must determine the extent to which it is reflected in the recommendations. However, in any survey it is well to look beyond the present boundaries in planning the locations of any new buildings or other changes near the edges of the school district. Insofar as possible, proposed new buildings within the school district should be in locations that would be appropriate in the event of any reasonably foreseeable change in district boundaries.

Occasional examples of sudden major shifts in enrollments are encountered. A large manufacturing plant, for example, may be permanently closed, and many families move away. Or a large federal installation or private industry may suddenly bring a large influx of new families into a school district. The crisis created by such events often causes confusion and hasty decisions which are regretted later and for which generations of school children suffer. The need for a long-range study is especially great in such instances, and the survey must aim particularly at the avoidance of makeshift measures of more than passing duration.

CRITERION 4. *The recommendations should take into account the applicable portions of any community plan which has been developed.*

The statement of this criterion seems to imply that planning school locations and attendance district boundaries should be subordinate to other provisions of a community plan which may have been developed with little or no consultation with school authorities. This should not be the case. There is as much propriety in saying that the locations of highways and parks should depend upon the locations of schools as that school locations should depend upon the placement of streets and railroads. Ideally, neither position is wholly tenable, since it would be best if the locations of all public facilities could be developed concurrently with full consideration of the total needs of the community. Be that as it may, the locations of streets, parks, railroads, and other public facilities are usually pretty well determined long before a school building survey is undertaken, except perhaps in new residential subdivisions. Therefore, it is necessary to a considerable degree that the school survey staff accept the situation and as best it can fit the school locations into the matrix which is already laid down and which cannot easily be changed.

There are other aspects of city or regional plans that may affect materially the number of children that the schools will have to accommodate in the future. Examples are the setting aside of large tracts of land for public use or for industry and the establishment of minimum lot sizes or other regulations affecting the density of population.

A common feature in city plans is the identification of small neighborhoods each with a considerable degree of sociological unity and cohesiveness. It is commonly assumed that the fostering of these neighborhoods will help restore many of the favorable social forces lost as small towns grew into cities. Insofar as this is true, the schools should try to keep their attendance district boundaries reasonably the same as the neighborhood boundaries, with interest in the school as one of the forces holding the neighborhood together as a social unit. There will be cases, however, when adherence to the neighborhood concept would result in isolation in a single school of some one racial or nationality group, and where violation of this concept would permit these children to attend schools with others of different backgrounds. This mingling of children of all kinds has been looked upon as one of the strengths of the public school system. Thus, in a situation of this kind the survey staff must choose between the values fostered by the neighborhood approach to districting and those implied in the concept of the school as a "melting pot."

There will be other cases where adherence to the social neighborhood boundaries will require pupils to cross major streets or face other hazards in traveling to and from school. Unless adequate safeguards can be established, the lines of hazard may have to take precedence over the sociological boundaries in establishing attendance districts.

CRITERION 5. *The recommendations should avoid any discrimination in favor of or against any segment of the population or section of the school district.*

The use of this criterion is suggested solely as a device for checking the tendency that sometimes prevails to provide less attractive and educationally adequate facilities for the older or less well-to-do sections of a school district. A certain amount of difference in the quality of the school buildings is difficult to avoid, since the people who live in the newer sections of the district, where the new school buildings are located, are the ones with money enough to buy or rent the better houses, whereas those who are less favored economically remain in the older sections of the city where the school buildings are older and often on smaller sites. These older school buildings may be too good to abandon, and lack of funds may prevent enlargement of their sites or other major improvements. All that can be insisted upon is that adequate consideration be given to this problem and that every reasonable effort be made to provide equal educational opportunities for all children regardless of their place of residence or socio-economic status.

CRITERION 6. *The recommendations should provide all needed facilities at reasonable cost and within such financial limitations as must be observed.*

This criterion emphasizes economy, which is defined to mean maximum educational value for every dollar spent. It does not indicate the reduction of costs to save money without concern for the other criteria which have been discussed.

Economy

A first approach to economy in formulating survey recommendations is to make the best possible use of every existing building worthy of continued service. This presupposes that it has, or can be made to have, all the facilities, including adequate site area, which are needed for the type of school to be housed in it. Considerations of economy require, also, that any such building be of such quality and design that it can be remodeled, if necessary, at reasonable cost; that it can be used without excessive costs of operation and maintenance; and that suitable safety and sanitary requirements can be met.

Numerous other suggestions for economy have been implied in the discussion in preceding pages. These include the following:

1. Shifting of attendance district lines to minimize new construction.
2. Changing the pattern of vertical organization or otherwise converting existing buildings to new uses to increase their utilization, and thus to reduce the amount of new construction.
3. Planning school facilities in relation to the total community pattern of needs and facilities so that economies can be

effected through joint use of certain properties of all community agencies and more extensive use of such facilities as the schools provide.

4. Purchasing of sites well in advance of need and securing sites that are large enough to permit future expansion of the outdoor facilities and building as needed.

5. Planning buildings which are reasonably flexible and readily expansible to accommodate future needs.

In seeking economy, the mistake should not be made of choosing the lowest immediate cost without adequate consideration of the more distant future. For example, an addition to an existing building might be less expensive than a new building at another location, and yet over the years may violate many principles of good planning or even result in a greater expenditure of money for the value received.

Reducing Cost

This criterion is concerned with the immediate dollar cost in relation to available resources, as well as with economy as defined above. As indicated in a previous chapter, there are often definite limitations on the amount of money available, and the survey recommendations must take this fact into account. This is particularly true of the recommendations for the immediate future. The long-range plan is more free of this restriction, but even here some thought must be given to cost. A long-range proposal that is so expensive that its ultimate realization is not a reasonable possibility is not the best plan, even though there are no financial obstacles to the first steps.

With the great need for new school building construction, and every prospect of increasing needs, the pressure upon available resources is quite likely to continue. A survey staff must often face the question of what to do when funds are insufficient to meet the most obvious immediate needs. There is, of course, no magic answer, but there are some helpful approaches. It is assumed at this point that the pattern of recommendations decided upon has already been tested for economy as suggested above and that no further changes can be made without serious impairment of the school program.

If costs cannot be reduced, one solution is to defer certain of the recommended improvements. The construction of certain parts of a new building may be postponed, or the purchase or installation of certain equipment, furnishings, or finishes may be deferred until a later date. It is particularly important that any such curtailment of the initial improvements be of such nature that the deficiencies can be remedied at a later date. Thus, it would be better to omit interior paint, finish floors, and built-in equipment than to reduce the size of classrooms. Also, it would be better to postpone the construction of a gymnasium or auditorium than to make it so small that it would never be satisfactory.

In deciding what facilities to postpone, consideration should be given to temporary joint use of certain spaces. For example, a combination auditorium-gymnasium might serve until a separate auditorium can be built, or the cafeteria dining room might be the assembly space for a few years. If this type of solution is sought, the design of the multi-use space should be as appropriate as possible for all intended uses. Also, it should be planned so that a minimum of loss occurs when certain activities are moved to new quarters.

In a building program involving a number of different projects, an obvious course of action when funds are insufficient is to establish some system of priorities for determining which projects can best be deferred. The manner in which it is done must vary with local conditions, but in general the correction of serious health and safety hazards should rank first. Beyond this, the need for increased capacity at different places within the school system would appear to have next claim upon the available resources. The establishment of a system of priorities may require that the survey staff outline the transitional steps involved. These, of course, must be subject to later change if the transitional period is to be very long.

In some cases, especially in small school districts, the problem of inadequate funds can be met by merger with an adjoining school district or by district reorganization of some other form. The district in distress is not able to dictate in such matters, and in some cases may not be a welcome addition to any of its neighbors. It must be kept in mind, too, that the merging of two or more poor districts does not produce one rich one. It is possible, however, that the joining of several districts of low wealth will reduce total building costs by making available to all some unused capacity in one. Also, at the high school level the total cost for one new building would be less than that for several small buildings serving the same geographical area and providing the same educational program.

In their consideration of Criterion 6, the survey staff will need estimates of cost of the various alternatives considered. These estimates must cover remodeling as well as new construction. Normally, the services of an architect or other specialist should be secured for making these estimates but exception might be made with an experienced survey staff if rough approximations of cost will suffice.

CHAPTER 6

THE EDUCATIONAL PLANNING OF A BUILDING

Meaning of Educational Planning
Essential Characteristics of Good Educational Planning
Major Steps in Educational Planning

IT HAS been pointed out several times that a school building should be designed to fit the activities that are to take place within it. This principle is basic in the evaluation of existing buildings and in the planning of new or remodeled facilities. A school building designed without proper educational planning can merit high praise for its aesthetic qualities, its economy of construction and ease of maintenance, and other features not closely related to function, but only by chance can it be equally deserving of praise for its contribution to a good school program over a period of years. Careful and thorough educational planning, as well as good architectural planning, is essential if the completed structure is to be a helpful tool, rather than a hindrance, to the many generations of teachers and pupils who will use it.

Meaning of Educational Planning

THE term "educational planning" as used in this volume is limited, as previously explained, to the planning which follows the survey and which is done to produce a statement of the facilities and qualities that a particular proposed building should include. Thus the term excludes many school activities which involve the making of plans with respect to the school program. Stated positively, the term as used here encompasses all planning activities, both before and during the architectural work, which are necessary to determine for a specific building project the number and general character of the facilities within the completed building and on the site, insofar as they have a bearing on the successful functioning of the desired school program and the efficient and safe operation and use of the physical plant. It includes, also, those activities required to see that the plans and specifications prepared by the architect provide in a suitable manner the facilities thus determined to be necessary.

Since the major focus in educational planning is on the school program, it follows that educational planning is an aspect of school administration rather than a branch of architecture. It follows, also, that the members of the educational planning staff should be essentially educators by preparation and experience, and should look upon themselves as colleagues, if not actual members, of the local school staff. It would be appropriate, however, and quite desirable, to have an architect work in close cooperation with the educational planner[1] throughout the process of educational planning.

The planning of a specific new building, then, breaks down into two parts, one primarily educational in nature and the other dealing with the architectural and engineering aspects. For the most part, the educational phase of the planning precedes the architectural and engineering phases, and provides the essential educational specifications upon which the architect and engineer base their proposals as to design and construction. The educational planning staff analyzes the school program to determine the number and nature of the physical facilities required; the architect and engineer then proceed to design a physical plant that will provide the needed educational facilities as well as satisfy certain important noneducational requirements.

The distinction is repeated at this point between the school-plant survey and educational planning, both of which are essentially in the educational field. The survey, which has been discussed at length in the preceding chapters, is a study designed to develop a comprehensive building program for a school district over a period of years. It is not concerned with the development of the detailed plans required for the construction of a particular new building. For example, the survey report might recommend that a new junior high school building for 750 pupils be erected at a certain location. It would not, however, indicate such things as how many rooms of each type should be provided, what facilities and interior arrangement they should have, how they should be grouped together and arranged within the building and on the site, or what materials and methods of construction should be employed in the new building. These details in regard to a specific building project are determined in the educational and architectural planning that follow the survey and the board's decision to proceed with a specific construction project.

[1] The term "educational planner" is used in the singular, but may include a group of people. See next chapter for discussion of this point.

Essential Characteristics
of Good Educational Planning

THE concept that detailed educational planning apart from architectural planning is required for each particular school building project is not new, but it has not been widely recognized and discussed until recent years. For this reason, the procedures involved in such planning are still quite varied and subject to change. There are, however, certain features which characterize all work of good quality in this area. The more important of these characteristics will be presented and discussed briefly.

RELATES TO THE SURVEY

The first essential characteristic is that the educational planning be done within the general framework of an approved over-all building plan for the school district. Such an over-all plan should result from a school building survey and be approved by the board of education. Obviously, some deviation from the survey plan as recommended or adopted may be necessary because of changed conditions, and this is quite appropriate if all necessary adjustments in the total plan are made. The important point here is that an individual building project should not be planned without knowing where it fits into the total scheme for the school district.

Failure to design a particular new building in relation to such an over-all plan involves substantial risks and can prove costly in terms of both money and educational effectiveness. The building may be of the wrong size or unduly expensive, thus causing overcrowding or waste of money. It may be in the wrong location, thus inconveniencing the children who must attend it and discouraging its use by older youth and adults whose use of the building is voluntary. Such a building, also, is more likely to be diverted at a later date from its intended use and made to house pupils of a different age and with a different educational program, thus resulting in a building which in many respects is a hindrance to good teaching.

ENCOMPASSES THE ENTIRE SCHOOL PROGRAM

A second requirement is that good educational planning include detailed analysis of every activity that will normally be housed in the building. Such analysis will include proper attention to possible future developments and will seek ways of providing flexibility and expansibility to meet unforeseen and unpredictable changes. It will encompass the total school program most broadly defined, including outdoor as well as indoor activities; vacation and week-end events as well as those occurring on school days; after-school and evening events as well as those during school hours; and activities of adults and out-of-school youth as well as those of regularly enrolled pupils. Lack of sponsorship by the board of education will not justify overlooking an activity that will use the school facilities over any extended period of time. In its consideration of the needs of various aspects of the program, good educational planning will maintain a proper balance and will not favor one activity unduly at the expense of others.

The analysis of activities must go behind the educational scene to encompass many supporting activities. Attention must be given to the operation and maintenance of the building and grounds; to the delivery, distribution, and storage of supplies and equipment; and to the removal of wastes. The routing and storage of buses, bicycles, and other vehicles on and adjacent to the site must be considered. Educational administration and supervision, guidance, library service, audio-visual aids, lunchroom program, and health service are other aspects of the program that require analysis as a part of the total planning process.

PROMOTES ECONOMY

The maximum educational return for each dollar spent (which is a sound definition of economy) can best be assured by designing a building which fits the needs of the school program. If this is done, there will be the maximum educational benefit both from each construction dollar spent and from each dollar devoted to staffing and operating the building throughout its years of service. Good educational planning promotes economy in this sense.

There are some who fear that the cost of a building will be greater if there are extensive educational planning activities. They often mistakenly assume that the process involves the adding together of the wishes of many people to determine what should be included in the new building. Such a process would, of course, be expensive, but it would not be good educational planning. While it is quite proper and desirable to secure the opinions of many people, these opinions are but one clue to the composite list of facilities finally derived.

It is quite possible that the educational planning activities will in the end indicate the need for a more costly building than would otherwise be planned, or in fact than can be financed. The final determination of the amount to be spent can be made after educational planning in the light of full knowledge of what is needed, rather than blindly as would otherwise be the case. Only by careful educational planning can the greatest economy be assured, regardless of how much or how little is spent.

PROMOTES GOOD ARCHITECTURAL WORK

Since the major responsibility for developing from the educational specifications a suitable design and the necessary drawings and other documents needed for construction falls upon the architect, it follows that a fourth essential characteristic of good educational planning is that it is done in such a way as to be most helpful to the architect. Good educational planning makes it possible for the architect to do a better job without unnecessary delay. The educational planner and other school personnel should be in a position at all times to provide promptly any information needed by the architect concerning the educational requirements. Most of this information should be provided in writing when the architect is directed by the board of education to proceed with the architectural planning, but there will normally be need for supplementary information as his work progresses.

The written materials presented to the architect at the beginning of his work are likely to be called the "program of requirements" or the "educational specifications." The latter term is more commonly used by educators, and will be used in this volume. If the educational specifications are to promote better architectural work, it is necessary that they be clear and concise, easy to use, and free of fixed requirements that stifle the creative imagination of the architect as he strives for the best solution to the problem at hand. The educational planning should be so thorough that changes of educational requirements are not made after architectural work begins.

CONTINUES THROUGH THE ENTIRE PLANNING PERIOD

A fifth characteristic of good educational planning is that it continues as long as there are planning decisions of educational import to be made by the architect or others. Throughout the architectural planning phase, questions will arise which have educational significance, and this may be true even later if changes are considered during actual construction. Also, it will be true during or after construction if the selection of educational equipment is delayed until that late. In any event, the educational planner should check all of the architect's drawings and specifications for conformity to the educational specifications and should recommend changes which he believes to be necessary and desirable to achieve a better educational plant. The very earliest time at which the services of the educational planner should terminate is when he recommends to the superintendent or board of education the approval of the architect's final drawings and specifications. If he is to be of maximum value, he should not be dropped by the board of education upon completion of the educational specifications, nor should he be bypassed either by the architect or by the school authorities at any stage in the architectural planning.

IS CLEARLY DISTINGUISHED FROM ARCHITECTURE

While there is a close relationship between the work of the educator and that of the architect in planning a school building, and possibly some twilight zone between them, there is an essential difference which must be maintained. A sixth characteristic of good educational planning is that this distinction is recognized and respected. The educational planner will carefully refrain from making decisions of architectural nature, and he will be tactfully insistent that educational decisions be made by the educators involved rather than by the architect. It is to be expected that an educational planner and architect who work together harmoniously on a project will come to the point where each raises questions and makes suggestions outside his own field of specialization, but neither should presume to make decisions or recommendations on such matters. To do so is to risk unsound decisions and invite friction which is likely to be reflected in a poorer building. The avoidance of such friction is extremely important because only by mutual understanding and wholehearted cooperation between educational planner and architect can the best school building be produced.

PROMOTES PROPER USE OF THE NEW BUILDING

A seventh characteristic of good educational planning is that it is done in such a manner as to promote understanding and effective use of the completed building and its equipment. An excellent school building designed by competent educational and architectural specialists may be severely criticized by teachers and citizens who do not understand certain of its features. Teachers may fail to make effective use of educational features which they do not recognize or appreciate. The teachers and other employees may inadvertently damage certain equipment or cause it to function improperly if they have not been adequately instructed in its care and use. The problem in all these cases is one of developing understanding. This can be accomplished in part by participation in the planning process, in part by proper publicity, and in part by suitable instructions at the time of opening the new building. The point made here anticipates the discussion in the next chapter of staff and citizen participation in building planning and the suggestions in a later chapter relative to the opening of the completed building. Therefore, these two aspects of the problem will not be elaborated at this point.

The publicity during the planning and construction of a new school building should be designed to promote widespread understanding without creating hopes or expectations that may have to be denied later. News concerning the decision to build, the employment of the educational consultant and architect, the presentation and acceptance of plans, the receiving of bids, the letting of contracts, and the like would always be in order. Decisions with respect to certain features of the building can be made known when they are reasonably final, and floor plans, perspective drawings, and models can be publicized. In developing understanding, it would seem helpful to give publicity to the planning process itself so that all know the orderly way in which the building is designed to fit the educational program. In fact, considerable effort should be made to give as much attention to the educational features of the building and the relationship of planning to program as to the attractive drawings or models which are so often used for publication in the newspaper or display in a public place.

USES TECHNICALLY SOUND PROCEDURES

Finally, but by no means of small importance, good educational planning employs technically sound procedures in a careful and painstaking manner. The educational planning of a new school building is a large undertaking with scores of detailed decisions to be made. Many of these decisions are based on judgment alone, while others require supporting calculations of various kinds. The use of faulty procedures or bad judgment, or failure to give attention to necessary details, can prove costly in terms of needless expense for construction or in impaired educational effectiveness of the completed building.

Attention is given in the remainder of this chapter to the nature of the procedures and technical processes involved in good educational planning.

Major Steps in Educational Planning

REDUCED to its simplest terms, there are two major phases of educational planning. The first is concerned with the determination of what facilities are needed in the building, while the second encompasses all activities designed to insure that the necessary facilities are actually provided for in the drawings and specifications prepared by the architect. For purposes of this discussion, however, the total process will be broken down into smaller steps as follows:

1. Review of school program planning.
2. Review of applicable parts of the building survey report.
3. Determination of the number of teaching stations of each type.
4. Determination of other quantitative requirements.
5. Determination of the qualitative design requirements for each type of room or space and its equipment.
6. Preparation of written educational specifications for the guidance of the architect.
7. Cooperation with the architect.
8. Checking and approval of architect's drawings and specifications.

Ordinarily, these steps are undertaken about in the order indicated and occur between the completion of the survey and the acceptance of final drawings and specifications for the building in question. There are, however, many exceptions. The survey may be so recent that Steps 1 and 2 are omitted entirely. The analyses of the educational program made as a part of the survey may be so complete or may have been extended to the point that all or much of Step 3 is done before the survey is finished and before Step 2 of the educational planning process is started. Decisions in regard to some of the equipment or furnishings may be postponed until construction is under way, or even completed. Finally, there is always the possibility that previous decisions made at any stage of planning may have to be reviewed in the light of financial limitations, difficulties encountered during construction, or other unforeseen conditions.

With these possible exceptions in mind, the several steps will be discussed and further explained in order.

REVIEW OF SCHOOL PROGRAM

It has been stated that program planning should precede the survey rather than be a part of it. In like manner, it should precede the educational planning of a new building. In actual practice, however, the program planning which has been done often provides an inadequate basis for many of the decisions which must be made with respect to a new building. This may be due to incomplete program planning or to the fact that considerable time has elapsed since such planning was completed. In either case, before the educational planning of a new building proceeds, the policies of the school with respect to the program should be reviewed and such additional study and deliberation undertaken as are needed to reach firm decisions.

The nature of such program study was discussed in Chapter 3 and will not be reviewed at this point.

REVIEW OF SURVEY REPORT

In a strict sense, any review of the survey findings and recommendations is not a part of educational planning. However, the amount of money involved is so great and a new building is so enduring in its effects upon the educational program, that no major school construction project should be undertaken without consideration of all pertinent developments since the completion of the survey. If this review should result in substantial doubts with respect to any aspect of the particular building project about to be undertaken, the time schedule for the educational and architectural planning of the building should be modified to permit these doubts to be resolved. Any educational planning work carried on during this period of re-study should be of such scope and nature that it will not in any way prejudice the answers to the questions raised about the survey recommendations. Perhaps the pitfall most to be avoided is the investment of so much time and money in the educational planning that there develops an unsuspected resistance to any change of over-all plan that would require starting over again.

DETERMINATION OF NUMBER OF TEACHING STATIONS

The first step in educational planning, after review of the educational program and the survey recommendations, is to establish the quantitative requirements. This includes determining the number of teaching stations of each type; the number and kinds of offices and other administrative rooms; the capacities of such facilities as auditoriums, lunchrooms, and gymnasiums; and the number and kinds of outdoor facilities. All questions with respect to "how many" or "how much" are answered at this point in the planning process. The answers depend upon such factors as anticipated enrollment, both for the school as a whole and by subjects; nature of the educational program, including courses and other activities offered, frequency of class meetings, kind of schedule, and size of class; extent of voluntary participation in certain activities; and various policies regarding school operation and maintenance.

Future Enrollments

The basic quantitative fact needed in the planning of any school building is the number of pupils to be housed. The planner must know not only the anticipated initial enrollment, but also the probable future number and the upper limits to be used in planning. In many instances, the answers to these questions will be furnished to the educational planner by the building survey report or by instructions from the school authorities. If instructions or survey recommendations are not specific as to the recommended size of the new building, or if it is deemed necessary for any reason to review the matter, new enrollment estimates should be made. Such new estimates should certainly be made if a year or more has elapsed since the survey estimates were prepared. Procedures for estimating future enrollments have been discussed in some detail in Chapter 3.

If there is no recently established or recently reaffirmed local policy with respect to minimum and maximum size of school, and the future enrollment seems likely to become quite small or quite large, the educational planner should seek some statement of policy by the board of education as to the enrollment limits within which he should plan the new building. While the board of education should determine the policy, the educational planner as consultant to the board should accept responsibility for making a recommendation.

Another aspect of the enrollment problem is to estimate how many will enroll in each subject in a departmentalized program. Unless a substantially new program is contemplated, a first step in estimating subject enrollments is to determine what percentage of the pupils in each grade have taken each subject in recent years. These percentages should be calculated year by year, and then examined for evidence of trends. Adjustments in the calculated percentages must be made by the educational planner as he deems appropriate in the light of any observed trends or other factors which might affect the distribution of enrollments among the various subjects. The offering of new subjects in the new building or the provision in the new structure of more adequate and attractive facilities for some subjects will result in a shift in the percentage distribution of subject enrollments. Changes in the counseling program could have a similar effect. Sound judgment based upon thoughtful consideration of previous experience and known factors that might affect the future is the only key to sound estimates of future subject enrollments. This, of course, does not assure complete success, but it tends to reduce errors in planning.

Elementary Schools

Once it has been decided how many pupils to plan for, the next step is to determine the required number of teaching stations of each type. The calculations necessary at this point require information with respect to the number of pupils who will use this type of teaching station, how much time they will spend in it each week, the desired average class size, and the nature of the weekly schedule.

In the typical elementary school, where each regular classroom is used by only one group of children during a given term, the determination of the number of regular classrooms becomes simply the determination of the number of classroom groups. The number of classroom groups can be estimated grade by grade, and a total derived by addition, or the predicted total enrollment for all grades or a group of grades can be divided by the desired average class size. If pupils of certain grades do not attend school a full day or every day of the week, as is usually true in kindergarten, separate calculations will be required.

For purposes of illustration, let us assume an elementary school of 350 pupils evenly divided among the kindergarten and grades 1 through 6. Let us assume, also, that the local policy is to maintain an average class size of 25, and to operate the kindergarten on a half-day basis. The 50 kindergarten pupils would make two groups. With each pupil attending only one-half of each day, the two groups would require only one kindergarten room. Above the kindergarten, each of the six grades would be divided into two class groups, making a total of 12 in all. Or the 300 pupils in these grades divided by the average class of 25 would produce 12 groups. Thus, the number of regular classrooms above the kindergarten would be 12.

Special rooms are usually provided in elementary school buildings for teaching physical education, and in some cases other special classrooms are provided. The use of these special rooms may be limited to certain grades, or they may be used by all grades. The regular classroom stands vacant while a given group of pupils is using the special classroom. In a situation of this kind, the number of special teaching stations of each type can be quickly determined by use of the following simple formula:

$$\text{Number of teaching stations} = \frac{\text{Total number of minutes or periods of use each week by all groups}}{\text{Total number of minutes or periods available each week in one teaching station}}$$

For example, let us assume that the only type of special classroom needed in this hypothetical school is for physical education, and that each class group above kindergarten will have three 30-minute periods of physical education each week. Assume, also a 27.5-hour (1650-minute) week or a 5.5-hour day. The number of physical education teaching stations required would be as follows:

$$\text{Number of teaching stations} = \frac{12 \text{ groups} \times 90 \text{ minutes each}}{1650 \text{ minutes per week}}$$

$$= \frac{1080 \text{ minutes of use}}{1650 \text{ minutes available per teaching station}}$$

$$= .65$$

Using periods instead of minutes, the calculation would be:

$$\text{Number of teaching stations} = \frac{12 \text{ groups} \times 3 \text{ periods each}}{27.5 \text{ hours in school week} \div .5 \text{ hours per period}}$$

$$= \frac{36 \text{ periods of use}}{55 \text{ periods available per teaching station}}$$

$$= .65$$

In other words, a physical education teaching station would be in use under these conditions 65 percent of the time, and only one such teaching station would be required.

Secondary Schools

In the typical secondary school, and some elementary schools, the calculations are complicated by such factors as departmentalization, greater specialization of classrooms, elective subjects, and more complicated schedules. The basic formula for use in such cases is the following:

$$\text{Number of teaching stations} = \frac{\text{Number of pupils enrolled in subject} \times \text{Number of periods per week in subject}}{\text{Desired average class size} \times \text{Number of periods per week each teaching station can be used}}$$

For the most part, separate calculations are required for each subject or subject area. Different subjects or subject areas should be grouped in the calculations only when all can use the same type of classroom.

Before calculations are undertaken, care must be exercised to establish firm data or policies relative to each item in the formula. With the advice of the educational planner, the school authorities should determine the subjects to be offered, the average size of class in each, which subjects are to be required and which elective, and the number of periods each course is to be taught each week. It is necessary, also, to decide whether each teacher is to be assigned a classroom and allowed to use it during his nonteaching periods, because this affects the number of periods each teaching station is available for class use. The anticipated pupil enrollment in each course is a matter of judgment based upon policies with respect to required and elective courses, trends in course electives in recent years, and anticipated changes in the total program which might affect the enrollments in the different subjects. It is obvious that no assurance can be had at any time that the subject enrollment pattern will not change or that other pertinent factors will not be modified in the future; all the planner can do is to strive for as firm information as possible and then proceed with the calculations accordingly.

Use of Formula. The use of this formula can best be made clear by an example. A hypothetical junior high school has a program of studies in grades 7 and 8 as follows:

Subject	Periods per week
English or language arts	5
Arithmetic	5
Social studies	5
Science	5
Art	$2\frac{1}{2}$
Music	$2\frac{1}{2}$
Physical education	$2\frac{1}{2}$
Industrial arts or home economics	$2\frac{1}{2}$
TOTAL	30

This program provides for no electives and no study halls. Lunch, assembly, homeroom, club, and similar activities are provided for outside the 30-period week. The total enrollments are 300 in grade 7 and 275 in grade 8, and are divided evenly in each case between boys and girls. The desired average class size in all cases is 25.

By using these data, the number of teaching stations for English in grade 7 would be calculated as follows:

$$\text{Number of teaching stations} = \frac{300 \text{ pupils enrolled} \times 5 \text{ periods per week}}{25 \text{ pupils per class} \times 30 \text{ periods of use per teaching station}}$$

$$= \frac{1500 \text{ pupil-periods of instruction}}{750 \text{ pupil-periods that can be provided in one teaching station}}$$

$$= 2$$

Since English, arithmetic, and social studies are all taught to the same pupils in the same sized class group for the same number of periods per week, the total number of rooms for these three subjects could be determined by one calculation using 900 in place of 300 in the numerator. If the building is to be designed to fit the program, it follows that such combined calculations are appropriate only when all the subjects so grouped can use the same type of classroom. For example, it would not be appropriate to combine English and science in the calculations if the science program should require a larger room or special equipment that would make the room inappropriate as an English classroom.

In these hypothetical calculations, it has been assumed that each room would be available for use every period of the week. For illustration, let us now assume that each teacher is assigned a particular room, has five classes each day, and has the use of his room during his nonteaching period. The result of these policies is that each teaching station is available only 25 periods each week instead of 30. The entries below the line in the above examples would become "25 pupils per class × 25 periods of use per teaching station," which would change the 750 to 625 and increase the calculated number of English teaching stations from 2 to 2.4 (1500 ÷ 625).

A similar adjustment would be required in event the number of class periods for a given course could not be divided evenly into the total number of class periods per week. For example, if a certain class were to meet 7 periods per week, the 30 in the divisor would have to be changed to 28. Another class group could not use the remaining two periods unless it were to occupy several different rooms during the course of the week.

Correction for Incomplete Utilization. Formulas of this type, as reported in the school-plant literature, usually include some correction for inability to schedule every room for 100-percent use, but the need for such a correction factor is not clearly established. Anderson found a correction factor to be required for special classrooms but not for regular classrooms, while Packer's conclusions were the opposite.[2] Conrad, on the other hand, decided against the use of any such a correction factor. He reasoned that the necessary margin would be achieved in one or more of the following ways, depending upon the program of the particular school in question:

1. The average class size used in the calculation would be less than the capacity of the typical classroom, since many classes would have to exceed the average. The difference

[2] Packer, Paul C., *Housing of High School Programs.* Contributions to Education, No. 159. New York: Teachers College, Columbia University, 1924. Also Anderson, Homer W., *A Method for Determining the Housing Requirements of Junior High School Programs.* University of Iowa, Studies in Education, Vol. 3, No. 3. Iowa City: The University, 1926.

between average class size and average room capacity would result inevitably in less than 100-percent pupil-station utilization.

2. A policy allowing each teacher to use his room during non-teaching periods or a lunch schedule which would keep some pupils in class while others were eating would result in less than 100-percent room utilization.

3. The necessary provision of a whole room where the calculations indicate a need for a fraction of a room would lead to less than 100-percent room utilization.

4. Less than 100-percent room utilization would occur when the number of periods for each class would not divide evenly into the total number of periods in the weekly schedule.[3]

Conrad's third point can be illustrated by using the figures for grade 8 in the example above. Calculations for English would be:

$$\text{Number of teaching stations} = \frac{\begin{array}{c}275 \text{ pupils} \\ \text{enrolled}\end{array} \times \begin{array}{c}5 \text{ periods} \\ \text{per week}\end{array}}{\begin{array}{c}25 \text{ pupils} \\ \text{per class}\end{array} \times \begin{array}{c}30 \text{ periods of use per} \\ \text{teaching station}\end{array}}$$

$$= \frac{1375}{750}$$

$$= 1.83$$

Obviously, two teaching stations would have to be provided, or some rooms would have to be designed to accommodate English and some other subject. Let us assume the latter and say that English, arithmetic, and social studies could be taught in the same classroom. The calculations for grade 8 would then be:

$$\text{Number of teaching stations} = \frac{\begin{array}{c}(275 \times 3) \text{ pupils} \\ \text{enrolled}\end{array} \times \begin{array}{c}5 \text{ periods} \\ \text{per week}\end{array}}{\begin{array}{c}25 \text{ pupils per} \\ \text{class}\end{array} \times \begin{array}{c}30 \text{ periods of use per} \\ \text{teaching station}\end{array}}$$

$$= \frac{4125}{750}$$

$$= 5.5$$

In this instance, it would be necessary to provide six teaching stations for these three subjects, since 5.5 rooms could not be built. These six rooms would have a capacity of 4500 pupil-periods (25 pupils per period for 30 periods for each room), but they would have only 4125 pupil-periods of

[3] Conrad, Marion J., *A Technique for Determining the Operating Capacity of Secondary School Buildings.* Doctor's thesis. Columbus: Ohio State University, 1952.

use. Thus, the rounding off to the next whole number of rooms results in 91.7 percent of utilization (4125 ÷ 4500).

Those who include a special correction factor in their calculations do it by inserting the appropriate factor as a decimal below the line. Without repeating the formula, this procedure can be made clear by repeating the last calculation with an 85-percent utilization factor included. The calculation then becomes:

$$\text{Number of teaching stations} = \frac{(275 \times 3) \text{ pupils enrolled} \times 5 \text{ periods per week}}{25 \text{ pupils per class} \times 30 \text{ periods of use per teaching station} \times .85}$$

$$= \frac{4125}{637.5}$$

$$= 6.5$$

Using the 85-percent correction produces a need for 6.5 rooms against 5.5 in the original calculations. The number of rooms built would have to be seven instead of six. With seven rooms, the capacity would be 5250 pupil-periods per week (25 pupils per class × 30 periods per week for each room), but the need is for only 4125 pupil-periods. Thus, the degree of utilization will be only 4125 ÷ 5250, or 78.6 percent.

In summary, then, the rounding off to a whole number of rooms would, in this particular instance, result in 91.7 percent utilization in spite of the fact that the formula seems to provide for 100 percent. When the correction factor is inserted to provide for 85-percent utilization, the rounding off causes the actual utilization to drop to 78.6 percent. In the latter case, two corrections have actually been made.

Another difficulty in the use of a correction factor in the formula is that there is no conclusive research that can be used in determining the size of the correction factor to be used. In other words, there has been no objective determination of what constitutes a reasonable percent of utilization. In fact, it might be inferred from the Conrad study that the percent of utilization which is acceptable depends upon the type of program, and that no optimum or ideal figure for all programs can be stated.[4]

The extent to which the rounding off to whole rooms will affect the percent of utilization will vary with the other factors in the formula. The margin which this procedure provides will be absent if the calculated number of rooms should come out to a whole number. For example, if the eighth-grade calculations above are repeated with 250 pupils instead of 275, the calculated number of rooms for English, arithmetic, and social studies

[4] *Ibid.*

will be 5.0 instead of 5.5 and there will be no rounding off. Also, where rooms are designed for any kind of multiple use, some of the calculated fractions of rooms are absorbed and the amount of rounding off is reduced. In these cases, there would be closer to 100-percent utilization, and therefore less leeway for scheduling difficulties. Because of this possibility, the resulting percents of utilization should be checked before finally deciding the number of rooms to provide. However, the mathematical chances of having the calculations for all subject areas result in whole numbers of rooms are so slight that they can be ignored. In other words, for all practical purposes it can be assumed that something less than 100-percent utilization will be achieved with no correction factor in the formula such as used by Anderson and Packer.

Use of Indexes. In Chapter 3 it was proposed that certain indexes be calculated which would indicate the number of pupils in total enrollment for which one teaching station would be adequate. If these indexes have been calculated, the number of teaching stations required for any given enrollment can quickly be determined by division. Thus, if the total anticipated enrollment in the school is 1200 and the index for chemistry and physics is 960, there would be need for 1.25 rooms for these subjects (1200 ÷ 960 = 1.25). Again, it should be pointed out, as it was in Chapter 3, that these indexes are not the same in all schools, but vary with policies and practices in regard to number of periods, pattern of subject enrollments, class size, and other factors. The indexes used here are based on hypothetical data chosen for purposes of illustration only.

Other Methods. All of the methods used for determining the number of rooms needed in a secondary school have the same essential elements. They vary in mechanical form and in allowance for scheduling difficulties. The formulas of Packer and Anderson, which were cited earlier, have been in use for a third of a century. Each makes a different correction for scheduling difficulties. Conrad's indexes were derived from the Packer and Anderson formulas but omit the correction. Castaldi published a nomogram to permit the graphic determination of the number of rooms, and used an 85-percent utilization factor to correct for problems of scheduling.[5]

DETERMINATION OF OTHER QUANTITATIVE REQUIREMENTS

Beyond the classrooms and other teaching stations where most of the group instruction takes place, there are numerous other rooms and

[5] Castaldi, Basil, *The Castaldi Nomogram.* Cambridge, Mass.: The New England School Development Council, 1953.

spaces provided in a modern school building. These must not be over-looked in the educational planning process. As in the case of the teaching stations, the first step is to determine "how many" and "how much" of each is required. If the latter is expressed in terms of number of people or the quantity to be accommodated, as is appropriate, these determinations are largely made by use of informed judgment rather than by mathematical calculations.

A great variety of rooms and spaces might be considered at this point, since the list would vary from one community to another and from one building to another in the same school system. Some of the more common facilities are now discussed under the following headings:

1. Nonclassroom facilities for pupils.

2. Administrative offices and staff rooms.

3. Custodial and service facilities.

4. Facilities for public use.

Nonclassroom Facilities for Pupils

In addition to classrooms, shops, laboratories, and other rooms where class instruction normally takes place, there are many spaces both inside and outside the building that need to be included in the list of requirements. Some of these are instructional in purpose, while others are more remote from the educational process. The following list includes the more common nonclassroom facilities for pupils and the type of decisions necessary at this point with respect to each:

1. *Library*—pupil capacity of reading room; number of reading rooms; number of conference rooms; number of listening booths; number of books to be shelved in reading rooms; facilities needed for librarian's office, workroom, and storage use, the number of persons and materials to be accommodated.

2. *Activity rooms for newspaper staff, student council, and similar student activities*—number of rooms of each type and number of persons to be accommodated in each.

3. *Lounges and other social rooms*—number of rooms of each type and number of persons to be accommodated in each.

4. *Assembly, dramatics, and speech facilities, including auditoriums, little theaters, audio-visual rooms, broadcasting studios, and the like*—number required and capacity of each.

5. *Cafeteria or lunchroom*—kitchen capacity in terms of total number of meals to be prepared, number and seating capacity of dining rooms, and number of serving counters of various types.

6. *Gymnasium facilities*—number of spectators to be accommodated for various events.

7. *Locker, shower, and dressing rooms*—number of rooms of each type, number of pupils to be accommodated at one time, number of lockers or storage baskets of each type, number of shower heads, and number of toilet fixtures.

8. *Other indoor athletic facilities*—number and capacity of special team rooms, equipment drying rooms, equipment repair rooms, and the like.

9. *Clothing storage*—number of pupils to be accommodated in lockers or wardrobes in each classroom or in corridor lockers.

10. *Toilets and restrooms*—possibly number of rooms and number of fixtures, but these matters should be left to the discretion of the architect except for mention of special requirements; most building codes establish generous minimum requirements.

11. *Health service rooms*—types of health service activities to be housed and number of staff members and pupils to be accommodated at one time; number of toilet fixtures, dressing rooms, showers, cots, etc.; need for and capacity of separate waiting room for the clinic.

12. *Outdoor facilities*—number of ball diamonds, tennis courts, football fields, practice fields, and other special areas that should conform to standard dimensions; number and size of other game areas; number of pieces and types of recreational equipment or size of other recreational facilities; need for and capacity of bus loading docks.

Administrative Spaces

The administrative office requirements will vary greatly from school to school. In the educational planning of a particular building, it is necessary to make decisions in regard to the following:

1. *Private offices*—how many private offices will be needed and for what officials? How many additional people will each have to accommodate for conferences and interviews?

2. *General office*—how many secretarial and clerical workers, including part-time and occasional workers, must be accommodated? What records and equipment must be housed in the general office? If teachers pick up mail here, how many mail boxes are required? For how many people must waiting-room space be provided?

3. *Other central office space*—what separate workrooms, storage rooms, vaults, or other supplementary spaces are required, and what should be the capacity of each?

4. *Quarters for guidance workers*—are these to be provided in connection with the general office or separately? How many people of each category must be housed, and how many additional people must each office accommodate for conferences or interviews? What is the need for separate waiting rooms, restrooms, toilets, conference rooms, record rooms, interviewing rooms, and other special rooms auxiliary to the guidance offices? What should be the capacity of each?

5. *Conference rooms*—if separate conference space is to be provided, the number of rooms and capacity must be established.

6. *Storage rooms*—if separate storage rooms are to be provided for educational and office supplies or books, how many of each type of room are required, and what should be the capacity of each?

Staff Rooms

In addition to the offices and meeting places for conferences, the staff members need separate rooms where they can work in privacy, relax or rest on occasion, and attend their personal needs. This is true of all staff members, even though common practice seems to reflect concern for teachers only. Among the decisions to be made at this point are:

1. *Teachers' offices and workrooms*—how many offices are to be provided for teachers, including offices for physical education teachers and coaches, and how many each should accommodate; if separate work or study rooms are to be provided for teachers, how many should there be and how many should each accommodate?

2. *Teachers' lounges, etc.*—how many teachers' lounges, restrooms, and toilets should there be and how many should each accommodate?

3. *Quarters for other staff members*—what toilet, locker, shower, and dressing room facilities should be provided for office workers, custodians, matrons, cafeteria workers, and others, and how many people must be accommodated in each room specified?

4. *Lunch facilities*—what provisions are to be made for lunches for teachers, office workers, custodial workers, and other staff members, and how many must be accommodated?

Custodial and Service Facilities

The facilities required for the operation and maintenance of a large school building are many and varied. The major items to which attention must be given are:

1. *Heating plant*—largely determined by the engineer, but fuel storage capacity, in terms of number of days' or weeks' supply, might be specified.

2. *Meters and transformers*—special rooms may be required by the utility company, but these questions can be left to the architect.

3. *Receiving and storage rooms*—number and capacities of rooms for receiving and storing supplies and equipment, including janitorial supplies, educational and office supplies, audio-visual equipment and materials, books and furniture, and other equipment.

4. *Custodians' rooms*—rooms needed for minor repairs at a central place in the building; utility closets and storage rooms needed throughout the building; and storage for lawn mowers and other equipment used outdoors.

5. *Elevators and lifts*—nature and extent of use anticipated.

6. *Communications system*—places where public telephones are needed; need for private switchboard, type and capacity; need for interroom telephones; need for public address system, space for controls, location of microphone and speaker outlets; need for fire alarm system.

7. *Bus garages*—number and size of buses to be stored and nature of repair facilities required.

8. *Parking facilities*—number of automobiles and bicycles to be accommodated.

Facilities for Public Use

For the most part, the general public will use the same facilities as pupils, but there may be significant exceptions. Public libraries, community canneries, and vocational shops are a few examples of facilities that are sometimes in school buildings solely or primarily for public use. For each such facility, it is necessary that the number and capacity be determined. If the public use of the facilities provided for pupils should require any supplementary spaces such as toilets in lobbies, separate storage rooms, or the like, these needs should be clearly indicated and capacities specified.

DETERMINATION OF QUALITATIVE REQUIREMENTS

The decisions in regard to quantitative requirements, which have been discussed in the preceding pages, cannot be made without some attention to the qualitative aspects, but major attention should probably be fixed first on one and then on the other phase of the problem. Once the list of needed rooms and spaces, and their capacities, has been completed, attention should shift to the qualitative side. By this it is meant that attention should be directed to questions dealing with size, location, arrangement, and equipment of the various rooms and spaces. Every room and every space on the quantitative list should now be re-examined and decisions made with respect to the qualitative details. For the most part, the decisions made at this point should be limited to the general features required, lest they restrict the architect to predetermined room sizes or shapes or to the use of fixed floor plans.

Location

A great deal of freedom ought to be left to the architect, but the educational planner should indicate for each type of room or space any necessary proximity to or separation from other rooms or spaces. Consideration should be given to location in relation to service driveways, street hazards and noises, playground noises, and other hazards or nuisances; to convenience of use outside of regular school hours; and to possible future expansions of the building or site.

Size and Shape

Theoretically, the determination of the size and shape of a room or space rests with the architect, with perhaps some general indication of what might be acceptable. This can be safely done only with a first-rate architect and then only after he has become thoroughly acquainted with the full range of activities to be carried on in each room and the numbers of persons and quantities and sizes of materials and equipment involved. Many educators and architects take the position that the educator should specify at least the size of classrooms. In any event, where some particular size or shape is especially to be desired or avoided, this fact should be determined by the educational planner and made known in the educational specifications. A case in point might be the stage, where it would be appropriate to specify approximate minimum or maximum dimensions. Dimensions of game areas on the playground and in the gymnasium should also be specified, since it is especially desirable to have these conform to accepted standards. For some storage rooms, maintenance shops, and other auxiliary rooms, the direct indication of approximate size would be most feasible and would not seriously tie the hands or stifle the ingenuity of the architect.

Functional Details of Interior Design

The heart of the planning process is the interior design of the different rooms and spaces, and especially of the classrooms. This requires careful attention on the part of the educational planner to the various activities that will go on in each room or space and to the physical facilities they require. In the case of instructional rooms, decisions must be made in regard to the amount of chalkboard, tackboard, and other display facilities; the nature and quantity of seating and desk space; the kinds, amounts, and sizes of supplies, equipment, books, and pupils' materials to be stored in the room; the preferences in regard to storage of pupils' clothing in the rooms; the special activity centers desired, such as a library corner in an elementary school classroom or a laundry center in a home economics room; and any special requirements in regard to the use of audio-visual aids or other teaching procedures.

Mechanical Facilities

While most details in regard to acoustics, heating, ventilating, and lighting should be left to the architect and his engineers, the educational planner should make decisions in regard to any special requirements necessary for proper functioning of the program. This should include decisions in regard to places where noise control is particularly needed, as in a lunchroom; where special heating or ventilating arrangements are necessary, as in a biology plant-growing room or an athletic uniform-drying room; and where special lighting is required, as in the stage area of the auditorium or where microscopes are being used extensively. The educational planning should also be concerned with the number and placement of electrical convenience outlets and radio and television connections; and with the location, type, and connections for mechanical building-cleaning equipment.

Materials of Construction

The educational planner should not presume to be an expert on building materials, but he should take responsibility for decisions having a direct bearing on the functionality of the building. In most cases where the educational specifications deal with materials, the desired qualities rather than specific products or brands should be named. For example, the educational planner should be concerned with the self-healing quality of the bulletin board materials, but not necessarily that cork be used to achieve this quality. Many decisions in regard to building materials will be based upon experience in operating and maintaining existing buildings. Unsatisfactory performance of certain materials should be noted, and lists prepared of features to be particularly avoided or especially to be desired in the new building.

PREPARATION OF WRITTEN EDUCATIONAL SPECIFICATIONS

The many decisions growing out of the educational planning process up to this point must be communicated to others. First of all, the board of education should be informed of the decisions and given an opportunity to raise questions and suggest or order modifications. In the second place, the decisions as approved by the board of education must be made known to the architect for his guidance in designing the project. Quite apart from the need for a written record, the volume of detailed information and its interrelatedness make it highly desirable, if not essential, that the major educational planning decisions be reduced to writing. It is obvious, of course, that the written document may, and frequently does, require oral interpretation and explanation, but all major educational requirements should be in written form.

As indicated earlier, the written document containing these educational requirements is usually referred to as the "educational specifications." This written document should be presented to the board of education, officially approved by the board as submitted or with revision, and transmitted by official board action to the architect as his instructions with respect to the planning of the building.

The content, organization, and method of presentation of materials in educational specifications is far from standardized, and no one pattern is advocated here. There are, however, certain standards or criteria which the authors do advocate for guidance in the preparation of educational specifications. These have to do with the content, organization and style of the written document, and the extent which the architect is challenged to do his best creative work. Each of these is discussed below.

Content

The educational specifications should provide the architect with all of the essential information which he must have to understand the architectural problem to be solved and the limitations under which he must work.

List of Desired Facilities. First of all, the information included in the educational specifications must include a list of the required facilities. This list should encompass all kinds of rooms and spaces to be provided in the building and on the site. It should not be limited to classrooms alone. Indication should be given of numbers of lockers required; the seating capacities of auditoriums, dining rooms, and similar spaces; the number of meals to be prepared in the kitchen or the kitchen equipment desired; number of automobiles to be accommodated in the parking area; and similar information which will tell the architect "how many" and "how much" of each type of facility is needed. It should not be necessary for the architect to look beyond the written educational specifications for the answer to any question regarding the quantitative needs.

In addition to listing the immediate quantitative requirements, the educational specifications should point out definitely the numbers and types of rooms and spaces that are likely to be needed in future additions, and should require the architect to show these additions in outline form on his preliminary drawings. Clear indication should also be given of any room or space in the original building which might need to be enlarged later by remodeling. Such information regarding possible additions and remodeling is essential if the architect is to design the building to permit such changes to be made with a minimum of cost and maximum of functionality.

Qualitative Requirements. Beyond these listings of the quantitative requirements, the educational specifications should describe the qualities desired in each type of room or space. Mention should be made of any special requirements as to heating, ventilation, electrical outlets, lighting, and plumbing; the types and amounts of chalkboard and tackboard; the types of seating and other equipment; the types of storage space and the quantities and sizes of the materials to be stored; the work counters, construction areas, or other special activity areas needed; and other similar information which will enable the architect to design the details of each room and space so as to satisfy the functional needs of the program to be carried on in it.

Another type of content to be included in the educational specifications is a statement of any preferences or requirements of the educational planner with respect to the locations of different facilities or groups of facilities. Mention should be made, for example, of the need for locating a shop near a service drive, if the problem of delivery of supplies requires it. A different type of example would be the listing of facilities that will be used frequently and at night and a statement that they should be so placed and possibly grouped as to facilitate such use. Other considerations which might be the basis for suggestions in regard to location are noise isolation, segregation of different ages of pupils, and grouping of facilities which need to be close together for proper functioning.

Limitations. Still another type of information which the educational specifications should include involves the limitations under which the architect must work. He must be advised of any financial limitations on the cost of the project, any restrictions on the utilization of the site, fixed dead-line dates of any kind, and any other mandatory requirements of the board of education. He needs to know, also, the expected relationships between himself and the educational planner and the procedures in regard to checking and approval of plans by the educational planner. Some or all of these limitations may be made known to the architect in some other way, or they may be included in the educational specifications. The advantage of the latter is that more of the instructions to the architect are thus to be found in one place.

Background Information. A final type of material to be included in the educational specifications is information designed to enable the architect to gain a sound understanding of the activities to be carried on in the building as a whole and in each part. It is difficult to generalize with respect to how much of this type of information to include. The better the architect, the more of such background information he wants. In fact, the truly great school architect will not only ask for extensive materials of this kind in the educational specifications, but will visit classes, confer with teachers, and engage in other activities on his own initiative to gain the understanding which he needs. The less able architect, on the other hand, would make less use of such background information in the educational specifications, and would prefer more specific suggestions as to the size, shape, and other features of the various rooms. The educational specifications should include a description of the major types of activities that will be carried on in each room or space and the number of people who will be involved, except in cases where these facts can be easily inferred. Thus it would be important to describe the types of activities that would occur in a classroom but not in a storage room. The written descriptions of activities can at best give only partial understanding and should be supplemented by direct observation by the architect in the classrooms of the school district in question.

Beyond the descriptions of activities, the background information might include statements about the nature and problems of the community, the school's role in the community, other aspects of the purposes and objectives of the schools, and the underlying point of view with respect to methods of teaching. All of these would contribute to better understanding of the total problem which the architect must solve, but again the effectiveness of their inclusion in the educational specifications depends upon the architect as well as upon the manner of presentation. As a minimum, these materials should be included in brief and simple form in the educational specifications, and should be supplemented by conferences with and observations by the architect. Whatever the means, it is essential that the architect acquire understanding of these background facts if he is to do a creative piece of work.

Organization and Style

The written educational specifications will be used primarily by the architect and his staff. If they are to be used most effectively, they must be logically organized and arranged so that the architect and his designers can readily locate specific information needed at any stage in the planning process. An analytical table of contents, an index, topical headings in the margin, and frequent cross references are all helpful devices, but writing from a logical outline is a basic requirement.

A direct, clear-cut style of writing, free of excess verbiage and vague or ambiguous statements, will facilitate the use of the document and prevent misunderstandings in many instances. If the architect has to guess what is wanted, or has to wade through a sea of words including unfamiliar pedagogical terms to find the answers, he is apt to substitute his own judgment for the wishes of the educational planner, and he would not be without some justification in doing so.

Challenge to the Architect

The most valuable thing which the board of education buys in employing an architect is his creativity—his ability to comprehend a complex problem and then create an architectural solution that satisfies in an imaginative way the many and varied aesthetic, technical, functional, legal, and financial requirements of the project. This creativity is most likely to emerge when the educational specifications are restricted to a statement of needs, without prescribing how these needs should be met. Rigid requirements as to size of room, details of room layout, or style and arrangement of buildings tend to stifle creativity and to reduce the architect to the status of draftsman and specification writer. Thus, they deprive the board of education of the architect's most valuable contribution to the project.

COOPERATION WITH THE ARCHITECT

The writing of the educational specifications which has been described up to this point can be done by the educational planner alone and then presented to the architect through the board of education. It is probable, however, that a better document would be produced with close cooperation during the preparation of the educational specifications. Certainly, as a minimum the architect should be present at meetings of the staff and others as they discuss what they need in the new building. This will contribute more to his later understanding of the written educational specifications than anything that can be written in the document.

Be that as it may, the architectural planning stage of the project is one in which close cooperation between architect and educational planner is essential. The best building will result when each feels free to go to the other with questions, criticisms, and suggestions to be considered together in a common effort to find the best solution. Mutual respect and confidence are the keynote.

One area of consultation will be the interpretation of the educational specifications. Even though every reasonable effort has been made to produce a perfect set of educational specifications, questions will arise regarding their meaning, and the architect will think of alternatives that will ease his problem or result in a building which he thinks will be better. There should be free and easy communication among the architect, the educational planner, and the superintendent on all questions and suggestions that arise in the architect's mind as he works with the educational specifications.

A second area of consultation has to do with the emerging plans of the architect. As he proceeds with his work on the problem, he will consider many possible solutions which he will express verbally or in the form of sketches or drawings. Time can be saved and a better building is likely if these tentative solutions are discussed with the educational planner before they are put into the form of drawings and specifications for formal presentation. This sort of informal consultation makes partners of the educational planner and the architect with each bringing his own special talents to bear on the problem.

CHECKING AND APPROVAL OF DRAWINGS AND SPECIFICATIONS

It is the position of the authors that the educational planning of a school building is as important as the architectural planning. If this be true, the board of education should not approve any drawings or specifications of any kind submitted by the architect without consulting the educational planner, whether the approval is an informal agreement with the architect's suggestion on some one aspect of the building or the formal acceptance of a complete set of drawings and specifications. It follows then, that the educational planner should meet with the board of education when it meets with the architect, and that the educational planner should have adequate opportunity to examine in advance any proposals to be made by the architect. It follows, also, that any written proposals sent to the board of education by the architect should be referred to the educational planner for analysis and report before any action is taken.

In all of this work in checking and approving drawings and specifications, the educational planner must function as an educator and not as an architect or quasi-architect. While he may go somewhat farther in private conferences with the architect, he must confine his formal checking and approval of plans and his reports to the board of education to the educational adequacy of the plans.

If educational planning has the importance that the authors have ascribed to it, and which it deserves, it would be well for the board of education to require the signature of the educational planner, as well as of the architect, on all drawings which it is asked to approve. This would give the board of education written endorsement of the plans as educationally sound.

CHAPTER 7

PROBLEMS OF STAFFING SCHOOL-PLANT STUDIES

Determining Who Should Participate
The Cooperative Study Approach
The Educational Consultant

P RECEDING chapters have discussed in some detail two types of school-plant studies, the survey and educational planning. Both have been presented as aspects of building planning that should precede, for the most part, the work of the architect, and it has been advocated that both be the responsibility of the educator rather than of the architect or engineer. Attention is now shifted from the nature of these studies to the personnel required to do them.

Determining Who Should Participate

The superintendent of schools as the chief executive officer of the board of education has the responsibility for making any necessary school-plant study, but it does not follow that he alone or with the assistance of his administrative staff should do the actual work. The decision as to the nature of their participation and the involvement of other people should depend upon the extent and complexity of the study, the advisability of postponing or leaving undone certain other work, the ability of the superintendent and his staff to handle the technical aspects of the study, and the need for an independent check on local thinking. If the administrative staff is sufficiently large and includes research and school-plant specialists, the entire study may be handled with no outside assistance or with occasional consultant service. Even in such a case, however, it is often advisable to arrange for participation by teachers and other school employees, citizens of the community, and possibly pupils. Whatever the decision may be in regard to the staffing of the study, the superintendent is responsible for general supervision and coordination of the project along the lines suggested in Chapter 1.

CRITERIA FOR SELECTING PARTICIPANTS

Since no one staffing arrangement will serve in all cases, certain guiding principles will be listed and then explained. The suggested principles are:

1. The staff of the study should include persons having the necessary professional understanding and technical competence.
2. The staff should be able to complete the study within the desired time limits and without undue detriment to other aspects of the school program.
3. The staff should be available for assistance as required from time to time after completion of the study.
4. The study should be staffed in such manner as to promote public understanding of the findings and recommendations and support of the building program resulting therefrom.
5. The arrangement should be consistent with principles of democratic administration, insofar as accepted in the local school system.

Securing Professional Competence

It must never be forgotten in the course of a building survey or planning project that the primary goal is to improve education through improvement in the physical facilities. Since this is true, the study staff must include persons in leadership positions who have thorough understanding of education in general, of instructional practices and procedures, and of certain technical processes in the school-plant field. The principal facets of this professional competence will be presented below together with brief comments regarding the qualifications of potential study staff members.

General Understanding of Education. An essential first step in any building study is a determination of the school program to be housed. To make such a program study, or to interpret and apply the results, requires understanding of the role of education in society, of the local factors affecting the role of the school, and of the possible directions of change that will have a bearing on school plant needs. Many communities have found that parents and older pupils can make significant contributions to the planning of school programs under proper leadership. It is the function of leadership in such a study to provide the background information required to understand the local problems; to make available any significant facts regarding practices, problems, and trends elsewhere throughout the country; to raise important questions regarding the local program; and to keep directing the discussion toward the school-plant implications of the program decisions. It is reasonable to expect a considerable measure of such leadership competence in the local school administration, but in a small system certain soft spots are to be expected without any discredit to the administrative personnel. The day-to-day operation of a school system is a confining job and the demands upon the administration are such that it is quite difficult to keep fully abreast of educational developments throughout the country. A specialist in the school-plant planning field, whether he be a member of the local school administrative staff or an outside consultant, can be expected by reason of his specialization to be more fully informed regarding educational developments as related to school-plant problems. A local school administrator, however, should have the advantage of greater familiarity with local educational policies and conditions.

Knowledge of Instructional Practices and Procedures. In a school-plant study it is necessary to make decisions regarding the content and organization of the curriculum, the organization of pupils into classes, the scheduling of instructional activities, and the general teaching procedures. The local superintendent and other administrators and supervisors can be expected to have considerable understanding of these problems, but teachers will have a more intimate knowledge of instructional procedures. The outside consultant might be expected to have more familiarity with practices and trends elsewhere which should be examined, especially in their application to school-plant planning.

Understanding of Public Administration. The point has been emphasized in earlier chapters that the planning of school facilities should be an integral part of general community planning. If this goal is to be realized, the staff of a school-plant study ought to be familiar with current thinking in the general field of city and regional planning, with local planning activities, and with the general problems and issues of public finance and administration. Most superintendents lack such familiarity. Since school-plant consultants are usually drawn from the ranks of school administration, many of them have the same weakness, except that they may be more inclined to seek and use assistance from public planning agencies.

Knowledge of School Buildings. The need for specialized knowledge about school buildings, while very important, does not overshadow the need for basic understanding of education, instruction, and public administration. It is important, however, that the staff of any school-plant study include someone who knows school buildings.

The required knowledge is of several kinds. First, it is important to know what kinds of facilities are and are not effective in fostering various phases of the school program. Extensive knowledge of the successes and failures of teachers and others in the use of various types of facilities and arrangements is extremely useful. Closely related to this is the need for knowledge of practical means of altering existing buildings to make them better adapted to the needs of the school program. Pupils, teachers, principals, supervisors, and other employees will have much first-hand knowledge of the suitability of existing facilities and will have certain suggestions regarding physical improvements. The superintendent, who is more likely to read school-plant literature and otherwise learn of practices elsewhere, will in general have a more comprehensive understanding of these matters, but he will lack the intimate knowledge that comes from day-to-day use of the facilities. The competent school-plant specialist should have both the comprehensive understanding and the intimate knowledge.

Another kind of school-plant knowledge required within the staff of a school building study is familiarity with health and safety standards. The study staff needs to be familiar with the major types of hazards encountered in school buildings and must know when and where to turn for expert assistance as required. This kind of knowledge might well be found in the local administrative staff, in the local fire department, or in some other public agency. The frequency with which readily observed and easily corrected hazards are allowed to continue year after year in school buildings throughout the country is evidence that these resources are not being used, even though probably available upon request. The educational consultant, while not an engineer, can normally be expected to call attention to these deficiencies and to urge suitable remedial procedures.

The third kind of knowledge of school buildings which might be included is familiarity with construction methods and materials. A general understanding of these matters is helpful, but there is an ever-present danger that the superintendent or the educational consultant will allow himself to become so intrigued by construction details that he loses sight of the essentially educational character of his job. He would have to be a true superman to keep adequately abreast of educational thinking and at the same time keep up to date with respect to details of architectural design and materials.

Command of Specialized Techniques. Chief among the specialized processes involved in a school building survey are: (1) the analysis of the educational program to determine its implications for school plant; (2) the estimating of future enrollments; (3) the calculation of the reasonable operating capacity of a school building, especially at the secondary school level; and (4) the calculation of percentages of utilization. In the educational planning of a new building, the calculation of room and space requirements and the checking of drawings and specifications are the two most specialized processes. These processes are not highly complicated, and can be learned by the superintendent or other local staff members as needed. However, there are many pitfalls that the experienced educational consultant will avoid. The seasoned worker will not waste time in the collection and analysis of interesting but irrelevant data, and he will be more alert to faulty data which are often very troublesome. The experienced worker is also more able to adapt his procedures to fit the data at hand.

The Time Factor

The need for haste is all too frequently a controlling factor in determining who should do a building survey or educational planning project. This is unfortunate because it often results in incomplete studies done by persons lacking the knowledge necessary to do them properly. The routine collection and interpretation of basic data by the superintendent would enable the administration and the board of education in most instances to foresee their building needs sufficiently far in advance to avoid this difficulty.

Another facet of the time problem is that a building study may divert the time and attention of the staff from other important duties which should not be postponed. The administrative and supervisory staffs of most school systems are quite modest in size, and any major diversion of attention to a special project requires that certain important tasks be postponed or remain undone. This is, of course, not so often true in a large system with a special research department, a school building department, or other specialized unit. The instructional program is the one most likely to suffer by any diversion of effort to a building study because other aspects of administration and supervision cannot be so easily put off. Since a child cannot relive a school day or a school year, any delay in the improvement of instruction is a permanent loss to the children then in school.

Promoting Understanding and Acceptance of Results

The purpose of a survey or educational planning study is to improve education by providing a better school plant. If the report is rejected, the project in this sense is a failure, no matter how well it has been done. A frequent and unfortunate consequence of such rejection is that the school authorities proceed without adequate study to modify the building program to meet the objections. A case in point is that of a midwestern city which three times rejected the advice of an outside survey staff and proceeded to erect a new junior high school building in a sparsely settled part of the city with little prospect of future growth. There is every indication that this school will for many years, if not for its full life, have too small an enrollment to permit any reasonably adequate junior high school program. It was erected by the board of education because of campaign promises made after the survey recommendations had been rejected at the polls.

One way of achieving acceptance of a survey report or set of educational specifications is by a "selling" campaign. The proper persons are persuaded by various arguments and appeals to give their endorsement. While a measure of understanding of the proposals is usually developed in this process, the attention of those in charge is often fixed almost exclusively on the gaining of approval by the necessary persons.

Another means of achieving support for the proposals is participation in the study by those whose support is needed or desired. If this procedure is used, no selling job is required to convince the participants. If others must be convinced, the participants in the study are usually enthusiastic and effective campaign workers. A case in point is that of an Illinois city where a building survey was conducted by a citizens' group under the leadership of consultants from a university. When the study was completed, the committee of citizens, which was fairly large, had the task of persuading the school authorities to submit a sufficiently large bond issue to finance the recommended improvements. The board of education thought the amount too high, and had to be convinced by a group of voters. This reversal of the usual situation resulted from responsible participation by a group of citizens in the actual study of needs.

The choice between acceptance based on a "selling" campaign and acceptance on the basis of understanding through participation is clear. If democratic values are prized, reliance must be placed on consent based on understanding rather than consent based on emotional appeal.

The use of an outside expert might or might not be an advantage in gaining acceptance of the results. Assuming an equally good quality of study, the attitude toward the expert may be one of awe and deference or one of resentment against intrusion by an outsider. If the former be true, the qualities of expertness and disinterestedness may loom large in the campaign for support of the recommendations. In communities where sharp differences of opinion have developed, the use of an outside expert may have particular value in gaining acceptance of any building program. Unfortunate as it may be, the discord sometimes reaches the point where the impasse can be broken only by such an approach.

In giving consideration to this need for gaining acceptance, other criteria for staff selection must not be overlooked. An unsound report may be accepted and bring peace to the community, but at the expense of children's education for years to come.

Securing Continuity of Service

At the conclusion of the best possible building survey, the task of providing better school facilities has barely begun. The survey by its very nature is designed to locate and define the needs and suggest in a general manner the solutions. It does not and cannot answer the scores of detailed questions that arise in the implementation of the survey. After completion of the survey, certain details of the recommendations must be filled in, sites must be selected, and educational and architectural planning must be done before construction can begin. Where the total program is large and extends over a period of years, the survey recommendations require rechecking and possibly revision several times before the building program is completed. The survey staff members in the course of their work acquire many detailed understandings of the problem which they cannot put into their oral or written reports, and these are lost if the staff leaves at the conclusion of the survey. As a minimum, the services of the survey staff should continue through the educational planning stage with the survey staff either serving as the educational planners or working closely with those who do.

In like fashion, there is need for the educational planner to remain in the picture after construction is started. He, too, holds in his head many details about the building and potentialities that may not be readily apparent to the teaching staff that moves in on the opening day. The educational planner can be helpful to the operating and teaching staff in learning how to make effective use of the new plant.

An outside expert might or might not be able to provide this continuity of service. Frequently, he is able, willing, and anxious to retain his connections, but is not called upon by the board of education after filing his survey report or educational specifications. This is shortsightedness on the part of the board, and it is not an argument against the employment of the expert to make the initial study. A local school administrator or other employee is likely to be available for continued service, unless he should accept employment elsewhere. If he should remain, the pressure of other duties will have a bearing on his availability for the purposes here contemplated. Groups of school employees, pupils, or citizens are quite certain to continue to be available after completion of the initial study. It does not necessarily follow, however, that they can be relied upon for frequent consultation after completion of the initial report. It may be difficult to regenerate the interest and drive of the group after the climax of submitting the "final" report.

Again, it should be pointed out that competent workmanship is essential, but that it is desirable also to staff these studies in such a manner that valuable ideas are not lost by early termination of the arrangements.

Promoting Democratic Administration

Much has been spoken and written during the past few decades with respect to wider participation by school employees and citizens in the determination of school policies and procedures. Also, there has been much experimentation with advisory or policy-making groups and councils of various types. Advocates of such procedures hold that better policies will result, that morale will be higher and the schools therefore more effective, and that the schools which teach democracy should practice it. The authors subscribe to this movement toward democratizing the schools, but with these qualifications. First, there must be a clear distinction between policy making and policy execution or administration. A group can formulate policies, but execution is a job for an individual, often an individual trained as an administrator. Second, the privilege of making policies must not be vested in persons who do not also accept responsibility for the consequences of the policies. At the present stage in our development of what we call "democratic administration," this would require that most groups organized for this purpose be limited to an advisory role. Finally, the judgment of the group in dealing with matters in which they are not specialists must not be allowed to crowd out the informed judgment of the qualified expert. We have in most cases yet to learn how to obtain both the benefit of the expert's knowledge and skill and the values of group participation.

The decision in regard to group participation in a building study must be made partly in terms of the readiness of the local school staff and community. If there is a history of such participation, there may be an expectancy that should not be ignored. If, however, there has been no such history, the school survey or planning project may or may not be the appropriate time to undertake to change the local pattern. It takes time and patience to develop comfortable and successful ways of working with such groups, and frequently such time is not available under the pressure of an urgent building need. In some instances, on the other hand, a school building study may provide an excellent opportunity to widen the circle of involvement in school planning.

If committees are not used, there should be other devices for securing the opinions of teachers and other interested parties. This is particularly important in connection with educational planning, since educational planning can hardly be adequate without consultation with teachers and others who will use the building.

Personal Qualities

A long list of desirable personal traits of school-plant workers could be prepared, but only three will be discussed.

Resourcefulness. Resourcefulness is important in locating sources of data, in modifying techniques to fit the data at hand, and in developing tentative proposals for analysis and testing. Resourcefulness at either the survey or educational planning stage can result in substantial savings without impairment of education. Often a single suggestion by a resourceful person will save in dollars alone many times the cost of his services. In one city, for example, two educational consultants in a few hours suggested a rearrangement of a physical education unit that eliminated 100,000 cubic feet of new construction with no loss of usable space or other desired quality. No one group of potential staff members has a corner on the resourcefulness market, but wide experience in handling school-plant problems is a distinct asset.

Objectivity. A second desirable quality is objectivity. The competent school-plant worker must approach his job open-mindedly and with a temperamental inclination to examine most critically any and all ideas, including his own. He must be tough-minded in insisting upon facts rather than hunches, and honest with himself and others in summarizing and evaluating the findings and recommendations. The needs of all aspects of the school program and all segments of the school population must be given due consideration and be met with no favoritism in the final recommendations. Obviously, the person who measures up to these requirements will not be a party to or be swayed by cliques or factions within the school staff or the community. This quality of impartiality is rare and is not related to length of experience in the school-plant field. Nor is there any one source from which workers with this quality are most likely to be available.

Ability to Work with Others. A survey or educational planning project is almost of necessity a cooperative undertaking in many of its aspects, and this requires an ability to work with others. The quality here envisioned is not the ability to sell one's ideas to others by persuasive language or gracious actions, nor is it the ability to gain acceptance through weight of position or domination in any other form. Rather, it has reference to an ability and willingness to work shoulder to shoulder with other people, sharing ideas freely, seeking and giving assistance as required, and offering and accepting criticism of ideas without involvement of personality. Essential ingredients are the ability to be selfless, a sensitiveness to the feelings of others, and a persistent focus on the job to be done rather than on who is to do it or get credit for it. No one source is superior to others in producing workers with this quality.

THE FINAL CHOICE OF STAFF

The preceding discussion of the several competencies required in the staff, of the strengths and weaknesses of various kinds of persons available, and of the other factors to be considered in the choice of staff has not resulted in any clear-cut advocacy of any one plan. No such advice can be given which will be equally applicable in all situations. However, the following generalizations are offered as a summary of the authors' views:

1. There is need in every school building survey and educational planning project for the services of one or more qualified experts in the school-plant field. As a minimum, expert advice should be secured on procedures and on the final recommendations. The expert should have a continuing relationship to the project from the start of the survey to the completion of the building program.

2. The local school administration should have a responsible role in planning and executing the study. The purpose of such participation should be to provide needed information, to check on the work of others, and to provide essential continuity and co-ordination as the program is executed.

3. Participation by pupils and by teachers and other school employees under competent leadership is essential in the educational planning of a new building and is helpful in setting up the school program as part of the survey process. Such participation will produce buildings more closely geared to local needs and will result in more effective use of the physical facilities when completed.

4. Participation by lay citizens under competent leadership and with expert advice is a valuable device for securing public interest in school planning problems and in gaining support for school-plant improvements. Since the public

determines the school program in the final analysis, such participation is likely to produce a general program of curriculum improvement.

5. The nature and extent of participation by school staff and lay citizens should be consistent with prevailing and emerging practices with respect to such participation in the local community.

These generalizations add up to a staff pattern that includes both expert assistance from the outside and participation by local school people as a minimum, and with citizen participation highly desirable. The balance of responsibility between outside experts and local persons must vary with local conditions.

The discussion to this point seems to leave no place for the architect or engineer in the survey and educational planning projects. These two aspects of planning are essentially educational in character and in general should be done by educators before architectural planning begins. However, the line of demarcation is by no means so sharp, nor should it be. During the building survey, an architect or engineer may be consulted with regard to the condition and future usefulness of existing buildings, especially when any question arises as to safety, the feasibility of extensive remodeling, or the cost of renovation in comparison with replacement. In the educational planning stage, the architect should participate in any way which will help him to understand better the educational specifications which finally reach him. He should be invited to attend committee meetings of all kinds at which the background information is discussed and should be free to raise questions and make pertinent suggestions. His participation at this stage, however, gives him no license of any kind to decide what the educational specifications should include.

The Cooperative Study Approach

IF committees of teachers or other school employees or groups of lay citizens are to be involved in the study of local building problems, careful planning is necessary to assure satisfaction both to the school authorities and to the participants. The board of education and superintendent must be convinced of the value of this approach and be prepared to give honest and full consideration to all committee recommendations. If the committees are not properly constituted, organized, and oriented to their work, the injured feelings and dissatisfactions which result may more than offset the advantages.

BASES FOR SELECTION OF COMMITTEE MEMBERS

As a first principle, it is suggested that committee members be selected from all major groups of people involved. There should be members from the principal school employee groups, particularly teachers and building service employees, and from all major segments of the population of the school district as a whole. A committee to take part in the educational planning of a new building should by all means include persons from all classes of school employees and of the major community groups which might use the building. If the school property is to be used for public recreation, which should be a normal expectancy, public officials responsible for recreation should also be involved.

The individual persons selected should be chosen mainly on the basis of the contribution they can make as members of a planning team. While teachers may be selected from certain departments and citizens may be chosen from certain organizations or groups, they should not represent these departments or organizations as such. Rather, they should all represent the entire school district and be of a mind and temperament that will enable them to take this broad view of their committee responsibility.

Another consideration of importance in the selection of committee members is their ability and willingness to continue to serve throughout the entire study. The building survey and the educational planning project are long and involved studies requiring the understanding and interrelating of many details. Intermittent service on such a project cannot be very effective, and may actually retard the group because of the repeated necessity of briefing someone who was previously absent.

MECHANICS OF SELECTING COMMITTEE MEMBERS

There are many possible methods of selecting members to serve on building study groups. Selection by the superintendent and the board of education is possibly most prevalent. This may be due to a natural reluctance to relinquish control, but it does have the advantage of permitting careful selection in terms of the principles suggested above. The school authorities can look over the various groups in the community and see that all are represented, and they can weigh different individuals in terms of their possible contributions and their probable willingness to see the job through. The weaknesses of selection by the superintendent or board are several. They often discover once they start the process that they do not have sufficient information about the various persons who come to mind and must therefore make their choices somewhat blindly. A second defect is that they may not know adequately the social structure of the population and may overlook significant groups that should be involved. It is particularly true that the unorganized segments of the population that are usually not prominent in civic affairs may be overlooked. Finally, there is always the possibility that such selection will result in suspicions in certain minds that the committee is "hand picked" to recommend the building program desired by the school authorities. If this should occur, some of the advantages of citizen participation are lost.

A second method is for the board to choose a small committee of widely respected citizens and have them choose the study committees. This partially offsets the charge of "hand picking," but perhaps not completely. Beyond this, the use of such groups would seem to have no advantage over direct selection by the board of education.

A third method of selection which might be used is to have different community organizations choose their own representatives. This avoids the charge of "hand picking," but it does introduce other flaws. The various organizations will have but little understanding of the job to be done and will not be able to select persons well in terms of their potential contribution. Persons who are not fully willing to serve may be drafted, and this will not be conducive to effective committee work. Finally, selection by organizations may result in a committee composed of individuals largely concerned with trying to secure certain things in which their own organizations are interested.

A fourth method, which avoids some of these difficulties and introduces some new ones, is to extend an open invitation to attend the initial meeting. At the first session, the job to be done and the essential qualifications of committee members are fully explained. Persons who then decide they do not wish to continue are permitted to withdraw. Those who remain set up an appropriate plan for recruiting additional persons to fill significant gaps. There can be no charge of "hand picking," nor can anyone assume that he has gained a place primarily to protect the interests of some one community organization. Persons who are not willing to devote the necessary time to the work are not likely to attend the first meeting, or will withdraw after the explanations made when the group first comes together. This voluntary approach may bring into the group certain people who will be trouble makers. This is a risk to be considered, but these people, and they do exist, are more likely to become supporters of the school program through such participation than by being constantly ignored or pushed aside. Another flaw in this approach is that the less favored economic groups of the population are not likely to respond to the invitation. They are, however, as apt to become involved by this process as they are by board selection, and there is little chance that they would ever get in as representatives of organized groups.

Many combinations of these three basic methods could be devised, possibly with one group responsible for making nominations and another for making the final selection. No generalization can be made as to any one pattern that is best for all communities.

ADMINISTRATIVE RELATIONSHIPS[1]

Before any decision is made to use a planning committee, the superintendent and board of education should clarify their thinking with respect to the duties and responsibilities of the committees and of their relationships to others involved in the total process. The decisions of the board of education in these matters should be communicated to all concerned not later than the first committee meeting. Failure to have such an understanding can lead to strained relationships at a later date, which are not conducive to the welfare of the schools.

One matter which should be made clear is the extent of the committee's responsibilities. There should be explicit understanding that the board of education is the final authority on all decisions as to school policy and the nature of the building program. The study committee members, however, should be true participants in the planning process, and not mere spectators or a sounding board. They should be free of dictation from the school authorities with respect to the interpretation of the facts, the formulation of the recommendations, and the preparation and presentation of the report. The committee should also be assured of complete access to all necessary records and of assistance in the preparation of needed statistical data and other facts. The committee should not be a device for securing cheap labor, or a form of "window dressing."

The foregoing should not be interpreted as a plea for unguided study by a group of amateurs. It has been emphasized earlier that certain professional competencies should be made available through an outside consultant, through someone in the local school system, or through some combination arrangement. Whatever the source of the expert help, there ought to be clear understanding at the beginning of the project of the nature of the help that can be provided and the conditions under which it should be used. There should be definite ground rules requiring that expert assistance be available and used at certain designated points, but of course no rule that would permit the expert to dictate procedures or recommendations. As a

[1] See Figure 1 in Chapter 1 for a chart of administrative and advisory relationships.

minimum, the expert should advise on all major study procedures to be used, should check the summaries and interpretations of all major blocks of information, and should check the preliminary report and recommendations. If it should develop that the expert and the committee disagree on some matter of major importance, it should be understood by all that the expert will have an opportunity to state his point of view orally or in writing to the board of education by arrangement with the superintendent.

It is important that arrangements be made for an outside consultant or some local staff member to provide the committee with essential background information, or sources of information, regarding the local school program and problems, significant trends elsewhere, and ways of attacking the problems which the committee will have before it. In other words, the plan should include measures to increase the competence of the committee members for the tasks at hand.

It is quite possible that some layman on such a committee will be an expert in his own right, say as an architect or contractor. In this situation, there needs to be an understanding that this person will function the same as any other member of the committee, unless he should be officially designated as an expert advisor to the group.

SUBCOMMITTEE ORGANIZATION

Usually it will be desirable to organize a study committee into smaller groups. In a survey, for example, there might be separate subcommittees dealing with the educational program, enrollment projections, evaluation of present buildings, and finance. In an educational planning project, there might be subcommittees responsible for different aspects of the total school program, such as lunch service or mathematics, to cite but two examples.

If subcommittees are used, provision must be made for co-ordination and intercommunication. The co-ordinator might be a committee member, a local administrator, the educational consultant, or a steering committee. Whoever he is, he has to be alert to gaps in the total process and to duplication and overlapping of the work of the various subgroups. Means must be devised for keeping all members of the total group fully advised of the principal findings and conclusions of each subcommittee.

The subcommittees responsible for the collection, analysis, and interpretation of data should not make the recommendations or write the report except in a tentative manner. A school-plant study, whether a survey or educational planning project, is complicated, and its parts are closely interrelated. It is necessary, therefore, that the recommendations be formulated by persons who are saturated with understanding of the facts revealed by all segments of the study. There might well be a subcommittee on recommendations drawn from all the other subcommittees, or the entire study group might prepare the recommendations. Whichever pattern is employed, it must be kept clear that the task is one of integrating the findings of all subcommittees and not one of merely adding together and editing the suggestions of the several subgroups. The drafting of the report is a job for an individual or very small subcommittee, although the draft may be submitted to the larger group for criticisms of the contents.

COOPERATIVE PLANNING AS THINKING TOGETHER

The essence of cooperative planning is *thinking together*. This is not the same as summing up the suggestions of individual committee members. Neither is it a process by which the suggestions of the more eloquent and persuasive members come to the top and are adopted by the whole group. If group action is to be most effective, there must be ample opportunity for all suggestions to emerge and receive full consideration.

If this is true, one of the first rules of a study committee should be to give ample and frequent opportunities for all ideas to be brought into the open, explained, and fully explored. This may require suspended judgment over a considerable period of time, but such a course will promote better feeling and often avoid loss of a fruitful point of view or proposal.

A second suggestion for the handling of ideas is that planning in the early stages be on a rather idealistic basis without too much concern for cost. This should be done with complete understanding by all that later cutbacks will be required or that some priorities will have to be established. This approach, if fully understood, will help to avoid the feeling of disillusionment that so often comes to committee members whose suggestions are not fully accepted. Another reason for proposing this approach is that it is likely to produce superior results, particularly in an educational planning project. This is true because in the final planning of a building certain features previously thought to be too expensive can often be secured at little or no extra cost if the desire for them is known. For example, in one city teachers expressed a desire for a small room where safety patrol members could keep raincoats, semaphores, and other paraphernalia. It was thought to be too expensive, but the desire was not forgotten by the educational planner. Shown on the first preliminary drawings submitted by the architect was a small space near an entrance which was designated for storage because of lack of any better use. In the completed building this space is an excellent safety patrol room which would have been missing if the original committee had been less idealistic in its planning. The added cost for making the space into a safety patrol room was not more than $100.

It is important, also, in the work of a study committee, that the planning of the school program not start "on the finished side of the middle." If maximum benefits are to occur from committee participation, it is essential that adequate attention be given to such basic considerations as the social role of the school and the nature of the learner and the learning process, rather than to superficial tinkering with the existing program.

Service on a study committee of this kind usually results in a considerable degree of enthusiasm, which is particularly in evidence at the time of submitting the final report. This *esprit de corps* is a valuable outcome of the project and should not be discarded. It is quite likely to be lost if the committee members never know the fate of their proposals, or if major changes are made without consultation with the committee. Therefore, it is a sound practice to inform the members of the group of every major development even after the committee work is done, and to consult them with respect to major developments affecting their proposals. Actual construction is often delayed, and the board or superintendent may lose many of the details of the committee's proposals. This may result in unwitting offense to committee members which could be avoided with adequate records of committee decisions and of the reasons behind them.

The Educational Consultant

THE educational consultant is a key person in many school-plant studies. He supplies in large measure the expertness required for the study and carries a heavy responsibility as educational advisor to the superintendent and the board of education. Since the impact of his work will be felt for many decades after the building program is completed, he should be chosen most carefully. Professional competence and the other personal qualities discussed earlier in this chapter should be the primary factors considered in his choice. There is no standardizing or accrediting agency of any kind to guarantee the competence of persons who assume the role of school-plant expert. As a consequence, they vary greatly in the degree of their expertness. Information about the quality of their service on other projects is probably the best single indication of their qualifications.

Since the educational consultant is an educator, state departments of education and the education divisions of colleges and universities are likely places to secure educational consultant services. There are also individuals or firms of educational consultants operating independently, and some firms of architects have educational consultants on their staffs. The employment of educational consultants by architects has met with some objection in educational circles. It has been argued that the educational consultant under such an arrangement might be tempted to recommend more costly facilities in order to increase the fees of his firm. There is, of course, this possibility, but the same can be said of the architect himself. It has been charged, also, that some architectural firms have used educational consultants more as bait to catch new clients than as professional workers to help design better buildings. These and other abuses can and do occur, but the remedy is to be found in the selection of architects and educational consultants of high ethical standards rather than in some gimmick in the details of the arrangements for employment.

EMPLOYMENT CONTRACT

The conditions under which the educational consultant is retained should be explicit and reduced to writing. If the service is provided by a college or university or a state department of education, an exchange of letters may suffice. A more formal agreement is usual when a private consultant is employed, and often when the service is provided by a university.

A formal contract, to be binding, must satisfy the usual requirements of contract law, which need not be discussed fully here. It is particularly important, however, that the duties and obligations of both parties be spelled out in detail, that the financial arrangements be definite, and that the date of termination of services be clear.

In stating the duties of the educational consultant, it should be made clear whether he is retained only to make a survey, to do educational planning, or to do both, and the scope of each should be briefly described in appropriate language. The contract should also specify what written reports are to be furnished, the number of copies of each, the date of completion, and the nature and place of presentation.

Financial Arrangements

The financial arrangements will depend upon the educational consultant chosen. Persons from state departments of education may be available without cost. Most universities make some charge for expenses or time or both, and the policies of the particular institution will have to be accepted by the school district. When a private consultant is selected, there is more choice of financial arrangements.

A per diem rate or a fixed amount can be agreed upon for a survey. The fixed sum is feasible in this case because it is possible to determine in advance approximately how much time will be required and what the incidental expenses will be. However, the flat rate is not applicable to the educational planning phase of the work. This is true because it is impossible to foresee the changes of plan which might be made and which would require major revision of the educational specifications. Also, it is impossible to predict how many different sets of architectural drawings will have to be reviewed and criticized before an acceptable plan is achieved. Because of these difficulties, the compensation for educational planning service is usually set at a stipulated percentage of the cost of construction or at a per diem rate.

Mention is frequently made of the desirability of a plan of reimbursement that does not tempt the consultant to perform his work in such a way as to increase his total compensation. This is pretty much a "will of the wisp." Additional construction can be advocated if a percentage fee is used, or additional time can easily be spent on a project if pay is on a per diem basis. The total fee cannot be increased if payment is on a lump sum basis, but the amount of time spent to earn the total can be reduced. This problem is not peculiar to this profession alone. Doctors, lawyers, and other professional workers have similar opportunities to inflate their charges. In employing an educational consultant, as in securing other professional services, reliance must be placed upon the professional integrity of the person rather than upon any phraseology that can be written into a contract document.

The agreement should make clear who is to pay travel and printing costs and other expenses and whether travel time and time on the project between trips are to be included in per diem charges. These items can mount to an appreciable total and should, therefore, be agreed upon in advance.

Termination of Services

It is particularly important in contracting for educational consultant services to stipulate the termination date or the events which will mark the end of the service. In the case of a survey only, the filing of the report usually marks the termination of the project. However, when educational planning is involved, the service may extend over a period of years before the entire building program is completed. Where such extended service is involved, provision might be made for termination of the agreement by either party under certain conditions. A fixed date might be set with the agreement subject to extension, or termination might be tied to some other foreseeable event. Whatever the details of the arrangements, provision should be such as to avoid termination of the consultant's services before the job is done. It is highly desirable that the consultant who makes the survey continue through the educational planning. Once educational planning is started, the consultant should continue at least until all architectural planning is completed and construction contracts are let.

CHAPTER 8

FROM EDUCATIONAL SPECIFICATIONS TO BUILDING DESIGN

General Nature of Architectural Service
Selection of the Architect
Agreement for Architectural Service
Architect's Services on School Projects
The Larger Issues of Architectural Design
Creating the Design of a School
Evaluation and Approval of the Design

DURING the building survey and educational planning studies, which have been described in detail in preceding chapters, educators have occupied the center of the stage and the architect has had a supporting role. With the completion of the educational specifications, the scene changes, and the architect takes the center of the stage, where he remains until the completion of construction.

Architecture serves to give physical form to the educational specifications, which are converted by the architect into the building and grounds that answer the specified objectives. This process produces the educational environment on which the proper functioning of the school program and the satisfaction and pride of the community depend.

Unfortunately, architecture is generally not well enough understood for the public to appreciate and demand the contributions which a good architect can offer toward the creation of a better human environment. Too often, he is considered as merely a technician who prepares the drawings and specifications and supervises the construction of buildings. This is an erroneous and limited point of view that has resulted in the many poor schools and the difficulties in their planning that are so often encountered.

Therefore, before discussing the processes of designing and constructing a school building, attention is directed toward the nature of the architect's role and the conditions of his employment and service which are essential if a school of the highest quality is to be attained.

General Nature of Architectural Service

THE architect has the responsibility of planning the school and handling the technical, administrative, and financial problems involved in its construction. He is indispensable to the execution of any school building project in that he co-ordinates the services of all the engineers and technicians involved in the design of the school and directs the execution of the building by the contractors. His preliminary studies are necessary to give a picture of the school and its cost before it is built, and his final drawings and specifications are the basis for contractors' estimates and for all construction operations on the site. His normal services include the impartial advice, technical guidance, and business administration of the project from the delivery of the educational specifications to him to the completion of the construction. He is available also for additional services that may be required in connection with the formulation of the educational specifications, the selection of a site, the utilization of existing buildings, or other special problems that may arise.

The language of architecture is design. Through design the architect defines the organization of the plan and the visual form of the building, its construction and equipment, and all details that affect the environmental conditions for the prescribed functions. The architect's problems in the design of a modern school building are highly involved, and their complexities are increasing not only with the demand for more articulate expression of the many specific needs prescribed by the educational specifications, but also with the advance of science and technology. The architect not only has to place rooms in their proper locations, determine their form in answer to functional and aesthetic needs, provide for safe and efficient circulation, and develop a pleasing appearance through architectural design, but he must also handle the technical problems involved in the choice of the methods and materials of construction, heating, ventilation, sanitation, illumination, acoustics, etc. In all his efforts, he is guided by economic limitations, building code requirements, demands of his clients, and the established practices within the building industry.

ARCHITECT'S QUALIFICATIONS

The architect's unique qualifications among the various design professions are that by talent and training in the art as well as in the science of building, he can work out a balanced solution to both the aesthetic and practical needs. His background is usually an education in an architectural school followed by a period of practical experience. A license to use the title of architect is required in most of the states of the United States in the interest of protecting both the public and the architectural profession. A practicing architect of good standing is usually a member of one or several organizations interested in the elevation of the profession and the improvement of its members. In addition to creative talent for art and the knowledge of scientific principles required for the design of buildings, he must possess the technical skill to prepare the construction drawings and specifications with the aid of his staff and consulting engineers. Further, he must have administrative and business ability to act as the agent of his clients, to direct the work of engineers and contractors, to deal with the problems involved in the control of expenditures for his clients, and to conduct his own office.

RELATIONSHIP WITH CLIENTS

The good architect, who has the proper combination of qualifications, can with relatively little direction convert well-conceived educational specifications into an excellent school building. He will bring imagination to the task confronting him and will explore the various possibilities for a solution to the school building problem with all the freedom at his disposal in the interest of achieving the best answer. If he is put into a strait jacket by unreasonable demands and needless interference, he cannot produce a good building. He cannot freely exert his creative ability, imagination, and artistic skill if forced to follow the dictates of laymen who feel that in "hiring" the architect they assume the right and duty to tell him exactly how to do his work. This attitude denies the citizens for whom the school is built the full use of the architect's professional ability and experience. To be satisfactory to the board of education and community, the architect's relationship with his client must be based on mutual trust, respect, and integrity.

To the good architect, every project offers a new challenge to create a building that will satisfy the needs of his client and make a contribution toward better architecture. This demands the cooperation of all involved in the planning and design process. The architect must listen to suggestions from his client and interpret and meet his demands and criticisms with patience and tact. The client must likewise try to understand what the architect aims to accomplish and allow him to employ his talent, technical knowledge, and experience to the fullest benefit of the building entrusted to him. The architect must also work in fullest harmony with consultants, engineers, landscape architects, building officials, contractors, and the workers on the construction site to accomplish a smooth and competent performance of all services involved.

BOARD'S INSTRUCTIONS TO ARCHITECT

Instructions and decisions from the board of education should be clearly stated and given without delay. The authority to express them should be vested by the board of education in a responsible person—preferably the superintendent of schools or his agent. When instructions result from committee meetings, the decisions reached should be summarized in clearly expressed statements and given to the architect in writing. In addition to written instructions covering the most essential points, the architect should have the opportunity to communicate informally with the superintendent and his staff, including the educational consultant, in order to obtain clarification of instructions and a better understanding of their intentions. His communication with the teaching staff, the board of education, citizens groups, and others should be through, or by arrangement with, the superintendent of schools or his delegated representative. Any other procedure is confusing and a cause for delay and poor service; it is also detrimental to efficient administration of the schools.

An infinite variety of solutions is possible for any given design problem. However, those that give excellent answers to the greatest number of objectives and requirements are extremely limited in number. Laymen may find it difficult to comprehend the architect's sketches, drawings, and specifications, and the problems encountered by him. Therefore, it is necessary that the person responsible for communication with the architect be someone who understands the nature of the architect's problems and the merit of his offerings. If this person conceives his role as that of a policeman rather than a collaborator, good architectural services can hardly be the end result.

RELATIONSHIP WITH OTHER DESIGN PROFESSIONS

Wherever the term "architect" is used in the text, it stands for a firm with a staff of designers, draftsmen, and other technical and clerical assistants that is entrusted with full responsibility for a building project. Uusually the work involves an association of the architect with one or several engineers who act as consultants or specialists in structural design, heating and ventilating, plumbing and sanitation, electrical work, and acoustics. Frequently, a landscape architect is added to this team for the planning of the school grounds. Further, consultation by experts on various specialties (like kitchen layouts) is included in the architect's services. The architect directs and co-ordinates the efforts of the various engineers and other specialists and integrates their work in his architectural plans.

Occasionally, suggestions may arise to engage an engineer for the full handling of a school project, to use stock plans that offer "ready-made" solutions to the problem, or to have the building planned by staff architects of the school board or building department. Though the engineer is qualified to deal with the technical problems of building, he is not expected to have the background for the art of architecture or the training in organizing of building plans which architectural education and experience provide. Hence, his approach to the design of a school building is likely to be one sided in the direction of emphasis on the utilitarian, with a disregard for human and aesthetic problems. There are engineering firms that have architectural departments, but in considering them as designers of a school building, one must carefully weigh the ability of the responsible individuals of this department to uphold the architectural interests.

The use of stock plans that offer ready solutions eliminates the fresh approach to design and thereby fails to meet individual needs. Similar shortcomings are likely to result from the complete handling of school building projects by staff architects of public bureaus. While it cannot be denied that the plans of public servants at times offer practical and expedient solutions to building problems, the outstanding examples of good school architecture in the United States and the greatest progress in the design of educational plants have been due to private architects with initiative, talent, skill, and knowledge for high professional achievement.

PROFESSIONAL NATURE OF ARCHITECT'S SERVICE

The architect renders services on a professional basis, and his conduct is governed by a code of ethics. This gives him a professional standing that must be carefully distinguished from that of the businessman who sells services or merchandise. Too often the differentiation between professional and business services is not clearly understood during the selection of and dealings with an architect. As a consequence, many an architect of high standing sometimes hesitates to enter into negotiations for services because he fears that the attitude toward him might be on a par with shopping for a bargain.

The architect's standing is equivalent to that of a lawyer or doctor. The fee he receives compensates him for impartial advice, creative design, and technical and administrative services. Though architectural fees are commonly a percentage of the construction costs, they must not be confused with a markup or commission on a product. The good architect works in the interest of his client to keep the cost of building within reason, even though the extra time and effort devoted to the achievement of savings actually reduces the sum he earns under a fixed percentage fee. On the other hand, the architect who considers—or is made to consider—his services solely as a business in the interest of his profit will devote only a minimum of time toward the study of the design, construction, and equipment, with a consequent adverse effect on the quality of the work and the cost of the project. These considerations must be borne in mind when selecting an architect. A low percentage fee usually does not result in savings on the total project cost, nor does it necessarily reduce the profit of the business-minded architect; it practically always harms the quality of the building.

Code of Ethics

The American Institute of Architects has adopted a code of ethics for the guidance of its members, and a board of education can expect a reputable architect to act within the limits of this code. This code of professional ethics is interpreted to place the following restrictions upon the members of the association:

1. An architect is not permitted to enter into a design competition unless the contest is authorized by the American Institute of Architects and adheres to special rules.
2. An architect is not permitted to compete with others on the basis of professional compensation, nor is he permitted to use donations as a device for obtaining competitive advantages.
3. An architect is not permitted to undertake a commission for which he knows another architect has been employed until he has determined conclusively that the original employment has been terminated.
4. An architect is not permitted to prepare sketches, estimates, or render any regular service without compensation.
5. An architect shall not attempt to supplant another architect after definite steps have been taken by a client toward the latter's employment.
6. An architect shall not knowingly injure the professional reputation and prospects of practice of another architect.
7. An architect shall not use paid advertising nor self-laudatory, exaggerated, or misleading publicity.
8. An architect shall conform to the registration laws governing the practice of architecture in any state in which he

renders professional services, and he shall adhere to the standards of practice established by the local professional body of architects.[1]

Selection of the Architect

THE architect may be chosen in several ways. In the interest of a higher type service and under recognition of the code of ethics of the profession of architecture, it is essential that an orderly process be followed. The American Institute of Architects recognizes various methods which, according to the principles they adhere to, fall into two categories: (1) the choice of the winner of an authorized design competition; and (2) open selection on the basis of general qualifications. Under the first method, the board with the guidance of a competent jury chooses the author of the best solution presented in a design competition. Under the second, which is the usual procedure for school projects, the board compares the work and qualifications of several architects and makes its selection.

SELECTION BY DESIGN COMPETITION

A design competition can be of value only if conducted under fair and equitable conditions. This method of selection is not common because it is relatively cumbersome, requiring a professional advisor, a design jury, and possibly the expense of prizes to the contestants. However, an owner receives in compensation the work of many architects representing a wealth of ideas. Competitions have the advantage of extending consideration for the award of a commission to a great number of architects and of bringing promising talent to the fore. However, the best drawing may not always result in the best building or the smoothest handling of the construction process.

OPEN SELECTION ON THE BASIS OF GENERAL QUALIFICATIONS

Open selection on the basis of general qualifications requires the comparative evaluation of a number of architects for which various methods of procedure have been recommended. The American Institute of Architects suggests that the qualifications of candidates be determined and compared on the basis of the following five questions:

[1] See *Handbook of Architectural Practice*. Washington, D. C.: American Institute of Architects, 1953, p. 166.

1. Has the Architect under consideration the experience necessary for the work in hand?
2. Has he the technical knowledge needed to control the design of the highly complex structure and equipment of a modern building, and to secure the best results without waste of space or money?
3. Has he executive ability and the force to compel the proper performance of contracts?
4. Has he successfully done work of like character or work from which his ability properly to serve the Owner may be inferred?
5. Has he such honesty and incorruptibility as are essential to the Owner's safety? [2]

Capabilities brought out by these five questions will assure a school board that the candidate is capable of producing an efficient, well built school, and that he has the capacity to administer the construction operations effectively and honestly. The authors suggest, however, the following additional questions to test other desirable qualities:

6. Has he the design ability necessary for the planning of a good school and the creation of aesthetic qualities?
7. Has he the necessary staff for the performance of the services?
8. Has he the ability and temperament to work cooperatively with others in the analysis and solution of the problem?

Use of Questionnaires

The answers to these questions must be sought by means of a fair tabulation of information received from the candidates, from persons for whom they have built, and from visits to buildings they have designed. Questionnaires will be helpful in obtaining uniform data from architects.

The National Council on Schoolhouse Construction and the American Institute of Architects have agreed upon a standard form of questionnaire for use by school systems.[3] This form requests the following items:

1. Information about the project: name of school district, name of superintendent, enrollment, general description of project, approximate time schedule for project.
2. Information about the architectural firm: name, address, tele-

[2] *Ibid.*, p. 16.
[3] Copies may be obtained by writing to the American Institute of Architects, 1735 New York Avenue, Washington 6, D. C., or to the National Council on Schoolhouse Construction, George Peabody College, Nashville, Tenn.

phone number, type of organization, names and qualifications of principals, staff organization, list of completed buildings, references, and supplementary information at option of architect.

In addition, the form indicates that in the event an interview is arranged the architect would be expected to furnish evidence that his organization and prior commitments would enable him to do the proposed work, that he would cooperate with the educational authorities, and that his drawings and specifications would be complete.

The information obtained in the selection process will be voluminous and possibly confusing. Difficulties will arise in comparing large firms with small ones, quantity of work versus quality, etc. It will also be hard to enter proper values for the various capabilities under the eight questions suggested above for the determination of the qualifications of the candidates.

Considerations Affecting Comparison

There are advantages in small firms as well as in large organizations. In small firms, the principal can give his personal attention to the individual jobs. The less cumbersome organization is usually more flexible in the meeting of new demands. The eagerness to expand business often results in greater initiative. On the other hand, large firms have within their staffs specialists with a broad experience in the various phases of architectural work. They have the facilities and the routine for the handling of big projects. In view of the fact that small firms can easily become large, while big organizations may decline, the choice of an architect merely on the basis of the size of his organization has little meaning. Of greatest importance to the quality of the work of an architectural organization is the capability of the member of the organization who will be responsible for directing the school building project. He establishes the policy, prepares or at least passes on the design, and controls the work of the office staff and consultants.

The choice of an architect on the basis of quantity of work performed should also be considered in the light of reality. Quantity is no indication of quality. Impressive lists of schools submitted by architects in their eagerness to obtain a commission should be given less weight than the observed quality of their buildings. Unfortunately, laymen entrusted with the selection of architects are often not sufficiently sensitive to architectural quality to prevent their falling into traps of salesmanship.

The Final Choice

To simplify the process of reaching a final decision, and to avoid confusion in the relative importance of the qualifications, it will be helpful to boil down the answers to the eight questions on pages 160–161 to three important factors—(1) design ability, (2) technical competence, and (3) executive reliability. This process applies only to the two or three final candidates after all others have been eliminated in a first screening by means of the questionnaire and careful review on the basis of all eight questions. These three factors are defined as follows:

1. *Design ability*—the talent and skill necessary to answer the functional needs defined in the educational specifications and to create an aesthetically pleasing building.

2. *Technical competence*—the knowledge, experience, and ability required for the translation of the design into the completed building. From this competence results the durability and practical efficiency of the structure and its low maintenance cost.

3. *Executive reliability*—the competence of the architect to administer the project efficiently and fairly.

The architect to be chosen should have the highest rating in these three qualifications. It must be borne in mind that administrative ability can be helpful only during the planning and construction phases of the building operation, while design ability and technical competence have a lasting effect on the school. On these depend the qualities of the building that contribute to education.

FAIR TREATMENT OF PROSPECTIVE ARCHITECTS

The treatment of architects during the selection process has an indirect influence on the kind and quality of services the school board will obtain. The rounding up of masses of architects for hasty interviews is useless and objectionable to the better type of practitioners. There appears little need for making contenders for professional work wait for hours in the presence of other numerous and sundry competitors for an inadequate opportunity to be heard. Interviews should be carefully scheduled, and an adequate time for a conference with the likely candidates for the work should be provided. The questions asked during interviews should be uniform and carefully worded to bring out pertinent information; it is futile to compare the knowledge, talent, and experience of one architect with the good fellowship, broad circle of friends, and other irrelevant attributes of another. Good architects justly resent being asked embarrassing questions about their fellow practitioners or having their own professional record, drawings, and photographs bandied about indiscreetly.

After an architect has been selected, all candidates should be informed of the board's action and thanked for their time and effort in filling out questionnaires, submitting exhibits of their work, and appearing for interviews. Whatever drawings or photographs they have submitted should be returned to them at the expense of the board.

Agreement for Architectural Service

A CLEAR understanding between an architect and his client as to their relations and obligations is of utmost importance. During any building operation many unforeseen situations arise that require a clear definition of the responsibilities of both parties. An oral agreement is not adequate, and even an exchange of letters does not provide a guarantee against misunderstanding. A formal agreement that is legally binding is the only satisfactory protection of the client (called "owner" in agreements) and the architect. "Owner" refers to the contract awarding authority, namely the school board, or in some cases it can refer to a school building committee or a municipality.

For the preparation of contracts, legal advice should be secured. Special attention must be given to the correct naming of the contracting parties and to their authority to enter into a binding agreement. In the agreement the project must be named, the extent of the services and obligations of the contracting parties defined, and the fee stipulated.

CATEGORIES OF ARCHITECTURAL SERVICES

The services an architect usually performs range from the complete handling of a project to consultation on some particular phase of it. The common types of services can be defined briefly as "normal professional services," "consulting services," and "occasional services."

Normal professional services usually extend from the point at which educational specifications are turned over to the architect to the acceptance of the finished building by the owner. They encompass the designing of the building, the preparation of drawings and specifications, the supervision of construction, and related duties which are stated in more detail in later sections of this chapter and in the following chapter.

Consulting services are of more limited scope. They may be restricted to some particular phase of work such as advice during site selection, the formulation of a building program, the selection of furnishings and equipment, or study of the utilization of existing buildings. Or, they may supplement the services of another architect in the capacity of expert on some particular problem, or some phase of it. Consulting services may involve in addition to professional advice the furnishing of technical information, sketches, drawings, reports, and estimates of cost; they may entail conferences, inspection trips, review of drawings and data, etc.

The occasional services an architect may perform include services as professional advisor on competitions; supervisory services in the direction of work by other architects, contractors, and others; and service as an expert witness or arbitrator in cases of disputes.

Sometimes it becomes desirable to engage two or more architects for one problem. They divide the responsibilities for the handling of a project and perform services as associated architects.

PERCENTAGE FEE AGREEMENT

For normal services, the most common form of agreement in reference to fees establishes a percentage of the cost of the project as the basis for the architect's fee. The percentage that applies to the bulk of the work is called the "basic rate." If several rates apply, as may happen, for example, if the project involves new construction and remodeling of an adjoining building, all the categories of work and the respective rates must be stated. Usually the basic rate covers the services of heating, ventilating, mechanical, and electrical engineers. It is best to have the fees of the engineers and specialists provided for in the architectural agreement because this leads to closer cooperation between them and the architect. Should it be unavoidable to have the engineers' services performed separately, the architect should be compensated for the integration and co-ordination of their work. The usual form of architectural agreement assumes that all construction on the building site comes under the direction of a general contractor. If separate construction contracts are awarded for any part of the work (such as plumbing or electrical work), arrangements should be made to compensate the architect for the extra time and effort consumed in co-ordinating the work of the separate contractors. The agreement should also be definite in regard to reimbursement of the architect for unusual out-of-pocket expenses, such as travel away from home under certain circumstances or extra sets of blueprints consumed during bidding. Normally the agreement should specify that should any extra work or expense be caused due to changes ordered by the owner, or should the project or any part of it be abandoned or suspended, the architect is to be paid for the services performed in connection therewith.

The payments to the architect under a percentage fee contract usually fall into three divisions. First, on completion of preliminary studies a portion of the fee (normally 25 percent of the basic rate computed upon a reasonable estimated cost) is due the architect. Second, upon completion of specifications and general working drawings, a sum sufficient to increase payments to 75 percent of the fee is due the architect, computed upon a reasonable cost estimate, or, if contractors' bids have been received, upon the lowest bona fide proposal. Third, upon the completion of the execution of the building, the balance of the fee is payable, based on the actual cost of the project to the owner, but not including professional fees or the cost of land.

The practice of architects in submitting bills varies. Some may be satisfied to bill only at the ends of the three divisions mentioned above, and some may consider it more favorable to both parties to send monthly bills on account toward the sums due at the ends of the divisions. The practice to be followed should be noted in the agreement.

Other usual clauses of the contract provide that surveys, borings, and tests are paid for by the owner; that the architect provides general supervision, but not the continuous personal superintendence by a clerk-of-the-works; that the architect's estimates of cost are not guaranteed as to their accuracy; that the drawings and specifications as instruments of service are the property of the architect; that neither party shall assign, sublet, or transfer his interest in the agreement without written consent of the other party; and that any questions in dispute shall be submitted to arbitration.

FEE-PLUS-COST AGREEMENT

The fee-plus-cost system has particular advantages when the extent of the work the architect is asked to perform cannot be predetermined. This may be the case in the alteration of an existing building or when the extent of a new project cannot be foreseen. Under this system, the architect is paid the cost involved in the preparation of drawings, the services of engineers employed by him, out-of-pocket expenses, and overhead, plus a fee of a stipulated amount for his personal and professional services. Frequently, architects are called on to perform exploratory services on a project, and for these the fee-plus-cost system offers an equitable method of payment.

SPECIAL AND SUPPLEMENTARY SERVICES

Special and supplementary services may be entered into under rates for consultative services. The latter may be lump sum fees or payments based on a per diem or hourly rate. A form of agreement suitable for the particular type of service requested must be mutually developed. The per diem rate may apply to some of the services performed in connection with site selection, the appraisal of existing buildings, the definition of space needs for a new school, or similar problems demanding a short-term employment of the architect.

TERMINATION OF SERVICES

The possibilities of termination of the architect's services before completion of the project are usually of some concern to the persons engaging architects. There is always the fear that the relations between the architect and his client may not be happy throughout the long and involved process of planning and constructing a building. There also exists a chance that the project may be abandoned or interrupted before the architect's services have been completed. At the time the architect is engaged, the question of termination of services should be discussed and a method agreeable to both parties arrived at.

ARCHITECT'S FEES

The charges under the various agreements for services vary according to the locality, the size and type of project, and the practice of individual architects. Suggested schedules of charges are available through architects and the local chapters of the American Institute of Architects. Wherever professional organizations have established a schedule of minimum fees, these rates are designed to give the architect a compensation that is adequate to carry out the normal amount of work with a reasonable profit. Higher fees are in order if greater services than normal are demanded. Lower fees may lead the architect to give less thought and effort to the project, to develop incomplete and vague drawings and specifications, and to devote a minimum of time to the supervision of construction. In these and other ways, lower fees often lead to increased construction costs and a less satisfactory building.

Architect's Services on School Projects

THE services of the architect on a school building project can be divided into six major phases. These start with the recognition of the need for a new building and end at the point at which the school is opened to teaching. The architect's advice and help on design and technical problems are of importance during each and every one of these phases. However, in the first and last phase, his contributions towards a better school extend beyond the normal services referred to previously.

These six phases are: (1) the programming phase, which encompasses the building survey, educational planning, and site selection; (2) the design phase, which establishes the general layout and form of the school, methods of construction and approximate cost of the structure; (3) the working drawings and specifications phase, which produces the documents necessary for construction; (4) the bidding and contract award phase; (5) the construction phase; and (6) the furnishing phase.

PROGRAMMING PHASE

The major responsibility during this phase rests upon the educator, since the primary task is to determine the extent and nature of the school-plant facilities needed. The processes and personnel involved have been discussed in detail in the first seven chapters of the book.

During the programming phase the architect's consulting services are usually necessary to evaluate proposed sites, to appraise existing buildings, to furnish information for construction budgets, and to advise on numerous technical problems that enter into the determination of school building needs and the drafting of educational specifications.

Unless the architect is engaged at this time for the entire services involved in the building of the school, it should be made clear to him that he will serve only on a short-term basis and that the information he provides may be made available to another who may be chosen at a later time. These preliminary services should be paid for, either by an extra compensation under an agreement for complete services or by a separate consultation fee. Some architects offer to do this work free in the hope of gaining an opening wedge to later professional services. However, while it is good and proper for any professional man to be helpful with any general information and advice that leads to better schools and architecture, it is considered a violation of the standards of ethics of the American Institute of Architects to supply sketches or any services that involve expense without due consideration.[4] Usually, there is little gained from free services in that good architects do not render them, and the poor architect in doing so may cause a poor start for a big and important venture.

In site selection, an architect can be of particular help. An architect with experience in land development and community planning problems is of considerable value in the choice of a location for a school. For the various sites considered, he can assist in studying the growth potential of the neighborhood, investigating transportation and highways, and studying the influences of existing land uses and the possibilities for protection against

[4] *Handbook of Architectural Practice*. Washington, D. C.: American Institute of Architects, 1953, p. 166.

undesirable encroachments. City planners may also be consulted, but architects are particularly well qualified to report on the relative suitability of various tracts of land in terms of the shapes and sizes of the properties in relation to the areas required for the building, playgrounds, walks, driveways, etc. With the aid of engineers or contractors, an architect is in a position to determine subsoil conditions that might require unusual expenses for special foundations or rock excavation. He can determine where borings should be made so they will come within the area to be built upon. An architect can also appraise topographic conditions and give information on the influence of the slope of the land on the placement of buildings and the drainage of the property. He can render technical advice regarding utility connections and the needs for sewage disposal. The need for competent professional advice and a careful consideration of all factors influencing site selection is emphasized by the many errors that have been made in the locations of schools.

Should there be a question on the possibility of using or converting existing buildings for the improvement of the school plant, the architect can advise on the technical problems and costs involved and the benefits to be gained.

DESIGN PHASE

With this phase the architect begins his normal services with the translation of the educational specifications into a design for the school. He first prepares diagrams showing the various possibilities for the organization of the space requirements in the plans for the building and site. Then he develops from the most promising diagram the preliminary plans, elevations, sections, perspective sketches, etc., that are necessary to enable a visualization of the physical aspects of the school and its grounds and an understanding of the costs involved. The architect's agreement for services usually refers to this phase as "the preparation of preliminary studies." The resulting design establishes the layout of the building and site, the appearance of the school in its setting, the general method of construction, and the approximate expenditures that must be anticipated. This indicates the significance of the step that is taken in the approval of the design by the board of education.

WORKING DRAWINGS AND SPECIFICATIONS PHASE

In this phase the architect develops from the approved design the working drawings and specifications. These are needed to determine the precise layout and design of the building and define the materials and methods of construction, the equipment, the dimensions, and all details so that contractors can prepare bids and execute the project. This is the largest phase of the work of the architect. Engineers work under him to design and plan the structural framing and the heating, ventilating, plumbing, and electric installations. If a landscape architect has been engaged, he will prepare plans and specifications for the development of the school grounds. During this phase every requirement of the educational specifications, the building codes, and other regulations affecting the design, construction, execution, and operation of the school are met. The board's approval of the working drawings and specifications signifies acceptance of all the architect's preparatory work for the construction of the building.

BIDDING AND CONTRACT AWARD PHASE

When the working drawings and specifications are completed, the architect obtains bids from contractors and directs the preparation of a contract for the execution of the work by the successful bidder.

CONSTRUCTION PHASE

During this phase the building is erected on the site from the architect's drawings and specifications. He provides supplementary detailed drawings and instructions, checks shop drawings, supervises the work, issues change orders, and approves payments to contractors. The acceptance of the building at the end of this phase completes the normal services of the architect.

FURNISHING PHASE

Under this phase the movable equipment, furniture, and fixtures are incorporated in the building, and the school is made ready for occupancy and operation. Supplementary services by the architect are of value in the selection, purchase, and setting up of the furnishings to assure harmony between the design, colors, and materials of the building and its contents.

The Larger Issues of Architectural Design

FEW man-made objects are as immovable as buildings. Hardly any tool has to function for as long a period of time as a schoolhouse has to serve education. Education changes. Social concepts, economic problems, science, and technology are all affected by the progress of the times, but an educational specification once converted to a building becomes frozen in the form given it by the architect.

Educational specifications are a definition of objectives and methods; when expressed in words, they allow for adjustments and are subject to differences in interpretation. While errors of assumption or judgment can be easily corrected in a written statement, they are difficult and expensive, if not practically impossible, to eradicate when they appear in brick and mortar or steel and concrete.

The architect's language is that of design by which he defines the physical form of the environment for education. In doing so, he creates a layout and appearance for the building and answers the functional and technical problems confronting him. He may satisfy the educational specifications with such skill and imagination as to provide a school that in all its aspects will stimulate the learning process and enrich the lives of teachers, pupils, and citizens. A good architect will consider this his ideal. On the other hand, a poor architect, even though he may carry out the educational specifications to the letter, may produce a building that is a distortion of all intents. As such, it can serve education only as a clumsy tool that demands unnecessary efforts in all the tasks it is called on to perform.

EVOLUTION OF FUNCTIONAL ARCHITECTURE

In architecture a blind following of fashion or stereotyped practice is destructive to lasting quality. Many school buildings of the pre–World War II era, with their now fully recognized inadequacies from an educational point of view, illustrate this point. In excuse for the architects of that time, it can be said that in the United States, as well as in many other countries, the schools were often built from standard patterns and their designs aimed to impress the citizens on the street rather than to satisfy the teacher or pupil inside the building. The mistake grew out of the then accepted traditional approach to design which relied on historic styles and antiquated methods of planning to arrive at a form for buildings. An improvement resulted from the architectural revolution of the second quarter of this century which brought the acceptance of modern architecture to the United States after World War II. Since then, design has aimed for a direct and honest expression of functional needs. However, many buildings of early functional design, while answering all practical needs, could be characterized as coldly utilitarian in character and criticized for lack of human qualities. Consequently, more recently the realization has come that not all that is functional is emotionally satisfying and that art demands more attention in design. The modern architecture that emerged after mid-century aims for the ideal to be both functional and aesthetically pleasing.

SEARCH FOR LASTING QUALITIES

In a search for lasting qualities, it becomes important to differentiate between the transitory and permanent considerations that enter into design. Anyone planning a school must keep in mind that a building is costly and remains in service for a long time. Early obsolescence will be prevented by the wisdom and farsightedness that have governed the design.

On the transitory side are short-lived fashions in style and novelties in installation and equipment. The life of a building extends far beyond the period when the appeal of novelties prevalent at the time of its completion has been eclipsed by new fads or become ridiculous in the light of better judgment. The gadgets and equipment that brought pride and joy when the doors of the building first opened may in the light of continuing progress become as quaint and inadequate as an antique car on a modern highway.

On the permanent side are the fundamentals of architecture that provide for the environmental needs of man. They fall into two groups—first, those answering psychological needs; and, second, those meeting the various physiological requirements. In the first group are the emotional reactions that grow out of the art of architecture. In educational building they offer the satisfying and stimulating environment for life in school. Within the second group fall all the practical demands that are met through the science of architecture. They affect the efficiency of the building and the health and safety of its occupants. The latter include the requirements for thermal comfort and fresh air; the avoidance of fatigue caused by eye, ear, or muscular strain; and all the factors that deal with the prevention of bodily injury from accidents, fire, etc.

While the terms art and science may be open to semantic discussion, they are commonly used to express the two aspects of architecture that must be dealt with in the design of buildings. Art supplies all the intangible qualities that make life in school pleasant and arouse the satisfaction and pride of the teachers, pupils, and public in the environment created for their use and enjoyment. The talent and feeling which a good designer devotes to the achievement of an artistic solution of an architectural problem are, unfortunately, all too frequently denied expression.

Science in architecture might also be called building technology. Whether or not it should be so named, the term here is used to express all definable conditions from which the practical efficiency of a building results. Its achievement depends on the knowledge and experience of the architect and the reasoning followed in his design. Efficiency can be measured, minimum requirements can be set up in standards, and formulas and data books can be used to answer these problems. The realism of scientific design is better understood and more appreciated in a materialistic age than the subtle qualities of art; for that reason, it usually receives ample attention.

Schools must serve their needs through a long period of changing times and attitudes. In the final analysis, the lasting merit of building design depends upon a balanced consideration of the factors that satisfy emotional needs through art and practical efficiency through science.

Aesthetic Qualities

The history of architecture is rich in examples of buildings that have kept their aesthetic qualities, while their standards of comfort have become inadequate or obsolete in the light of technological progress. The beauty of a building contributes aesthetic pleasures that go beyond mere visual satisfaction. They are the total reactions one feels through all one's senses that make the difference between drabness and cheer, between monotony and liveliness, between calmness and restlessness. To deny the building these attributes is equivalent to depriving the environment of all pleasant aspects that contribute enjoyment to life and work and that are necessary to avoid institutional traits. Full aesthetic merit is not derived from the outward appearance of the building alone, but also from the stimulating atmosphere and good working conditions within and from the order and logic with which the functional needs have been expressed in the planning and construction of the building. In this broad concept, aesthetic qualities are not affected by changes in architectural styles and the building will hold its merit throughout the wanderings of fashions and fancies that will occur throughout its life.

Practical Efficiency

The practical efficiency of a building is influenced by scientific and technological developments which are in a continuous and rapid state of progress. The latest mechanical devices of one year will be out of date in the next. There is a perpetual effort to elevate standards and to increase by mechanical devices the conditions of comfort in buildings. For example, while 15-foot candles of artificial illumination were considered adequate in the standards prevailing after World War I, 30-foot candles became the minimum after World War II. Fortunately, this deficiency can be corrected by additional light fixtures, but there is no cure for the fundamental defects of the earlier architecture, such as lack of space in classrooms, poor daylight distribution, and heavy walls that prevent changes.

CONCLUSIONS ON APPROACH TO DESIGN

Modern architecture answers the needs of progress. Functional design, which characterizes it, meets the fundamental requirements of a building program and provides flexibility for adjustment to changes that may have to be made in the future. However, the achievement of superior architectural quality demands a striving for ideals in all aspects of design by the architect and a sympathetic attitude to his efforts by his client. The large issues should at no time be overlooked or sacrificed to small matters. A distinction must be made between the fundamental aspects of design that become fixed in a building and the detail that can be altered by simple remodeling. These considerations enter into the choice of the design which is more fully discussed in the following pages.

Creating the Design of a School

THE architect is enabled to begin the design of a school upon receipt of the educational specifications and the survey of the site. He proceeds under the realization that he must satisfy certain objectives, and that there are definite limitations confronting him. To avoid harmful compromises in the usual conflict between ideals and realities, the architect must choose a method of approach that leads him to the solution of the design problem which best satisfies the demands under the unalterable restrictions.

OBJECTIVES

The educational specifications define the educational objectives the architect must meet in his design. They are the program from which he develops the layout of the school. They give him the list of facilities to be provided, the specific qualities desired in them, and a statement of general objectives and limitations.

The objectives are educational and architectural in nature. The architectural objectives, in addition to meeting the educational demands, are the achievement of quality in construction and good inner and outer appearance.

A good architect strives for new heights of achievement with every building design entrusted to him and realizes his opportunity to enrich the environment in which people live and work. He aims to give the architecture he creates those lasting qualities of aesthetic satisfaction and practical efficiency which have been discussed earlier in this chapter.

The best design results when the educational specifications are confined to a clear statement of requirements that can be met and challenge the architect to find the most imaginative and skillful solution to them. A mediocre design at best can be expected if educators, either in conferences or in the educational specifications, "step over the line" and tell the architect how to solve his problem. A creative individual suffers from frustrations that are damaging to his work if his sincere efforts toward obtaining a good school are impeded by unreasonable or ever-changing demands.

THE LIMITATIONS

The limitations are primarily financial, but may also be inherent in the conditions of the site, in the community, in the climate, in construction techniques, or in regulations and restrictions affecting building. The financial limitations should be made known to the architect before he starts his design. Though it would seem obvious that the allowable project cost must be sufficient to meet the demands of the educational specifications, this is frequently not the case. By obtaining the help of an architect for the preparation of a budget of expenditures before the board commits itself to what it intends to build, later difficulties and disappointments can be avoided. The good architect can be expected to be familiar with the technical limitations of the various methods and materials of construction and the requirements of building laws and labor practices.

THE SITE SURVEY AND BORINGS

The survey of the site is a drawing prepared by a civil engineer which shows the boundaries of the land available for the school project, its physical characteristics, and the available roads and utilities. It gives the architect the dimensions of the property lines and the angles between them; the slope of the land in terms of contour lines; the position of outcropping ledges, wells, trees and woods, existing buildings, roads, walks and paved areas with their curbs, and other surface features; the location and size of utility lines, such as sewer, water, electric, telephone, and gas; the names of the owners of adjoining properties, and the positions of such neighboring buildings as may affect the planning of the school; and any easements and restrictions on the use of the site.

The borings are recorded on drawings which show the subsoil conditions with their load-bearing capacity, the position of ground water, and the types of soil to be encountered in excavation.

The usual contract for architectural services requires the board of education to provide the survey and the borings at its own expense, but the architect may be called on to provide instructions for the preparation of the survey and the locations of the borings.

THE DEVELOPMENT OF THE PLANS

In the development of the plans for the school building and grounds, the architect first analyzes the educational specifications to arrive at a grouping of the required facilities according to their kinship in use or space form. He then combines rooms that have an affinity into building blocks or wings housing classrooms, science rooms, shops, auditorium and related facilities, gymnasium, etc. These units are affected in their shape by whether a string of rooms is placed beside a corridor (single-loaded corridor), or a corridor is inserted between two rows of rooms (double-loaded corridor), or whether they are combined in a cluster of two or more rooms, or placed back to back, etc. The length of the wings or blocks of the building is limited by the efforts to avoid excessively long straight corridors (preferably not over 200 feet). Their height is governed by the number of stories, the play height requirements of gymnasiums, or the sightlines and acoustical dictates of auditoriums. The resulting units are then combined in a compact arrangement (compact plan), or spread out in varying degrees (open-plan types), or joined loosely—possibly completely separated—to form a campus. The shape of the site, topography, orientation, segregation of community facilities from the classrooms, the areas suitable for playgrounds and parking, and the approach road location all have their influences on the development of the plans. In addition, a number of other considerations enter, which at times are in conflict with each other and which demand of the architect judicious treatment and a constant effort to let the important issues govern the minor ones.

These considerations entering into the placement of the facilities listed in the educational specifications are:

1. *Functional affinities.* Certain facilities need to be close to one another because of the functions they serve. A locker and shower room, for example, should be near the gymnasium and also the outdoor playfields. The band room should be near the stage, to cite another example. The particular functional affinities desired will depend upon the program of the school in question, and should be stated in the educational specifications.

2. *Circulation and traffic control.* This requires careful study of the numbers of pupils who will use the corridors and stairways at times of peak load. Trial daily schedules and room assignments may have

to be set up to estimate the traffic volume at different places. Similar tests may be needed with respect to occasions when large groups of people assemble in the auditorium, gymnasium, or cafeteria. The grouping of rooms may be one solution to such traffic problems as are revealed by such studies.

3. *Grouping for public use*. A frequent need is that certain facilities be readily accessible for public use for assembly, adult education, or other purposes. They must allow separation from the rest of the school, while they must be properly located for regular school use.

4. *Segregation of age groups*. In a building in which a great divergence in the ages of the pupils exists, there should be some grouping by age to avoid conflicts.

5. *Expansibility*. The arrangement of the building and its placement on the site should be planned to permit easy future expansion of the site, of the building as a whole, or of particular facilities within the building. Such expansions as might reasonably occur within the lifetime of the building should be explained in the educational specifications and the arrangement of the building should be designed to facilitate them.

6. *Flexibility*. The planning and structural design should permit some internal alterations or changes in the use of the facilities to anticipate the possibility of future changes in the educational program.

7. *Safety*. This affects the placement of playground areas and locker rooms with respect to traffic ways and other sources of danger; the location of places of assembly; and the placement of boiler rooms, shops, and other areas of high fire hazard.

8. *Noise control*. This suggests that noisy areas such as band rooms, shops, gymnasiums, and outdoor play areas be so located as to minimize the interferences with other school activities.

9. *Odor control*. Kitchens, laboratories, and other sources of odors should be located to cause the least transmission of odors to other parts of the building.

It is recognized that it may not be possible to harmonize some of these considerations affecting the grouping of facilities in the development of the plans for a school. Wherever this is impossible, some means available in modern building technology may be resorted to for the purpose of achieving the required objective. For example, satisfactory results in noise control can also be achieved by sound insulation, and in odor control, by proper artificial ventilation.

Last but not least, the architect will consider the sculptural effect of the building masses and the shape of the spaces between them to give artistic expression to the functional arrangement of the plans. He will consider the attractiveness of the views experienced while passing through the building, the pleasing shape of the rooms and views from them, and the visual appeal of the exterior to the passerby. A good architectural design depends on a balanced emphasis on all these considerations.

VARIOUS TYPES OF SCHOOL PLANS

There are several ways in which building spaces may be combined. They may be concentrated in one simple building block, distributed throughout several wings, or placed in a series of isolated structures. Each of these different types may be one or several stories high. Each one has particular advantages and disadvantages that must be weighed before a particular diagram can be selected as the basis for the development of the design. The different forms of these basic types of school plans are identified under various names, some of which are illustrated in Figure 3.[5]

The core-type plan consolidates the spaces of the building within a rectangular single story block and places the classrooms back to back with a utility core between. The roof is the medium through which daylight is brought into the rooms along with the windows. Occasionally, interior courts occur in structures of this type. The loft-type plan is a variant of this

[5] The sketches in Figure 3 on pages 178–179 show in diagrammatic form the diverse principles followed in the plans for schools of various sizes. The sketches are based upon the following:

1. *Core type:* Junior High School, Laredo, Texas. Caudill, Rowlett, Scott, & Associates, architects. A. A. Leyendecker, associate architect.
2. *Loft type:* (a) Junior High School, Electra, Texas. Caudill, Rowlett, Scott, & Associates, architects. (b) Hillsdale High School, San Mateo, California. John Lyon Reid, architect.
3. *Wing type:* (a) Suggested plan for an elementary school, courtesy of *American School and University.* (b) West Columbia Elementary School, Brazoria County, Texas. Donald Bartholme & Associates, architects. (c) Rugen Elementary School, Glenview, Illinois. Perkins & Will, architects. (d) Melvindale High School, Melvin-

dale, Michigan. Eberle M. Smith Associates, architects.
4. *Finger and pavilion types:* (a) Andrew Jackson Elementary School, Ferndale, Mich. Eberle M. Smith Associates, architects. (b) High School, San Jose, California. Ernest J. Kump, architect. (c) White Oaks Elementary School Annex, San Carlos, California. John Carl Warnecke, architect.
5. *Cluster type:* (a) Hollow Tree Elementary School, Darien, Conn. Ketchum, Gina, & Sharp, architects. (b) Heathcote Elementary School, Scarsdale, N. Y. Perkins & Will, architects. (c) Elementary school plan developed by Caudill, Rowlett, Scott, & Associates for Time, Inc. and published in *Life* for February 1, 1954 and *Architectural Forum* for March, 1954.
6. *Campus type:* Comparative studies by Walter F. Bogner, architect.

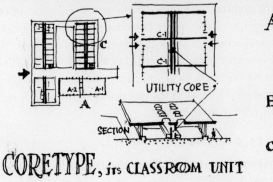

A GENERAL ACTIVITIES
- 1 AUDITORIUM ETC.
- 2 GYMNASIUM ETC.
- 3 ADMINISTRATION
- 4 LIBRARY
- 5 CAFETERIA

B SPECIAL ROOMS
- 1 SHOPS
- 2 HOME EC, ARTS-CRAFT

C ACADEMIC UNITS
- 1 CLASSROOMS
- 2 KINDERGARTENS

UTILITY CORE

SECTION

CORE TYPE, its CLASSROOM UNIT

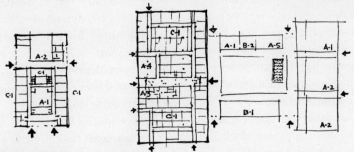

LOFT TYPE, SMALL and LARGE SCHOOL EXAMPLES

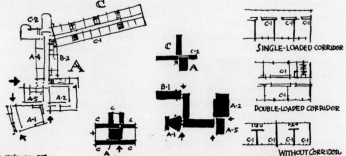

SINGLE-LOADED CORRIDOR

DOUBLE-LOADED CORRIDOR

WITHOUT CORRIDOR

WING TYPE, A FEW OF INFINITE VARIATIONS and CLASSROOM WINGS

Figure 3. Examples of Types of School Plans. (For identifying information and credits, see Note 5 on page 177.)

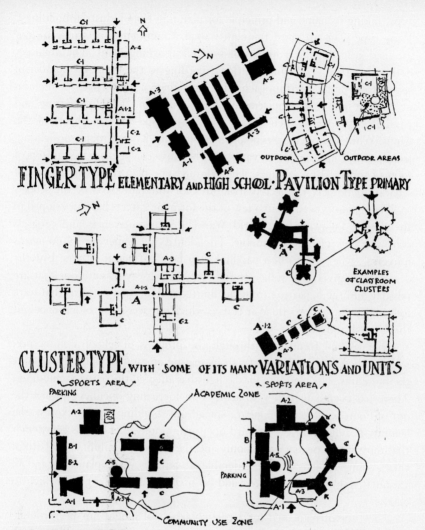

FINGER TYPE ELEMENTARY and HIGH SCHOOL · PAVILION TYPE PRIMARY

EXAMPLES OF CLASSROOM CLUSTERS

CLUSTER TYPE with SOME OF ITS MANY VARIATIONS and UNITS

CAMPUS TYPE with CIRCULATION OUTDOORS and ENCLOSED

type, taking its name and principle for planning from industrial buildings.[6] Wing-type plans are most frequently used. Commonly, the wings are not grouped according to a formal or symetrical arrangement. The architect determines their shape and position according to the type and number of spaces to be housed within each. He places them according to the dictates of the lot and the requirements for circulation. The finger-type and pavilion-type derive their names from the shape and placement of the wings. While the pavilion-type plan has single or pairs of rooms protruding from connecting corridors, a variation, the cluster-type plan, has clusters of rooms connected by passages. The campus-type plan resorts to a series of separate or loosely connected structures for different parts of the school.

These plan types are but a few of the forms architects have developed in the decade following the World War II. As inventiveness and progress continue, new plan types emerge. The identifying names are by no means universal; what some call a pavilion may be a cottage to others. But the descriptions given will suffice to indicate the variety of solutions that are possible and the departure from the limited stereotyped patterns that were followed in the pre–World War II days which one sees in the older schools of the United States.

One general trend runs through the progress of school architecture, namely the effort to distribute an increasing amount of light throughout the buildings. The planning for daylight has affected the shape of buildings. There has been a tendency to achieve an increasing openness toward the out-of-doors, and the irregular, spread-out building forms express the leaning of some architects toward open planning. Other trends counteract that movement, primarily economy and the need for flexibility; for both of these, compact plans offer considerable advantages. Each plan type and all variants have their *raison d'être* and no precise rule can be given which to choose.

The type of plan used for a particular school should not be predetermined but should emerge from the architect's examination of all facets of the problem. Frequently, many different schemes are developed, tested, and modified or discarded until a satisfactory solution is found. Then, and only then, is it possible for the architect to state with any assurance the shape of the building which he will recommend. If the best building is to result, the board of education and school staff should give the architect full freedom to explore various design possibilities.

[6] The term "loft" designates open floor space, usually simple in outline, which lends itself to a great variety of division by the insertion of partitions.

Evaluation and Approval of the Design

THE architect's design establishes what the school will be like and what it may cost before it is built. Hence, the approval of a design by the school authorities is one of the most important steps in the entire planning process. The final decision is based on a review of the architect's preliminary studies which consist of plans, elevations, sections, perspective sketches or a model, a construction outline, and approximate cost estimates. From these illustrations and the accompanying information, it should be possible for laymen to visualize the building and the site development that has been proposed and to check on the compliance with the requirements of the educational specifications. Of course, this depends on how well the illustrations have been prepared and how familiar the observer is with the reading of plans and architectural data.

The design of a building is arrived at in gradual stages. The architect first explores the various possibilities for the organization of the building spaces on the site in diagrammatic plans. Then, after the scheme that offers the most promising solution to the program has been decided upon in discussions with the educational planner and possibly others, he develops the preliminary plans and other illustrations that are needed for a portrayal of the design.

DIAGRAMMATIC PLANS

The architect may or may not ask the board of education to approve his diagrammatic plans. Should the building be simple and the plan type obvious, he may not need a board decision at this time. However, when two or more greatly differing solutions are possible, as may well occur with the diverse plan types that can be used for larger schools, a policy decision must be made that will involve the board in the selection of one of several diagrammatic plans submitted. For example, the board may be asked to make a policy decision in choosing between a campus-type plan and one which is more compact.

Whenever the board of education or other school authorities are asked to consider the diagrammatic drawings, they should give foremost attention to the larger issues. No consideration of irrelevant detail should be allowed to confuse the important considerations or detract from a subsequent, logical progression toward the final architectural solution of the problem. The fundamental objectives and the long-range needs should be kept in mind at all times, and the details subordinated to them. The building of a school is often a new and strange venture for many persons who become involved in it. It may be hard for them to adhere to the significant factors. For example, they may devote an undue amount of time to an inconsequential detail like the use of glass blocks or sloping roofs while slighting basic functional requirements.

The acceptance or rejection of a plan type expressed in diagrammatic drawings should primarily be governed by the suitability of the scheme for the objectives of the educational specifications. This will depend on the proper relationship of the various units or wings of the building to each other. First, therefore, the juxtaposition of the rooms and play areas for their affinities—internally as well as externally—along with the other considerations affecting their placement must be analyzed. Incidental thereto is the consideration of the architectural effectiveness of the composition of the building masses. Second, the amenities offered to the individual rooms by the proposed plan types in relation to orientation, conditions for natural illumination and ventilation, views, and isolation from noise and other interferences will have to be scrutinized. Third, the site plan will have to be evaluated in terms of the position and space for playgrounds, roads, parking, future extensions, etc. Fourth, the advantages of the different schemes from the point of view of cost will have to be compared.

The architect may be asked to carry out revisions of the diagrams submitted, to present additional ones, or to develop one of those submitted. He should be given a clear-cut understanding of the direction he is to pursue in his next move so that the choice of the plan type can be driven to conclusion without wasting time and increasing his drafting expenses. The diagram chosen will be his basis for the organization of the preliminary plans. It will contain the principles and the nucleus of the ideas from which he will proceed in the preparation of the final design.

COMPLETE PRELIMINARY STUDIES

When a diagrammatic scheme for the plan has been decided upon, with or without board approval, the architect completes the preliminary studies and prepares them for presentation to the board of education. The drawings and other documents submitted to the board at this point should give a clear impression of the school he has designed and its approximate cost. They usually include:

1. Plans for all floors of the building.
2. Site plan showing the proposed development of the land.
3. Perspective sketches of the exterior and some of the principal interiors (classroom, auditorium, entrance, etc.).

4. Sections showing the story heights, the profile of the roof, and the placement of openings for daylight distribution.
5. Construction outline defining the systems of structural framing, heating, ventilating, plumbing, and illumination. This should also designate some of the principal materials and types of equipment so that a policy decision can be reached on the quality of construction in reference to durability, safety, economy, and other basic objectives.
6. Approximate estimate of the cost of construction.

The architect will use his individual method of illustrating the building and presenting the submittals. He may also resort to models to show the entire building complex or details of it and may augment or elaborate the usual submittals with drawings of important features and statistical data.

Cost Estimates

The approximate cost estimate submitted by the architect with his drawings illustrating the design of the building will indicate whether the anticipated construction is within the budget. A check must be made of the amounts included in the architect's estimate against the allowances for the various items in the budget for the complete project cost.

The complete project cost is made up of many items which fall under the following headings designating the major divisions of the budget: (1) cost of land and site improvements; (2) cost of building construction; (3) cost of equipment and furnishings; and (4) fees and incidentals.

The fees include payments to the educational consultant, architect and engineers, landscape architect, lawyers, and any other consultants that may be called in. The incidentals include minor expenses occurring during the programming phase, such as title search, appraisals, condemnation proceedings, borings and surveys, travel expenses, etc., and other items arising later, like elections, advertising for bids, blueprinting, insurance, salary of the clerk-of-the-works, dedication expenses, etc. The largest incidental expenditure may be for contingencies that might arise during construction due to unforeseen conditions and changes involving extras. For these an allowance should be carried in the budget.

The architect in presenting approximate estimates will usually give only the costs of the construction contracts coming under his services. He may or may not include site improvement costs. Even though the architect will aim for reasonable accuracy in his cost estimates, he obviously cannot guarantee them. The architect's preliminary estimates are made on the basis of various unit prices, such as the cost per square foot of floor area, per cubic foot of space, per pupil, per classroom, etc. From experience and cost records kept by him on other schools, prices for these various units can be assumed, and the total cost approximated.

As the plans for the building progress into the working drawings and specifications phase, a greater amount of information becomes available on the basis of which costs can be determined with greater accuracy. When partially completed working drawings and an outline of the specifications are ready, an estimate based on a quantity survey can be prepared. Estimators are then able to compile a lengthy list of the quantities of labor and material involved in the construction and price the various items according to prevailing rates. Since actual costs are determined only by the contractors, the architect can never give an absolutely accurate quotation, but the quantity survey is a reliable way of determining what the building may cost before the final plans and specifications are sent out for bids. Its cost involves an extra expense to the architect which should be recognized in his fee or borne by the board as a reimbursable expense. Should the budget be tight and should additions or elaborations during the preliminary design phase have resulted in excessive costs, there still remains an opportunity to make cuts during the completion of the drawings and specifications from which the contractors will prepare their bids. This will eliminate disappointments, delays, and extra costs which would arise if the bids should run too high.

APPROVAL OF PRELIMINARY STUDIES

It bears repeating that the approval of the preliminary plans by the board of education is a very important step. When these plans are approved, the basic design and general method of construction are fixed, and the architect proceeds on this basis to develop working drawings and specifications. He rapidly incurs sizable financial obligations for drafting and engineering services, which would be wasted in event of any later substantial change in the basic design. It is for this reason that the architect's contract usually provides for reimbursement for any extra expenses caused by changes ordered by the board of education after the preliminary plans have been approved.

In considering the completed preliminary plans for approval, the larger issues as well as the details are appropriate for discussion. However, if the plan type has previously been approved by the board, a change should not be ordered except for a very good cause.

In deciding whether to approve the design, the following principles must receive foremost consideration:

1. The merit of the building design in terms of the correctness and completeness of the space requirements and their grouping, the features which the layout offers in relation to the educational objectives, and the appearance of the school as a pleasing expression of the functional requirements.

2. The merit of the site plan in terms of present and future requirements for the school and its likely extensions; the playgrounds, roads, parking, and other outdoor areas; and the practical and aesthetic advantages offered by the shape and position chosen for these various elements.

3. The merit of the solution in terms of the relative efficiency with which needs have been met under the budgetary limitations and the desired qualities have been achieved. This demands consideration of initial cost and likely expenses for maintenance and operation due to the types of construction and mechanical installations proposed.

CHAPTER 9

FROM THE DESIGN
TO THE COMPLETED BUILDING

Problems in the Building of a School
Methods of Building
The Architect's Documents for Execution
Selection of the Contractor
Execution of the Building Operations
Time Consumed in Design and Execution

THE approval of the architect's preliminary studies by the board of education permits the starting of working drawings and specifications. The design is now frozen; there may be minor changes or adjustments later, but in principle the building when built will represent what the architect has shown on his preliminary drawings and described in the construction outline. The preparation of working drawings and specifications is a production operation that is best accomplished when large staffs in the architect's and engineers' offices can work with the certainty that their involved tasks will not be impeded by continuing requests for revisions or delays.

During this phase, the methods for construction and mechanical installations are developed and the materials and equipment chosen. They are depicted in great detail on drawings and are described in specifications. The details of the design are developed to establish the exact locations, kinds, and dimensions of all walls, doors, windows, foundations, floors, roofs, and a multitude of other items of construction and building finish, along with the position and sizes of all piping, duct work, light switches, heat outlets, boilers and fans, sanitary fixtures, and all other parts of the mechanical installations and equipment. The architect is assisted by engineers and specialists who compute and lay out the structural framing and the heating, ventilating, plumbing, electrical work, and other specialties. He gives them the necessary instructions and co-ordinates their work. All told, he is responsible for the preparation of a complete and correct set of plans and specifications from which precise estimates can be prepared and construction work be executed by contractors. The work the architect and his engineers perform must result in such a complete definition of the building that every item of labor and material is either shown on the drawings or described in the specifications. Only if this is done thoroughly can the work of the contractors be performed smoothly and without requests for extra payments for whatever was forgotten or inadequately planned.

Problems in the Building of a School

THE fundamental problem of construction is the achievement of a suitable enclosure and the best conditions for life within it. In other words, it involves the creation of an architecturally and functionally satisfying barrier against the outdoor elements, the partitioning of rooms, and the provision within them of the thermal conditions, fresh air, illumination, sanitation, acoustics, etc., which the use of the building demands. Usually economic limitations dictate that the most efficient way for the accomplishment of these objectives be found and used.

PROBLEMS OF BUILDING METHODS AND MATERIALS

Building is one of the oldest human skills, and methods employed by the earliest civilizations still find their applications today. The heavy masonry walls, the sloping roofs, and the crude heating and sanitation found in the schools that were built up to the beginning of this century are vestiges of the past. The building of a brick wall today is little different from what it was at the time of the Persians and Romans. Only in recent years has technological progress led to the mass production of building materials, the use of prefabricated parts, and considerable achievement in the mechanical production of indoor comfort under controlled conditions. Though the prefabrication of entire buildings is not yet fully practical, a sufficient number of prefabricated building parts is available to simplify the construction process and reduce costs. However, there exist some retarding influences to these developments. In part, they are due to building regulations and trade practices that have not kept up with progress and often still require methods that are antiquated. In part, they are due to the fact that manufactured materials like metals, plastics, etc., are still more expensive than materials like wood, clay, cinder, or cement products.

Nevertheless, advance and expansion in the available techniques of construction and materials have been tremendous, and the complexities of the problems of architects and engineers have increased in proportion. Construction has become very much lighter; where formerly a heavy wall and a roof with an attic served as barrier against the cold and wet, today a thin curtain wall and a roof that also serves as ceiling have to answer the same purpose. While formerly leaks were absorbed in the thickness of walls and attics, today they appear in the rooms unless the design of the construction, waterproofing, and careful workmanship keep them out. The thin walls, roofs, and floors also produce problems of condensation and noise penetration, which again demand precautions that were not needed in the past. There are difficulties resulting from the corrosion of metals, the cracking of concrete floors and masonry blocks, the warping and shrinkage of wood with expansion and contraction, and innumerable other inherent deficiencies in materials and methods. All these have to be reckoned with so that defects may be prevented by the architect's precautionary measures.

PROBLEMS OF SUPERVISION OF CONSTRUCTION

Other problems arise in the execution of construction by contractors and building trades workers. All construction operations must be carried out by labor that may worry too little about defects that might arise as a consequence of inadequate care in workmanship and by contractors who, after having submitted the lowest bid, may aim for the least number of labor hours on their payrolls and the lowest bills from their material dealers. Hence, even the best architect occasionally has difficulties to correct after the building is completed, and with an inexperienced one serious defects may arise that require excessive outlays for repair and maintenance.

While the architect can be selected on the basis of qualifications, including an evaluation of his technical competence, the contractor is usually chosen solely on the basis of the lowest bid. Therefore, it becomes particularly important to make him adhere meticulously to the requirements of the drawings and specifications on which his price is based. This stresses the necessity for the completeness of these documents and the need for strict supervision and control—all being the concern and responsibility of the architect.

Supervision by the architect includes periodic inspection trips, but not daily tours or continuous presence. On any but a small or simple job there should be a full-time clerk-of-the-works present who is constantly on the alert for defective material and workmanship that may be concealed before the architect or his superintendent appears.

Many contingencies may arise during construction. There is the chance of unreasonable extra charges by contractors; the possibility of a contractor's financial difficulties or business failure; disputes about correction of defective work; accidents; fire; damage from windstorms, frost, and floods; inability of the contractor to execute the work; unauthorized changes in the work; etc. All these must be anticipated, and ways of dealing with them must be provided before construction starts.

PROCEDURES FOR HANDLING PROBLEMS

A competent architect can avoid serious problems during construction by the exercise of reasonable care, provided he has the support and cooperation of his client. The usual precautionary measures are carried out as follows:

1. The methods, materials of construction, and mechanical installations must be carefully planned and shown in great detail on the working drawings and described in the specifications. These documents form the basis of the construction contract.

2. An established process for the selection of contractors, often prescribed by laws regulating bidding on public work, must be carried out, followed by the signing of legal agreements and the furnishing of performance bonds by contractors.

3. The specifications must provide ways of dealing with various contingencies and be made a part of the construction contract. (This part of the specifications is called the "general conditions of the contract.")

4. The architect's supervision and the continuous inspections by the clerk-of-the-works should enforce honest execution of the work in accordance with the plans and specifications.

5. The architect's administration of the construction contract must provide a record of authorized changes, keep a running account of the financial obligations to the contractor, periodically check the quantity of labor and material represented on the site, and verify the contractor's bills for them.

The conscientious following of the course outlined above will usually lead through the complex and entangled building process without major obstacles.

A great number of firms, public bodies, and individuals representing diverse and often conflicting interests, together with a large and mixed labor force, highly specialized and frequently organized to work under union regulations, are involved in the operation. Under these conditions, and under the uncertainty of strikes, storms, or some other unforeseen event, it is never safe to predict completely smooth sailing. However, one of the major contributions of a good architect is to lead an owner with a minimum of difficulties through all problems that can be reasonably anticipated.

The members of the school board, the superintendent, the educational consultant, and anyone else having or claiming to have a voice in the building of the school must at all times painstakingly recognize the authority of the architect. As appointed agent of the owner, he has full responsibility for the direction of the building operations. He receives his instructions from the owner and carries them out through his office or has them followed out by the construction contractor whose work he controls. This may be a general contractor who is in charge over several subcontractors or it may be a series of separate contractors. The contractor in turn channels instructions through his general superintendent on the job, to the foremen for the various trades, and finally down to the workmen. This chain of command establishes an orderly procedure which must be carefully adhered to in order to prevent conflicting instructions and to enable the keeping of orderly records by the architect. Deviation from systematic channeling of instructions through the responsible individuals causes errors, extra expense, delays, and ill-feelings.

There are numerous examples of undue difficulties that have resulted from a break in this chain of command. Owners have received bills from contractors for extras which neither the architect nor a responsible representative of the owner has authorized. Board members or clerks-of-the-works have asked contractors on the job to make changes without going through the formalities of requesting written change orders from the architect. As a result of these and many other irregular procedures, annoying disputes have arisen involving unforeseen expenses and often work stoppages.

The superintendent of schools, or his officially delegated agent, is the logical person to carry the responsibility for the school board, and all instructions, decisions, and correspondence should be channeled through him to the architect who controls the building operation.

Methods of Building

THE construction methods and the systems for mechanical installations involved in the building of a school are so greatly varied and technically complicated that they demand the knowledge and experience of the architect and engineer for a sound handling of the problems. These technical experts will be governed by certain basic objectives in the selection of suitable types of construction and proper materials and equipment. Some understanding of these objectives will be helpful to members of the board, the superintendent, and educational planners in properly appraising and following the building process.

THE OBJECTIVES IN CONSTRUCTION

The first basic objective is functional suitability, or the appropriateness of a method for a given purpose. For each purpose definite performance and aesthetic requirements exist that can be defined so that the suitability can be determined on the basis of how well each of them is answered. To clarify this statement by an example, the choice between light steel construction and concrete can be made on the basis of the requirements for fireproofness, cost, appearance, and several other factors.

The second basic objective is durability and strength. This is partly inherent in the materials and partly dependent on how they are used. The materials must be chosen and the details of construction must be developed to prevent the deterioration of the building under the attack of the elements of nature (primarily moisture, frost, storms, and earth tremors), the wear and tear of hard usage, and damage by vermin and rodents.

Cost constitutes the third basic objective. This involves the consideration of types of construction which are relatively inexpensive though some of them may demand a high cost for upkeep. Therefore, it is important to take a long-range view in regard to economy and to realize that carrying charges on the initial cost of a building plus the expense for maintenance determine the cost-in-use which is a continuing financial burden.

The fourth basic objective is safety. The safety of a building is in part governed by the layout of the plans and in part by the method and materials chosen for construction. First, it will depend on the exit provisions and the avoidance of hazardous conditions that might result in accidents on stairs, in corridors, and in rooms; second, it will hinge on the structural strength provided in the engineering computations; and third, it will be derived from the fire protection facilities and other safety measures.

Maintenance Costs

Maintenance costs are primarily affected by the manner of meeting the objective of durability and strength. There are numerous causes for repairs and replacement which are discussed in the paragraphs that follow.

Many substances employed in the building process are subject to deterioration and dimensional changes from the influences of the humidity or acids in the air or from moisture they themselves emit. There exists the problem of shrinkage cracks resulting from green lumber or improperly cured concrete, cinder blocks, and concrete blocks. Most of these are not serious defects and some are unavoidable. There also is difficulty with the corrosion and electrolysis of metals. Further, some wall boards and fibrous materials do not remain inert under humidity changes, and unpleasant consequences appear in buckled surfaces and unsanitary joints. The very earth on which the building rests may produce settlements and more serious cracks if the bearing capacity of the soil is inadequate, or if any part of a footing is not placed on firm ground, or if an earthquake occurs.

Moisture is one of the most critical problems. The most common difficulties that arise in buildings are because of moisture penetration from the outside or to condensation within. The frequency with which leaks appear indicates how hard it is to combat nature and how important it is to take measures to deal with the problem in the preparation of plans and specifications. Frost causes the greatest difficulty in connection with moisture and produces problems by cracking foundations, outdoor slabs, steps, and area-ways, and frequently by causing pipes to freeze.

Storms endanger the stability of a structure that is not designed to withstand them, and commonly their high wind force subjects the outer surfaces of buildings to severe attacks and carries water, snow, and airblasts through the windows, walls, and ventilators with consequent leaks or drafty conditions. Preventive measures have to be taken not only in the construction, but also in the heating and drainage layouts to prevent damage to the building and hardships to its occupants.

Likewise, protection against damage from termites, rodents, etc., must be provided. The wear and tear under human use is of greatest concern in the choice of materials. Also, cutting used by building trades workers for clearances for pipes and ducts through structural supports, may have serious consequences. There are technical solutions and preventatives to most problems. They must be incorporated in the plans and specifications if maintenance costs are to be kept at a minimum. Later difficulties can be minimized by the architect's careful attention to detail, and by good supervision.

The four basic objectives given are but a general and arbitrary classification of the principal factors that affect the choice of materials and methods of construction. It must always be borne in mind that in the choice of any method or material, the objectives must be given primary consideration, and the ways of accomplishing them must follow. In other words, the first question to be asked should be— What must be accomplished? The second— What is the best way to do it? The answer to the latter query should appear in the architect's plans and specifications.

THE OBJECTIVES IN MECHANICAL INSTALLATIONS

The mechanical installations provide environmental comfort and they contribute to the health of the occupants of the building and to the efficiency with which work is performed. These are the basic objectives that govern the planning of the heating and ventilation, the plumbing and sanitation, and the illumination and electric work.

Technological progress has made higher standards of comfort possible. The building industry produces and constantly develops new mechanical devices that not only aim to answer man's need for thermal comfort, fresh air, light, etc., but also allow for automatic control. While progress continues, it must be borne in mind that the ideals sought are not yet achieved and are perhaps not fully attainable. Though we find a movement toward controlled, constant conditions in temperature, air supply, and illumination, the psychological demands of man are such that constancy produces dullness. Hence, an entire reliance on artificial environment does not in itself produce the most ideal conditions for living or work. For example, it was found that in industrial buildings the windowless plant did not satisfy workers, and vision strips have had to be installed in the more recent structures. Likewise, high-intensity, shadowless illumination was found to have shortcomings. The even light eliminated the delicate shading required to discern form. Beyond that, the human value of contact with nature must not be disregarded. In general, there are no mechanical substitutes for windows that bring in views, daylight, and fresh air.

There is much that could be said about the various methods for mechanical installations. Detailed information is published by the American Society of Heating and Ventilating Engineers [1] and the Illuminating Engineering Society.[2] In these reference texts the engineering problems are discussed and the methods for dealing with them are thoroughly described and illustrated.

The architect must attack all problems arising in mechanical installations. For example, he must consider how natural light and air can be

[1] *Heating, Ventilating, Air Conditioning Guide.* New York: American Society of Heating and Ventilating Engineers, published annually.

[2] *I. E. S. Lighting Handbook.* New York: Illuminating Engineering Society, 1952.

supplemented by artificial illumination and ventilation. He has to integrate the ducts, pipes, radiators, grilles, and light fixtures into the design of the rooms and the construction of the building. He must plan for ease of maintenance so that cleaning and replacement of lamps and rusted pipes can be readily accomplished. He has to consider the flexibility of the installations so that changes and extensions can be carried out. He has to provide places in the construction for all mechanical equipment, feeder and return lines, etc., so that no unsightly effects or hazardous obstructions are created in classrooms, gymnasiums, etc. There are plumbing pipe spaces, raceways for cables and conduits, recesses for radiators, and innumerable similar details to be incorporated in the drawings and specifications. The thin walls arising in the newer types of construction present particular difficulties in this direction. The thoroughness of the architect's services can be detected in the clean, unobstructed interiors in which no blemishes from pipes and wiring, etc., appear. Therefore, it is important to have the architect handle and integrate into his plans all equipment that must be installed in the building. This also includes loud-speakers, fire extinguishers, kitchen equipment, etc., which some boards may unwisely consider as part of the furnishings that can be installed by dealers without requiring the architect's services.

WALL-BEARING AND SKELETON CONSTRUCTION

The architect in preparing the documents for the execution of a building must decide whether wall-bearing or skeleton construction is to be used.

Wall-bearing construction is the traditional way of building. This system has many limitations, and for that reason is gradually being discarded. In this type of construction the walls that carry the structure have to be heavy. If windows or doors occur within them, the lintels covering the openings are broad and the piers between the windows obstruct the passage of light. Changes in the building are more difficult to execute because the removal of bearing walls causes loss of the support for the structure above. The fact that the walls are heavier involves additional materials and labor and increases the cost. Some advantages of wall-bearing must not be overlooked. If heavy walls occur between classrooms, their weight and thickness produce an excellent sound barrier.

Skeleton construction resorts to a framework of columns and beams for the support of the floors and roof. The walls have no further function than to form a curtain against the out-of-doors and to separate the rooms; therefore, they can be much thinner. The interior of the building can be divided at any place and the partitions can be easily relocated. Hence, the flexibility offered gives this system of building its appeal. There are additional advantages. The absence of piers between windows allows for continuous ribbons of glass and thereby increases the amount of daylight that can be brought into the rooms. The erection of the building can proceed faster and entails less cost due to a reduction in the mason's work. The columns can be spaced at regular intervals, or modules, that are suited to the dimensions of prefabricated wall and floor panels.

FIRE-RESISTIVE AND FIREPROOF CONSTRUCTION

Safety from fire in schools depends, roughly speaking, on the exit provisions and the resistance of materials in the building to burning and heat. Frequently, buildings are called fireproof if the materials used in their construction are incombustible. However, tests show that most materials that do not burn still suffer in their stability from exposure to fire after a certain period of time. For example, steel bends under heat. Therefore, the National Fire Protection Association refers only to fire resistance and gives ratings for various materials and methods of construction.[3] Building laws frequently use the term "fireproof" for types of construction and materials that have high resistance ratings. To the architect, fireproof construction expresses a method of building that withstands flames and heat for at least three to four hours. What many laymen call fireproof may be only a fire-resistive construction of incombustible materials with a much lower rating. In local and state building laws several categories of construction are differentiated according to their fire safety and durability.

For clarification, five principal types of construction are described, though many building laws subdivide these into a greater number of categories.

Fireproof Construction

This is usually a construction of masonry and concrete with metal doors, windows, and trim. If a steel skeleton is used, it must be protected by concrete, masonry, or metal lath and plaster. No part of the structure is combustible. While this type offers the highest degree of safety to life, damage to property may still result from a fire that burns the furnishings or equipment. It is primarily used in schools of multiple stories.

[3] *Building Construction and Equipment.* National Fire Codes, Vol. III. Boston: National Fire Protection Association, 1951.

Fire-resistive Construction

This type uses incombustible materials for the structural framework of the building. Wood occurs only in nonsupporting members according to the varying limitations of different building regulations. The structural frame is usually a steel skeleton without fireproofing. This type of construction is much lighter in weight and in appearance, less expensive, and more flexible than fireproof construction. For this reason it is commonly used in school buildings.

Ordinary Masonry Construction

This type uses masonry walls for carrying the floors and the roof but allows the use of wood for the construction of the floors, roofs, etc. This is the traditional method used for the building of schools. However, what little fire resistance and safety it provides depend upon the use of incombustible materials for the wall and ceiling surfaces and the insertion of barriers to the spread of fire in the hollow spaces of the construction.

Heavy-timber Construction

This is not as commonly used in school building as it has been in mill construction. It resorts to a skeleton of columns, girders, and floor beams of heavy timber and employs thick wood planks for the floors and roof. The advantage from the point of safety is that heavy timber chars without burning through. Laminated wood beams frequently used in school buildings have this same advantage.

Wood-frame Construction

This is the traditional method for building dwellings in the United States with light wood studs and floor joists. The lumber used in the walls, floors, and roof is only two to three inches thick and for that reason burns through easily.

CHOICE OF A TYPE OF CONSTRUCTION

The choice of a type of construction does not depend on fire resistance alone; safety to a large extent is provided by good exits. The other objectives of construction—namely, durability and strength, functional suitability, and cost—are of major influence in the decision regarding the materials and methods for the execution of the architect's design.

The durability and strength of fireproof, fire-resistive, and ordinary masonry construction are somewhat greater than that of heavy-timber and wood-frame construction. Though frame houses have stood in the United States for hundreds of years and the early little red schoolhouses were built of frame construction, this type finds application in modern school building only in smaller structures or units of schools that are isolated against the spread of fire.

In the consideration of functional suitability, one has to recognize that ordinary masonry construction often does not offer the desired flexibility in that it relies on the wall-bearing principle. The solidity of fireproof construction is somewhat of an obstacle to later changes or enlargement of the building.

In regard to cost, fireproof construction is generally the most expensive and wood frame the cheapest; the higher the fire resistance, the greater the cost. Safety from fire in wood construction can be greatly increased by the installation of sprinklers, with a consequent additional cost.

Frequently, it is stated that a school built of an industrial type of construction is the cheapest. This claim demands a distinction between industrial type of construction and industrial type planning. Industrial construction stands for an exposed steel skeleton, with the least expensive windows, crude heating and ventilation, and only rough walls, floors, and ceilings; it comes under the category of fire-resistive construction. It is a fact that the unit price per square foot of factory floor area is perhaps less than one half that of a school. However, while there are many things to be learned from the industrial type of construction regarding economy, it must be remembered that the standards of environmental comfort, the number of walls and partitions, the interior finish, etc., that are represented in the square foot price are greatly different for the two types of buildings. This is reflected in the higher unit cost for schools.

The feature of factory construction that does offer considerable savings and can be adapted to schools is industrial-type planning. The simple outline of factory buildings results in the greatest amount of floor area for the least amount of exterior wall. Rectangular or square buildings are also the easiest to subdivide; hence, they offer great advantages in regard to flexibility. The loft-type school is based on these concepts and consequently is one of the least expensive. However, one must weigh this against the features of the irregular plan types in which the longer exterior walls produce closer relationship with the out-of-doors and the spread-out wings provide greater separation of noisy rooms. Thus, in the industrial plan types, qualities that make a school pleasant and quiet are sacrificed in favor of lower cost.

The Architect's Documents for Execution

THE design of the school, its construction, and mechanical installation are defined in great detail on the working drawings. Whatever cannot be shown graphically on the drawings is described in the text of the specifications. These two documents are parts of the contract for the execution of the building. They are the basis for the contractors' bids and serve as layouts and instructions for the erection of the school.

THE WORKING DRAWINGS

The working drawings are usually subdivided into several sets, as follows:

1. The architectural set, which contains the basic drawings for all the construction operations, and shows labor and material involved in the erection of the building and the development of the site. It serves as a key to the integration of the other sets; as a layout for the work of all contractors, subcontractors, and fabricators; and as the basis for the contractors' material orders from suppliers.
2. The structural set, which shows the framing of the floors and roofs, and all structural supports and details thereof.
3. The heating and ventilating set.
4. The plumbing set.
5. The electrical set.

The last three sets of drawings indicate the mechanical installations and provide the layout for the work of the various contractors involved in them. For smaller buildings, some of these sets may be combined; for larger projects, a greater number may be employed in order to deal with special installations. There may also be a separate set of drawings for the landscape work, showing the general layout, the construction, and the planting.

The extent of the work of each of the various contractors is accurately defined in the drawings and specifications. Should there be a landscape construction contractor in addition to the general building contractor, it must be clearly established where the work of one ends and the other begins. Also, for the work of the various trades this definition must be made, as usually the general contractor sublets different parts of the construction to a number of subcontractors. Disputes arise if their individual responsibilities are not made clear in the drawings and specifications.

A well-organized procedure in keeping with established practices for building operations is followed in the preparation of drawings and specifications. After basic dimensions of the layout are established on the architectural set, the engineers start on their phase of the work. They prepare the structural and mechanical sets of drawings, which in turn are integrated by the architect into his drawings. Wherever spaces for pipes, heating equipment, ducts, electric fixtures, wiring, etc., are required, the architect makes provisions on the architectural set for their installation. The architectural set is the most complete of the working drawings. It consists of a great number of separate sheets that show plans, elevations, sections, details, and schedules indicating all the work involved in the erection of the building. The structural set limits itself to layouts for the structural framing and supports of the building; the heating and ventilating set to layouts and details for all equipment, piping, duct work, etc., and all devices for the control of thermal comfort and fresh air; the plumbing set to all plumbing fixtures, and any work incidental thereto, and all pipe lines for supply, drainage, etc. Finally, the electrical set locates the wiring distribution panels, switchboards, switches and receptacles, electric fixtures, clocks, intercommunicating systems, conduits, motors, oil burner and fan connections, and the like.

This description, though incomplete, serves to indicate the profusion of information that has to be developed, compiled, and marked on the drawings. The preparation of working drawings is an intricate and complicated process that demands an organized presentation of a vast quantity of information on the numerous sheets of the various sets—all of which must be understood by an owner.

During the preparation of the working drawings, numerous studies and computations are made by the architect and the engineers to find the best solutions to the details of the design and construction of the building and the structural framing, mechanical installations, acoustics, and built-in equipment. The most efficient answer is constantly sought by the competent architect. He compares prices of the various ways in which the desired objectives and the requirements of the educational specifications can be met. He never loses sight of the fact that the details of the working drawings and the materials described in the specifications give the building its final quality.

THE SPECIFICATIONS AND GENERAL CONDITIONS OF THE CONTRACT

The specifications are written descriptions of the materials, methods, and equipment used in construction. Every type of material, light fixture, etc., is described in a way that clearly designates the type and quality of the product so that it is identifiable and substitutions by the contractors can be detected and prevented. The specifications are broken into chapters, each dealing with the work of a separate building trade. Every chapter is tied by reference to a set of regulations governing the work of all contractors and entitled "General Conditions of the Contract."

The division of the specifications into chapters recognizes established practices of building trades workers and subcontractors in the performance of construction work. The general conditions are divided into standard clauses that are normally applicable in the execution of building contracts and supplementary general conditions pertaining to the construction of the particular project. For the former, the printed form of the American Institute of Architects is generally used; the latter are drafted by the architect to meet special and local conditions.

The 44 articles of the printed form of the general conditions, published by the American Institute of Architects,[4] define the documents of the construction contract and the status of the persons involved in their preparation and use; they include stipulations governing detail and shop drawings, samples, royalties and patents, surveys, permits, building ordinances, inspection of work, changes in the work, claims for extra cost, methods for the correction of work, the rights of the various parties to stop work, methods of payment, the various forms of insurance and guarantee bonds, claims for damage, liens, assignment, mutual responsibility of contractors, arbitration, etc.

Supplementary general conditions cover special problems that might arise in the execution of the particular job, such as temporary enclosures, temporary heating, temporary buildings on the construction site, and progress photographs.

With the aid of these documents, the construction operation should proceed without undue difficulties, provided that the parties involved exercise reasonable skill and care in doing their work and are mindful of their responsibilities.

PROVISION FOR ALTERNATE PRICES

Often questions arise as to whether the architect's documents will produce bids that come within the budget, or whether a different way of executing some items of the construction or installation might not be less expensive and equally good. Both of these situations are dealt with by requesting alternate prices from contractors.

[4] *The Handbook of Architectural Practice.* Washington, D. C.: American Institute of Architects, 1953, p. 127 (Form A-2).

Alternates involve extra work for the bidders and are apt to produce confusion unless clear instructions for them have been incorporated in the drawings and specifications. They can be omitted or reduced in number if a quantity survey is prepared by the architect before the bidding period starts, as discussed in the preceding chapter. However, the attitude of architects toward alternate prices varies; there are some who like them for a certain flexibility they provide in the selection of the lowest bidder and in adjusting the kind of construction to the budget. The latter should pertain only to minor items of work; as, for example, the use of metal versus wood for door frames, plaster versus acoustic tiles for ceilings, etc.

APPROVAL OF DRAWINGS AND SPECIFICATIONS

At the completion of the working drawings and specifications by the architect, a school board is in a position to ask for a minute description of every item of construction and equipment used anywhere in and about the building. By pointing to any room on the plans, it should be possible to obtain a clear understanding of the size and appearance of the space, its construction, the materials used on the floor, walls, and ceilings, the extent and design of built-in equipment, the types of lighting and heating units, the method of control provided for them, the grilles for ventilation, the number and kinds of coats of paint, etc. The index to the specifications and drawings and the clear marking system for the sections and details on the drawings should make it possible for anyone concerned with the building, including the ordinary worker, to find his way through this cumbersome set of documents. The clarity, completeness, and accuracy of the information is essential to the preparation of close estimates by the contractors. When these documents are completed, they must be officially approved by the school board. The placement of signatures of the contracting parties on each of the drawings and sets of specifications will identify them as parts of the contract and will prevent the contractor from alleging that additional requirements were inserted after the bidding.

Selection of the Contractor

THE usual method for the selection of the contractor for public work is competitive bidding, with the award of the construction contract going to the lowest responsible bidder. This is usually regulated by state or local statutes. To obtain bids, it is first necessary to invite the bidders to submit a proposal and then to furnish them with drawings and specifications for preparation of their estimates. Invitations are usually issued through advertising in the press or construction news organs as required. In addition, the architect may send invitations to bidders he would like to have participate. The advertisements or invitations must give the name of the project and mention when the drawings and specifications will become available and where they may be procured. It must also state when and where the bids must be filed and the documents returned and whether a deposit for the drawings and specifications is required. Usually, an assurance is also required from the bidders that they will accept the contract for the work if selected. This is accomplished through the deposit of a certified check or the filing of a bid bond. The amount for these is usually determined by the regulations governing contracts for public work and varies in different localities. The bid bond has the advantage that the bonding company will usually ascertain whether the bidder qualifies for a later performance bond should he be awarded the job. The various states and localities may also require written evidence of the contractor's competence for the execution of the work. The drawings and specifications are furnished the bidders along with instructions. The latter stipulate how, where, and when the bids must be submitted and call attention to a form of proposal prepared by the architect which all bidders must fill out.

A reasonable time should be allowed for preparing bids. In general this should not be less than two weeks. In large or complicated work three weeks or longer may be desirable. If extension of the time for bidding becomes necessary, bidders should be notified of the new opening date of bids at least 48 hours prior to the original opening date. The instructions also require that bidders must write to the architect for any clarifications or corrections of the drawings and specifications that may be needed and that they must familiarize themselves with the site, the drawings and specifications, and all conditions that affect the execution of the contracts. Should any clarifications or corrections of the drawings be needed, the architect will issue during the bidding period supplementary instructions to all bidders.

The form of proposal which each bidder is required to complete states that, after having carefully examined the instructions to the bidders, the drawings and specifications, and the general conditions affecting the execution of the contract for the work, the bidder submits a price of a given amount for the execution of the entire work, or a definite part of it, depending on whether the work pertains to a general contract or to one of several separate contracts. The form of proposal also states the period for which the price named is binding and the time required for the execution of the contract. The form of proposal may request unit prices for certain items of the work to aid the architect in checking the contractor's bills and quotations on extra work and changes.

Usually, the bids are opened in public and tabulated by the architect. After a comparison of the prices and the various alternates to them, the successful bidder is selected. Several days may be necessary to accomplish this because the architect must first verify the information received with the proposal.

Each bidder has been made aware through the specifications or the instructions to bidders that should he be selected for the execution of a job, he must submit a performance bond. This bond is usually made out in the full amount of the contract and is a guarantee from an insurance company that it will assume the risk of the contractor satisfactorily completing the work. Other formalities are laid down in the statutes governing bidding on public work. These must be meticulously followed in order not to hold up the progress of a building over some technicality.

AWARDING OF THE CONTRACT

The contract for the construction of a building is signed by the awarding authority and the contractor. Legal counsel is recommended for the preparation of the contract. It must be ascertained that the persons signing the contract are authorized to do so. The document must give the names of the parties to the contract; stipulate the contract sum, the scope of the work, the time of completion, the method of payment, and the procedure for acceptance of the work and final payment; and list the contract documents by an enumeration of the drawings and specifications.

When the contract is signed and all legal formalities are completed, the contractor will be requested to submit to the architect a breakdown of his estimate into the items carried for the work of the various trades listed in the specifications. This is necessary to check later requisitions for payments. Further, the contractor is requested to submit a schedule of dates for the execution of the various phases of the construction operations. From this, the architect will be able to check the progress of the work; it also helps him to prepare and issue the necessary detailed instructions at the times they are needed.

Execution of the Building Operations

THE execution of the work rests in the hands of the contractor and normally comes under the supervision and control of the architect. While in rare instances the supervision may be handled by the owner, this procedure is not recommended and has, therefore, not been discussed in this text. The architect can only assume the responsibility for his product if he has the authority to insure that the intent of his plans and specifications is faithfully carried out. As explained previously, a clerk-of-the-works is usually essential to the satisfactory execution of the work. This is an employee of the owner, responsible to the owner through the architect. He will be requested to submit daily reports on the progress of the construction, the number of men working, the materials delivered or required, instructions or drawings needed, difficulties that have arisen, and actions taken or demanded. He does not have the authority to request additional work beyond the plans and specifications nor to permit changes from them. The power for these rests solely with the architect.

SUPERVISION BY ARCHITECT

The architect will issue during the execution of the construction supplementary detailed drawings and instructions about procedures to be followed in the execution of the work. He will also verify the shop drawings made by the fabricators or producers of various components of the construction.

During all operations, confusion in instructions must be avoided, and the members of the school board, the superintendent, and the educational consultant must deal through the architect and adhere to the chain of command that has been discussed previously. Should any changes in the work be required, authorization for them must be issued in a written form signed by the architect and owner. The architect's change orders serve as a record of extra costs or savings and as such avoid later disputes. Contractors are not permitted by the general conditions of the contract to claim extra costs unless a written authorization to perform additional work is given. Change orders should be issued for any departure from the plans and specifications, even if they do not involve extra costs. From time to time the contractor will be required to submit samples of the materials which must be approved. This may involve tests by laboratories, the cost of which is provided for in the specifications or borne directly by the owner. At the end of each month the contractor will prepare a requisition for payment for the work completed and materials suitably stored on the construction site. The architect will check the correctness of the request and issue a certificate of payment to the owner. A sum of 10 to 15 percent is withheld on the contractor's monthly requisition as a guarantee against overpayment and assurance of the completion of the work by the contractor. Should any difficulties arise due to the failure of the contractor to correct work in accordance with the architect's instructions, payments to the contractor may be withheld. These procedures are covered by the stipulations of the general conditions of the contract. The contractor will be obligated to carry liability insurance, and usually the owner carries the fire insurance. The contractor must also obtain the building permit and pay all fees in connection therewith.

Among the many problems that occasionally demand the architect's attention during the execution of the construction is the inability or failure of a contractor to carry out the work shown in the drawings and specificacations, substitution of inferior material, poor workmanship, bad expediting, request for a greater payment in the requisitions than represented in the amount of work performed and materials stored on the job, and failure of the contractor to pay his subcontractors and material dealers. Most of the difficulties can be avoided by the architect's clear and complete working drawings, specifications, and instructions, and by the competent supervision and control of the contractor by the architect and the clerk-of-the-works.

COMPLETION AND ACCEPTANCE

Construction operations ultimately reach their end. The number of workers from the various trades dwindles, and only the painters remain inside the building to complete that last and final coat of finish which will give the school its fresh appearance.

Outside, the lawn is being seeded, and if the season is right and the budget adequate, the shrubs and trees that blend the building with the land are being planted. The unsightly construction shacks and rubbish piles are being removed, and the school construction appears to be finished. However, the construction operations are only at the point of "substantial completion," as it is referred to in the agreement with the contractor. The school is not quite ready for occupancy, and neither furniture nor pupils should be brought in until all the last-minute touching-up and final adjustments have been made. Were furnishings set up too soon, and should blemishes develop in the process, disputes would arise as to the responsibility for damages the architect must ask the contractor to repair during the period set aside for final corrections. The recording of the date of substantial completion is important because the general conditions of the contract provide that the contractor continues to be responsible for faulty materials and workmanship for a period of one year from this day.

Good practice demands that the architect prepare a careful list of all touching-up, adjustments, replacements, and incomplete work at the beginning of that period. At that time the building and the grounds should be carefully gone over by the architect and the representatives of the owner who will finally be involved in the operation of the new school to assure that all points that have a bearing on the final acceptance of the contractor's work are properly taken care of.

After the final corrections have been carried out, the construction is completed and the school is ready for acceptance. The architect will have checked off all the items that have appeared on his list of required adjustments. A final inspection takes place by the authorized representatives of the owner, the architect, and the contractor. Provided everything is satisfactorily completed, the owner formally agrees to accept the contractor's work. The architect usually asks his consulting engineers to participate in the final inspection so that their advice in regard to the full completion of the mechanical installations will be available to him. With acceptance of the building, the construction phase ends and the school is now ready for the furnishings. The period that elapses between substantial completion and acceptance is stipulated in the agreement between the owner and the contractor. Upon acceptance, the contractor is entitled to the final payment for his work.

RECORD DRAWINGS AND OPERATING INSTRUCTIONS

At some future time it may become necessary to refer to drawings that show how the construction was finally carried out. There may have been departures from the working drawings and specifications during the building of the school, and incorrect information may complicate later repairs or changes.

The architect's drawings will not be of much help to the execution of any future work unless they have been kept current by continuous revision during the entire construction process. This can be done because every change demands a written authorization which can be recorded on the drawings. Continuing revision of the working drawing set and the notation of change orders on the drawings is an inherent part of good architectural practice.

Operating directions for mechanical installations can be requested in the specifications. The specifications for these trades can include clauses that require contractors to provide suitable instructions for the equipment they have installed. Whether or not suitable provisions have been made for this can be verified at the time of approval of the plans and specifications.

OWNERSHIP OF ARCHITECT'S DRAWINGS
AND SPECIFICATIONS

The agreement between an owner and an architect normally states that drawings and specifications as instruments of service are the property of the architect. This clause is often misunderstood and causes undue concern. The erroneous impression arises than an architect only lends his blueprints to an owner and that they must all be returned to him. The emphasis in the statement should be on "instruments of service." That means that the design and all methods the architect has devised for the building construction remain the property of the architect. This is his protection or copyright, so to speak, against anyone executing several other buildings from the same plans and specifications.

Time Consumed in Design and Execution

WITH the acceptance of the building, the normal architectural services end and the balance of the fee is paid. The cost of the work by which a percentage fee is governed is now established by the sum of payments to contractors who have worked under the architect. Unless it was previously taken care of, adjustments are made to change the basis of the fee from the estimated costs to actual costs.

The period the architect has served the school board may have extended over a year and a half to two years or more. The time depends on the size of the building and the speed of progression through the various phases of the operation. During the design phase decisions demand careful deliberation, and the progress may be relatively slow. Though it is perfectly possible for the architect to complete his preliminary studies in one or two months, it seldom happens. Only with small buildings, or in cases where there is pressure for time, will such a short period for the preliminary studies be feasible. This is not the fault of the architect nor that of the school board or the educational planners. There must be adequate time for arriving at the approval of the architect's sketches in this critical period. However, avoidable delays that interrupt the continuity of the work should be prevented, as there is little opportunity to make up for lost time later on.

The period required for the preparation of working drawings and specifications again depends on the size of the project and the number of men engaged in the work at the architect's and engineers' offices. Two months may be adequate for a small building; three to five months is the minimum for the average. Bidding takes several weeks, and at least another week will pass before the contract is signed and excavations are begun on the site. The construction phase alone may consume nearly a year or more, depending on the size of the project, the weather, and time lost through unforeseen interruptions.

The variables are too great to make a definite statement on the total time consumed in the planning and building of a school. However, the times mentioned for the various phases of the work will indicate that planning must start early if the school is to be ready when it is needed. Further, it must be recognized that the annual enrollment increase continues for at least two years between the time the space needs are determined in the educational specifications and the time the new school is ready to meet them.

CHAPTER 10

FROM COMPLETED STRUCTURE
TO FUNCTIONING PROGRAM

Selecting Furnishings and Equipment
Selecting and Training the Staff
Presenting the Building to the Public
Assembling and Keeping Important Building Documents
Final Adjustments and Corrections

W HEN the architect certifies to the board of education that the building is ready for occupancy, the scene changes and the educator returns to the center of the stage. During the early part of the planning process, when the survey was being made and the educational specifications were being prepared, the planning was primarily the responsibility of the educator. With the approval of the educational specifications by the board, the major role shifted to the architect, who proceeded to design the building and prepare the drawings, specifications, and other documents necessary for bidding and construction. With the letting of contracts, the various contractors emerged as the prominent actors under the supervision of the architect. Now, with the completion of construction, the educator takes over again and proceeds to put the building into use.

All that has gone before has been done in order that a carefully developed and defined school program might be so housed that it can flourish. The manner in which the building is initiated into service and the handling of it over the years will determine in large measure whether or not its full teaching potentialities are realized. While plant operation and maintenance are relevant at this point, they are beyond the scope of this book, and attention now will be directed to those tasks to be performed by the school administrator as the new building is put into use. These are five in number, as follows: (1) selecting furnishings and equipment; (2) selecting and training the staff; (3) presenting the building to the public; (4) assembling and keeping safely the necessary records and operating instructions for the building; and (5) arranging for the final adjustments and correction of defects during the period of initial use. It is assumed at this point that the grading, seeding, planting of shrubbery and trees, paving, playground surfacing, and other site work have been done as a part of the construction phase of the project.

Selecting Furnishings and Equipment

WHILE the architect may have had responsibility for specifying all furnishings and equipment, a more common practice is to divide the work between the architect and the school administrator. A reasonable basis for such division is to have the architect specify any item of equipment attached to the building or permanently connected to utility lines. Thus, by way of example, he would be responsible for folding bleachers, basketball backboards, kitchen equipment, built-in lockers, and laboratory tables, but not for pupil seating, teachers' desks, and draperies. In practice, the division should not be so sharp and rigid as this might imply. The architect needs to confer with the school administrator regarding the selection of the items of fixed equipment which he specifies, and the architect should advise on furnishings and movable equipment so that they harmonize with the remainder of the plant.

The selection of equipment and furnishings should precede by some weeks or months the completion of the structure in order to allow ample time for ordering and delivery. Failure to start early enough may result in embarrassment in not being able to open a much needed building when construction is completed, or, perhaps even more serious, may lead to hasty selection and acceptance of undesirable substitutes for the articles really wanted.

A frequent error in budgeting for a school project is failure to make adequate allowance for furnishings and equipment. Sometimes this item is simply overlooked; at other times the available building funds are so limited that it is decided to purchase these things from current operating funds, to use furniture from an existing building, or to do without some things, hoping that a parent-teacher association or other benefactor will come to the rescue.

CRITERIA FOR SELECTION

It is not intended to discuss completely the sizes, materials, and design of school equipment and furnishings, since this would require a volume in itself. However, attention will be called to a few general principles that should be observed.

Should Fit the Program

The new building presumably has been designed to implement an educational philosophy and program, and the equipment and furnishings should be selected with the same end in view. Suppose, for example, that the new building is to house an elementary school and that it has been designed to stress informality and flexibility in a self-contained classroom stituation. The room cannot express informality if the furniture expresses formality and regimentation; it cannot express flexibility if the furniture cannot be rearranged as needed. Small group activity requires tables, chairs, and other furniture that can be easily rearranged; science activities require a variety of equipment and suitable work and storage space, which may be movable in the interest of flexibility; small group reading instruction requires movable chairs which can be grouped in a corner of the room away from other activities; and the use of projected audio-visual aids requires drapes or other devices for the control of daylight. These are but a few examples of how the nature of the program should be reflected in furnishing and equipping the building.

In some cases, because of lack of funds, it has seemed necessary to use old furniture from a building which is being discarded or from surplus which is on hand. This is unfortunate unless the furniture is in good condition and can be adapted to the educational program to be operated. It is distressing to see 50-year-old desks fastened on wooden strips and set in rows in a new school building which is obviously intended for an informal and flexible type of program. The use of such furniture defeats in part the purpose for which the new building was designed.

Where building funds are so limited that furniture must be purchased from other sources, it would be preferable to anticipate the need and purchase the furniture in advance as circumstances permit. It could then be used in the old building temporarily, and would be suitable for transfer to the new one.

Should Be Safe and Healthful

An important requirement is that all furniture and equipment used by pupils be of proper size. Since the children in any one room differ greatly in height and other body dimensions, a variety of sizes or adjustable furniture is necessary.

It is essential also that equipment be as free of hazards as possible. Draperies should be flame resistant, sharp instruments should be avoided where others will do, power tools in shops should have proper guards, gas appliances should have automatic shut-offs, and playground equipment should be free of sharp corners and other hazardous features.

The character of a school building has an important bearing on the well being of a child, and the recognition of this fact is presumably reflected in the design of the building. It deserves equal consideration in the selection of equipment and furnishings. The design, materials, and colors should blend with the room itself to make a pleasing total environment. Reasonable variation from room to room adds much to the attractiveness of the building with little or no extra expense.

Should Be Durable and Economical

Children are hard on a school building and everything in it which they use, and the selection of equipment and furnishings should be made with this in mind. Furniture and equipment of all kinds, therefore, ought to be sturdy and so designed that mischievous hands cannot make unwanted adjustments, remove parts, or mar surfaces. Drapes and other furnishings should not be of flimsy materials and should be securely hung lest they be inadvertently pulled loose. Ease of cleaning and making repairs should be sought. It is not necessary to sacrifice aesthetic qualities in the search for durability.

Should Be Complete

If at all possible, a new building should be furnished completely when it is put into use because experience has shown that items not purchased at this time may never be obtained. It is common practice to omit some of the furnishings with the thought that the money can be raised by other means to complete the job. A teachers' lounge, for example, is frequently left for a teachers' club, a parent-teacher organization, or other group to furnish. This may result in considerable delay before the room is ready for use, and, because of limited funds or personality difficulties, it often leads to the selection of items which are not of acceptable quality, taste, or usefulness.

This does not mean that public participation and interest are not valuable, nor does it mean that every last detail has to be provided so nothing will be needed later. There will always be opportunity for the purchase of extra things for the school and for participation by the teachers and public in other constructive ways.

COOPERATIVE APPROACH TO SELECTION OF FURNISHINGS AND EQUIPMENT

An earlier chapter advocated a cooperative approach to the planning of a building, with participation by teachers and other school employees, pupils, and parents. It was also advocated that technical assistance be provided from within the administrative staff or by the employment of an outside educational consultant. This approach is as applicable to the selection of furnishings and equipment as to the earlier steps in the planning of the building.

The advice of the architect is also important, as mentioned earlier, in order that the equipment and furnishings will fit the atmosphere which the architect has tried to create in his design.

Selecting and Training the Staff

In the designing of the new building, it is quite likely that innovations of program and building operation were contemplated. The building might have been designed for a different approach to teaching than has prevailed in the community in the past and it may have new kinds of mechanical equipment or other physical features not familiar to the building operation and maintenance staff. Insofar as there are such innovations, there is need for selecting and training the teaching and custodial staffs so as to realize the maximum good from the new plant.

THE TEACHING STAFF

If the new building has been properly planned, it has been planned so that teachers can work with children in certain ways. It is important, then, if the maximum educational value is to be achieved, that the teachers for the new building believe in working with children in these ways and can do it capably. To the extent that choices are available in the selection of the staff, the administrator when seeking teachers should have this objective as his goal. As a further assurance of success, he should arrange for an appropriate in-service education program.

If the building has been cooperatively planned, some or all of the persons who are to teach in the new building may have had a part in its planning. If so, they will have some understanding of the underlying educational philosophy and of the purpose and usefulness of the building features. Such participation is one of the best means of assuring most effective use of the new building.

The in-service training activities for teachers should include such instructions as are necessary for proper use of the mechanical facilities. They need, for example, to know in a general way how the ventilating system works and what they should do or not do to keep it functioning properly, and they should have similar information regarding the heating controls, the public address system, and the interroom telephones. If there are classroom toilets or similar innovations, there will be need for some discussion of how to administer them most effectively. Some of this in-service education of teachers might be handled on a tour of the building followed by a short orientation meeting, but much of it will occur as principals and other supervisors visit classrooms, conduct teachers' meetings, and perform other supervisory duties.

THE CUSTODIAL STAFF

Similar consideration is necessary in the selection and in-service training of custodians. It is not unlikely that they will need to learn how to operate and care for new types of equipment, and there may be new kinds of floors or finishes that they must learn how to clean and keep in proper condition. New kinds of chalkboard may require different care. Instruction on many of these matters will be given by the installers or manufacturers. Also, some universities arrange short courses for custodians, and some school systems are large enough to operate their own instructional programs for these employees. Wherever the assistance is obtained, it is important that capable custodians be selected, receive proper initial instructions, and then be kept up to date by a continuing program of in-service training.

The custodian's role in the proper functioning of a school is likely to extend beyond the care of the physical facilities. He has many contacts with pupils and frequently meets visitors to the school; he does much to create a lasting impression toward the school. If the custodian's performance in these areas is to be most gratifying, it is essential that capable people be selected, that they be taught the importance of their responsibilities, and that they be so treated that they perform all of their duties with pride.

RELATIONSHIP OF TEACHERS AND CUSTODIANS

The relationships between teachers and custodians are often marred by misunderstanding and friction, which is sometimes not kept within the walls of the building. A lengthy discussion of this problem does not belong here, but it is appropriate to point out that proper orientation of the teaching and custodial staffs to the new building should forestall some of these difficulties. There should be common understanding of who should operate certain mechanical controls, who should determine room temperatures, and the like. The teachers should know in general the work load and schedule of the custodians so that they do not make unreasonable requests or develop unreasonable expectations. Custodians, on the other hand, need to understand and accept the educational reasons for movable desks, classroom toilets, art and construction activities, after school use of rooms, and other features of the building or program which add to their cleaning problem or otherwise complicate their work schedules.

The goal of the administration is a smooth running organization with the entire staff working together for common purposes. This does not just happen; a good time to start making it happen is when the new building is opened.

Presenting the Building to the Public

THE good school administrator never forgets that the schools belong to the people, and he makes great effort to keep the public informed through a continuous program of interpretation. Such an administrator will not neglect the opportunities for public relations presented at the time of opening a new school building. News stories, formal dedication ceremonies, and open-house programs are commonly instruments for this purpose. Generally speaking, the principal objectives of these activities will be:

1. To let the public know what the building is like.
2. To increase public understanding of the educational program.
3. To impress the public with the importance of education and solicit continued interest and cooperation in solving the school's problems.
4. To say "thank you" for the building and for assistance in planning it.

EXPLAINING THE BUILDING

The public can be informed about the building in the public press, over the radio, at public meetings, or by an open house or dedication program. While all of these means should probably be used, it is especially helpful to get the public to see the building. The timing of the open house or dedication should permit the maximum number of citizens to attend and also permit the best viewing of the entire plant. Sunday afternoon is frequently chosen for these reasons.

The program of an open-house ceremony usually includes a tour of the building, frequently with members of the staff or older pupils serving as guides. It is good practice, also, to have informed persons stationed at certain places to explain unusual features which might not otherwise be understood or concerning which there might be some question raised. A printed brochure including a simple floor plan would also be helpful on these tours. It could contain information regarding costs, unusual features, planning procedures, and other items of interest.

If there are features which are not fully accepted by the public, there might well be some explanation either in the brochure or orally. In one community, for example, the new elementary school building contained an entrance lobby with a fireplace. Rumors about the cost of this feature and the extravagance of the board of education spread and grew until some people thought there was an expensive fireplace in each classroom. Actually there was but the one fireplace, and it had cost an extra $400. Armed with this fact, the friends of the school were able to refute the rumor successfully.

Many people will not find it possible to attend the formal opening ceremonies, no matter when they are held, or they may prefer to visit the building when school is in session. There will also be visitors from out of town in many instances. These visitors should be made to feel welcome, should be given copies of any available literature, and if possible should be given the services of a guide. Older pupils can serve effectively as guides and gain educational values as well.

EXPLAINING THE SCHOOL PROGRAM

The second objective mentioned above is to increase public understanding of the school program. This is more difficult to do if school is not in session. However, during the inspection of the building teachers can be stationed in their rooms and evidences of pupil work and activities can be shown and explained. Display spaces can be used for the same purpose. Certain aspects of the program can be explained in the printed brochure or in other printed materials, and oral explanations to the entire group can be a part of the open house program. These various displays and explanations can probably be made more effective if the dedication is postponed until the building has been in use for a few weeks. This will give the staff and pupils a chance to plan and to prepare displays and other media for explaining the program. At the time of the formal opening it should be emphasized that visitors will be welcome while school is in session.

SOLICITING INTEREST AND COOPERATION

Another objective in the opening ceremonies is to impress the public with the importance of education in society and to ask for continued interest and cooperation in the solution of the problems facing the schools. This can be done in many ways including displays, printed materials, pageants by pupils, and formal addresses. The latter is a standard way, with a prominent speaker. There is considerable merit in local participation in this part of the program with local people presenting in simple, well-organized fashion the salient facts about the long-term goals, the progress to date, and the difficulties to be overcome in the future. This would be an appropriate time for accounting to the people for the expenditure of building funds, or other money already provided, and for explaining the careful planning and sound controls employed in the use of their money.

"THANK YOU"

The successful completion of a new building is achieved only through the efforts of many people, who frequently serve without compensation or who add this service on top of an already heavy work load. This is particularly true when the building has been planned cooperatively with many school employees and citizens participating. Words of appreciation publicly expressed are certainly in order, but they must be sincere and not unreasonably profuse. The occasion for such expressions may be the open-house program, or any of the usual means of mass communication in the community may be used.

Assembling and Keeping Important Building Documents

AT THE completion of construction the architect will turn over to the school authorities a great many documents which may be of much value in future years. Among these are guarantees and bonds, manuals for the operation of certain equipment, parts lists, and drawings and specifications. Most of these documents can be accommodated in the regular school files, but in practice many of them are lost. A piece of equipment fails after a period of several years, and the operating manual or the guarantee cannot be located. Or the drawings may be needed and cannot be found. The value of many of these documents and the chances of their being lost both increase with the passage of time. It is the responsibility of the school administrator to see that these documents are secured promptly and are properly and safely filed.

It is especially important that a complete set of drawings and specifications be obtained, and, as indicated in the preceding chapter, that it be corrected to show the building in every important detail as actually constructed. This is needed for making repairs and additions throughout the life of the building, which may be a half century or more. Photographs of the building at various stages of construction are also useful in this connection. The importance of these documents is shown by the experience of one city which remodeled and enlarged a 40-year-old building. Since the structural drawings were missing, the architect had to cut into walls and columns to determine the size and capacity of the weight-bearing elements, and for this extra work he was paid an additional fee of several thousand dollars.

The storage of construction drawings is troublesome because they vary in size, and most school systems have too few of them to justify special files. Small scale photostatic copies are sometimes made, but the scale is often distorted by this process and the drawings are hard to read. Microfilming is also used, and the drawings then can be examined in a viewer or enlarged photographically if necessary.

Another problem involved in the storage of drawings is that they become brittle with age, and important details are lost as the edges are broken off. Drawings or tracings on linen cloth are relatively permanent but expensive unless produced photographically. This whole problem is one upon which the advice of the architect should be sought.

Final Adjustments and Corrections

A SCHOOL building is a large and complicated structure erected by a great many different craftsmen. It is reasonable to expect that some defects will show up after the building is put into use. This is particularly true with clock systems, heating plants, and other mechanical systems, but there may also be flaws in roofs, flashings, floors, or other parts of the structure itself. It is important that the school administration be alert in detecting these flaws and having them corrected during the guarantee period. Failure to take reasonable precautions may prove to be expensive when repairs are made later.

PART TWO

The School Plant and Its Features

CHAPTER 11

THE SCHOOL PROGRAM AS THE KEY TO SCHOOL PLANT DESIGN

The Relationship of Program to Plant
General Aspects of the School Program
School Program Trends
Planning for Change

THE first part of this book has dealt extensively with the planning process from the initial survey of needs through the development of educational specifications and the architectural planning to the construction and dedication of the building. In this discussion it has been emphasized repeatedly that the starting point in school-plant planning must be the school program and that the program will be the main factor in determining the type of building; the kinds of space; the size, shape, arrangement, and equipment of the various spaces; and many other features of the building. However, the discussion up to this point has been relatively devoid of comments regarding program per se. This has been deliberate in order to keep attention focused on the processes themselves.

The authors now, in the second part of this book, turn to a discussion of the school program and the implications of different program features for the design of a school building and its parts. Because there are often many ways to reach a desired end, the authors have not attempted to describe for any type of building or any feature of a building a particular plan as being the only successful solution to the problem. The authors believe in experimentation. They do not believe that the perfect school building ever has been built or ever will be built. Neither do they believe in any one way, any stock plan, or any standard solution. Each building should be an improvement over the one built previously; it should be different not for the sake of being different but because the planners of that building think there is a better way of interpreting program into plant in that situation.

The Relationship of Program to Plant

THE truth of the principle that the school plant should be designed to fit the desired program has so long been recognized that it can well be taken as an axiom. It has been stated and emphasized time and again in school-plant literature and has already been repeated several times in this volume, yet in practice it is still honored as much in the breach as in its observance. The reasons for failure to heed it are many and varied. All who have responsibilities in the planning of schools must share the blame.

The authors have known of cases where conscientious architects have tried to get specific information about program needs from local school authorities without much success and have been told to design a building similar to one that they designed for some other community. Or they have been told that they were engaged because they were school architects and therefore they must know the answers and should go ahead and plan the building. In other instances architects apparently did not want much information lest it upset preconceived notions which they had regarding the building or lest it cause them to abandon a stock solution. In some cases they have belittled the efforts of educators to supply information by dealing directly with the board of education and by raising the excuse of excessive cost whenever any suggestions for changes were made.

It takes concentrated creative thought to develop the educational specifications and the same kind of thought by the architect to translate them into a good building design. It also takes time. It is much easier and quicker to let the matter go by default and hope that the experience of the architect with other buildings will produce another school building which will do the job well enough. But lack of attention to the relationship of program to plant may well be the most extravagant defect in the building program.

As an introduction to the second half of the book, this chapter will emphasize the continually developing school program and its relationship to school plant.

General Aspects of the School Program

BASIC to any discussion of the school program must be an understanding of what is to be included in it, definitions of certain terms, particularly if they are interpreted variously in different localities or regions, and a focusing of attention upon concepts and characteristics which may be overlooked.

THE SCHOOL PROGRAM: WHAT IS IT?

Too often the school program is considered as an accumulation of courses or subjects. While reading, writing, and arithmetic, as well as science, social studies, music, art, and physical education, are prominent aspects of the school program, they are not the entire program. There are many other areas of learning which cannot be so simply organized into subjects or courses, including those with such objectives as the development of citizenship, respect for property, respect for the rights of others, ability to work cooperatively, social graces, good work habits, and other desirable attitudes, appreciations, and habits too numerous to list here. Some of these are developed coincidentally with the development of skills and the mastery of content in organized courses. Others are even more intangible and their realization must come bit by bit from various phases of the total complex of actions and reactions of pupil to pupil, pupil to teacher, and pupil to total school environment.

Such intangible factors as the development of attitudes of sportsmanship and fair play, for example, may be fostered not so much from work in the classroom as from competition in such extracurricular activities as dramatics, athletics, and student elections. An understanding of the services which are provided in everyday life by nurses and doctors may arise through the school health program in its service aspect rather than through its direct instructional phase. Accordingly, it may be seen that the school program is a very complex whole. Moreover, in its noncurricular or extracurricular, as well as in its purely curricular aspects, the proper functioning of the program to a large extent depends upon the provision of suitable plant facilities.

THE ELEMENTARY AND THE SECONDARY SCHOOL

Any discussion of school program or school plant must make frequent references to the elementary school and to the secondary school. These terms do not have the same meanings for all persons. A distinction receiving common acceptance is the use of the term elementary school to cover that portion of the school career of each child which is spent in the kindergarten and the first six grades. Regardless of organization by buildings in any particular school district the term secondary school is accordingly applied to grades 7 through 12. For convenience these definitions will be the ones followed in this book. In some places school buildings are used to house groups from the kindergarten through the seventh or eighth grades. The term elementary is sometimes applied to these situations, but by the above definitions such a school is a combined elementary and secondary school, the seventh and eighth grades being a portion of the secondary school housed with the elementary school group.

Except in smaller school districts where six-year secondary schools are fairly common, the secondary grades are often divided into two sections, the junior high school and the senior high school. In the most common pattern the junior high school includes grades 7 through 9 and the senior high school includes grades 10 through 12, although two-year junior high school and four-year senior high school combinations are not uncommon. Many other patterns besides the ones here described exist, largely for convenience of housing rather than for reasons attached to the educational program.

There are educational authorities who propose that the 13th and 14th grades be considered as secondary school grades, while others refer to them as junior college grades. Any attempt to discuss junior college housing is beyond the scope of this book.

THE CONCEPT OF AN ARTICULATED PROGRAM

The organization of school systems into elementary and secondary divisions is a source of many problems in the education of boys and girls. Increased understanding of the learning process and of the principles of child growth indicates that continuous sequences of learning activities based upon individual needs and keyed to each child's rate of progress and achievement are necessary. However, the fact that school systems are organized on this dual basis works directly against articulation and tends to cause a severe break in each pupil's educational career. For example, much has been done in the elementary school to adapt the program to individual needs, but the results generally do not carry over smoothly into the junior high school.

This is an important problem which is perhaps too little recognized in education today. Each of the two school divisions has its own historical background, and their integration into a single continuous system has been only superficial. The gap is very commonly perpetuated through customary administrative and supervisory organizations (witness the prevalence of the elementary school supervisorship), and distinctions in teacher education courses, in certification requirements, and perhaps worst of all in school district organization in many states.

This is not the place to try to solve this problem, and it must be admitted that the solution will not be easy to find. It is important, however, that those who are engaged in defining school programs as a basis for school-plant planning, who perhaps have an opportunity to develop educational specifications unrestricted by the patterns of the past, and who may be correspondingly and concurrently developing administrative and supervisory organizational patterns, should bear in mind the evils which result from this lack of articulation. And they should plan as far as possible to close the gap in the interest of developing a smoothly flowing program of learning activities for each boy and girl.

NONINSTRUCTIONAL ASPECTS OF THE PROGRAM

The total program of activities which must be accommodated by a school plant will include many which have primarily service rather than instructional functions. Among these are feeding pupils at noon; health services, including first-aid and physical examinations; promotion of physiological and psychological comfort; administrative and guidance activities; recreational and social functions; and various forms of community service. While many of these program phases have learning values if properly organized and administered, their primary purpose is that of service. They are, however, important and their plant needs can only be properly determined if they are carefully studied in the planning process.

School Program Trends

THE schools, like all social institutions, change as years pass by. Some of these changes are quantitative; others are qualitative. One has only to reflect upon the great increase in the number of boys and girls who have extended their educational careers into high school and college in the past half century to recognize the extent of the quantitative change. In terms of the character of the program, the schools have changed the content and methods of instruction to keep abreast of new knowledge and the changing needs of society.

Educational changes are not made for the sake of change itself, for actually the public school system is probably one of America's most conservative and traditional institutions. Changes, however, occur, although slowly and with a definite lag behind need. Changes will continue to occur, mostly through experimentation. This is one of the valuable outcomes of local control of educational programs under the framework of American democracy.

GENERAL ASPECTS: ALL LEVELS

The early ungraded school was a simple and friendly institution, and its simple organization permitted maximum attention by the teacher to the needs of each individual pupil on the basis of his current state of achievement and progress. The growth in number of pupils and the development of mass education led to the organization known as the graded system, and inherent in it are many of the educational problems which trouble educators and parents today. If the numbers of pupils were small enough that the ungraded school could be revived, and if to it could be applied today's understandings of psychology and child- growth, many of these problems would disappear. There is a great need in the field of education to put into effect theory which is well established but too little practiced in the organization of the curriculum and in instruction.

Considerable attention is also being paid to psychological and social theory which is peripheral to the curriculum itself. Much of this has relation to psychological and social attitudes on the part of the pupil. One of the trends arising from this thinking is a reaction against large schools, both in terms of pupil enrollment and in terms of the mass of structure of the building. Elementary schools with a thousand or more pupils bring together in one spot too many youngsters to make it possible to give each individual child the attention which he merits both in the classroom and elsewhere in the total school situation. With large groups it becomes more necessary to have an excessive number of rules and regulations, rigid routines for the handling of crowds, and a cacophony of gongs and bells to distribute and redistribute the pupils in the spaces to which they must be assigned. This too massive school society, too easily fraught with the emotions of the crowd, is not psychologically desirable.

Similarly there has been a distinct trend away from large, compact, and monumental buildings which tend to become institutional, unfriendly, and even frightening to small children. Elementary schools in particular have been scaled down in height and spread out in area wherever it is possible to find enough land. Even in congested areas the provision of more and smaller schools is the tendency. Generally, where larger groups must be brought together, larger sites are obtained, and the building is spread out into several units or wings, each one of which in its psychological effect on the child may be somewhat the same as a separate small school. Along with this there has been a tendency in design to remove institutionalism and coldness. In some cases it may even be necessary to sacrifice easy maintenance in some features of the building to keep it from appearing too "antiseptic."

Even in schools for children on the secondary level these same needs and trends hold true, and the tremendously large secondary school is no longer desired. Again, the most important reasons are that, in a very large institution, the individual loses his identity, there is a lack of cohesiveness of school spirit and morale, the school tends to become excessively structured in its program and routines, and the emotionalism of the crowd tends to replace the companionship of the small group.

TRENDS IN THE ELEMENTARY SCHOOL PROGRAM

If there is any one characteristic of the modern elementary school program which distinguishes it most from that of the past, it is the emphasis upon learning through activity. Activity work in units of instruction serves to give both meaning and motivation to the basic skill program. Furthermore, the integration of learning from various subject matter fields is brought about by the concentration of activities about a natural center of interest to the end that the whole child and his growth in all aspects become the objectives of teaching.

To realize the desired integration, departmentalization has been almost completely eliminated from elementary schools in favor of the self-contained classroom organization. Under this arrangement one teacher has major responsibility for the complete education of one group of children for a school year or more. This teacher may need and receive help from other teachers or specialists in certain areas, but in general is responsible for the entire program. The job of the teacher is to understand each child as a total personality and to guide and stimulate his learning in all areas, rather than to be responsible only for a particular segment of subject matter accomplishment. This teacher is a specialist in children rather than in teaching only one branch of subject matter.

The self-contained classroom attempts to be a complete learning laboratory and school living space for the teacher and a group of pupils. It is spacious, or should be, and of a shape which encourages flexible and informal arrangement. It should facilitate individual and small group work with the teacher in a helping role, as contrasted with a formal arrangement of seating with the teacher at the front of the room lecturing and hearing recitations. The self-contained classroom is in essence the school-day home of the child, as well as a laboratory in which he experiments in such fashion that his learning is promoted.

Unfortunately, most of the elementary school buildings erected during the 1920's and the 1930's, when the emphasis was so heavily upon construction of the so-called standard classroom, are not well adapted to the self-contained classroom approach because the rooms are almost always too small. The newer buildings, beginning with some erected in the late 1930's, and planned with the activity program in mind, provide much larger classrooms and make it possible to break away from the stereotyped program of the older school. Actually many of the school buildings constructed before World War I have larger classrooms and for that reason are better for modern use than those built between the two wars. The buildings which are being erected today are designed generally for the self-contained classroom approach.

There are some learning areas in which a self-contained classroom cannot entirely meet the requirements. Obviously instruction in instrumental music given to individuals or small groups will require a space so located and so constructed that the work will not disturb other pupils. Also, provision must be made for those large group activities which involve at any one time the pupils of more than one classroom. Among these may be included physical education, certain forms of dramatics, and some of the choral work.

In the truly self-contained classroom the free reading or library work will be provided for by a library table or library corner. If the self-contained classroom purpose is to be carried out in full, there will not be a separate library-type space in the elementary school building. There may be, of course, a book or a resource center where library books not in current use may be stored and where other resource materials may be kept when inactive.

In subsequent chapters in the discussion of sites, classrooms, and special facilities for elementary schools, the effect of the school program upon the school plant will be brought out in considerable detail. The brief discussion which has been introduced here has been primarily for the purpose of giving the reader a basic understanding of the nature of the elementary school program as the authors of this book view it.

TRENDS IN THE SECONDARY SCHOOL PROGRAM

That section of the public school program now generally referred to as the secondary school has had a mixed history. The lower third of this program, roughly that part usually assigned to grades 7 and 8, still bears traces of the terminal learnings assigned to these grades in earlier years when only a relatively few pupils continued through high school. The upper two thirds of today's secondary school program had its beginnings in the early academies and high schools whose primary purpose was preparation for college. As more and more pupils, not college bound, strove to get a high school education, and it was found that many of these pupils did not have the intellectual capacity to succeed in college preparatory work, there were introduced various types of hand work or manual training. For the same reasons, schools began to offer other work of a practical nature including bookkeeping and other early courses intended to prepare pupils for business vocations. Also, there came the introduction of various other subjects presumably intended for election by the pupils who did not plan to go to college or who were unsuccessful in college preparatory courses, and who had no interest in practical arts or business education.

All these changes were in response to a recognition of the needs of the pupils who were flooding into the high schools. The currently existing conglomerate programs of the high schools of America represent attempts to meet the requirements for education of all the boys and girls of high school age. The present program is truly an aggregate whose parts have historical justification in earnest endeavors to meet the needs of pupils. For many these needs are relatively well met; for others there are serious gaps in the learning program—a fact that is well recognized by educators.

Aims of Secondary Education

There have been many attempts to establish a coherent body of objectives for secondary education around which a well-integrated and carefully articulated program could be developed. In this respect the complexity of modern civilization has presented the schools with a very difficult task. In recent years emphasis has been placed upon a number of general competencies required for citizenship in all of its various phases. These range from the performance of one's obligations as members of a democratic society to the development of occupational abilities. Attention is directed to leisure time satisfactions, ethical values, consumer competence, and many other abilities which are deemed desirable as preparation for living in the modern world. Statements referring to these competencies are not phrased in terms of subjects, and new courses have not been organized around these competencies. In fact, these statements of competencies have not been intended to promote new courses in "leisure time satisfactions," "ethical values," etc. The result to date has been a continuation of the existing framework of subjects with some new ones added, and with varying emphasis in all courses on the newer objectives. This has been accompanied by decreased emphasis upon subject requirements in such major fields as mathematics, English, and science.

Criticisms of Secondary School Programs

The secondary schools have been subject to criticism from many angles. There are those citizens who wish that more emphasis would be placed upon various subject learnings and who cite deficiencies in spelling, writing, and arithmetic among high school graduates as a basis for their criticism. On the other hand, there are those who blame the schools for the social ills and delinquencies of youth and call for greater emphasis on social habits and the attributes of good citizenship. Among educators, there are those who, taking their cue from psychological learnings which emphasize the need for wholeness in the educational process, condemn departmentalization and belittle any emphasis on the teaching of separate subjects or subject matter per se. At the other extreme, there are educators who believe that there are serious deficiencies in the teaching of fundamental skills needed in later life and who clamor for more emphasis upon basic subjects.

In all this welter of conflicting demands, there are a few bright spots which stand out as signposts toward a goal which is not yet clearly discerned. It is probably true, for example, that modern teaching methods have brought about better learning of basic skills on the part of the average pupil. It should also be noted that gains have been made in reducing extreme compartmentalization and that general curriculum organization is moving toward a broad fields pattern. There seems, however, to be a limit to the extent to which progress can be made in this direction because of general acceptance of the need for differentiation of programs tailored to meet the needs of different pupils.

The Need for Integration

There can be no denying that extreme discreteness of learnings should be avoided and that instruction which results only in an accumulation of isolated facts or skill elements without meaning or understanding of relationships among them is of little value. For many years attempts have been made to organize instruction so that learnings can be tied together and draw meaning from one another. Early attempts were aimed at "correlation," and subsequently there was a brief flurry of efforts to obtain "fusion." Later the word became "integration" and eventually one arrived at the "core curriculum." All of these attempts have had value in the breaking down of the rigid barriers between subjects and in the development of an understanding on the part of teachers that rich meaning is essential to learning.

In the elementary school where all pupils study substantially the same subjects, the development of activity units and the self-contained classroom organization have been highly successful mechanisms for achieving integration. However, in the secondary school similar efforts have not been so successful because of the need for more highly specialized preparation of the teacher and for greater differentiation of program to meet the needs of different pupils. The so-called core curriculum, for example, has often been limited in practice to a mixture of English and social studies in grades 7 and 8 and occasionally in higher grades.

General Education and Special Education

General education is an accumulation of learnings which are of value to all pupils, whatever may be their purpose or their future. Special education may be defined as including that instruction which has a rather specific purpose in terms of the future needs of certain individual pupils. As school courses are usually organized, there are some which are largely general education and others which are largely special education. The problem of classification is not simple, however, because there are items or fields of learning which are of general education value for all pupils, but which when pursued to a higher level have special education values for some pupils. In some courses or subjects, as customarily organized, the learnings have mixed aims. It must also be recognized that the educational planning for individuals will vary in the relative emphasis on general education and special education. There is reason to believe that the more able pupil should postpone his specialization and work at more advanced levels in general education. It is on these higher levels that the distinction between common learnings, as usually defined, and general education tends to break down and that general education is extended to include much of what is often called the "liberal arts."

Problems of Organization

The organization of the instructional program on the secondary level is exceedingly complex and involves many difficult problems. By the advent of the ninth grade pupils are beginning to differentiate their programs instead of all taking the same courses. It is on this level generally that foreign languages are introduced and that the more complex mathematics courses such as algebra are offered. The need for advanced preparation of teachers in special subject fields gave rise to the organization of the instructional program by courses, and it has been the major factor in the survival of this pattern.

Courses and course credits have been criticized and even ridiculed for years as evidence of overemphasis on technicalities of organization. Nevertheless, changes in the secondary school program have largely taken the form of addition or substitution of courses. And unfortunately the effect of the demands of society for the introduction of new courses has been largely to dilute the program. There are many who urge a new form of organization to solve this problem, and the core curriculum is one attempt in this direction. But the core curriculum has not prospered because of the scope of the program and the difficulty of securing teachers with a sufficient breadth of preparation and a sufficient understanding of the nature and needs of children. These attempts to find new patterns of organization, however, have not ceased. And it is well that they have not because from them it is possible that some plan will arise which will reduce some of the existing evils, perhaps knit the program more closely together, and develop a pattern which will better meet the needs of all boys and girls.

There is good reason to believe that the pupil needs, rather than a series of teachers of different divisions of subject matter, one person who really knows him. This person would have an interest in him, help map out his learning program, guide him in his learning, and encourage him to develop according to his interests and abilities. This need is no less for a youth of secondary school age than for a younger child. This suggests that the trend may be toward one teacher for a particular group of children in the secondary school for general education in one general-purpose classroom, with suitable provision of other teachers and classrooms for the special education learnings.

There are also those who think that integration may be achieved by having a team of three or four teachers assigned primarily to one group of several scores of children. The major emphasis in this enterprise would, of course, be upon the field of general education or common learnings. The group would frequently assemble as one for planning and for other activities of common interest and would then break up into subgroups for other purposes. Various resources of the total school plant and of the total faculty would be available for special education purposes.

In both of these schemes the central theme is a grouping of general education learnings in a sort of self-contained classroom situation with special-purpose teachers as resource persons for such specialized work as instruction in science, higher mathematics, foreign languages, bookkeeping, office practice, home economics, industrial arts, etc. Plans of this nature have been introduced in one form or another, but none has gained common acceptance. Possibly these are transitional devices which can be used between the self-contained classroom plan extending through the 8th grade and the specialized course pattern in the upper secondary school years. The one caution is that the substantially differing needs of individual pupils must not be neglected in attempts to achieve integration.

Needs of More Able Pupils

It might be worth while to mention that one basic problem which is perhaps not given enough attention in the planning of secondary school programs is how to satisfy the needs of the more able pupils. These boys and girls in particular will pursue programs involving much mathematics, science, and foreign languages as preparation for later advanced (collegiate) learning. There is some evidence that sequential and continuous programs in basic areas of learning, perhaps in some form of broad fields organization geared to individual advancement at will (or at the natural rate of achievement), may be the key to their needs. These folks have an important role in society, since it is to a large extent through their discoveries and inventions that progress is made in medicine, engineering, industry, and other fields of endeavor which are so basic to the advancement of the American way of life.

Guidance

One of the more important problems in the area of secondary education at the present time is the prevalence of maladjustment between the individual pupil and the instructional program which he has chosen or which has been chosen for him by his parents or which he has had to take because of certain inflexibilities in the offerings of the school. This problem long has been evident to those concerned with the instruction of youth, and the need of adequate guidance services to reduce this maladjustment has also been apparent for a long period of time. There has been a great deal of development in the field of guidance theory and in the educational psychology and principles of learning upon which it is based. Guidance practice, however, tends to lag seriously behind theory, and general practice tends to lag even more seriously behind best practice.

Uncertainties in Present Thinking

The difficult problem of the secondary school program is further complicated by the current rapid growth in enrollment which is forcing new secondary school construction upon school systems which have not yet found a new and workable pattern proved to be superior to the one which evolved, perhaps haphazardly, over the past few decades. The crux of the problem is that there is no widespread agreement among educators or the public as to the role of secondary education in our society or how it should be organized. Citizenship education may be accepted by many as a simple definition of the principal objective, but there is no clear picture of this objective translated into organization or into the framework of instructional methods. Many think that the course-unit-credit-period form of program organization stands in the way of realization of the comprehensive objective. There is considerable agreement that basic thinking about the purposes of secondary education in our society, rather than tinkering with schedules and courses, is needed if present uncertainties are to be resolved in a satisfactory way. But to date no one has found an alternative organizational pattern which is generally regarded as workable. Accordingly, and perhaps unfortunately, the only available answer to those who must build seems to be the provision of general and specialized classrooms with as much flexibility built into the structures as possible.

Planning for Change

THOSE who have struggled with the problem of planning school plants for school programs which are changing or are expected to change have found no way in which the future can be forecast with infallibility. There are, however, a few points which are generally accepted as valuable in trying to plan for the unforeseeable. One of the most important things to do is to be certain that the probability of change is not only realized but freely acknowledged. It is well for school program planners to speculate freely about the scope and nature of possible changes, and to examine critically the plant implications of all reasonably possible future changes in each and every aspect of the school program. If this exploration is freely and fully carried out, the building planning is most likely to take into account every possibility of insuring flexibility of structure, internal and external expansibility of spaces, convertibility and interchangeability of facilities, and avoidance of hindrances to changes in arrangement and assignment of building spaces or site areas. Obviously, adequate site area is essential for this purpose.

The problems of planning secondary schools to meet the needs of the program are today much more difficult than for elementary schools because of the greater uncertainties regarding the future shape of the secondary school program. Only within the limits of present practice and reasonable estimates of modifications to be expected will it be possible to talk about the secondary school building and site.

In the next few chapters the total school plant and its various important features (site, classrooms, special areas for instruction, and service areas) will be discussed in detail. Throughout this discussion references will be made to the school program, both elementary and secondary as may be applicable, to illustrate how the functioning of the educational program is the key to school plant design.

CHAPTER 12

THE SCHOOL SITE

Importance of Selecting a Good Site
Characteristics of a Good Site
Development of the Site

O NE cannot erect a school building unless there is land upon which it can be placed. With this statement, there can be no quarrel, but one can hardly go further in describing a school site to the citizens of an entire community without risk of sharp disagreement. Particularly in small and medium-sized localities an intense public discussion of a school site problem often develops, even to the point of acrimony and vituperation and sometimes gross distortion of facts. These discussions are usually centered on such matters as location, size or cost, or identity of the owner of the property in question. Much less frequently is there sound public debate on the educational adequacy of a proposed site or its suitability for public recreation or other intended uses.

Importance of Selecting a Good Site

WHILE the site must, of course, provide space for the building, this is only part of its purpose. The outdoor facilities and the rooms and equipment within the building are part of the same school plant, and together they either facilitate or restrict and impede the development and operation of a good educational program. To select a site which is educationally inadequate is essentially the same kind of error as omitting some important room or space within the building. A school building otherwise well planned and well constructed, but erected on a site which is poorly located or otherwise unsuitable, may actually represent a considerable waste of public funds.

UNSATISFACTORY SITES

The many unsatisfactory solutions of the site problem which are found throughout the country stem usually from lack of knowledge and understanding of the purposes and uses of the site and what these imply by way of space, topography, and other site features. The community disputes usually arise when some educator or other individual has a vision which is not shared by the board of education, municipal authorities, or other community leaders.

An illustration of the kind of dispute which often occurs is that of an eastern city of more than 30,000 people with a school system of enviable reputation. A new building of 17 classrooms was to be erected some 25 or 30 years ago as an elementary school and designed for later conversion to a junior high school. At the time there was available a tract of 15 to 20 acres of vacant land, suitably located and otherwise desirable for school purposes. The superintendent of schools, a wise and farsighted educator, tried hard to convince the board of education to acquire a substantial portion of this tract. The school program of that day was not sufficiently developed to require the immediate use of a large site, and it was difficult to impress the board and citizens generally with the need for it. Also there was a strong feeling on the part of the municipal officials and other influential citizens that only a minimum of land should be removed from the tax rolls. The outcome was that only $4\frac{1}{2}$ acres were purchased. Today the physical education, recreation, and athletic activities of this school and of the neighborhood it serves, which are much more highly developed and extensive than when the building was erected, are greatly handicapped. This situation is now acknowledged in this community as an outstanding example of lack of foresight because the adjacent land is almost completely occupied by relatively new and fairly expensive houses, and expansion of the site would be so costly as to be quite impossible for all practical purposes. Strangely enough, such is the perversity of human affairs, attempts to obtain adequate school sites in this city are still met by the argument that land cannot be freely spared from the tax assessment lists.

Characteristics of a Good Site

It must, of course, be recognized that there is no standard pattern which can be applied in judging all school sites. It is as true of the site as of the building itself that the nature of the school program should be a primary determinant of the nature of the physical facilities. Conditions vary from community to community with respect to school programs, public recreation programs, nonschool facilities available for recreational use, financial resources, and other significant conditions. Because of these variations, the definition of a good school site will not be identical in all places. There are, however, certain commonly accepted criteria, or ways of looking at a prospective site, which are reasonably applicable in all cases. These relate to location, suitability for the school program, suitability as a place for construction, and aesthetic possibilities. Each of these is discussed below.

The characteristics of a good site must be consistent with the emphasis in Chapter 11 upon emerging patterns or even unforeseen features of future school programs, which must be taken into account in designing new school plants today. In site selection and development, as in designing the building itself, it is necessary to plan for today's program and still keep the door open for future growth and change.

LOCATION

In considering the location of a school building, attention must be directed to two important aspects—accessibility and environment. The first has to do with the convenience and safety of pupils and others in traveling to and from the building; the second with the attractiveness and whole-someness of the surroundings of the school.

Accessibility

The evaluation of an existing or proposed site as to its accessibility requires first of all a knowledge of the boundaries of the geographical area to be served by the school. If the site is one already accommodating a school building in use, the determination of the area served is simple enough. If, on the other hand, a new site is being sought or new uses of an existing site are being studied, the whole problem of determining a suitable attendance district must be faced. This requires examination of such diverse factors as density of pupil population, desired maximum and minimum size of school, capacity and enrollment of other school buildings in the school system, travel distances and provisions for transportation, existing layouts of streets and other public facilities, natural geographical boundaries, proposals of official planning agencies, and the like. The weighing of these many factors and the establishing of a suitable pattern of attendance areas throughout the school district are part of the survey process, and as such they are discussed earlier in this volume.[1]

[1] Consideration of this problem permeates the whole process of formulating recommendations which is discussed at length in Chapter 5.

With the boundaries of the attendance area known, the evaluation of a site in terms of accessibility is reduced to a consideration of travel distances, methods of travel, and conditions along the routes of travel within that area. The best site from the standpoint of accessibility alone is the one which permits the greatest number of pupils to travel in comfort and safety over the shortest routes to and from school. There is, of course, much room for subjective judgment on these matters, as is evidenced by the fact that walking a long distance to school was much more accepted a generation ago than it is today. In general, the trend has been and continues to be toward shorter distances for pupils to walk and greater concern for the hazards encountered en route.

Travel Distances. The generally accepted limit for pupils in kindergarten through the sixth grade to walk to and from school is three fourths of a mile each way, but there are many who would advocate a half-mile maximum. For pupils of junior high school age, the commonly accepted limit is one and one half miles, while for senior high school pupils this is extended to two miles.[2] These limits must, of course, be adjusted in the light of any adverse conditions along the routes of travel. For example, even a quarter mile might be an excessive distance for a pupil to walk along a heavily traveled highway where there are no sidewalks. Where transportation is provided, the distances of travel can be substantially extended. It seems to be generally agreed that 30 minutes is a satisfactory maximum time for elementary school pupils to be on a bus each morning or afternoon and that for secondary school pupils the time limit can be increased to one hour.[3] If the population is sparse or if otherwise suitable sites are not available, these distances or travel times may have to be extended, but the goal should be to locate the sites so that the greatest possible number of pupils live within the suggested limits.

Centrality of Site. Other things being equal, the location of a site should be reasonably central within the populated portion of the area to be served, with due allowance for future residential developments or other shifts of population. However, the desire for centrality must be weighed against the hazards and other obstacles encountered in reaching the site. For pupils who walk to school, thought must be given to the streets and railroads which pupils must cross and the volume and speed of traffic they carry, to

[2] National Council on Schoolhouse Construction, *Guide for Planning School Plants.* Nashville, Tenn.: The Council, 1953, p. 25. Also, American Association of School Administrators, *American School Buildings.* Twenty-seventh Yearbook. Washington: The Association, 1949, p. 73.

[3] *Loc. cit.*

factory districts and undesirable neighborhoods through which pupils might have to pass, to isolated tracts of vacant or wooded lands where a molester might lurk, to the presence or lack of sidewalks, and to steep grades or other adverse conditions along the way. For pupils who use public transportation, there should be concern for safety in getting to and from the buses, for the number and nature of places of transfer, and for the possibility of avoiding travel at times when large numbers of shoppers or workers are traveling in the same direction on the same bus routes. If pupils are transported by school bus, there are fewer occasions when travel hazards must be considered, although there are situations where a bad bridge, a dangerous hill, or a busy thoroughfare can be avoided by proper location of the site. In all of the concern for travel conditions it is extremely important that adequate consideration be given to possible future changes; full cooperation with public officials responsible for planning such changes is essential.

Often, there will be a choice between a small site which is centrally located but educationally inadequate and a large site which is educationally superior but not so central. It is generally considered better in such instances to sacrifice centrality for the other desired qualities, even if some added transportation cost is involved. A site which is too small or otherwise inadequate will hold a heavy hand for many, many decades on the development of a suitable program for the children and the adults of the community. The welfare of people is more important than mere centrality of location.

Environment

A wholesome emotional outlook, an appreciation of beauty, and a respect for the property and rights of others might possibly be developed in pupils in drab and ugly surroundings, but they would seem to be much easier of attainment in a school environment which is attractive and quiet. Wherever possible, a school should be located in a residential or park district, rather than a business or industrial area. Barrooms and other places which might have undesirable influences on youth should be avoided, and the school should be away from busy, noisy thoroughfares or places where crowds pass to and from work or on other missions. The streets and residential areas around the school should be attractively landscaped and well maintained. The view in any direction from the building should be pleasing. A clean, uncontaminated atmosphere, free of smoke and undesirable odors, should always be sought.

Since a neighborhood is likely to change considerably in the lifetime of a school building, it is emphasized again at this point that every effort should be made to foresee future changes in the area around the site under consideration. Present zoning, proposed zoning changes, and other aspects of the plans of public authorities as well as the opinions of informed persons, should be taken into account before a final choice of site is made.

SUITABILITY FOR SCHOOL PROGRAM

To the man on the street the relationship between program and physical plant is most readily apparent with respect to the outdoor facilities. As he passes some buildings, he sees hordes of children trying to play in a small, barren area, often pushing and shoving one another because there is insufficient space for games and other more orderly activities needed to provide exercise and release of energy. At other buildings, where the land area is more ample, he sees more organized play with less rowdyism and he may also see evidences of such educational activities as planting a garden, studying plant or animal life in the field, or learning principles of conservation by actual outdoor experiments.

The "postage stamp" sites on which many of our still-used nineteenth-century urban schoolhouses are located are mute testimony to the need for foresight with respect to the program to be accommodated on the school grounds. The persons who selected these small tracts of land a half century or more ago did so in terms of the limited school programs of that day. Outdoor activities were a very minor part of the school program; hence, sites did not need to accommodate physical education classes or week-end or vacation playground activities. Adults were so busy making a living that they had little time for an evening or week-end game of softball or other kinds of recreation for which space is now so eagerly sought. Those who select new sites today should learn from this experience and look upon future expansions and changes of program, especially in the fields of physical education, athletics, and recreation, as a normal expectancy.

Size of Site

The most important single question that can be raised about the suitability of a proposed site is whether it provides sufficient and appropriate space for all of the in-school, evening, and vacation activities of the children and adults of the area to be served, as well as the building itself and the related service facilities. Since the programs to be accommodated vary from place to place and from school to school, no standard list of site facilities can be given. However, the following list of possible needs may serve as a starting point in local planning. The site should provide:

1. Space for the original building and any future additions which might reasonably be made to it.
2. Space for lawns, preferably with no part of the building or any future addition closer than 100 feet from any edge of the site.
3. Space for walks from the street, from drives and parking areas, and possibly from one portion of the building to another, with proper separation of walks from drives and other vehicular areas.
4. Space for bicycle entrances and storage racks, with proper separation from pedestrian areas and spaces used by motor vehicles.
5. Space for drives and parking lots for employees, pupils, and patrons, including persons who come to the school for community affairs within the building or on the athletic fields.
6. Space for drives, loading docks, and turning areas for trucks making deliveries of fuel, cafeteria supplies, or other items used in the building.
7. Space for bus garages.
8. Space for outdoor play, physical education, and athletic activities of children, with suitable separation of areas for different ages and different kinds of activities, and with enough room for alternate use to permit rest and renewal of turf on heavily used play areas.
9. Space for nature study, gardening, farming, and conservation activities where required by the program.
10. Space for general recreational activities of the community which are to be accommodated on school grounds.
11. Space to provide a suitable margin for future expansion of present activities or the development of activities not now foreseen.

Number of Acres. No categorical statement can be given regarding the number of acres required to provide these spaces. An obvious factor affecting the acreage is the number of pupils, but there are many others. Before the size for a given school can be determined, there must be a local decision with respect to each type of space suggested in the preceding list, and quantities and sizes of spaces must be determined. The shape, topography, nature of soil, and other characteristics of the site may render parts of it unusable or difficult to use effectively, and thus affect the acreage needed. Finally, the design of the building itself and the placement of the building and other facilities on the site have a very definite bearing on how much space they require and thus on the total number of acres needed.

With all of these variables to be considered, the only satisfactory way to determine the acreage needed is to make trial layouts of each site under consideration to see whether all of the facilities can be provided on it. Templates cut to scale to represent the building and the various outdoor facilities are useful in this approach, since they can easily be arranged in various ways on drawings of the different sites. The services of an architect or landscape architect and of an educational consultant can be very helpful in this process.

Recognizing the impossibility of setting any absolute standards of size, some national groups have proposed as a general guide certain minimum acreages for schools of various sizes. The American Association of School Administrators [4] and the National Council on Schoolhouse Construction [5] are in agreement in recommending for an elementary school at least five acres plus one acre for each 100 pupils in ultimate enrollment and for a secondary school at least 10 acres plus one acre for each 100 pupils. Thus, an elementary school that will ultimately have 300 pupils should have a site of at least eight acres, while a secondary school of the same size should have 13 acres. It must be kept in mind that these are minimum sizes and that larger areas are usually advisable where they can be obtained.

Before accepting these minimum sizes, it would be well to make a trial layout of facilities as suggested above because all too often the space required for facilities other than the building itself is underestimated. Also, it would be well to think carefully about possible future expansions of the program and the added space they will need. Sites of 10 to 20 acres for elementary schools and of 25 or more acres for secondary schools are being selected with increasing frequency, and the uses to which they are put should be of interest to anyone trying to decide how much land to acquire. The long-range plan for the development of one 80 acre secondary school site is shown in Figure 4. This site is in a small suburban community of only a few thousand people, but one which has the possibility of becoming a large city within the period of usefulness of the school buildings now being erected. Many thousands of children and adults in future years will profit from the farsightedness of those responsible for the decision to build on this large tract of land and to plan in advance its future development.

[4] American Association of School Administrators, *op. cit.,* p. 75.

[5] National Council on Schoolhouse Construction, *op. cit.,* pp. 26–27.

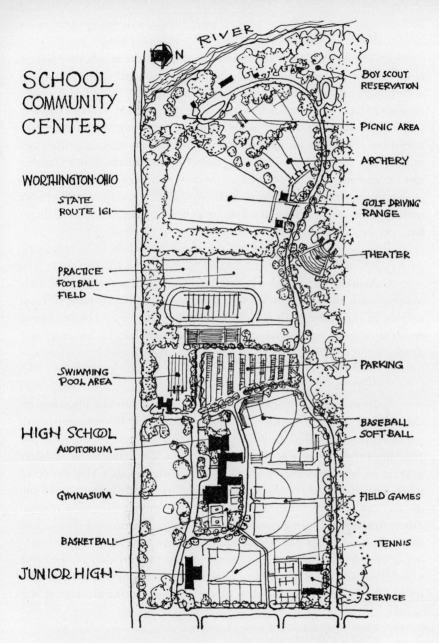

N RIVER

SCHOOL
COMMUNITY
CENTER

WORTHINGTON·OHIO

STATE
ROUTE 161

PRACTICE
FOOTBALL
FIELD

SWIMMING
POOL AREA

HIGH SCHOOL
AUDITORIUM

GYMNASIUM

BASKETBALL

JUNIOR HIGH

BOY SCOUT
RESERVATION

PICNIC AREA

ARCHERY

GOLF DRIVING
RANGE

THEATER

PARKING

BASEBALL
SOFT BALL

FIELD GAMES

TENNIS

SERVICE

*Figure 4. Plan for Development of an 80 Acre High School
Site. (From Daniels, Arthur S. and Packard, Marion V., A*
Plan for the Worthington School-Community Recreation
Center, p. 7. Columbus, Ohio: The Authors, 1954. (Mimeo.)

Other Physical Characteristics

Acreage alone will not satisfy the needs of the school program. A large tract of irregular shape, uneven topography, rocky and barren soil, or swampy land is sometimes available at low cost, but it may be extremely expensive over the years in terms of restrictions on the school program. Presence of these features on a site, however, need not bar it from consideration. They can be ignored if there is adequate acreage with more suitable characteristics, or if suitable spaces can be obtained at reasonable cost by grading, drainage, or other corrective measures. It should be kept in mind, also, that some of these seemingly adverse conditions could prove quite useful in the teaching of science or other subjects, and should, therefore, not be categorically rejected.

SUITABILITY FOR CONSTRUCTION

Another criterion is that the school site should permit the construction of a building at reasonable cost and at an appropriate place in relation to the other facilities to be developed on the site. The services of an architect and related specialists are especially valuable in judging a proposed site on this criterion.

Proper Site Layout

It is of primary importance that the site permit the placement of the building and other facilities in proper relationship to one another. All too often this is ignored during selection of the site and sometimes is not faced until the floor plan of the building is fixed. The result of such neglect is likely to be an awkward and unsafe arrangement over a long period of years. Drives may be so located that supplies have to be carried long distances to a supply room within the building, pupils may have to cross drives to reach the playgrounds, the outdoor play areas may be so close to the classrooms that playground noises interfere with classes in the building, or the playgrounds may be so far away that they are difficult to supervise. These are but a few illustrations of the need for the most careful study of a proposed site in terms of the arrangement of facilities it will permit.

Cost of Improvements

Quite apart from the purchase price of the land, there are many site features which affect cost, some to a minor extent and others very greatly. Insofar as possible, these should be ascertained in advance and considered along with the purchase price. Among these conditions are:

1. The need for extensive hauling of dirt because of a surplus or shortage on the site.
2. The presence of rock or other conditions affecting the cost of making necessary excavations and ditches.
3. The presence of quicksand or other unsatisfactory subsoil conditions requiring special footings or piling to support the building.
4. The need for removal of large boulders, trees, and other obstructions or the filling or capping of old wells or pits.
5. The need for drainage of unduly expensive nature.
6. The need for constructing and maintaining special installations because of distance from public water and sewer lines and gas, electricity, and telephone service.
7. The need for constructing and maintaining long access drives.

These and other adverse conditions can usually be overcome by modern construction methods, but they should be accepted only when the cost of remedial measures is reasonable.

Since so many of these conditions are not readily apparent from the surface, it is important that competent technical advice be sought. In most instances, test borings or test pits should be made to determine subsoil conditions and the results should be analyzed and interpreted by a competent engineer or architect before the land is purchased. The files of most architects will yield numerous examples of thousands of dollars of unanticipated costs during construction because the board of education did not think it necessary to spend a few hundred dollars in advance for test borings to determine what was beneath the surface.

ATTRACTIVENESS

A final criterion is that the site should permit the development of an attractive school plant. This is not a plea for a monumental building with extensive applied ornamentation or for putting the school building on a main thoroughfare where more people can see it. However, in avoiding these evils which have so often prevailed in the past, it is not necessary to hide the school building in an old gravel pit or place it in ugly surroundings. The site should permit the pleasing location of an inviting building in an attractive setting. This requires a location in a desirable neighborhood and on a sufficiently large site to permit setting the building back from the street and away from adjoining structures. It also requires soil that will support a good lawn, trees, and shrubbery.

Development of the Site

A POORLY arranged or underdeveloped site, like a badly designed or partially equipped classroom, defeats in part the very purpose for which it was designed. A tract of land outside the building or a bit of floor space within can help or hinder the work of the school, can promote safety or invite accidents, and can engender pride and enthusiasm toward the schools. Not infrequently the opposition to the purchase of large tracts of land for school purposes is due to failure to make effective use of even smaller sites at existing buildings in the same community.

Before a tract of raw land can be transformed into an attractive and useful educational tool, there must be a concept of its potential and a willingness and ability on the part of the people to provide the necessary funds for proper site development. If the concept and willingness are present and the funds are short, at least the planning for the future development of the entire site should be done before the first construction is undertaken. This tends to prevent later regrets regarding the design or placement of the early construction, and at the same time it sets up desirable goals toward which later efforts can be directed. The 80-acre site shown earlier in this chapter is at present only partially developed, but the entire plan was prepared early by an educational consultant and a landscape architect, and is gradually being executed.

PLANNING THE SITE

The creation of a plan for the development of the entire school site should not be something apart from the planning of the building itself and its immediate surroundings. To be most acceptable, the site plan presented by the architect should encompass the total site and show future developments the same as future building additions are indicated. Unfortunately, this is all too seldom done, and only a partial site plan, or even none at all, is presented for approval as a part of the preliminary drawings when the basic design scheme is established.

Since building and site are part and parcel of the same school plant, the same general planning procedures are appropriate for the outdoor facilities as for those within the building. The processes of educational planning, writing educational specifications, and architectural designing, all of which are described in detail in Part One are as applicable to one as to the other. The one difference, if there be any, would be that the site offers more opportunity and greater need for cooperative planning with other community agencies. This is true in part because the school grounds are often used by nonschool groups, but the same could be said of the auditorium and certain other parts of the building. The main distinction is that the planning of the outdoor spaces is likely in more instances to involve joint use, and even joint control or operation, of certain facilities. Also, park and recreation boards frequently have landscape architects and other specialists on their staffs that can be of much assistance in planning a school project to promote effective community use as well as service to the pupils of the school.

It is not unusual to find communities where a park or recreation board owns and operates sizable playgrounds, while the schools have only meager facilities. This may be evidence of lack of foresight on the part of school authorities, or it may result from other causes. In any event, it indicates a need for cooperative efforts in the interests of the entire public, which pays the total bill for all agencies in the field. Happily, there are evidences of a trend toward a more rational approach. Some communities place all public recreation under the board of education, others give the schools official representation on the recreation or park board, and some depend upon the good will and insight of the several boards to work together. The best pattern, if there be one, has not yet been determined. The important thing is not the pattern itself, but rather that school sites, parks, and other recreational areas be integrated into a pattern that serves most adequately all the needs of the community.

There are, to be sure, certain difficulties in any such cooperative approach. There may be deed restrictions or other impediments to be taken into account, and there may be community traditions that cannot be ignored. There are also many practical operating problems that must be solved. The schools, for example, must be concerned that there be no undue interference with regular school activities, that school property be safeguarded against vandalism, that proper financing be arranged, and that there be proper co-ordination of effort to avoid undesirable duplication or gaps in the program. Other agencies will have similar concerns of equal merit, but all of the problems and concerns of all the agencies will fall into proper perspective if the welfare of the entire community becomes the primary goal of everyone involved.

GENERAL PRINCIPLES OF SITE DEVELOPMENT

Since the planning of the site is but part of the planning of the total plant, there is no need to repeat here the discussion of the planning process in Part One of this book. Rather, a few basic principles will be repeated, with different phrasing, and used as the framework for the remaining discussion of site planning. A proper plan for the development of a school site is one which:

1. Promotes economy of construction, operation, and maintenance.
2. Promotes convenience and safety in operation and use.
3. Produces a total plant which is attractive and can easily be kept so.
4. Makes adequate provision for all the needs of the complete program of activities of the school.

ECONOMY IN SITE DEVELOPMENT

In many ways a good plan of site development can save money without impairing the usefulness, safety, or attractiveness of the finished product. Part of the savings can be effected in initial construction costs; others in the expenses of operation and maintenance over the years. Since the possible economies are so numerous and varied, only a few illustrations will be cited at this point.

The economies in original construction that can be achieved by good site planning are largely related to the placement of the building. Costs for excavations and foundation walls can be reduced by fitting the building to the contours of the land, and extra expenses for special footings and special drainage can be avoided by placing the building on high ground and where subsoil conditions are known to be favorable. Proper placement of the building will reduce the length of utility and drainage lines and drives and walks, and thus reduce costs. On the operation and maintenance side, good planning can reduce the steepness of banks that might be subject to erosion, can divert surface water that might affect the foundations of the building or damage drives and parking lots, and can reduce the amount of paving and sidewalk that must be kept in repair and free of snow.

CONVENIENCE AND SAFETY THROUGH SITE DEVELOPMENT

This aspect of planning, like the preceding one, requires no great elaboration here. Many of the applications pertain only to a specific site and will normally emerge with good architectural services. Also, discussions in later chapters will deal more fully with service facilities and with safety. For these reasons, only a few examples will be given to illustrate the principle involved.

A site plan designed for convenient use will place service drives near storage rooms, kitchens, shops, stages, and other places within the building to which deliveries must be made. It will locate parking areas in convenient places and playgrounds within a reasonable distance from the exits through which the users will leave the building. On the safety side, the good site development plan will provide separation of areas used by pedestrians, bicycle riders, and vehicular traffic, and will avoid a driveway arrangement that makes access to the street unduly dangerous. It will avoid places where a tardy and speeding delivery truck and a group of pupils hurrying to the playground might meet, especially where the view of either is obstructed.

AESTHETIC CONSIDERATIONS IN SITE DEVELOPMENT

This principle, too, needs no great elaboration at this point. As indicated earlier in the chapter, all that is proposed is an arrangement of facilities and simple plantings to make the entire plant attractive and pleasing without undue extra expense. Thought must be given not only to initial cost but also to the expense of maintenance. Trees, shrubs, and other plantings should be selected with an eye to the amount of care required and their resistance to wear and tear of children at play. In placing shrubs close to the building or vines on the building, added difficulty in painting, washing windows, and making repairs must be anticipated. Varieties of trees which have a tendency to clog sewers or create excessive litter on the ground should be avoided.

SITE DEVELOPMENT TO IMPROVE SCHOOL PROGRAM

Whatever merit there may be to the other principles of site development which have been discussed, the fact remains that the whole purpose of having a site is to provide suitable facilities for conducting the program of the school. It follows, then, that the site should be developed in such a way as to foster a good program. All of the other principles of site development, except where safety is involved, are secondary in importance to this. As has been said so many other places in this volume, the program should be decided first, and the site development plans should then be made accordingly. Also, the probable program of the future as well as that of the moment must be considered. The school program to be considered in planning the site includes many different kinds of activities. Among them are the outdoor play and recreation of pupils and others, athletic contests, activities such as gardening and nature study, and community use of the school plant.

Play and Recreation

It is generally recognized today that the growing child needs much play to foster his proper physical and social development, and that an adult as well needs to play in order to maintain his physical and emotional well-being. School programs encompass many play activities for children ranging from the completely unsupervised free play of a spontaneously formed group on the playground before school or at the noon hour to outdoor classes in physical education or formally organized field days. Many of these play activities are continued over the week-end and through vacation periods, with or without formal organization and supervision. Older youth and adults frequently use the school grounds for organized games such as baseball or tennis or for other recreational activities. The games played vary greatly from region to region and from school to school, and will change from time to time in a given place. This being the case, the list of outdoor play areas for a given school must be tailor-made for that school and must allow for future changes.

Zoning of Playground. One of the problems which arises in the planning of any site is that of zoning the playground for children of different ages or sex. It is generally considered desirable to set aside a separate place or places for the very young people, often with a completely separate space for the kindergarten and possibly for each room in the lower grades. Special play areas are considered desirable for upper elementary school children, junior high school pupils, and senior high school pupils, if all are housed in one building. For each of these older groups, there should be a separate area for each sex. The justification for such zoning is that the play interests of children change as they grow older and differ for the two sexes after the middle of the elementary school period.

When any building or its site is intended to provide for various combinations of grade levels, the separate requirements must be added together. For example, for a junior-senior high school there should be separate accommodations for the junior high school and the senior high school levels. Certain play fields, however, may overlap. The areas laid out for soccer and field hockey in the fall may be baseball fields, softball fields, or archery ranges in the spring. However, the diamond part of the baseball field or portions of a running track should not overlap any other field.

Playfields should not encroach upon each other when simultaneously in use, and there must be for certain sports suitable space for stands for spectators. Schools having any substantial enrollment may require more than one space for each activity, since there may be a number of athletic squads in each season. In the case of football, separate practice and game fields may be needed.

Location of Playgrounds. Where to locate the various play areas is another problem common to all site planning. For kindergarten and primary grades, where play is not boisterous and noisy and where the play periods are short, the play areas should be quite close to the classrooms and preferably adjoining them. For older pupils, there is need for a greater distance from the building to the playground in order that the normal noises of children at play will not disturb classes in the building. For physical education classes which are followed by showers or change of clothing, ease of access to the locker room is essential. For children of all ages, safety is a factor to be considered in locating the playground. The most common hazard is the crossing of a driveway or parking lot in going to and from the play area.

Playground Equipment. Some equipment is normally involved in a play program. Some of it, such as baseballs, hockey sticks, and tennis rackets, can be stored within the building and brought out as needed. Other equipment, such as jumping standards and hurdles, cannot be transported so easily, and the site plan must provide some convenient storage space either within the main building or in an auxiliary structure. Other equipment, such as swings and climbing devices, normally remains outdoors and presents no storage problem. The hazards of the various pieces of equipment must be considered in their placement on the site as well as in their choice, and this must include the hazards to onlookers or children playing as well as to those using the equipment. The safety aspect is discussed in more detail in Chapter 20.

Playground Surfacing and Marking. The plan of site development should specify the type of surfacing. For most games sod is ideal, but to maintain suitable sod it is necessary to have a large enough area to spread the load and to permit periodic nonuse of each section of the site to rejuvenate the grass. In most cases there is need for some paved area for use in wet weather, and possibly for very young children to use for wheeled toys such as tricycles. Frequently one paved area can serve as a rainy weather playground, as an outdoor basketball court, as an area to be flooded for ice skating, and as an overflow parking space for special occasions.

Certain games for older children require some marking of the field, including baseball, hockey, volley ball, and football. These areas should be laid out according to standard dimensions if possible, especially when they might be used also in connection with an interscholastic athletic program.

Nonschool Use of Playgrounds. Most school playgrounds are extensively used outside of school hours by children and by adults. This is quite proper and should be encouraged by appropriate site planning. For the most part, no special facilities are required, since these participants use the facilities already provided for regular school use. If the nonschool use requires the keeping of special equipment on the site, a separate storage space may be advisable. There may also be need for a small space for a supervisor to keep records and store supplies. In most cases, there will be need for access to toilets. These requirements can usually be met at little or no added cost by an arrangement of site and building spaces that permits limited entry into the building under supervision. Vandalism and other misconduct by playground users can be reduced by an arrangement that offers few opportunities for small groups to be out of sight of the main body of participants and the person in charge.

Interscholastic Athletics

Programs of interscholastic athletics in the major sports introduce special problems of site development, largely due to the crowds that must be handled. Extra parking space must be provided and the arrangements must permit the rapid movement of people between the parking lot and their seats without damage to play areas, shrubbery, and other site features. Facilities must be provided for rapid sale and collection of tickets and often for sale of refreshments and other items. Flood lighting, public address systems, first-aid rooms, special offices for coaches and officials, special team rooms, and toilets for participants and spectators are among the other items to be considered. These special facilities may be in the main building, if total site plan permits, or may have to be in a separate stadium or other structure.

The extent to which the site development plan provides such special facilities for interscholastic athletics must depend upon the emphasis placed upon the program in the particular school in question. Recognizing that there is gross overemphasis in many cases, the authors firmly believe that the physical facilities should be consistent with the emphasis which the local school authorities and community decide is appropriate. The use of makeshift and often filthy locker, shower, and toilet facilities in stadiums and the perpetuation of other similar unsatisfactory conditions cannot be condoned.

Other Outdoor Activities

In addition to informal play, games, and sports, there are other potential uses of school sites which deserve more attention by educators and architects than they have received. A small wooded tract, a ravine, or a hillside may offer many opportunities for instruction in science or conservation, and a garden plot or experimental planting beds would seem to deserve a place on many school sites. Places for outdoor classes in sketching or for music or dramatic performances in the open would also seem to be appropriate in most parts of the country. While the authors would not suggest the inclusion of such features in the site plan unless required by the local school program, they would urge that questions be raised about such activities. They would suggest, also, that the site plan leave opportunity for future developments along these lines.

Camping is another outdoor activity that is being added to the program of some schools. Camping experience is valuable because of the social learnings involved in around-the-clock group living and because of the premium it places on self-reliance. It also offers, especially for the city child, rich opportunities for learning to understand natural phenomena and the problems of conservation. An occasional school site will be large enough to provide a relatively isolated section for camping, but in most instances a separate location in the country will be necessary. The camp will need not only buildings to house and feed the children and staff, but also indoor and outdoor assembly areas, game areas, nature trails, and the like.

Community Use of Building

Attention has already been called to the need for anticipating public use of the outdoor facilities. There are also certain indoor facilities which are often used by the public and which affect the over-all site plan. Chief among these are the auditorium, gymnasium, and cafeteria. The plan of site development should be such that large groups of people can move easily from the parking areas to these parts of the building. Sidewalks and suitable outside lighting should be provided and steep banks, long flights of stairs, and other obstacles should be avoided.

The discussion at this point has moved back to the building itself, which serves to emphasize again that outdoor and indoor facilities are and must be planned as a integrated whole. If the best results are desired, the site development planning cannot be put off until the building plans are completed or the building is erected.

CHAPTER 13

THE CLASSROOM

The Development of the Modern Classroom
Needs of the Emerging Elementary School Program
The General Elementary School Classroom
Secondary School Classrooms
Important Features of All Classrooms

———————

THE basic element in every school building is the space where learning activities are carried out. Since learning activities vary widely in nature, the spaces devoted to it differ in size, shape, and the way in which they are equipped for instruction. Some of these spaces are quite specialized in nature, as, for example, gymnasiums, shops, and laboratories. The majority of the learning spaces, however, are the classrooms in which the boys and girls spend the greatest proportion of their school time. For purposes of convenient reference, instructional spaces in a school building may be classified as (1) regular or unspecialized classrooms, generally more or less alike throughout a particular building; (2) special classrooms, a category including shops, laboratories, and classrooms requiring a great deal of special equipment and generally used only for particular groups, classes, or activities; and (3) special activity areas, which would include gymnasiums, auditoriums, libraries, and student activity rooms. This chapter will examine the first of the above categories—regular classrooms. Subsequent chapters will consider the special classrooms and special activity areas.

The Development of the Modern Classroom

THE classic prototype of the American school building, and truly the acorn from which the oak has grown, was the "little red schoolhouse." Regardless of its color, which varied, the original American school had one classroom. The development of school buildings with more than one room followed certain common patterns. Two-, three-, and four-room buildings were generally single story, with the four-room building usually square with a center hall and a room in each corner of the square. There were, of course, exceptions—two-room buildings, one room over the other, and four rooms, two over two. Most of the earlier buildings of more than four rooms were of the two-story type. Four over four made eight, and three floors in a square form, provided twelve rooms. Beyond twelve rooms this scheme broke down. Some of the earlier secondary school buildings, needing more rooms, squeezed in a few additional rooms about a central hall, but the development of longitudinal corridors with rooms along both sides proved to be the answer.

With a building consisting only of corner rooms, it was possible to have windows on the two outside walls. Moore a half century ago said:

> Three windows at the rear and four at the left of the pupils give a very good light for the ordinary sized school-room, lighted from two sides.
>
> When only lighted from the left of the pupils' desks, five windows are preferable if the construction of the building will allow it.[1]

In these buildings of the late nineteenth century and early twentieth century, it was common to have relatively large rooms designed to accommodate either 48 or 49 pupils' desks and seats screwed to the floor, either as six rows of eight or seven rows of seven.

The earlier buildings having longitudinal corridors also had large rooms. Moore said:

> The standard generally adopted for a class-room in Massachusetts, for what is usually called a fifty seat room, is 32 feet long, 28 feet wide and 12 feet high.
>
> In the lower grades sometimes 56 seats are provided, but this large number is not recommended.
>
> Grammar and the high grade rooms are commonly seated for 42, 47, 48 or 49 pupils.
>
> Twenty-eight by thirty-two feet gives a floor space of 896 square feet, and allows 21.33 square feet of floor space for 42, 19.06 for 47, 18.66 for 48, 18.28 for 49 pupils.[2]

Subsequently, however, with the movement to reduce class sizes, there developed a trend toward smaller classrooms. Three factors were involved, namely:

[1] Moore, Joseph A., *The School House*. Boston: The author, 1905, p. 16.   [2] *Ibid.*, p. 17.

1. Rooms strung like beads along a corridor could have light from only one side, and hence must be more narrow.
2. Smaller rooms cost less.
3. Educators began deliberately to promote smaller classrooms in order to limit class sizes.

THE STANDARD CLASSROOM CONCEPT

This trend eventually led to the advocacy of the so-called "standard classroom," which was generally about 22 feet wide by approximately 30 feet long and designed to accommodate not more than 35 pupils seated in five rows of seven seats each. Several other prescriptions accompanied this standard. It was specified, for example, that the seats must be so arranged that the light would come from the pupils' left side. With dark finishes and great brightness contrasts there were strong shadows. Accordingly, because most children are right-handed and the shadow would obscure what has been written as the hand moves across the page unless the light comes from the left, the "light over the left shoulder" legend has had a long existence. This same statement has been customarily applied to reading, although with the absence of glare and shadow conditions the importance of the direction of incidence of light is relatively unimportant. The left-handed child, being in the minority, received little consideration in the standard classroom.

The breaking away from the learning situation in which the teacher was a taskmaster and the chief virtue of the pupil was to sit still and keep quiet to a new pattern in which children were encouraged to be active finally forced the abandonment of the standard classroom with its fixed seating. In its place, particularly in elementary schools, came classrooms having nearly 50 percent more floor space with movable equipment replacing the screwed-down seats and desks. The unfortunate circumstance is that so many small classrooms were constructed during the period between World Wars I and II.

RECENT CHANGES IN ELEMENTARY SCHOOL CLASSROOMS

It is in the elementary grades particularly that the change in the nature of the educational program has demanded a change in the character of the classroom accommodations. The emphasis upon creative and constructive activities, upon children working together in projects which give meaning to many types of learning, and upon general freedom of movement called undeniably for more floor space. These and other factors proved to be powerful enough to bring about experimentation and change.

Some elementary schools which constructively broke away from the standard classroom tradition appeared before World War II. The distinguishing feature generally was a design which provided a work alcove or partially screened-off activity space. Subsequent to the war, the accumulated thinking of several years took shape in a wide variety of designs based upon much freer consideration of many factors relating to program—considerations of comfort, health, and safety as affected by lighting, heating, and ventilation; and, above all, considerations of flexibility in use and arrangement of internal fixtures and facilities. During this period there have appeared L-shaped rooms, square rooms, various types of bilateral and multilateral daylighting, emphasis upon single-story construction, separate or partially separate workrooms, work areas in corridor spaces, buildings without corridors, separate single-room units, cluster plans, and a host of other schemes which show the use of intelligent and imaginative experimentation by school building planners.

Needs of the Emerging Elementary School Program

THE most significant difference between the earlier elementary school program and the program dictated today by increasing knowledge of educational psychology and child growth and development is the replacement of *passive* learning by *active* learning. This has been accompanied by a continuing effort to reduce the size of classes. Achievement in this endeavor has been variable and not yet generally as successful as could be desired.

Two phases of the elementary school program make important demands upon the classroom. One is the continuous program of skill development in such subjects as reading, writing, and arithmetic. Chief among the requirements for these learning activities are good, well-lighted work surfaces, convenient storage for books and materials, chalkboard, chairs and space for the reading circle, and a library corner with chairs, tables, and book-shelving. For the purpose of giving meaning to the skills and opportunities to exercise them in interesting and meaningful situations, the elementary school program includes much more creative and constructive activity in the nature of project or unit work than formerly. This work is generally organized into units based on themes or problems which are natural centers of interest for the children, and which contribute to the development of desirable attitudes, appreciations, and other valuable outcomes, as well as help tie together the skill learnings. They also serve directly certain emotional and psychological needs of children.

It is this activity work which has been responsible for the greatest change in the design and general nature of the elementary classroom. No longer do the pupils spend the school day sitting in enforced silence, working only with books, pencils, paper, and chalk. More freedom to converse and move around requires careful acoustical designing of the room, more space, and as much movable equipment as possible. Work counters, fixed and movable, sinks with hot and cold water, and a variety of equipment such as workbenches, library tables, bookcases, aquariums, and easels are essential for this type of program.

Another change which has affected classroom design has been the greater emphasis upon the self-contained classroom. Under the influence of this trend, departmentalization in the elementary grades has largely disappeared. The self-contained classroom movement, like the activity movement, has brought with it greater room size and more variety and flexibility of equipment. This is true because under this plan all instruction is carried on in the regular classroom except those few activities which require very large or specialized areas, such as physical education, dramatic and musical projects requiring a full stage, and instrumental music. The new concept of the elementary school classroom is, therefore, a school-hour home for the children which is at the same time a largely self-sufficient learning laboratory.

The General Elementary School Classroom

In the modern elementary school operating on a self-contained classroom basis, all of the rooms are generally similar except for those items, mostly movable and interchangeable, which must conform to the sizes of the children in each room. This general classroom provides all facilities for the learning activities of the pupils including space and equipment for work in the fundamental skills; for creative and constructive activities, including projects in arts and crafts, nature study, and science; and for classroom library, storage, and display purposes.

THE KINDERGARTEN ROOM

The concept of the kindergarten is often that it is an introductory year to the school career of the child, a year for the development of readiness for later school experiences. A better concept is that it is the first year of a well-developed sequence of learning activities, during which the child makes a transitional adjustment from the home environment to school environment. The kindergarten program, as a natural result of its aims, involves more socializing activity, including much group play and other group endeavors. There is almost no consideration of the abstract; nearly all endeavors are related to concrete objects, and the learning space must provide for the accommodation of play equipment, building blocks, etc., which require a large floor area per pupil.

Some people, including the authors, hold to the point of view that any substantial and abrupt distinction between the kindergarten and first grade is artificial. These people say that it is a fallacy to provide a large well-equipped room for the kindergarten and assume that all children will be equally well adjusted at the end of one year, or that any children should go from the kindergarten into a first-grade room and program which are suddenly greatly different from the kindergarten. According to this point of view the kindergarten room should not be regarded as a special classroom. Rather, it illustrates well what a lower elementary grade classroom should be.

FLEXIBILITY IN USE

The elementary school classroom should be designed for maximum flexibility in use. This is necessitated by the great and changing variety of activities now included in the school program, which requires frequent changes in the arrangement of the room to accommodate new activities. Flexibility is essential, also, because a given room may have to be assigned from time to time to a different age group needing different sizes or types of equipment.

This need for flexibility has led, to a large extent, to the abandonment of the separate or partially separate workroom adjacent to classrooms. In its place, an equal area is added to the classroom itself.

Sufficient floor space being assumed, the criterion of flexibility requires that there be a minimum of fixed equipment which limits the use of floor and wall areas. It allows only such built-in storage, shelving, work counters, and other equipment as will be permanently needed by any group of pupils assigned to the room and as can be placed around the perimeter of the room in spaces where there can be no more desirable alternative use. Wall space is considered to be functional space for teaching and, after allowance for windows and doors, there is usually too little left for all desired uses. Chalkboards, tackboards, and sink counters, for which fixed locations seem desirable, are usually attached to the wall, and the area under the windows is often used for bookshelving and other storage, since it has little other value.

All other items of equipment are designed to be movable. This applies generally to pupils' desks and chairs, teacher's desk and chair, work counter units or work tables, library table, library bookshelf units, aquariums, sandtables, workbenches, easels, clay bins, wardrobe units, etc.

SIZE

It has already been indicated that the trend has been to increase the size of elementary school classrooms. Most of the rooms built between the two wars had net floor areas ranging from 650 to perhaps 725 square feet. Efforts to increase the size met resistance because of cost. Nevertheless, the endeavor has been largely successful, particularly in communities where the public has supported the efforts by the school people to design school buildings to fit the needs of the program.

For elementary classrooms except kindergartens, educators have generally been recommending a minimum net floor area of 900 square feet. While this goal is not always achieved, areas closely approaching and sometimes substantially exceeding this figure are becoming relatively common. It is generally accepted that kindergarten rooms should be considerably larger than the rooms for grades 1 through 6. Various "standards" ranging from 1,200 to 1,500 square feet have been recommended, and the 1,200-square-foot mark is quite commonly achieved or exceeded in new construction.

Those who believe that the transition from kindergarten to first grade is too abrupt present a substantial argument for designing rooms for the first two or three grades which in size will be closer to that of the kindergarten room. There is some logic to this point of view, but there are also some practical obstacles. It is, for example, not always possible to designate a particular classroom permanently for a particular grade. One way in which this difficulty can be avoided is to have all elementary classrooms as large as kindergarten rooms, and certainly this would provide excellent learning situations. Some designs, such as those which are incorporating into the working area of the classrooms space previously segregated for corridor use, tend to make this possible with little or no increase in cost.

Sometimes attempts are made to establish the size of a classroom in terms of square feet per pupil. It is said, for example, that an elementary classroom should provide 30 square feet per pupil. This presumes a choice of some figure for class size, probably the maximum rating for the room. If this is assumed to be 30 pupils, the recommended area is 900 square feet. Class sizes, however, vary from school to school, from class to class, and from year to year. Actual situations also vary from desirable situations, and often cost factors prevent the reduction of class sizes to optimum ranges. Accordingly per-pupil area standards have only limited application. The number of square feet needed depends also upon the requirements of the local program and to some extent upon room shape and the locations of windows, doors, and other features which affect the usability of the floor space. The soundest approach is to use scale templates representing the desired equipment in trial layouts on scale drawings of floor and wall surfaces. The use of scale models for trial layouts is also a good approach. With either of these procedures, the area per pupil is properly reduced to an incidental product of the planning process rather than the starting point.

When workrooms or work alcoves are constructed as part of the classroom space, their area plus the general classroom area is usually included in the comparisons with standards. The chief arguments for separate workrooms are isolation of noise, protection of project work, and avoidance of mess in the classroom. The construction of a workroom between two adjacent classrooms, to be shared in use by both, is sometimes advocated as a means of economizing on total floor area. Workroom arrangements, however, restrict the space they occupy to only certain types of activities and hence reduce the flexibility of use of the total area. Jointly shared workrooms are even more inflexible, since their use by either class is contingent upon the schedule of the other class. Furthermore, activities which carry over from day to day, requiring that materials or project work be left in place for a considerable period of time, will prevent the other class from using the work area.

SHAPE

Years ago, the corner-room type of building had nearly square classrooms. Emphasis upon unilateral lighting with rooms strung along a corridor tended to produce oblong rooms. The trend to larger rooms tended to make the rooms longer at the same time that efforts to provide better natural light tended to make them more narrow, or at least kept them from becoming wider.

The development of various forms of bilateral lighting or top lighting broke the restrictions upon width and the square classroom is returning. Various arguments have been advanced in favor of the square classroom, including (1) maximum area in proportion to perimeter, (2) greater flexibility in use and arrangement of activities, and (3) less corridor length per classroom. In terms of cost factors alone, it has not been conclusively proved that the square classroom is more economical. The economies listed above might be offset by increased costs of framing and daylighting.

Barring cases of extreme length and narrowness and designs having awkward angles or obstructions to flexibility in use, it is difficult to make an absolutely convincing case for or against any particular shape. The shape should be the outcome of the planning process rather than a premise.

TOILET ROOMS

Until relatively recently the toilet needs of school pupils have been customarily met by general toilet rooms conveniently located in the building. Generally the basement toilet of a generation or more ago has gone the way of the outdoor toilet building. Attractive modern sanitary fixtures in tiled, easily cleaned, well-lighted, and well-ventilated toilet rooms on the classroom floors of the building have become standard practice.

It early became good practice to provide kindergartens with separate toilets located near by. From this evolved the provision of kindergarten toilet rooms directly connected with the kindergarten room, usually with two toilet seats but without differentiation by sex. The next development was the provision of separate toilet rooms directly connected with the elementary grade classrooms. At first, and still most commonly used, came the design of toilet rooms attached to the primary grade rooms. In many cases this arrangement covers only the kindergarten and first and second grades. Less often it covers all classrooms through the sixth grade.

Opinions differ. Some contend that there will be embarrassment if pupils above, say, second-grade age go directly from the classroom through a toilet room door. In some states further upward extension of this arrangement is not at present approved, although the opposition seems gradually to be losing strength in the face of satisfactory experience with separate room toilets for all elementary grades. One of the authors remembers his own skepticism about this point, which proved entirely unwarranted after administrative experience with several new elementary school buildings in which separate toilet facilities were provided for all rooms from kindergarten through grade 6.

Questions arise as to whether or not each classroom should have one or two toilet rooms, and whether or not they should, in the case of two, be separately designated by sex. Again, there has been successful experience to indicate that one toilet per classroom is sufficient.

Secondary School Classrooms

THERE is a general similarity of secondary school classrooms to those which have been described above for elementary school purposes. Although the unspecialized secondary school classroom is usually not as large as the rooms now being planned for elementary school purposes, there is a tendency to make it larger than during the period between the two world wars. The tendency today is to provide general classrooms of 800 square feet or more, but the pressure of costs too often results in a floor area somewhere in the range of 700 to 750 square feet. This size, however, is substantially better than the results achieved prior to World War II.

VARIATION IN SIZE

Secondary class groups vary in size considerably more than do elementary school classes. While the upper limit for the usual academic classes (excluding physical education, band, and choral groups) generally is in the range of 25 to 35 pupils, there will be many which are much smaller. Notable among these are classes in advanced languages and mathematics, which in small and medium-sized secondary schools may be as small as 10 to 15 pupils. Because of this almost universally existing situation, it has been advocated that there be a few small classrooms in any secondary school building, with the expectation that the small classes will be assigned to these rooms.

Such variation in room size has not worked well in practice for several reasons. First, a given teacher usually has both large and small classes, and this plan would require that he teach in more than one room. The usual result is that the teacher fails to take with him the variety and quantity of instructional materials that he could use if he had all his classes in one room, and the instructional program suffers accordingly. The second objection is that the small rooms soon come to be used by large classes because of the resistance of teachers to frequent changes of room. The resulting overcrowding of the small classrooms leaves little opportunity for more than the study-recite, question-and-answer type of teaching, and sometimes creates hazardous conditions.

CLASSROOMS FOR THE FUTURE SECONDARY SCHOOL PROGRAM

Attention was called in Chapter 11 to the considerable dissatisfaction with some aspects of present-day secondary school programs and to the existing uncertainty regarding the future course of developments. This uncertainty poses an exceedingly difficult problem for the school building planner; in fact, it is probably the greatest single problem in the school-plant field at the present time. Somehow secondary school buildings must be designed to accommodate today's programs and yet be sufficiently flexible that they do not retard the development of new, but not now foreseeable, programs in the future.

Some persons, looking approvingly at the self-contained classroom in the elementary school, would like to adopt this plan at the secondary school level, and thus would like to have much larger classrooms. Others see many objections to this plan, and some of these objections have been discussed in Chapter 11. However, even those who favor this approach see a place for specialized rooms for certain purposes, such as science or crafts.

Whatever program emerges in the future, classrooms will be required and many of them will not be too unlike the regular or unspecialized classrooms of today as far as basic structure is concerned. If today's secondary classrooms are made adequate in size, preferably approaching the size of elementary school classrooms, and are expansible, they might be a step toward the future and most likely would not be an obstacle to the emergence of a new program. These rooms would need also to be so designed that sinks, work counters, and other equipment could be installed if desired. The various special classrooms, which are discussed in the next chapter, would also have to incorporate more elements of flexibility than are now customary. A general rule, applicable to all kinds of secondary school classrooms, would be that no unnecessary degree of specialization be built into the structure of any new building now erected.

Important Features of All Classrooms

THERE are many design features common to all kinds of classrooms, both elementary and secondary. Among these are storage facilities, chalkboards, tackboards, electrical outlets, and audio-visual facilities. The more important of these features will be discussed below, as they apply to classrooms in general. Some of them are also discussed later with particular attention to features requiring extra emphasis in special classrooms.

CLOTHING STORAGE

The problem of storing pupils' clothing varies according to the demands of the local climate. The following discussion is based upon maximum need; in more favored climates, the facilities can be much simpler. The methods most commonly used are:

1. Open storage in corridors, either on hooks on the wall or on semi-partition screens.
2. Banks of lockers in alcoves opening off corridors.
3. Lockers in or along corridor walls.
4. Wardrobe units in the classroom wall.
5. Separate cloakrooms adjacent to and opening into the classroom.

6. Open storage on hook strips along the classroom wall.
7. Open storage on free standing movable units in the classroom.

Open Storage in Corridor

Earlier schools generally provided for the storage of pupils' clothing on hooks on the corridor walls, sometimes on metal mesh semi-partitions or on the walls of partial inclosures in corridor spaces. There were various disadvantages, among them the fact that corridors were generally dark, poorly ventilated, and not designed for ease of supervision. Other criticisms of this method were that one pupil's clothing touched that of others, rubbers and overshoes got mixed up, clothing and headgear fell upon the floor, and wet clothing did not dry well.

Lockers in Alcoves

One of the early departures from hook strips was the provision of individual lockers in alcoves off the corridors. This was more common in secondary schools than in elementary schools. The great difficulty was the problem of supervision.

Lockers in Corridor Walls

With the development of well-designed and well-constructed lockers and the growth of the trend to put supporting members and duct work in thicker walls between the classroom and the corridor, it became common practice in secondary schools to recess pupils' lockers into the corridor walls. In recent years this practice has been frequently followed in elementary schools.

In favor of this procedure has been the saving of cubage over separate cloakrooms and the saving over classroom wardrobes of expense and of valuable classroom wall space. At first there was concern that in the elementary schools supervision would be a problem for the teachers, particularly in the case of younger pupils who might need help in putting on or taking off clothes. This fear, however, seems to have been unjustified.

Another question about which there has been debate is whether or not corridor lockers in elementary schools need to be locked. Since individual keys would present problems of loss and combination locks would be difficult for younger children to use, schemes have been developed for master locking arrangements to be operated by the teacher. In most elementary schools, however, locks have not proved necessary. The lockers are usually adjacent to the classrooms, thus allowing for general supervision by the teacher; also elementary school pupils do not spend much time in the corridors without supervision. For corridor wall lockers in secondary schools, a combination lock (not padlock) with a master key is the preferred arrangement.

A common plan is to exhaust the air from corridor spaces through the lockers. The scheme is supposed to air out the clothing and dry it if it is wet. The effective functioning of this plan, of course, requires a carefully designed ventilating system. The air is discharged to the corridor through vents in doors and then through the lockers to ducts leading to the out-of-doors. Not all of these schemes work as planned, particularly if the teachers open windows or if the wind pressure is adverse. Except under ideal conditions and with superior engineering, it may not be unreasonable to question the superiority, as far as airing of clothing is concerned, of locker systems over open hanging of clothes on hooks. The chief disadvantages of metal lockers in corridors are the noise attendant upon their use; the continual need for repair to hinges, doors, latches, and locks; and the need for greater corridor width to avoid congestion.

Wardrobe Units in Classroom Walls

This arrangement is one of long standing. The major portion of one wall (in the so-called "standard classroom," the rear or side wall) of the classroom consists of swinging or sliding doors opening into a closet with overhanging tiers of hooks. In some cases all the doors open or close when an end door is operated. The usual provision for ventilation in this otherwise tightly closed-off space is to exhaust the air from the room through the wardrobe to the outdoors.

The advantages of this scheme are: (1) hiding the clothing from sight; (2) adequate ventilation providing the teacher keeps the door to the corridor closed and does not disarrange the calculated air flow; and (3) convenience of access under the immediate supervision of the classroom teacher.

The disadvantages most often noted are: (1) except for the most expensive and highly engineered mechanisms, the doors gradually lose their precision of operation; (2) the necessary cubage and the installations are expensive; (3) something about the hanging of clothing, etc., in a recess leads too often to a messy melange of caps, rubbers, lunch boxes, etc., on the floor; and (4) the use of classroom wall area for wardrobe doors not only reduces its utility for other purposes, except for separated small tackboards, but also makes it impossible to use the floor area in front of the doors for any project work.

The trend in the more informal elementary school classrooms of today is away from classroom wall wardrobes. For secondary schools with departmentalized programs they have not been and are not now in favor.

Separate Cloakrooms

Many older buildings have a separate cloakroom at the end of each classroom, extending from the corridor to the outside wall. Usually there are two doors, sometimes one at each end opening into the classroom and sometimes with a door into the corridor at one end and one into the classroom at the other. The superiority of this scheme over classroom wall wardrobes is that the wall between the cloakroom and the classroom is functional. The greatest disadvantage is the waste of cubage, the cloakroom itself often having 20 percent as much cubage as the classroom. At present the installation of separate cloakrooms is not common, except in kindergartens.

Open Storage in Classrooms

In many older schools recessed wardrobes have become open clothing storage because the wardrobe doors have become inoperative and have been removed and not replaced. No important difficulties have been observed in these situations except the loss of wall space for other use and the unsightliness of a wardrobe recess originally designed to be enclosed.

Movable Racks

Some elementary schools have simplified the clothing storage problem considerably by disregarding the problems of hiding the clothing from sight, providing special ventilation, and providing one fixed place for storage. This opens the way for the provision of free-standing movable storage units. Properly designed, they appear to be satisfactory. They can be moved about as desired to put them in the most convenient location for loading and unloading and can be left during the day in any part of the classroom where they will not interfere with other activities. Sometimes these are racks with tackboard on one side. They are functional as screens to separate activity areas. In the larger, more flexible elementary classrooms of the present day, they offer an inexpensive and seemingly satisfactory answer to what has at times been an expensive and troublesome problem.

OTHER STORAGE

Few school buildings have adequate provision for the storage of the many items for which space must be found. The result is that all kinds of spaces are pressed into service—attics, basement areas, boiler rooms, areas under stairways, and even crawl spaces and pipe tunnels. These practices are often detrimental to the stored materials and all too often create fire hazards. In the pages that follow, consideration will be given to the storage facilities that should be provided for classroom use; other types of storage will be discussed in later chapters.

Storage of Supplies

For every classroom it is necessary to have a certain amount of storage space immediately accessible for various school supplies, books, pupils' project work, and equipment temporarily not in use. This is particularly important in the modern elementary school because of the great variety of materials which are used.

Most older schools have some closet space with shelving built into one of the classroom walls, sometimes accompanied by built-in drawers of various sizes. A later trend has been the installation of shelves under the windows. Standardized units of shelving are available to match the ventilating and heating units commonly used. This arrangement is useful in both elementary and secondary schools. With the installation of sinks and work counters in elementary school classrooms and workrooms, it has become common practice to use the space under the counters for storage. Additional storage cabinets may also be hung on the walls above the work counters. Actually, the types of storage installations to be selected for an elementary classroom must depend upon the design of the room. The demand for wall space for windows, tackboard, and chalkboard has made it necessary to use considerable ingenuity in planning storage space. The emphasis upon flexibility has led to the development of movable storage units, usually of counter height, in sections which can be put together to make counters of various lengths or project work tables of various shapes and sizes. This facilitates the changing of use of the room from one age group to another by the substitution of sections of a different height.

Whatever may be the locations of storage spaces, whether fixed or movable, it is desirable to keep in mind the dimensions of the various items to be stored. Large sheets of art paper, large items such as clay buckets, long objects such as maps and charts, and such varied materials as playballs, paints, and tools all require specially designed storage areas. Because not all rooms need all of these items all of the time, it is especially fitting that movable storage units be employed. These movable units, then, may be used when and where needed. They have value in both elementary and secondary schools.

In secondary schools where classrooms for the same subject are usually grouped together, it is convenient to have storage rooms in each of these areas. Nevertheless, there is also need for storage for paper, chalk, and other general supplies in each classroom. On the whole, the amount of storage space required for the unspecialized secondary school classroom of today is less than that required in an elementary school. Shelving or cabinets along the window wall, perhaps with a wall closet, should be sufficient in most cases.

Storage of Books

It is essential that there be sufficient book storage in each classroom. A convenient arrangement is to provide bookshelving as part of the cabinet work under the windows. Bookshelving in the movable storage-work-counter units is also a very satisfactory arrangement. Use of these units, perhaps with casters or wheels, permits the placement of as much shelving in any room as necessary at any time and facilitates the moving of books from place to place or from room to room.

Miscellaneous Storage

There are also many miscellaneous items which are permanently or temporarily related to a particular classroom but not in continuous use. Accordingly, storage in or adjacent to the classroom must be provided for them. Among these are tools, lumber, completed or partially completed pupils' projects, projection equipment, rolls of wrapping paper, and wooden or cardboard boxes. It cannot be expected that every classroom can be furnished with a large storage room; hence there must be provision for general storage for the entire school or for groups of classrooms.

Storage for the Kindergarten

The great variety of materials used in a kindergarten requires much more storage space than for any other elementary school classroom. Such items as dolls, carriages, tricycles, building blocks of various types, and carts demand substantial space. For each kindergarten, a walk-in closet may be required. Except for the fact that there will not be as many books in the kindergarten, shelving and cupboard space will be nearly as abundant as in other classrooms. Special storage must also be planned for cots, pads, or blankets where it is considered necessary to have the children relax during the kindergarten session.

Teachers' Personal Storage

It is considered the best practice to have a closet of reasonable dimensions for the teacher's own personal use. This closet should have a rod for coat hangers, one or two shelves above, and a good lock. A three-quarter or full-length mirror on the inside of the door is generally appreciated. It is essential that the teacher's cloak closet be deep enough that coats hung on coat hangers will not be crushed.

Some schools have been planned with the only storage for teachers' clothing consisting of lockers in or adjacent to the teachers' lounge. The trend seems to be away from this arrangement with preference for the closet in each room, since this appears to be more convenient and more satisfactory to the teachers.

CHALKBOARDS

The chalkboard in schools of previous generations was largely slate, which provided an excellent surface for chalk. The dark grey or black surface, however, contributed heavily to the lack of light reflection and provided irritating brightness contrasts. This blackboard often extended in a band all the way around the room, broken only by windows and doors. In many older buildings where wide piers existed between windows, these surfaces were covered with blackboards even though they were virtually unusable because of the glare of the adjacent windows. In cheaper installations painted plaster or composition board was substituted for the slate, but the color was always black.

The first trend to bring about a change in the area devoted to chalkboard was the use of more and more display material, particularly in relation to activity-type instruction in the elementary schools. This resulted in a demand for more tackboard, and school building planners began to restrict the chalkboard generally to the front of the classroom and eventually to only a portion of that space. Like many other trends, this one occasionally went to an extreme, and in some cases classrooms were constructed with as little as 12 linear feet of chalkboard space. Teacher reaction against too little chalkboard, particularly in some junior high school and senior high school rooms where science and mathematics are taught, led to a retreat from the extreme. Today it is considered advisable to install a minimum of 18 linear feet of chalkboard in the average classroom; less, of course, in the kindergarten where a minimum amount can be supplemented, if necessary, by portable chalkboards; and more in various secondary classrooms where the nature of the subject matter requires substantially more wall writing space.

As greater attention began to be paid to the visual efficiency of the classroom, the objections to the black surface of slate were more clearly recognized. Various expedients were tried, including the use of black and colored crayons on white or light-colored enameled or porcelainized surfaces, painting the slate with a green paint including abrasives, and the use of green glass or plastic with an abrasive surface. Subsequently, the development of a green porcelain coating on a metal surface gave additional variety to the materials for choice. One advantage of this latter type is that magnetized indicators and holders can be used for bulletin board purposes if the porcelain coating is on a steel base. ;

The major criteria for judging any type of chalkboard are that it be: (1) sufficiently abrasive to take chalk well, (2) smooth enough and sufficiently impermeable to clean well, (3) heavy and rigid enough (and mounted with sufficient backing) to eliminate vibration or resonance, and (4) properly colored for effective contrast with chalk and minimum brightness contrast with the remaining visual environment.

Heights of chalkboard should conform to the size of the pupils using the rooms. However, the fact that an elementary classroom may be used for various grades from year to year has led to a tendency to drop the chalkrail to lower grade levels and depend upon the vertical dimension of the board to accommodate older pupils.

TACKBOARDS

The best tackboard surface developed to date is a good grade of cork, the self-healing properties of which appear to be unmatched. Commonly used substitutes are various composition boards of pressed fibers and panels of softwood. One suggestion for concealing the tack-holes in inferior materials is to camouflage them with a pin-point stippling over the basic coloring. Traditionally, corkboard has come in a neutral brown color. Recently, perhaps to conform with the growing predominance of green chalkboard, there has been an increasing use of green corkboard. Other colors also are available.

Tackboard is generally applied in bands to match the chalkboard in its width and mounting height. Sometimes, however, for younger children installations reaching to the floor have been made. In some cases portions of the classrooms or corridor wall have been finished in softwood panels for tacking purposes.

A fairly common installation, in addition to the basic tackboard areas, consists of a strip of tackboard several inches wide mounted above the top of the chalkboard. Tackboard strips of this type are of greatest value only if their dimensions are such as to allow use of paper 12 inches wide. Actually, at the height involved, the usefulness of this tackboard strip is largely restricted to decorative purposes. Another less pretentious but very useful tacking device is a narrow strip of cork inserted in a metal channel designed to support movable hooks along the top of the chalkboards. This cork strip is sufficient to carry the tacks which may be used to hold the top edges of display materials.

Various types of reversible panels, chalkboard on one side and tackboard on the other, have been designed. Use of these devices, however, has been relatively rare.

HOOK STRIPS FOR DISPLAY

Reference has already been made to hook strips with an insert of cork for installation along the top of chalkboard areas and tackboard areas. These can be obtained in some variety, with or without the cork insert. Usually the hooks have bases which can be slipped into a metal channel either at the time of installation or, by turning at an angle, at any time. The installation of these devices allows for the hanging of maps, charts, and many other display materials when and where desired. They should be a part of the original design of every classroom.

ELECTRICAL OUTLETS

The use of various projection devices, record players, and other equipment requiring electricity has made it necessary to pay careful attention to the location of electrical outlets in every classroom. General practice favors at least three double outlets, conveniently located. One of these may well be over the work counter in an elementary classroom or in the workroom if there is one.

AUDIO-VISUAL NEEDS

The major justification for the use of audio-visual aids must lie in their contribution to the learning situation. The realization of their purpose requires their use in the classroom and not in a special room or auditorium to which the pupils must travel. The grouping of classes of pupils to see films is advisable only when the material to be seen is of educational value to all pupils or of entertainment value. Overemphasis upon the entertainment aspect inevitably creeps in when the only place for projection is an auditorium.

The darkening of a classroom for projection requires opaque or nearly opaque light control drapes or curtains. This runs counter to the use of extensive fenestration, especially in the bilateral or multilateral installations. Attempts to resolve this difficulty have taken the form of various types of screens for daylight projection, but these have generally provided only marginal satisfaction, particularly for certain types of materials. The best available solution to this problem appears to be the installation of darkening drapes in every, or almost every, classroom. With the new materials available this installation is relatively inexpensive, being more economical than the provision of a separate visual-aids room. On the other hand, further development of projection and screen equipment may make it possible to obtain more satisfactory results in full daylight.

WORK COUNTERS

The increased emphasis upon constructive and creative activities has led to the installation of sinks and work counters almost as standard practice in kindergartens and elementary grade classrooms. The best installations are undoubtedly those in which the sink is set into the work counter so that there is a substantial amount of counter area on each side. Controlled hot and cold water should be available through a swinging mixing faucet. Sometimes a hose is provided, but it is not necessary. There is probably no better counter top presently available than the newer surfaces commonly used in kitchen counters. A single sink, fairly large and not excessively deep, is all that is usually needed.

For the sink in the work counter, soap may be provided and a suitable holder or dispenser should be properly and conveniently located. A paper towel dispenser should be mounted in a position easily reached by children. A splashboard installed along the wall behind the sink and work counter is a must.

The sink counter height should be scaled, as far as possible, to the size of the children who will occupy the classroom. The practical difficulty is that, except for the kindergarten, class or grade allocations may vary from year to year. Too fine an adjustment to pupil-scale may defeat its own purpose. Furthermore, convenient stand-up heights are somewhat more flexible than sit-down heights. And, above all, there are great differences in the sizes of children of any one grade. For these reasons, there is a tendency to average the counter heights, generally with some tendency to lean toward the convenience of the younger pupils. A sink counter height of 24 to 26 inches will be reasonably satisfactory for all grades above the kindergarten. For the work counter in a kindergarten a counter height of 22 inches is favored. It is possible to design a counter and sink unit, not rigidly built into the wall, which can be adjusted in height at little expense through minor changes in the plumbing.

The counter should have storage cupboards underneath, with suitably spaced shelving in accordance with its height. Sliding doors with high-grade hardware are preferable to swinging doors, and a toe space should be provided along the base. Either enameled metal or high-grade hardwood should form the counter and cabinet units. If metal is used, it is essential that the doors have a double facing and that all edges be turned and corners smoothed to avoid sharp places. The minimum counter length at the sink installation should be sufficient to permit three or four pupils to work together and to accommodate materials, tools, and utensils. There may well be other counter space in the classroom.

DRINKING FOUNTAINS

There should be a drinking fountain in the kindergarten, and preferably in every elementary room, possibly as part of the sink unit, although opinions differ as to its location. It may well be a separate unit. The installation of drinking fountains in each elementary classroom versus convenient corridor locations is sometimes considered a debatable matter. Either arrangement appears to be generally satisfactory, although the trend seems to be in favor of the room location. Cost may be a factor to be considered. The advantage of the corridor location is that the number of fixtures may be reduced, and automatic water coolers may be provided at reasonable cost. Obviously, in the installation of automatic water coolers the thermostatic control should not allow the water to be too cold. Central cooling systems serving all drinking fountains are also used.

WALLS

A carefully designed classroom will not have a great deal of plain wall space, except above the chalkboard, tackboard, and doors. Various wall finishes are used, ranging from wood to plaster to brick or other forms of masonry. Whatever material is used, the walls should be attractive, light in color for the purpose of suitable light reflection without excessive brightness or uncomfortable contrast, easily cleaned and not collectors of dust and dirt, and of suitable acoustical properties. The seeming increasing tendency to use painted blocks should cause no apprehension providing the specifications and the supervision insure that the blocks are carefully selected and properly laid. Unless precautions are taken, however, the painted block wall may be unsightly because of broken corners or uneven masonry work. Where plain surfaces exist in the lower walls, as is usually unavoidable below the chalkboards, it is essential that materials be used which are not easily marred or scarred.

FLOORS

With the advent of movable desks and chairs for pupil seating, it is no longer necessary to have a material into which screws can be driven. At the same time, bare concrete floors have not proved to be desirable because of lack of resilience and the difficulty in keeping them clean. The overwhelming trend is toward the use of a concrete floor base to which some sort of a tile floor is applied. Whatever may be the floor covering, it is desirable that it be fairly light in color with a substantial light reflection in order that it may not unduly clash with the rest of the visual environment.

CHAPTER 14

SPECIAL CLASSROOMS

Special Elementary School Classrooms
Special Secondary School Classrooms

THE discussion in the preceding chapter of regular or unspecialized classrooms naturally covers many features of all classrooms including those which are for special purposes and hence are more or less specialized in design. The purpose of this chapter is to discuss problems and issues in the educational planning of special classrooms and to point out the features which are peculiar to each type of special room. Since limitations of space prevent full discussion of each type of special classroom, only the major aspects will be discussed and reference will be made in the bibliographical notes at the end of the book to more detailed publications.

Special Elementary School Classrooms

GENERALLY today elementary schools (kindergarten through grade 6) provide for all instruction in the self-contained classroom, except for activities requiring such larger areas as are provided by a gymnasium or auditorium. Some vestiges of departmentalization, usually only in the upper grades, remain in a few places. These are most likely to be found in schools housing eight grades where the programs of pupils in grades 5 through 8 may be organized on a departmentalized basis. For such programs there will be need for some special classrooms, the choice and design depending upon the nature and organization of the local school program. Among the types of special rooms to be found are a woodworking or general shop, a science room, an art room or arts and crafts room, and a music room.

In some older elementary school buildings with small classrooms which cannot be readily enlarged, the shift toward the self-contained classroom type of program has been handicapped by classroom inadequacy. In these situations some activities, such as arts and crafts, must of necessity be assigned to special rooms.

In most elementary school buildings, unless they are exceptionally large, vocal or instrumental work of a group nature, in which the group is too large to use a regular classroom, will be carried on in the auditorium, playroom, or multipurpose room. However, in systems in which the music program calls for instrumental instruction on an individual or small group basis, it is well to have a space specifically designed for the purpose because sound might otherwise interfere with other activities. Rooms for this purpose will vary in size according to the character of the program, perhaps from 120 to 200 square feet in area. There may well be space for a piano. Needless to say, this room should be designed to prevent excessive reverberation and to reduce sound transmission to adjacent spaces.

Provision should also be made for one or more small rooms for such individual and small group work as speech correction, remedial reading, and psychological testing. These small special rooms are usually located near the office. They may be alternately used for conference purposes, and a conference room in the office suite may serve many of the purposes listed above. If the school has a library room, some of these activities may be scheduled there.

ROOMS FOR ATYPICAL CHILDREN

Special education programs for handicapped children are most prevalent on the elementary school level. In the secondary school, particularly at senior high school ages, these children, especially the physically handicapped, are usually integrated into the general student body as closely as possible. Arrangements must differ in accordance with local needs and policies.

There are many varieties of specialization of care and instruction which can be included in this general program area. For mental handicaps provisions range from classes for slow learners to programs for children who are severely retarded. The variety of physically handicapped pupils is great, including the blind, the partially sighted, the deaf, the hard of hearing, orthopedic cases, cerebral palsies, cardiacs, and pupils with low vitality.

A good general classroom has most of the features necessary for the instruction of atypical children, but for the physically handicapped there may be need for some special equipment and facilities, including ramps for wheelchairs, elevators, provision for noon lunches, and apparatus for such therapy as may be a part of the school program. For the mentally handicapped there is usually provided such special equipment as work benches, tools, looms, games, etc.

School programs for the handicapped are constantly being given more emphasis. Practice and emphasis vary widely from place to place and full coverage of atypical programs and facilities is much beyond the scope of this book. It should be pointed out, however, that there is a marked trend to integrate the program of activities for these children as closely as possible into the general program for all pupils at all levels.

Special Secondary School Classrooms

IT HAS already been indicated that the so-called general, or un-specialized, secondary school classroom will accommodate instruction in many of the usual secondary school subjects with variation only in equipment and furniture. This, of course, is subject to some qualification. For example, rooms which are to be used mainly for mathematics may need substantially more chalkboard area than rooms which will be used largely for instruction in English and social studies. Also, rooms which are to be used generally for instruction in English and in social studies, and perhaps also in foreign languages, should have accommodations for extensive reference book collections, and in some it may well be desirable to install a work counter for activities required in project work. By and large, however, specialization is limited to classrooms and laboratories for science, home-making, business education, music, fine arts, industrial arts, and vocational education. Even in these special areas, changes in program can be anticipated, again indicating the need for flexibility in design.

The changing nature of the secondary school program and the need for clear thinking about the program of the future have already been discussed in previous chapters. In the design of special classrooms, particularly, it is important that thought be given to direction of change and relationships among parts of the program. Too often, in the design of secondary school buildings, has there been undue emphasis on special fields and lack of thinking about the program as a whole. Some questions are peculiar to a particular field of study and some are applicable to all fields. If the design is to be forward looking, these questions must be faced. Some of them are:

1. Will emphasis upon departmentalization increase or decrease in the future?
2. If such emphasis increases, what does this imply as to size, location, and design of special facilities?
3. If emphasis upon departmentalization decreases and a trend

toward greater integration prevails, what plant implications does this have? What will be the relationship of a department and its special facility to the program as a whole? Will part of the learnings in the special field be acquired in the general education classroom? What will be the function of special instructors and the special facility?

4. How can balance be assured? What steps can be taken to prevent overemphasis on facilities for a popular or over-aggressive department at the expense of others with less aggressive staffs or less popular appeal?

5. Knowing that the secondary school program is certain to change, but not knowing just what the future program will be like, how can a school building be designed so that it will fit today's best programs and yet be readily adaptable to unknown future requirements?

As indicated in the preceding chapter, appropriate ways of hedging against these uncertainties are to keep to a minimum the degree of specialization of these special classrooms and to build into them as much flexibility as possible with the minimum of expense for alterations. The importance of this approach cannot be overemphasized.

SCIENCE FACILITIES

The typical secondary school science program today consists of what is usually known as general science in grades 7, 8, and 9, followed by a sequence of biology, chemistry, and physics, and, in large schools, other more specialized courses, with a choice and sequence for each pupil in the upper years selected in accordance with his needs and ability.

Science Classrooms

The science courses in grades 7, 8, and 9 require instructional spaces whose chief modification from the unspecialized classroom is the installation of a demonstration desk fitted with a sink and gas and electric services. These rooms also should have an adjacent storage space for the accommodation of chemicals and apparatus. A desirable addition in the classroom is counter space, preferably including a few acid-resistant sinks and service outlets for gas and electricity. This counter and the demonstration desk should have a chemical-resistant surface. The counter space will serve as a pupil work area and a place for aquariums, seed flats, animal cages, etc.

The traditional instructional arrangements for the advanced science courses of biology, chemistry, and physics consisted of specialized laboratories plus one or more lecture rooms with a demonstration table in front and tiers of seats for the pupils. Over the years this arrangement has given way first to specialized combination laboratory and recitation rooms containing laboratory desks for the specific science course plus an arrangement of tablet-arm chairs for the nonlaboratory aspects of the program. This arrangement in turn has been superseded by multipurpose science rooms with laboratory desks designed to accommodate work in biology, chemistry, physics, or other sciences, and with each room also providing seating for other classroom instruction. Figure 5 illustrates such a multipurpose room.

One of the problems in the design of science laboratories is the installation of water services, drains, gas services, and electrical services for laboratory desks arranged in various formations over the floor area of the room. Recently, there have been more installations wherein the services have been arranged along the sides of the room. In some cases a counter around two and sometimes parts of three sides of the room has been set up with movable working surfaces in the form of tables, which can be placed perpendicular to the counter when laboratory work is in progress and arranged in various formations in the central floor area when other instructional activities are in progress. In other cases fixed laboratory desks project from the walls. These arrangements promise some economy in utility installations and considerable flexibility in use, and the relative absence of utility connections in the center of the floor makes the rooms particularly adaptable to conversion to other purposes to keep abreast of future program changes. These arrangements are well worth further experimentation and trial.

Auxiliary Rooms for Science

A science suite requires a considerable amount of storage, and a common arrangement is to provide a storage and preparation room between each two science rooms. It is common practice to design and install a plant-growing area or greenhouse, and sometimes an animal room, available to the laboratories which are to be used primarily for the study of biology. Similarly, in the areas which are designated for work in the physical sciences, consideration should be given to a darkroom, a room for work in radio and electrical activities, and in a large installation a workroom containing a work bench and simple power tools such as a lathe, drill press, and saw for the construction of student-designed apparatus and working models illustrating scientific principles.

Where the storage and preparation rooms are arranged between adjacent

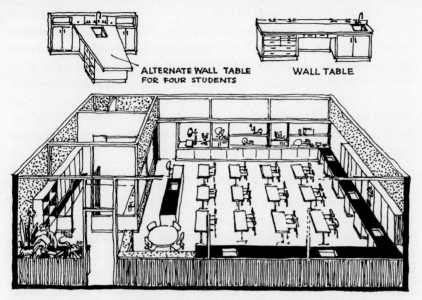

ALTERNATE WALL TABLE
FOR FOUR STUDENTS

WALL TABLE

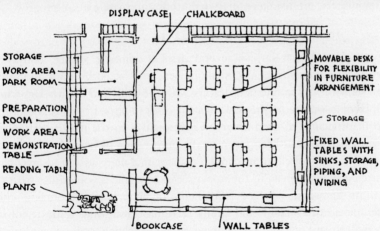

DISPLAY CASE   CHALKBOARD

STORAGE
WORK AREA
DARK ROOM

MOVABLE DESKS
FOR FLEXIBILITY
IN FURNITURE
ARRANGEMENT

PREPARATION
ROOM
WORK AREA
DEMONSTRATION
TABLE

STORAGE

FIXED WALL
TABLES WITH
SINKS, STORAGE,
PIPING, AND
WIRING

READING TABLE

PLANTS

BOOKCASE   WALL TABLES

Figure 5. A Multipurpose Science Room.

science laboratories, it is desirable that there be a door opening into each of these laboratories from the preparation room, and the equipment should include a table on casters or a rolling cart which will make it convenient for the instructors to set up apparatus in the preparation room and wheel it into either of the adjacent laboratories. The storage or preparation room should be specifically designed for the apparatus and supplies necessary for the adjacent laboratories. Special storage should be provided for balances, heavy apparatus, lengthy and odd-shaped apparatus, glass tubing, etc., as well as for chemicals and other supplies.

Other Requirements for Science

Science laboratories require special consideration with reference to ventilation, and in such areas as those devoted to instruction in chemistry it is necessary that special provisions be made for removing irritating or poisonous gases and for preventing their circulation in the laboratory and other parts of the building. Special attention should also be given to safety provisions in science laboratories, including the installation of suitable fire extinguishers, fire blankets, master shutoffs, alternate exits, etc.

HOMEMAKING LABORATORIES

Under such various general titles as domestic science, home economics, and homemaking, it is common to find on both junior and senior high school levels instruction dealing with the skills and knowledges which will be of assistance to girls, and in some cases to boys, in the establishment and maintenance of good homes. Traditionally, on the junior high school level instruction has been given in the preparation of foods and in textiles and the making of clothing. Similar courses on a more advanced level have customarily been given in the upper secondary grades, sometimes with the addition of courses selected from home nursing, home decorating, child care, home management, and family relations. From these separate courses in cooking and sewing has evolved in some schools a more generalized program of homemaking. More recently the concept has broadened further in title and purposes to "home and family living." It is realized that all youth live in families and have problems of relationships, understandings, adjustments, and participation in family life. Moreover, they will continue to live in families and will marry and create families of their own. So, home and family life education under this concept is a basic part of general education, certainly reaching far beyond activities in cooking and sewing for girls.

How best to organize and provide learning experiences in this field is not clear as yet. Solutions will vary from school to school. It is certain, however, that those faced with the responsibility of building planning must think carefully about the implications for plant in the changing nature and broadened concepts regarding this part of the secondary school program. Among the questions to be considered are: How can the home-making facilities be designed to provide maximum flexibility of arrange-ment? Does setting the department off in a separate building or "home-making house" help or hamper flexibility and integration with the rest of the school program? Should there be separate courses in foods and in clothing, with separate specialized laboratory facilities for each? Should home decorating or homemaking be taught in a homemaking apartment? Or, to suggest an opposite approach, which is presumably an outgrowth of the urge toward integration of learning activities, should all instruction in these areas be provided in generalized homemaking laboratories?

Foods Laboratory

The cooking laboratory generally associated with the traditional program in its earlier form consisted of stoves and work tables with storage space underneath, usually arranged in orderly rows down the middle of the classroom, sometimes with sinks in each row and sometimes with one or more sinks provided only along some convenient wall space. This arrange-ment of equipment gave way to the development of so-called "unit kitch-ens." Each unit kitchen consists of a grouping of kitchen equipment, such as stove, sink, counter, and cabinets, generally in locations along the laboratory wall. Each is designed to serve the instructional needs of from two to four pupils. A very common installation consists of six of these unit kitchens in one laboratory designed to serve the instructional needs of a class of 24 pupils. Accessory equipment, such as refrigerators and special storage spaces, is conveniently situated usually to serve the needs of more than one unit kitchen. Often both gas and electric stoves are provided so that by rotation of stations pupil groups can obtain instruction in the use of various types of cooking equipment.

Sewing Laboratory

The essential features for a laboratory space devoted to a course in sewing or clothing include:
1. Sewing machines, today generally electric machines of various types.
2. Electrical outlets for the machines.
3. Tables for laying out cloth and patterns and for cutting.

4. A storage system providing "tote boxes" or drawers or trays of suitable design to keep materials being used by each pupil.
5. Wardrobes for storing completed or partially completed garments.
6. A fitting space or room with one or more sets of triple mirrors.
7. Fitting forms.
8. Sink and counter.

It is essential that the light, both natural and artificial, provide a high degree of illumination and be so distributed that glare or shadows are at a minimum. The minuteness of the visual task puts a premium upon the provision of a high level of illumination, and the need for color discrimination requires a wealth of natural lighting. The principles of visual comfort and efficiency discussed in Chapter 21 should be carefully observed. Fifty foot-candles upon the work surface should be considered the minimum.

Homemaking Apartments

With the growth of instruction in the courses related to homemaking, some senior high school homemaking suites came to include an apartment with a living room, a dining room, a bedroom, sometimes a bathroom, and occasionally a kitchen, although usually the apartment was located close to the cooking laboratory and the kitchen was omitted. The purpose of this suite was to provide facilities for instruction in the arrangement of furniture, setting of tables, serving of meals, making of beds, sometimes interior decoration, etc. The extent to which the installations were used varied, depending upon changing emphasis in instruction and the capabilities of the instructors. There has, however, been a growing opinion that the actual functional value of these special apartments does not warrant their cost. Experience has shown that in many cases they are not used as intended, and are converted to other activities of entirely different character.

Generalized Homemaking Laboratories

A more recent trend is to place less emphasis upon separate courses with separate specialized laboratories for each course in the general field of homemaking instruction. This movement toward integration may take the form of shorter unit courses through which a pupil or group of pupils may during a year receive instruction and experience in the use of various types of homemaking equipment, or of courses consisting of unit activities each involving many phases of homemaking and the use of many types of equipment. When the instruction is organized in this more highly integrated fashion, the instructional space requirements call for a more generalized laboratory. In this laboratory may be found equipment for cooking, possibly arranged in a number of unit kitchens, laundry equipment, equipment for work on clothing, and a home living space in which various room arrangements may be provided as needed. It is also common for facilities to be provided for discussion or recitation in the same area through the provision of suitable seating.

Actually, the difference between the segregated laboratories and the generalized laboratory is not as great as might appear from this description. Excellent installations have been designed in which the cooking laboratory includes laundry equipment, and the clothing laboratory includes space for discussion purposes and for projects relating to the housekeeping of typical rooms. These laboratories may be in adjacent rooms or actually in one large space with provision for one or more movable partitions or folding doors so located that the entire area can be divided into two, or perhaps three, instructional spaces as needed at any particular time. An arrangement of this sort is particularly flexible, since it is adaptable to either point of view of instruction or to any variations between them.

Health and Safety Requirements

Foods laboratories or generalized homemaking laboratories are areas where hazards must be carefully considered. Fires may start in the kitchen, and it is desirable to have a master gas shutoff, suitable fire extinguishers, fire blanket, and a first-aid cabinet. Special ventilation should be provided for the kitchen. Each homemaking laboratory should have at least two exits.

BUSINESS EDUCATION CLASSROOMS

Is ability to use a typewriter with some skill desirable and necessary for everyone? Is some rudimentary knowledge of accounting procedures needed by everyone? Is family budgeting important? Is intelligent buying important? Is some knowledge of business practices and business law necessary for the average citizen?

How shall these things be taught? What kinds of facilities are necessary? Beyond this, what kind of vocational training in this field should be offered in a specific community? And what kinds of facilities does the program require? In what direction is the program in this field likely to move? Will the secondary school facilities be used increasingly for late afternoon and evening instruction in the business education field? Will there be a cooperative training program with local commercial establishments?

Answers to these and similar questions must be obtained if intelligent planning of the business education facilities is to be achieved. Although those faced with the planning problem may obtain some help by studying layouts used in other schools, basically each community has to develop its own facilities in terms of its own program.

Typewriting Rooms

Instruction in typewriting, which is found in both junior and senior high schools, and occasionally in elementary schools, requires on the secondary levels a classroom with a typewriter and a suitable table or desk for each pupil in the class. For senior high courses both manual and electric typewriters should be provided, and it is general practice to have a variety of the major brands represented.

Because typewriter tables take up more room than ordinary classroom furniture, the use of a room of ordinary size involves congestion, and too often elimination of all aisles except those at the sides of the room. This can be avoided by providing oversized rooms. Perhaps the equipment should be chosen first, in order to make it possible to determine the proper width and length of the room to accommodate the desired number of rows of desks with suitable aisle spaces. The usual procedure, however, because of the structural factors which make it more costly to vary room widths in the usual school building, is to make a longer room and reduce the number of aisles.

Naturally, a satisfactory solution could be reached by reducing the number of pupil stations, but the tendency is to keep typing classes fairly large. From 30 to 36 is no uncommon assignment, although in some cases the number runs substantially higher.

A typewriting room should have superior lighting, extra acoustical treatment, convenient outlets for electrical machines, and a sink and counter. A separate, perhaps smaller, practice room which can be used by typing pupils in their free time during and after school hours is a very desirable adjunct to the business education suite.

Bookkeeping and Accounting Rooms

The larger size of desk surfaces generally provided for instruction in bookkeeping requires more space per pupil and hence oversized rooms are usually necessary. A sink and counter should be included in each room, and more than an average amount of chalkboard should be provided.

Storage space should be abundant and to a large extent should be specifically designed. Space and suitable desks and counters should also be made available in this room for adding machines and calculators.

Office Practice and Business Machines

Business is becoming more and more mechanized, and the machines involved are becoming more varied, more complex, and more refined. Business education in schools requires more emphasis upon familiarity with machines and training in the use of general types. The office practice or business machines courses accordingly are receiving growing emphasis and more and better equipment is being provided for instruction.

The room or rooms provided for instruction in the use of business machines in office practice courses should have special attention given to acoustical properties and should have an abundance of electrical outlets conveniently located, adequate natural lighting supplemented by artificial lighting specifically designed for each machine station, and an abundance of counter work space and storage space. A clean-up sink with mirror, towels, and soap should be conveniently located. The use of protective aprons in working with mimeographs and duplicators suggests the installation of a few lockers or a closet for their storage. In small schools the space for work on business machines may be an alcove off the bookkeeping or typing room or a small room separated from it by a partition with glass panels to allow easy supervision of both areas by a single teacher.

Instruction in stenography may be in a general classroom in its beginning stages and perhaps in its advanced stages. Typewriters must, however, be available for transcription both from shorthand notes and from machine recordings.

Office practice courses may include instruction in filing, use of the telephone, receiving people, dress and make-up, and many other areas. It is essential that the local program be fully outlined and the instructional areas designed accordingly.

Distributive Education

Business education is to a large extent special education and has some fundamental vocational aspects. This is particularly true of courses in retail selling or distributive education. The space needed for instruction in this field has many laboratory characteristics. The area should be larger than the average classroom and should provide for the installation of a display window, display counters and showcases, sales counters, shelving for arrangement of stock, wrapping counters, cash register, clothes racks, dressing booths, etc.

General Requirements for Business Education

In small schools where one room must serve for instruction in various business courses, it may be advisable to have typewriter desks of school size, with a recess in the top into which the typewriter may be dropped, leaving a level desk surface suitable for use by other classes.

The business or commercial education rooms should be grouped together in a suite with the room designated for teaching of stenography adjacent to a typing room and with the business machines laboratory adjacent to the spaces designated for instruction in bookkeeping and accounting and to the distributive education laboratory if one is included.

Business education facilities are in heavy demand for adult education. For this reason they should be located to provide easy access for adults in after-school and evening hours. In small schools it may be advisable to have the business education suite near the office so that its facilities may supplement the often too limited facilities and service of the administrative offices. However, the school program in such cases should, in taking advantage of the opportunity for pupils to gain practical experience, avoid exploitation of pupil labor.

MUSIC ROOMS

Generally, special rooms for instrumental or vocal music, or both, are a feature of secondary school buildings, both junior and senior high school. In a small school unit one room may suffice for both purposes. In a larger school two or sometimes even more may be required. Where there are two rooms, one of them generally is designed specifically for work in instrumental music and the other for vocal or choral groups. There may, however, be some merit in having them interchangeable. If the school has a suitable auditorium, some of the music work may be carried on there, but the many demands upon an auditorium may make it necessary to have additional spaces specifically designed for work in music. Some schools may have elaborate ones. It should be obvious that the requirement for any particular school must be worked out in terms of the total load upon the spaces designed for auditorium purposes and music purposes.

In the design of music facilities, as with any other facility, careful thought must be given by the planners not only to the present program, but also to the future program. In considering the present program, such questions as the following will need to be considered. What are the objectives of music education? How do they contribute to the total objectives of the school? What are the music education experiences that every child should have? How can all children be helped in developing a finer sense of music appreciation? How can the ability to create original music be encouraged? Does the present music program accomplish these aims? If not, how should it be changed and strengthened? Is there an overemphasis upon performance aspects and not enough emphasis on other objectives?

Consideration of such questions as these by the planning group may bring about desirable program developments and may point the direction in which the program will continue to develop and change during the years ahead. Such consideration cannot help but have an effect on the kinds of facilities to be provided for music education. The result should be not just another facility like one built in a neighboring town, but something unique and better for the kind of program to be developed in the particular school.

Instrumental Music Room

An instrumental music room preferably should have more width than the usual oblong classroom, and while it does not need to be exactly square, and perhaps should not be so, neither should it be too long and narrow. As a matter of fact, its shape may vary considerably and there is no particular necessity that it should be a rectangle at all. Instrumental music rooms are sometimes designed with tiers or terraces of platforms either fixed in construction or designed so that they may be removed section by section when desired. In some cases there is a preference for the use of a flat floor with an elevated podium for the instructor. If tiers of platforms are to be used, it is desirable that they be removable, lest they interfere with flexibility of use of the space. Each platform should be wide enough to accommodate the seated musician with a music stand without interference from those on the next tier of seats. This width should be approximately four feet, with a wider platform on the upper rear level for the use of large instruments.

Rooms for Vocal Music

A secondary school, either junior high school or senior high school, may have a number of vocal music groups of varying sizes. In a small school a single classroom, perhaps somewhat larger than the average, may provide sufficient instructional space for this activity. In a larger school there may be some choral groups having as many as 200 pupils. Supplementing a vocal music instructional space with the use of a small auditorium and occasional use of the large auditorium may cover the needs for these larger groups. As in the case of instrumental music rooms, terraced platforms may or may not be provided; but if provided, they should be removable. A good piano should be available at all times.

Other Music Instruction Needs

Many secondary schools include in the music program courses in harmony and music appreciation. For instruction in theory, the room provided for vocal music instruction or one similar to it will be sufficient. Some programs in music appreciation call for the provision of sound-proofed spaces in which individuals or small groups can listen to records or transcriptions at any time.

It is common practice to install adjacent to the instrumental music room some practice rooms for individuals and small groups. For individual use, a minimum floor area of 60 square feet is recommended. If several of these rooms are installed, it is recommended that they vary in size.

Storage of Music

Instruction in instrumental or vocal music generally involves the accumulation over a period of time of extensive collections of music. It is good economy that these be stored in such fashion that they are well preserved, yet readily accessible. The storage facilities may be built into or against the wall of the music room, or may be in a separate music storage room or the office for the instructor. It is an excellent idea to have a counter conveniently available for sorting and laying out sheet music.

Storage of Instruments

The number and value of musical instruments owned either by the pupils or by the school makes it essential that suitable storage facilities for them be provided in, or adjacent to, the instrumental music room. Sometimes this storage is provided in an adjacent room, but it is most economical and perhaps most effective to have suitably designed cabinets along one wall of the instrumental music room. Spreading these cabinets out along an entire wall, or a large part of it, makes it possible for several pupils to be putting away or taking out instruments at one time without the congestion which may result if all of them have to enter a separate room for this purpose. If a separate room is planned, it must be remembered that the plotting of pupil traffic must consider the fact that one pupil stopping to remove an instrument from a cabinet will hold up the line. Obviously, in either arrangement, the storage cabinets for instruments need to be specifically designed for the various types and sizes of instruments which will be involved.

Storage of Uniforms and Robes

Generally, a secondary school band has uniforms. It is common practice for these to be used extensively during the fall season and periodically through the rest of the school year. Proper storage should be provided in order that they will be suitably protected from fading, dust, and moths. At the same time, they must be easily accessible. There are several possibilities involving use of fixed or movable racks with coat hangers. If the racks are movable, they can be brought out into the music room when needed and pushed back into specially designed closets after use. Robes for choral groups also require suitable storage facilities. They may either be hung on hangers or folded and stored in boxes, drawers, or cabinets, depending upon the nature of the material. Spaces used for storing uniforms and robes require adequate ventilation.

Miscellaneous Features

Consideration should be given to the possibility of microphone outlets for the public address system and for equipment that will permit recording or the transmission through the public address system of programs arising in the music room. All music rooms should have suitable and properly located electrical outlets and be provided with high-fidelity record players. The design of the room should take into account proper locations for the piano or pianos. Because of the large numbers of pupils accommodated, each of these rooms should have at least two exits.

Acoustics is very important in the case of all types of music rooms. The problem is a double one. First, it is essential that the acoustical treatment keep reverberation inside the room within proper bounds. Since too much acoustical treatment is as bad as not enough, technical help is advisable. Second, it is of prime importance that sound transmission to other spaces be prevented. Attention must be given not only to the insulation of walls against sound travel, but also to the prevention of sound transmission through ventilating ducts, floors, and ceilings. Location also plays an important part in the solution of the problem of sound transmission. It is unwise, for example, to locate music rooms immediately adjacent to the library, the offices, or to other classrooms, or under or over any of these spaces. A design which calls for isolation of the music rooms in a separate wing may fail in this respect if it is necessary to open the windows in warm weather and other facilities needing a quiet atmosphere are located near by.

Affinities

Inasmuch as music groups will be involved from time to time in programs in the school auditorium, it is desirable that the music room be located close by and easily accessible to the stage. Under these conditions, groups of pupils waiting for cues during performances may be held in the music room. If the stage has good dressing room facilities, they will be of value to the music groups when the band is changing into uniform. Accordingly, it is desirable that the access from the instrumental music room to the dressing rooms and the stage be direct and ample to avoid congestion. It is also desirable that there be direct, or nearly direct, access to the out-of-doors from the instrumental music room.

ART ROOMS

Instruction in art in the secondary school includes not only drawing and painting with various media, but also modeling or sculpturing and work with ceramics, fabrics, and many other materials and objects. Closely related to the drawing phases of art instruction, and sometimes in small schools taught by the same instructor and in the same room, is the work in mechanical drawing. In larger schools, and with more diversified courses, the work in drawing of the mechanical or technical nature, particularly in the upper levels, will be more closely related to the instruction in mathematics and in industrial arts and vocational work. Accordingly, it is necessary before the facilities for instruction in art and drawing can be worked into the plans for a new school building, that the local school authorities provide a careful analysis of the contemplated school program in these related fields.

Art rooms, because of the more active nature of the learning process and the need for use of model stands, easels, and displays, will require more room area per pupil than is provided in the average classroom. This ratio of size may well be in the nature of one and one half or two to one.

Lighting

It is sometimes specified that the art rooms should have a northern orientation, the assumption being that north light will not require shading from direct sunlight and will not cast strong shadows. This is not a necessary condition, if the room is designed in accordance with the principles of visual comfort and efficiency discussed in Chapter 21. It is important that as much reliance as possible be placed upon daylight in preference to artificial light in order that colors may be seen at their true value. This is a problem requiring ingenuity on the part of the architect, and with the variety of design and flexibility of structural planning and construction now available, no rigid specifications can be delineated here.

Equipment

Suitable art benches or drawing tables should be available for each art instructional space in accordance with the work which is to be carried on there. Each art room should have clean-up counters with a sink or sinks providing hot and cold water, and should have a moderate amount of chalkboard and as much tackboard as possible. Other equipment will include easels, paper cutters, work tables, modeling stands, filing cabinets, display provisions both within and without the classroom, connections for gas and electricity, and special storage spaces for drawing boards, picture files, unfinished projects, and models.

Affinities

If the local program heeds the relationship between the constructive and creative arts and the fine arts, the instructional facilities for art work will be closely related and adjacent to the industrial arts shop. If the industrial arts sequence includes a laboratory for arts and crafts, or handicraft work, it is the fulfillment of a natural relationship to locate the art room adjacent to the arts and crafts facilities. Projects involving ceramics, leathercraft, jewelry, art metal, and furniture will be developed in their constructive aspects in the arts and crafts room, and in their decorative aspects in the art room.

In small schools one large room may serve for work in art and in arts and crafts, an excellent arrangement to emphasize the integration possible in these fields. Where two separate but adjacent rooms are planned, they may be separated only by a folding partition which will enable them to be used in conjunction.

Similar considerations apply to the relationship between art and homemaking activities. Because of the variety of possible arrangements and the dependence of plant design upon the program, it is very essential that the scope and purposes of the local school program in these areas be fully developed and that proper specifications be given to the architect.

INDUSTRIAL ARTS SHOPS

Industrial arts in the secondary school is generally considered to be an integral part of the general education program for all pupils. Earlier program design ordinarily included only a few specific courses. A junior high school program of this nature, for example, might have included one year of woodworking, one year of metalworking, and perhaps a course in printing. A senior high school program of the same type might have included advanced courses in woodworking, metalworking, printing, and machine shop. The larger the school, the more differentiated the program, and large city schools generally offered a wide variety of specialized courses.

Perhaps because of the growing emphasis upon integration in the educational program, there has been a continuing tendency to organize general or comprehensive shop courses. Under this arrangement the program in junior high school might include general shop courses in the seventh and eighth grades and even in the ninth grade, sometimes supplemented by a few more specific courses on an elective basis. The same trend continued into the design of the senior high school program provides a pattern of broad comprehensive shop courses followed on an elective basis in the upper years by advanced courses of a more specific nature.

While one school system may have an industrial arts program based almost entirely upon special unit courses and another may have a program heavily endowed with general or comprehensive shop courses, it is possible to have a great variety of patterns containing aspects of both of these designs. Here again it must be emphasized that the design of the program is a matter for local determination, and building plans must take into account the program specifications thus developed.

Regardless of the general nature of the program organization, it can be expected that the work done with woods and metals in the earlier junior high school grades will be largely that which can be done with hand tools. Such power tools as will be installed will be used largely by the instructor or in some instances by more advanced or skillful pupils under his immediate supervision.

It must be emphasized again that industrial arts courses should not be confused with vocational shop courses. The latter are specifically designed to prepare for a certain specialized occupation or trade, whereas industrial arts courses are a part of a broad field of practical arts developing skills and knowledges which have substantial values for all pupils regardless of their future work.

Drawing Facilities

In the industrial arts curriculum, or related to it, there are two rather distinct types of work in drawing. One is that which is specifically related to the work of the course or the project which the pupil is carrying out in the shop. For this purpose, it is desirable to have some drawing tables either directly in the general shop or in an area very convenient to it and under the supervision of the same instructor. The second type is a separate course in drawing. In this case the work is regarded as a separate subject commonly referred to as mechanical or technical drawing. A course of this nature may well be chosen by a pupil whose program is heavily elective in the industrial arts fields, and it is practically a basic requirement for pupils who are taking work in most areas of vocational shop. An instructional space for the specialized course in mechanical drawing will need specially designed drawing tables with storage for drawing boards and for the drawing materials and projects of individual pupils. Blueprinting or other reproduction equipment is often provided. This drawing room requires special attention to both natural and artificial lighting.

Woodworking Shops

For the earlier years of instruction in woodworking the equipment will consist largely of woodworking benches with suitable vises, cabinets or lockers for the storage of projects, and lumber racks. There also is usually a separate space or enclosure for painting and finishing, and possibly one for tool storage which may take the form of a separate enclosure in which hand tools may be stored and inventoried. For the upper grades there will be a substantial amount of power tool installation. Here the segregation of areas for storage of tools, for storage for particular types of materials, and for the finishing of work will be more sharply defined.

Metal Shops

The program of metal work in industrial arts will usually include several fairly distinct divisions, such as sheet metal work, bench work, casting, welding, forging, and machine work. In a comprehensive shop set-up a single large instructional space will provide areas set aside for work in these various fields. In large installations there may be separate shops and separate courses in sheet metal work, welding, machine shop, and art metal.

Other Shops

The term power mechanics is sometimes employed as a title for a course covering the general fields of electricity, motors, engines, mechanisms, and vehicles. Work in such courses is usually organized around various sources of power and the application of these forces in structures, vehicles, communications, etc. There may also be shop courses in electricity, auto mechanics, and other specialized areas. Graphic arts is a term used to embrace a broad field of work which will include not only printing but photography, various processes of duplication, etching, and a study of related materials and their use. The general crafts program area includes the study of the use of textiles, leather, ceramics, plastics and similar materials, and the design and preparation of novelties, jewelry, accessories, utensils, and other items.

All of these courses need shop facilities designed to facilitate the learning activities selected for the program. For work with automobiles, trucks, and tractors, it is necessary to have one or more large doors to the shop, to install hoists, and to provide special tools and testing equipment. For printing or graphic arts the trend is away from concentration upon letterpress printing toward instruction in many forms of reproduction. The equipment is varied accordingly, including offset and various forms of photographic reproduction.

Size and Layout of Shops

It has already been emphasized that the design and specifications of the local school program must always be a matter of local responsibility. This applies particularly to the industrial arts program, which will vary from school to school. To the same extent that there will be differences in the program, so must there be variations in the facilities which are provided.

Industrial arts shops may be of various sizes and shapes. There is an increasing tendency to use an industrial type of construction for shop areas to permit future flexibility in the location of partitions and equipment. These areas are often wider than the typical secondary school classroom. For a junior high school general shop 1,800 square feet of floor area will generally accommodate equipment, special storage, and a discussion area. From 1,500 to 1,800 square feet of floor area is a fair approximation of the minimum size requirements of a junior high school woodworking shop, including all necessary accessory areas. For all upper secondary levels the size will vary to a greater extent in accordance with the number of pupil stations contemplated and with space needs of equipment which is to be installed. Obviously, it is good practice to leave some margin of space for future additions to the curriculum and the equipment which may be made necessary by them. There is, however, danger in listing definite minimum figures or ranges of sizes for shop spaces. No set of specifications can be given that will meet the varying needs of different school systems, and it is not possible to set a standard size for industrial arts shops.

It is generally considered good practice to have in a shop not only floor space for the benches and equipment but also space where the pupils may be assembled for discussion and group instruction not involving use of equipment.

Location and Affinities

Industrial arts shops are generally located on the first or ground floor of a school building. This is particularly desirable for ease in moving in equipment and in the delivery of materials. With reference to these items, it is necessary that most shop instructional spaces have wide doors leading directly to the outside of the building, with easy access from a service drive. Within the building, passage from the delivery point should be direct and simple. The delivery of lumber, for example, should not require complicated maneuvering around corridor bends or through doorways set at angles.

Even though it may be expected that good acoustical engineering will be applied to industrial arts shops, attention must be paid to the fact that these are noisy places and the location of the shops, usually in a wing by themselves, should be such that transmission of noise either through the building or across open spaces between wings will not interfere with the quieter activities in other parts of the building.

In a school having a shop installation of substantial size, it is common practice to locate the shops in a separate wing or section of the building. There are, however, various other instructional activities with close relationship to industrial arts work or drawing upon such work for contributions. Courses in graphic arts and creative arts and crafts have an obvious relationship to instruction in fine arts, and the affinity between industrial arts shops and the auditorium stage is well recognized. In the latter case, it is essential that intervening doors and passageways, as well as storage rooms, be located and sized to accommodate scenery and other stage properties that may be of awkward size or shape.

Equipment

It is essential that all the equipment and tools used in industrial arts shops be up to date and in good working condition. All installations of power equipment should be in strict accord with best industrial practice, and every safety precaution should be observed, including guards, power shut-offs, and proper location of equipment to minimize accidents which might result from interference in passage of pupils or in manipulation of materials. Suitable provisions should be made for the disposition of sawdust and other hazardous wastes, for ventilation, and for immediate and effective control of fire. Particular care must be taken in the installation of forges, kilns, and furnaces. First-aid equipment must always be at hand.

Toilets and Washrooms

When toilet rooms are located in the wing planned for industrial arts shops, it must be remembered that this work may not be confined to boys alone, although the participation of girls in industrial arts, whether justified or not, is traditionally in the minority. However, on the assumption that the participation of girls may be encouraged in the future, toilet rooms for both sexes should be provided.

Because shop work will soil the hands, washing facilities should be installed within each shop. These should include sinks or clean-up stations, with towel cabinets, soap dispensers, and mirrors conveniently located. In some shops, special clothing will be worn and lockers should be provided.

VOCATIONAL SHOPS

The space requirements for vocational or trade education are highly specific with regard to each of the many possible vocational education areas. Strictly speaking, vocational education is special education, and, except in its most elementary phases, participation is on the basis of a choice by the pupil of his intended future occupation. No prescription can be given with reference to the courses which should be provided in any locality, since these must be chosen in direct response to local needs.

This concentration upon preparation for a specific occupation represents the great difference between vocational education and industrial or practical arts. The latter are essentially aspects of general education, and participation by a pupil implies no choice of future occupation.

Because of the provision of state and federal aid for instruction in vocational education, there are often legal or administrative requirements which may to a great extent shape and regulate the form of the instructional program for each trade. One of the things the community will have to decide is whether it will shape its own vocational program to meet its own needs as a planned part of the total community educational program or whether it will allow an outside agency to impose its program requirements in order to obtain reimbursement. There need be no incompatibility and in some instances there is none. This is mentioned here because the decisions made will have an influence on the facilities to be provided. In addition to the number of trades or vocations which may be involved, there are also many varieties of programs depending on the age and status of the pupils. These include day school trade courses, closely woven into the framework of the secondary school program, apprenticeship courses, continuation school programs, and cooperative work-study programs in many fields.

Another issue that will have to be decided about the program is how much specific trade training should be the responsibility of the public schools. Is it the responsibility of the school to train men to operate a new machine or new process in a local industry or is this the industry's responsibility? Should the school train bricklayers, toolmakers, die sinkers, plasterers, carpenters, painters, electricians, television repairmen, practical nurses, and beauty operators? It is beyond this book's province to answer these questions, but the physical facilities cannot be designed without answers.

Spaces for Related Work

The total program of a student enrolled in the usual vocational education program in a secondary school involves three major types of learning activities. One of these is the shop work which generally requires about one half of the total school time, either one half of each day's program or alternate days or weeks. In addition to the shop work, there is for each trade course certain specifically prepared related instruction which will vary from course to course, or from trade area to trade area, but generally including related instruction in science, mathematics, and drawing. There will also be instruction in such fields as English, social studies, and physical education, all of which activities, whenever possible, are shared with the nonvocational pupils of the school. This last arrangement is generally regarded as important in order to prevent, as far as possible, the segregation of the vocational and nonvocational groups of the same age.

For the instruction in so-called related courses, regular classrooms of a secondary school can be used, but there is a tendency to provide special classrooms with one related classroom for each vocational shop and located close to it. It may be possible for one related classroom to serve the needs of two such shops. There are two factors affecting the size of a related classroom. One is the size of the average vocational class group which may be smaller than the average class of the school. This would allow a related classroom to be smaller than a regular classroom. However, a related classroom, because of the nature of the work carried on in it, must provide for a considerable amount of demonstration work by the instructor and space must be provided for equipment varying in nature from course to course or shop area to shop area. This factor tends to require a larger room with larger doors. Where funds and space permit, the related classroom for each shop area is generally at least as large as and sometimes larger than the average secondary school classroom. The related classrooms should be designed for projection of audio-visual materials.

Shop Spaces

Vocational shop areas for many courses require a considerable amount of floor space. A vocational shop devoted to instruction in auto mechanics, for example, must be large enough to permit work upon several automobiles at one time. Space in such a shop is also necessary for the housing of a number of automobile engines, chassis, steering assemblies, wheel assemblies, brake assemblies, greasing facilities, testing equipment, work benches, and a great variety of special machine tools which are involved in the repair of the modern automobile. Similar consideration is applied to the vocational shop in agriculture or farm mechanics, where tractors and a great variety of farm machinery will be used in instruction. Vocational shops in boat building will naturally require dimensions which can be determined only by the scope of the program and size of the boats to be constructed. Vocational machine shops contain a large amount of equipment in the nature of lathes, drill presses, milling machines, etc., generally with several units of each and with various types of each machine tool. Some shop areas require less space, generally because the items of equipment are smaller.

Location

Because vocational shop facilities are generally designed for industrial type construction which will provide large floor areas and which will be extremely flexible with reference to the changing of interior partitions or the relocation of equipment in terms of changing needs, it is usually considered good practice to place the vocational shops in a separate wing of the secondary school building or sometimes in a separate building. The location should be such that there will be a minimum of sound transmission to the rest of the school unit and that there will be easy access from a service road. In a school unit providing both industrial arts and vocational shops, the two may be more or less closely grouped together in a separate wing. Because of the varying natures of the programs, however, there is generally not much overlap in use or interchangeability of facilities. A frequent exception in small schools is the combined use of facilities for industrial arts and vocational agriculture work. Vocational shops, as well as industrial art shops, are subject to a great amount of use outside the normal day-school hours and should be located so that they can be accessible without making it necessary for night school students to pass through the other parts of the school building.

Auxiliary Spaces

Toilet rooms for boys and girls should be provided in the vocational shop area. Storage rooms, specifically designed for the service they will give to the various trade instruction centers, must be provided, including tool storage, material storage, with suitable racks, bins, and cabinets, supply storage, and project storage. Because of the requirements of the shop situation, it is generally advisable to provide an instructor's space where his desk and files may be protected by a partition. For many of the vocational shop areas it is desirable that locker and shower rooms be easily available.

Health and Safety Aspects

Particular attention must be paid to ventilation, to the avoidance of fire and accident hazards, to acoustics, and to the provision of good lighting properly arranged for each item of equipment or at each work station.

Some vocational shops present particular hazards for which precautions must be taken. In automobile shops, for example, special provision must be made for removing exhaust fumes from running motors. There should be no grease pits. All shops using gasoline, paints, and volatile and inflammable liquids of all sorts must have positive and powerful ventilation, protection against electrical sparks, and suitable fire-fighting equipment.

Shop areas used at night should have supplementary emergency lighting. Paint spray booths should have vapor-proof lamp fixtures, be constructed of a fireproof material, have self-closing doors, and be especially well ventilated. There should be special storage for paints, oils, and gas cylinders. State and local codes should be consulted on these points.

Generally, as a safety precaution, all machinery, piping, and controls in shops should be painted to conform to a color code. Some paint companies will provide free consultant service on this matter. Guide lines for machine operation stations and foot traffic are a valuable safety device.

CHAPTER 15

THE AUDITORIUM

Analysis of Local Program Needs
Determination of Capacity
Audience Facilities
Facilities for Performers
Location and Relationships

IN ANY school having more than one classroom, it is desirable that there be a place where pupils can be assembled in larger groups for various purposes. Except for very small schools this building feature assumes major importance and requires serious attention in the planning process. Facilities may vary from small assembly halls with simple stage accommodations to large auditoriums having most or all of the features of a large theater.

Analysis of Local Program Needs

THE determination of the assembly room needs for any projected school requires analysis of the major purposes of such facilities in terms of the needs of the local situation. The planning must give full recognition to these needs as they may be classified under three major categories, namely: the needs of the instructional program, the needs of the social life of the school, and the needs of the community. Each of these must be carefully examined to determine the capacity of the required assembly space, its design, and the facilities and equipment to be provided.

NEEDS RELATING TO THE INSTRUCTIONAL PROGRAM

The primary need for including an assembly space in a school is to meet the requirements of the instructional program. Included here are musical presentations, dramatic enterprises, talks, and projections of films and slides, all meant to convey information, understanding, and appreciations to the pupils assembled as the audience. Also to be considered within the scope of this purpose are the learnings achieved by pupils who are involved in various types of presentations for which a stage and audience are necessary.

NEEDS RELATING TO THE SOCIAL LIFE OF THE SCHOOL

A second and very important need is that which relates to the social life of the school, including not only the integrative needs of the group but also the entertainment values. In this category are included those activities which contribute to the enjoyment of school life, to the development of pupil morale, and to the general aims of school government. Common examples are moving pictures, lectures by humorists, shows by magicians, sports rallies, student council assemblies, and drives for the sale of student activity tickets.

CIVIC AND COMMUNITY NEEDS

A third major need for an auditorium space in a school unit is the fulfillment of civic and community requirements, either for the community as a whole or for that fractional but often tightly knit portion of the total community known as a neighborhood. Included under this heading are those events in which parents and citizens participate either in presentations or in audience situations. These include community concerts, recitals, parent-teacher meetings, civic meetings, and all sorts of group gatherings where stage and audience space are needed.

Determination of Capacity

On the basis of the analysis of local needs in terms of the purposes of assembly spaces, it is possible to determine such factors as the capacity of the audience space, the nature and size of the stage facilities, and the character of auxiliary spaces. One of the most important questions to be settled is that of capacity. Because an auditorium is a relatively expensive facility and one which is extremely difficult to enlarge after once built, it is essential that its original capacity be properly established. Capacity must be considered for both school needs and community needs.

CAPACITY FOR SCHOOL USE

By and large the variables which serve to establish the proper size for a school auditorium are the grade level of the school and the number of pupils to be enrolled. A small auditorium is more suitable for small children with immature voices and offers a less formal and less overwhelming situation to them. A reasonable minimum capacity for a six-grade elementary school is one half of the expected ultimate enrollment, since assemblies of upper elementary and primary grade children may, because of differing interest levels, be scheduled separately.

In small schools where there is a chance for expansion, whether elementary or secondary, it appears to be desirable to provide an assembly room which will seat all pupils with some margin for growth in enrollment and with the thought that the original provision will seat at least half the ultimate enrollment of the school. Except in rare cases, few auditoriums with full stage facilities would be constructed to seat less than 350 or even 400 persons. Anything smaller would hardly justify the expense of building a good stage and would too often take the form of an assembly hall with a platform or incomplete stage.

A 350- to 400-seat auditorium will more than accommodate the needs of a six or seven room elementary school. It will allow for growth in enrollment and for community needs. For a school twice as large it will just about meet the seating requirements for all pupils. If the school grows further in enrollment, it will be necessary to hold duplicate assemblies, and the same will hold true for schools initially larger.

Many educators believe that the minimum desirable enrollment for a secondary school is about 500 pupils in a four-year school or 400 pupils in a three-year school. An auditorium seating capacity of 400 to 500 pupils will satisfy the initial needs of a school of minimum size yet accommodate an enrollment of 800 to 1,000 pupils. A space seating 800 pupils will meet needs for an enrollment up to 1,500 pupils. Many authorities prefer not to have a capacity in excess of 1,000.

In a large school or in a school where the main auditorium is large, it is well to plan a smaller assembly room with a complete stage. This room will be used by dramatic groups and choral groups, for speech instruction, for certain audio-visual purposes, for pupil and other group meetings, and for many other purposes for which the main auditorium is too large.

CAPACITY FOR COMMUNITY USE

The high school auditorium is generally the only suitable place in the community, particularly in a small town or village, for large community or civic group meetings. In such a case, it might be advisable to plan an auditorium larger than that required for school purposes. In a large city there may be a municipal auditorium or arena which will serve the needs of the city for events having extraordinarily large audiences, but it is quite likely that there will be so many community activities that there will also be a great deal of community use of school auditoriums. Under such conditions a high school auditorium seating as much as the total school enrollment, or perhaps more, may well have extensive use for community concerts, recitals, local theater groups, and performances by various types of organizations. However, facilities planned to seat more than 1,200 tend to become excessively expensive. Beyond this capacity, furthermore, the effectiveness for instructional purposes and its value for the audience are diminished.

In large communities there is also a consistent need for meeting places on the neighborhood level. The number of organizations in a modern city in need of meeting places of only moderate size is almost endless. To serve community needs the auditoriums of junior high schools or elementary schools in a metropolitan area are generally in great demand. Good school policy requires that they be made available freely for educational and civic purposes.

Audience Facilities

IN TERMS of function the auditorium must provide two major types of service. One of these is the accommodation of the audience; the other is the accommodation of those involved in the performance. From the point of view of the audience, the design of the audience space—including its shape, the slope of the floor, the nature and arrangement of seats, the lighting, ventilation, and acoustics, and the supplementary accommodations provided for audience use—demand careful planning if the auditorium is to fulfill its purpose successfully.

SHAPE OF AUDIENCE SPACE

School auditoriums are, and have been, built in all sorts of shapes. The typical small auditorium in an elementary school, and often those provided for secondary schools, are oblong, generally with the stage on an end of the rectangle. In older buildings the oblong was a typical design because it fitted easily into the total mass of the building. Newer designs present audience spaces in a great variety of shapes, and there is no one plan which can be considered superior to all others.

However, the shape of an auditorium, at least of its interior, is important from the point of view of acoustics and sight lines. It is very important that competent professional advice be obtained in the planning of the audience space. The design of an auditorium and stage is a highly involved problem demanding that a good architect be given freedom to use his creative skill and draw upon experts in acoustics, illumination, and ventilation.

THE AUDITORIUM FLOOR

Unless the level of the stage floor is excessively high, seating on a flat or level floor will provide good vision of the activities upon the stage for only a very limited distance. Accordingly, only the smallest assembly halls should be designed with level floors. School administrators are acutely aware of the problems arising from auditoriums planned to seat four or five hundred people without a sloping floor. Beyond the tenth or twelfth row the members of the audience are very limited in their view of the stage. Under these conditions pupils easily lose interest in the action on the stage and mischief prevails. When interest persists, those in the rear will half stand or kneel upon the seats in order to see over the heads of those in front. These actions, particularly with the usual type of movable seating, make considerable noise which in turn interferes with the general conduct of the audience and the ability of all to pay attention to the performance.

The proper design of an auditorium floor is a technical problem requiring careful planning in order to provide good sight lines. The slope of the floor and the correct height of the stage depend upon the size of the auditorium and must be considered together.

Generally, orchestra pits are not provided in school auditoriums, but the first row of seats is set back far enough that the school orchestra may be accommodated in front of the stage when it plays accompaniments for school dramatic enterprises.

The older secondary school auditoriums, and in some cases those provided for larger elementary schools, had balconies. Sometimes the balcony was extended straight across the rear of the audience space, although many cases may be found where it was carried across the back and also along both side walls. Where these side extensions were of any great length, there were usually many seats which were of little value for observation of stage performances. Modern design has made balconies unnecessary within ordinary size ranges for school auditoriums. This is fortunate because they have always presented administrative problems and generally have added substantially to the expense of construction.

Recently some consideration has been given to the planning of spaces which resemble an arena with seating on all sides of a central area where the action takes place. This so-called "theater-in-the-round" has a quality of informality and is suitable for certain types of school presentations. However, because of its lack of utility for many school and community uses, it would seem advisable to have this feature included in a school building only if there were also available a standard auditorium with a standard stage. Actually, the theater-in-the-round arrangement can be installed in the

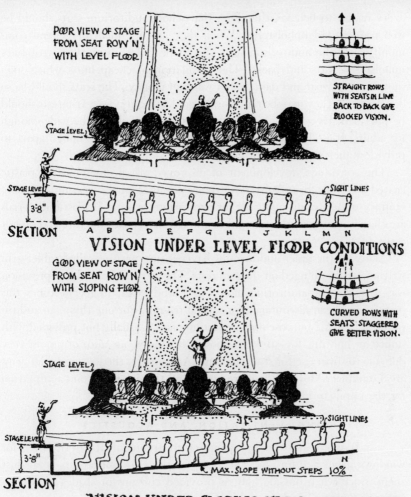

POOR VIEW OF STAGE FROM SEAT ROW 'N' WITH LEVEL FLOOR

STRAIGHT ROWS WITH SEATS IN LINE BACK TO BACK GIVE BLOCKED VISION.

STAGE LEVEL

STAGE LEVEL

SIGHT LINES

3'-8"

SECTION   A B C D E F G H I J K L M N

VISION UNDER LEVEL FLOOR CONDITIONS

GOOD VIEW OF STAGE FROM SEAT ROW 'N' WITH SLOPING FLOOR

CURVED ROWS WITH SEATS STAGGERED GIVE BETTER VISION.

STAGE LEVEL

STAGE LEVEL

SIGHT LINES

3'-8"

MAX. SLOPE WITHOUT STEPS 10%   N

SECTION

VISION UNDER SLOPING FLOOR CONDITIONS

Figure 6. Auditorium Sight Lines.

cafeteria or in the gymnasium when wanted, if suitable provision is made for lighting and acoustics.

AUDITORIUM SEATING

In the well-designed auditorium with a suitably sloping floor, it is essential that the seats be securely fixed to the foor. Youth of school age are inevitably hard on furniture, and unless the seating is securely fastened, it is invariably worked loose. If the seats are comfortable, there will be less restlessness of the pupils and better attention to the performance. There is every reason to believe, therefore, that school auditorium seats should be well padded and upholstered. When they are intended for general community use, the auditorium seats should be full theater type with fully upholstered seats and backs. The installation of cheap units which soon show signs of wear and damage is a waste of money. The seats should be so designed that they may be raised or lowered without noise. Arm rests should be provided. Even in elementary schools the seats should be wide enough for adults. It is also essential that the rows be placed far enough apart to provide sufficient knee room for adults.

The continued development of improved plastic materials or plastic coated materials for upholstery purposes promises longer wearing and more sanitary upholstering materials for auditorium seating. If plastic materials are chosen, however, they should be those which resist puncture and do not easily tear.

Many of the older auditoriums have seating with so-called tablet arm writing surfaces hinged on the arm rests. The purpose behind this provision was to make the auditorium useful as a study hall. In recent times this practice has been discouraged for several reasons. For one thing, an auditorium for its basic purpose does not require and is usually not provided with sufficient lighting for study purposes. Secondly, an auditorium is very difficult to supervise for study hall use. And finally, the folding tablet arms are a nuisance. Most of them are noisy, and there is a constant temptation for the pupils to manipulate them.

LIGHTING, VENTILATION, AND ACOUSTICS

It is not unusual to encounter an argument about the need for windows in an auditorium. The trend of thinking appears to be against them, since when outside light is provided curtains or shades are drawn when the auditorium is in use.

The artificial lighting in the seating space should be adjustable in intensity, with perhaps two or three levels of illumination. Some or all of these should be controllable from the rear of the auditorium as well as from the stage. At least some light should be controllable from each entrance. Exit lights should have separate circuits, preferably with provision for emergency current from an auxiliary source. Particularly if the auditorium is to be used for large commercial productions, there should be shaded directional lighting in the aisles.

The auditorium must be well ventilated, and there should be no discernible noise from the ventilation equipment. The ventilation, the heating system, and the acoustics should be carefully designed to meet the needs when the auditorium is either partly or completely filled. These are technical engineering problems requiring the services of experts.

THE LOBBY AND RELATED FACILITIES

The larger the auditorium, the larger must be the lobby. Also, the greater the community use, the larger must be the lobby. The lobby is, in essence, a gathering place of persons waiting to purchase tickets or greeting and conversing with friends prior to taking their seats. As far as the learning activities of the school are concerned, the lobby is largely waste space, and for this reason it is often slighted in the design of school plants. When such facilities are used by the public, the inadequacy of the lobby often leads to criticism. Sometimes the lobby to the auditorium, if suitably located, may serve as a pupil lounge, pupil activity space, or as a waiting room for bus pupils. It is desirable in planning that a careful evaluation be given to the relative importance of school use and community use.

Obviously, any lobby should be tastefully decorated, carefully arranged with reference to traffic flow between the outside entrance and the entrance from the lobby into the auditorium space, and devoid of awkward shapes and wall angles or corners interfering with smooth traffic flow.

Ticket Booth

For community use and for school presentations where admission is charged to the public, it is essential that there be a place where tickets may be sold in the lobby of the auditorium. The location of this facility requires considerable thought. If it is just inside the entrance, the lining up of patrons for the purchase of tickets may well cause congestion and force some to stand outside the door. It is better to put the booth well inside the lobby away from the outer entrance so that such lines as may form may be accommodated completely inside the lobby. Often one person out of a couple or group will get in line at the ticket window, and his companions will wait while the tickets are being purchased. For this reason, it is desirable that the ticket booths be so located that the public may come into the lobby and be well away from the entrance doors while those who are to purchase the tickets form in line.

Public Toilets

It is often possible to place pupil toilet rooms in locations convenient to the entrances to the auditorium in order that they serve not only the pupils but also the parents and other citizens who will comprise the audience at evening functions. In large auditoriums it is desirable to have a separate set of public toilets located near the lobby or entrances to the auditorium. In such cases it is essential that the toilet rooms be ample in size and adequately equipped to serve large numbers of people when the demand is heavy during intermissions. Too often the design of auditoriums makes only a slight concession to this need, with inadequate equipment tucked away in spaces left over during the planning of the lobby and auditorium space.

Check Rooms

In small and medium-sized schools the requirement of space for the checking of outer clothing is very often met by the use of an adjacent classroom. Coats and hats are placed upon desks or tables brought in for that particular purpose. Portable racks may be brought in when necessary. In larger installations it is sometimes desirable to have a specially designed cloakroom similar to those provided in theaters, hotels, or other public places. Inasmuch as these spaces have no relation to school use and are utilized infrequently, it is difficult to justify the added cost of their installation and make them adequate for large group use. If they are provided, they must be specifically designed to meet the demand upon them. It is false economy to devote any space to checkrooms which may prove inadequate for the load imposed upon them by a full audience.

Facilities for Performers

A GOOD auditorium must not only furnish comfort and convenience for the audience, but it must also include properly designed facilities to insure that the presentation to the audience may proceed smoothly and efficiently. For this it is essential that the stage, the projection facilities, the lighting, and all other necessary backstage accommodations be properly designed and provided.

THE STAGE

Too often learning values of an otherwise satisfactory auditorium are severely reduced because the stage is made too small. One does not have to visit many older buildings to find cases where a shallow stage has been altered by building a wide apron across its front, even in many cases with the installation of false fronts or curtains to shelter the wings. These rebuilt stages are generally makeshift and rarely satisfactory. Many school buildings of recent design, particularly elementary schools, include stages which have suffered from false economy in the building of a storeroom or a stairway for an exit at one side of the stage, completely removing the wing space on that side.

Except under unusual conditions, it is probably a good rule of thumb to say that the width of the stage, including the wings, should be approximately the same as the greatest width of the auditorium seating space. It is also good practice to design the stage so that the wings as far as possible are unobstructed by partitions or fixed equipment. The practice in older buildings of extending a partition from the edge of the proscenium arch to the rear of the stage on each side, with a door in each partition leading to a side room, has largely been abandoned. Yet this design is occasionally found in relatively new buildings.

The dimensions of the stage must depend upon the sizes of the groups and the nature of the activities to be accommodated. Normally a school stage will at times be used by large choruses and for pageantry, and a size ample for such occasions will be sufficient for other uses. A minimum depth (front edge to rear wall) of 18 to 20 feet is commonly recommended for elementary schools and 25 to 35 feet or more for secondary schools. Twenty-five feet is often suggested as the minimum width of the proscenium arch for small auditoriums, but in some large secondary school auditoriums a width of 40 to 50 feet may be provided. The height of the proscenium arch must provide suitable sight lines from the rear seats of the auditorium. Expert technical advice is necessary. The best procedure is to specify all desired uses of the stage in terms of nature of performance, number of performers, etc., and allow the architect to evolve a proper design.

For a school auditorium, including even large secondary school auditoriums, it is generally unnecessary to have a stage attic or gridiron for the purpose of "flying" scenery. It is not needed for school use and represents an uneconomical expenditure of considerable magnitude. There should be no catwalks or high-level platforms accessible to pupils.

The Stage Floor

While the front and center sections of the stage floor are desirably built of hardwood, it is convenient to have the surrounding area made of softwood in order that the scenery may be anchored easily by nailing or by using special screws and braces which are available for the purpose.

Sometimes the front part of the stage consists of sections or boxes which when in place are level with the rest of the stage. These sections can be arranged to form two or more steps or terraces, which are useful for choruses and other large groups. This design is largely restricted to small elementary schools. Its desirability is questionable.

WORK SPACES FOR STAGECRAFT

Part of the educational value of stage presentations of a dramatic nature lies in the construction of stage scenery and stage properties by pupils. For this purpose there should be additional available wing space or an adjacent stagecraft room. This purpose can also be fulfilled by locating the arts and crafts room or industrial arts shop close to the stage. In these auxiliary spaces the stagecraft club or the students who are preparing the scenery may build and decorate the various flats and drops for such stage sets as are necessary for any particular enterprise.

STORAGE

It is also very essential that suitable storage space adjacent to the stage be provided for the storage of scenery and properties. While it is common practice to store more of these materials than is necessary, since the anticipation of future use for some materials never is realized, nevertheless they will be stored somewhere, and it is better to have a properly designed and located storage space than to have them lying around in corridor ends, under stairways, and in other makeshift storage places which are frequently hazardous.

ACCESS AND AFFINITIES

The stage should be so located and designed that it will be directly accessible from the school corridors on both sides or from one side and the rear, with side access from the audience space. It should not be necessary to go through the audience space to reach the stage. There should be at least one large door for direct access to a service delivery or loading platform. There should also be easy access to the arts and crafts room or industrial arts shop and to the music suite. Obviously, in the design of a school building, it is impossible to get everything immediately adjacent to everything else, but careful planning can supply the relation of spaces according to their affinities.

LIGHTING AND COMMUNICATIONS

The electrical equipment for a stage in a school auditorium should provide adequate lighting, preferably including rear and ceiling spot lights with suitable controls, and except in a very small school, provisions for overhead colored lights and for the dimming of lights. There is a growing tendency to omit footlights. In schools where public address systems are installed, it is sometimes recommended that provision be made for wiring the stage microphone into the public address system. There is, however, some question about the utility of this arrangement and probably it should not be done if there is considerable expense involved. The design of stage

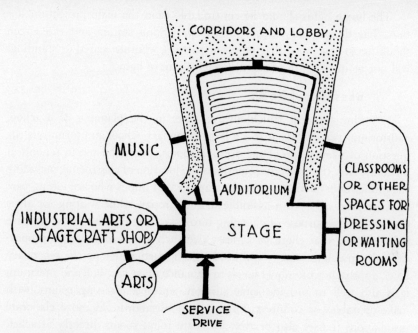

Figure 7. Facilities with Important Relationships to the Stage.

lighting and public address equipment is a relatively complex problem requiring the services of specialists. Good judgment must be used in order that these facilities are neither too elaborate nor so meager that makeshift arrangements are later installed.

PROJECTION FACILITIES

A station or stations where projection equipment may be located is essential. Inasmuch as it is now universal practice to use 16-mm. safety-type film in schools, it is generally considered unnecessary to provide for a 35-mm. projector. By the same token, it is not necessary to install the absolutely "fireproof" projection booth which was considered a must in the early years of motion picture projection. However, it is a great convenience to have some sort of enclosure where the projectors and accessory equipment may be both used and stored. It is also convenient to have a station in the central aisle not too far back from the stage, where short-throw projecting devices can be used with small audiences. There should be a suitable screen for the showing of motion pictures, and there is good evidence that the provision of a motorized screen results in less wear and tear than hand operation. Suitable connections should be made to speakers properly located for use with sound movies.

The house lights should be controllable from the main projection station. The design and location of the projection station and the screen should be so developed that pupils or patrons, whether seated or standing, will not be in the path of the projected beam of light.

DRESSING ROOMS

One problem which always arises in the planning of a school auditorium, particularly if it is a large secondary school auditorium, is the question of what to do about dressing rooms. For pupil use in schools of moderate size, the answer is sometimes the location of classrooms, including the music room or rooms, near the stage so that pupils who are taking part in stage productions can assemble in these rooms while waiting for their cues or for the purpose of changing into costumes. For this latter purpose it is desirable that there be at least two such spaces of generous proportions. Inasmuch as many pupil productions, particularly on the secondary level, approach professional levels in demands upon costume and make-up, it is also well to provide some suitably equipped dressing rooms, with make-up tables or counters, mirrors, and washbowls. In more elaborate installations it may also be well to locate toilet rooms directly attached to each dressing room and to design the dressing rooms so that there may be as many as six or eight make-up stations in each one. This provision is of particular value if the auditorium is to accommodate to a large extent community productions or professional groups which are brought in from time to time by community concert associations or theater guilds. Even with dressing rooms, it is important that there also be conveniently located large spaces which can be utilized as waiting areas for large groups such as choruses. No prescription can be made of facilities which will fit all situations. It is desirable that the school planners in any particular community make a careful study of community and civic needs.

If dressing rooms are provided, it is desirable that they be on the same level as the stage. The building of dressing rooms in the wing spaces, piled up in several stories accessible only by stairways from the stage, is an undesirable arrangement.

Location and Relationships

IN THE schools of an earlier day the assembly hall or auditorium was often located on the top floor. The construction of an auditorium space over a gymnasium or over a cafeteria was also a rather common arrangement, perhaps on the assumption that the two elements in each case should have the same floor area and hence would fit more easily into the building shell if one were placed over the other. Gradually the auditorium has been brought down to the ground floor. Considerations of safety and convenience of access have been instrumental in this movement. The trend toward more flexibility and openness in design has made this placement possible, and the rapidly growing acceptance of the single-story building has been a compelling force in this trend. The auditorium of the present-day school is most likely to be one of the distinguishable elements of the total building complex, designed specifically to fulfill its purposes and facilitate its functions, located for greatest convenience, and integrated into the total building design in a free and simple fashion.

Inasmuch as a school auditorium may be used extensively for community purposes, whether it is a large auditorium in a secondary school of considerable size or a small auditorium in an elementary school, it is essential that it be so located that it will be easily accessible to the public without making it necessary for people to use an entrance at some distance from the auditorium and to travel through school corridors to reach the audience space. The general layout of building and site should bring the auditorium, access drives, and parking spaces into convenient relationship.

In order that the school building may be properly supervised, it is also desirable that arrangements be made so that the auditorium and lobby may be physically separated from the rest of the school building by gates or doors.

It is particularly important in cold climates that the heating and ventilating systems of the school be so designed that the auditorium may be used whenever necessary when the rest of the school is closed without making it necessary to heat the entire building. This is done with relative ease with modern heating systems, but unless provision is made in the planning for zoned heating, it may be found later that the auditorium cannot be used on cold evenings without heating the entire building.

LITTLE THEATER

It has been suggested that in a big school the large auditorium be supplemented by a small auditorium or little theater. The location of the small auditorium depends upon the layout of the total building plan. There are close affinities with both the language arts and the music areas. This facility is also likely to be in great demand for community use, particularly for activities for which the large auditorium would be greatly out of scale. Accordingly, there should be convenient public access.

PHYSICAL AND HEALTH EDUCATION FACILITIES

IN THE all-around education of the child it is necessary to provide instruction relating to the physical aspects of living as well as the intellectual. This has been long realized in theory, but, in general, the physical education program has achieved only spotty, and generally far too scant, consideration in the schools of America. Too often and to too great an extent interscholastic athletics, because of its popular appeal, has received a preponderance of attention to the detriment of, and even in place of, a well-planned instructional program in physical education. In addition to the direct effects of this misplacement of emphasis, there has been developed in the minds of some educators, and even in the thinking of some school building planners, a tendency to "throw the baby out with the bath." This takes the form of a de-emphasis upon physical education programs and the development of suitable facilities for instruction in this field.

The Physical Education Program

THESE conflicting points of view and the high public interest in many aspects of the physical education program, particularly in interscholastic athletics, make it especially important that those who plan facilities for physical education give thorough consideration to the purposes to be achieved and to the activities which they require. In a general sense, athletic activities are a part of the physical education program, and they will be so considered in this book. Health instruction, too, is included for convenience, even though it is not so considered in all schools.

PURPOSES AND TYPES OF ACTIVITIES

The first important purpose of the physical education program, and one which has undoubtedly been of great value in promoting the well-being of the current generation, is the development of physical fitness. Included in this general category are the development of muscular strength and tone, the improvement of physical co-ordination, the development of agility, and the acquisition and maintenance of good posture. A second major aim is the development of the ability of each pupil to maintain health and physical fitness throughout life. For this purpose it is essential that proper health habits be established as a result of suitable instruction and practice and that the many and varied health facts be learned by the pupil in such fashion that they will contribute to his present and future betterment.

It is essential that every boy and girl include in his program suitable individual or team games in which he can actively participate not only during his school career but also in later life. For the latter, it is essential that emphasis be given to those physical recreation activities which do not require large numbers. These so-called "carry-over" or individual sports include golf, swimming, tennis, bowling, etc. It is advisable that instruction in these fields be given considerable emphasis and that these activities not be minimized in favor of the more spectacular team games.

The team sports, which have not only participation values but spectator interest as well, have become an integral part of the American scene of life. As school activities, they contribute to such worth-while objectives as the learning of cooperative team work, sportsmanship, fair play, timing, co-ordination, and the following out of instructions in group activities.

In some schools the physical education program has been developed to include a considerable breadth of activities on a rotational basis through the week. Such a weekly program in a secondary school, for example, might include for girls one period each of gymnasium floor work, swimming, dance instruction, health instruction, and games. A parallel program for boys might encompass the same or similar activities, but possibly with more emphasis upon games or floor work or on such special and more rigorous activities as wrestling, tumbling, and weight lifting. Games for children in the lower elementary grades are simpler and less highly organized than those for older children.

Many schools have programs including what is known as "corrective" or "adapted" physical education. This varies from generalized activities designed to develop and maintain good posture for groups of selected pupils to special exercises individually prescribed for handicapped pupils.

There is no uniform pattern for health instruction. In elementary schools it is usually taught in the self-contained classrooms, and often is closely integrated with other subjects. At the secondary school level it may be a separate course or it may be part of the science program. An arrangement preferred by some is to schedule a period of health instruction in a typical classroom situation in the weekly physical education program. Still another alternative is to combine health instruction with the daily gymnasium period.

Determination of Program and Facilities

THE pattern of activities will vary from school to school depending upon age of pupils, local interests and customs, and climatic conditions as related to the possibility of outdoor play. These differences in program require, in many cases, differences in the plant facilities. Since the physical education facilities within the building are relatively costly to construct and difficult to remodel, it is essential that they be as nearly right as possible when the building is erected. This requires careful planning.

LOCAL RESPONSIBILITY FOR PROGRAM

It is the responsibility of the local school authorities and local citizens to determine the scope and character of the physical education program, but it is reasonable to expect that in this process the advice of educational consultants may be sought. It is particularly important that the program already existing not be used as a basis for planning a new building if the program has been in any way restricted by inadequate accommodations. Also, it seems to be only common sense to give as much attention to the needs of girls as to those of boys. It has been a common experience of the authors to find situations in which the boys in a high school may have three, four, or five periods of physical education each week while the girls may be restricted to perhaps two periods. Many school administrators have struggled with this problem but have found themselves blocked in any attempt to provide for the girls as good and as full a program as for the boys because of lack of instructional spaces.

The decisions to be made locally must deal with such questions as the following: How much time per day or per week shall be devoted to instruction in physical education and health education for boys? For girls? In what size classes shall such instruction be given? What shall be the program in the elementary schools? In the junior high school? In the senior high school? What part shall interscholastic athletics play on each level for boys? For girls? What emphasis shall be given to intramural competition, and what activities shall be be included for boys? For girls?

DETERMINATION OF NUMBER OF INSTRUCTIONAL SPACES

For the calculation of the number of teaching stations necessary it is possible to use the formula already described in Chapter 6. However, particular attention must be given to the following in the application of this formula to physical education, especially at the secondary school level:

1. If there are several physical education teaching spaces, it is necessary to analyze the program carefully in order to determine how many should be gymnasium floor areas and how many should be of other types.

2. A realistic choice must be made of the desirable class size. If the figure is set too low, it may be impossible to raise funds for the number of instructional spaces required by application of the formula. On the other hand, it should not be set too high, lest the conditions become unworkable and teaching effectiveness be impaired.

3. In the calculations it must be remembered that there will be an average of perhaps 5 to 10 percent of the pupils absent each day throughout the school year, and that some will provide doctor's certificates which in many cases will require that they be completely excused from all forms of physical activity.

4. It is also necessary to note that a certain proportion of the girls, especially in the senior high school, may be expected to be excused periodically from physical education.

5. Many secondary schools also have the practice of excusing from the regular physical education program the groups, both boys and girls, who are engaged in athletics.

DETERMINATION OF TYPES OF SPACES

To a large extent in the United States, particularly in northern climates, the rigors of winter make it necessary to conduct much of the physical education program indoors. Many other aspects, however, can be conducted out-of-doors. Indoor spaces and equipment for various types of floor work, dancing, tumbling, and rhythmic activities will usually be required. Spaces will also be needed for such games as basketball (including modified forms for younger pupils), volley ball, handball, softball, and many special games for younger children. The indoor competitive sports program, particularly at the secondary school level, will often require facilities for wrestling and swimming. The outdoor activities requiring consideration in planning are many and varied, and encompass far more than competitive sports and games for older pupils. Specific types of spaces that might be required are suggested later in this chapter.

A thorough study of the activities which may be included in the physical education program will indicate the variety of instructional spaces which may be called for and point out the fact that generally much more than a gymnasium floor is necessary. The most important types of indoor teaching spaces are the gymnasium floor, the health classroom, the swimming pool, and miscellaneous instructional spaces for a variety of special purposes. All of these will vary in type, size, design, and equipment according to local needs and financial resources; hence no standard pattern is advisable. Recognizing this need for variation, the major types of instructional spaces are described below as an aid to local planning.

The Gymnasium Floor as an Instructional Space

IT IS obvious that most of the basic indoor activities of the physical education program require a large, unobstructed floor area—that is, a gymnasium floor. A space of 2,400 to 2,800 square feet is generally considered desirable for a secondary school teaching floor. For elementary schools a somewhat smaller area, possibly 1,500 to 2,000 square feet, will usually suffice because of the simpler nature of the games and rhythmic activities at this level. This is particularly true for the kindergarten and primary grades.

If the gymnasium is to be used for basketball, which is quite likely at the junior and senior high school levels, somewhat greater floor areas will be needed to allow courts of standard size. Extra area may also be required for spectator seating space. These two aspects are discussed later in the chapter.

For schools which require two instructional areas on the gymnasium floor, an area large enough for a standard junior high school or senior high school basketball court, including the necessary area at the sides and ends of the court, will be sufficient, if divided by a folding partition or other similar device. The two instructional areas can be thrown into one when necessary. It is desirable that a suitable recess in the wall of the gymnasium be provided to receive the partition when it is folded back. A motorized partition, designed for ease and durability in use, is to be preferred.

For larger schools in which more than two gymnasium floor instructional spaces are needed, the solution may be found in making the main gymnasium floor somewhat wider and slightly longer to give a total floor area approximating 10,000 square feet. Such an area can be divided into four instructional spaces. Another solution is to build a second gymnasium. Sometimes this latter procedure is favored, with one gymnasium generally designated for use by boys and the other by girls.

Theoretically, in a growing situation the need for expansibility can be left for satisfaction by the later erection of a second gymnasium. The difficulty is that too often the second gymnasium is not built, and the physical education program in the enlarged school is restricted to the original space. Another solution is to design the original structure so that an end or side wall may be removed and the floor area increased.

CONSTRUCTION OF THE GYMNASIUM FLOOR

No better floor material has been found than properly laid hard maple. The lumber should be rigidly selected for quality and uniformity of color, and the specifications should call for narrow widths of the finished flooring boards in order to prevent the strips from cupping.

The finished floor should be laid to provide resiliency, and suitable provisions should be made along all sides to allow for expansion and contraction. A metal shoe attached only to the wall is the usual procedure for covering the joint and protecting the base of the wall.

The floor should be laid in such fashion that moisture from condensation will be prevented as far as possible from accumulating underneath. Maple floors should be treated with a penetrating seal. Over this should be painted the lines for game areas, and the final treatment should be a high quality gymnasium floor finish.

HEIGHT OF SPACE

For gymnasium spaces in which basketball will be played, there should be a minimum unobstructed height of at least 20 feet. Heights substantially in excess of this figure are unnecessary. Playrooms designed for use only by primary grades will not need a ceiling height in excess of

12 or 14 feet. The upper elementary grade program may include some modified form of basketball, and a ceiling height of approximately 18 feet will be necessary.

WALLS

The walls of a gymnasium space are subject to rough treatment, and to a height of at least 6½ feet, and preferably as much as 8 feet, should be finished in a material with great resistance to marking and scarring. All corners should be rounded, and there should be no obstructions in the form of doors swinging into the activity space, columns, pipes, ducts, or radiators. Upper portions of the walls may be painted cinder block, painted plaster, brick, or any other material that may be easily cleaned.

LIGHT

Throughout the gymnasium suite there ought to as much natural light as can be obtained and suitably controlled. This is especially important for locker rooms and team rooms. It is also generally preferred for the gymnasium floor area, but the daylighting must be designed so that it will not interfere with the clear vision required for basketball, badminton, etc. Various arrangements of top or monitor lighting have been used satisfactorily. Diffusing glass or glass blocks properly located may be used, but high brightness contrasts should be avoided. Because of the difficulty of controlling natural light and the fact that it usually is supplemented by artificial light even during the daytime, there are some who suggest that natural light may be unnecessary. This seems, however, to be a minority opinion.

Artificial lighting should be ample and designed to give an even distribution of illumination without shadows. Glass areas and electric fixtures in the range of game activities should be protected by heavy wire mesh guards. Thermostats, telephones, etc., if mounted where they can be struck by balls or equipment, should also be guarded.

ACOUSTICS

Physical education activities are noisy activities. Accordingly, the gymnasium space, the pool area, and the locker and shower rooms should be carefully designed acoustically. In any of these areas subject to moisture, any acoustical materials used must be moisture proof.

SPECTATOR SEATING

The determination of the proper amount of spectator seating is a difficult problem, and the solution will vary from place to place in accordance with the local community opinion. In an elementary school, unless the location involves out-of-the-ordinary community use, little spectator space is necessary beyond a bench along the side walls for pupils temporarily not engaged in activities on the gymnasium floor.

For junior high schools some spectator space is required, largely for pupil groups who wish to watch their classmates perform in intramural games. Ordinarily there will be sufficient seating if the number of seats equals from 50 percent to 100 percent of the enrollment of the school.

On the senior high school level more spectator space is required. Spectators will be present largely for basketball, but also very often for gymnasium exhibitions, wrestling, and other activities. Except in situations where community public interest in the competitive aspects of inter-scholastic basketball is excessive, the provision of a total number of seats equal to approximately one and one half times the enrollment of the school should be satisfactory. Reference to this question will be made again in the section of this chapter relating to athletics.

The most economical arrangement, and that which is preferred in terms of most efficient use of available area, is the installation of folding bleachers along one or both sides of the main gymnasium floor. When spectators are not present, the bleachers can be folded back, allowing more floor space for physical education use. When interscholastic games are played, the bleachers may be opened without infringing upon the area required for the game. Properly designed, a gymnasium for a reasonably large school can usually accommodate the necessary number of seats in folding bleachers along both sides of the main gymnasium floor. The design and arrangement of these bleachers should give adequate attention to safety factors.

Other Instructional Spaces

CONSIDERABLE emphasis has been given to the gymnasium floor as an instructional space because it is the one which is always provided whether or not other teaching spaces for physical education are included in the plans. In secondary schools particularly, except in very small units, there will be need for various other instructional spaces such as health classrooms, swimming pools, wrestling rooms, and corrective rooms. These will be discussed briefly below.

HEALTH CLASSROOMS

Health may be taught in a room having the general characteristics of a regular classroom, including chalkboard, tackboard, storage cabinets, and other customary classroom features. A demonstration desk similar to those used for science instruction may be helpful. In some cases, it may be advisable to provide a somewhat larger health classroom, possibly as much as 1,500 square feet, so that it can be also used for corrective or adapted physical education, wrestling, tumbling, and other activities. If such combination use is contemplated, storage space must be provided for chairs and other equipment, there must be suitable safeguards against damage, and a higher ceiling may be advisable.

SWIMMING POOL

A swimming pool may be provided as one of the physical education teaching spaces, or solely for recreational use outside the regular instructional program. The relatively high cost makes a pool difficult in many cases to construct and operate, but the teaching of swimming is generally considered important. Such instruction cannot be left to haphazard self-learning through visits to lakes and beaches by those boys and girls whose families can afford to send them, nor to the opportunities available to the favored few who can attend summer camps. Except where outdoor swimming is possible during most of the year, an indoor pool is highly desirable.

Most pools in American secondary schools are designed to meet National Collegiate Athletic Association standards, which require a minimum length of 75 feet. Often they are made an inch or so longer to make certain they qualify for official records. The width is recommended to be in multiples of 7 feet, generally allowing five or six 7-foot swimming lanes. Depths vary, but standard practice is $3\frac{1}{2}$ feet at the shallow end with at least one half of the pool having a depth of not over $4\frac{1}{2}$ feet. The depth at the diving end varies. For a low diving board, a depth of 10 feet is desirable, with greater depth allowed for higher boards. Ceiling heights should provide at least 13 feet above the highest board, preferably more to eliminate mental hazards.

There seems to be a tendency toward variety in swimming pool design, including L-shaped pools and multiple units which separate diving areas from swimming areas.

The floor or deck around the pool should be of nonslip tile; the pool itself should be of tile designed for that use; and the walls of the room in which the pool is located should be a glazed brick or glazed tile block to a height of 6 to 8 feet. The deck should be at least 10 to 15 feet wide on each side of the pool, with somewhat greater width at the ends. It should not drain into the pool.

The finish of all wall and ceiling surfaces should be impervious to moisture and be rust proof. The use of wood in the pool area should be minimized, and no veneered stock should be used. Precautions must be taken to avoid condensation on ceiling areas.

Pools require filtration and sterilization equipment, for which suitable space must be allowed in planning. Generally the temperature of the water is kept within a certain range by thermostatically controlled heat exchangers.

Spectator space, if provided, should be separated from the pool and deck area, and entrances to the seating should be direct from the out-of-doors or from school corridors without requiring travel through locker

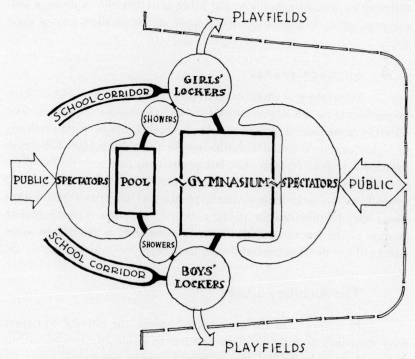

Figure 8. Space Relationships in the Physical Education Suite.

rooms or across the pool deck. Separate toilets should be installed for spectators.

The swimming pool should be so located that it is conveniently served by the locker and shower rooms. (See Figure 8.) Provision should be made for storing and drying swimming suits outside the main locker room. Also, it is desirable for girls to have hair dryers in the locker room or some other area located conveniently near by. There should be one unit for every two or three girls in the largest class group expected to use the pool at any one time in the regular physical education program.

MISCELLANEOUS INDOOR INSTRUCTIONAL SPACES

In addition to the main gymnasium floor, the health classroom, and the swimming pool, there are other specialized indoor instructional rooms which may be provided in the physical education suite. These include areas devoted to corrective work (generally floor spaces of 1,000 to 1,500 square feet equipped with special apparatus) and rooms specifically designed for wrestling, bowling, and other activities not requiring a full-size gymnasium. In a small school one space may serve all or most of these needs.

OUTDOOR SPACES

Many physical education activities can be carried on out-of-doors for portions of the school year which vary with the climate. The out-of-door activities range from free play and use of wheeled toys by young children to highly organized games and athletics for the older pupils. The spaces required vary from place to place but generally include areas for free play, especially at the elementary school level, and fields for baseball, softball, football, soccer, field hockey, track, tennis, and sometimes golf. Other spaces may be provided for public recreation purposes. The design and location of these outdoor spaces must be considered in relation to other aspects of site development, and these have been discussed in Chapter 12.

The Auxiliary Spaces

IN ADDITION to the instructional spaces, the physical education suite must include many auxiliary features to insure effective operation. Among these are locker and dressing rooms, showers, and storage spaces for gymnasium and athletic uniforms and equipment. For the most part these are basic necessities, although there will be some room for choice in determining the needs of different grade levels.

LOCKER AND DRESSING ROOMS

In order to determine when locker and dressing rooms are required and the scope of the functions they must serve, it is first necessary to consider the general structure of the typical physical education program from grade to grade.

The Earlier Grades

In the primary grades, and perhaps through the fourth grade, it is common and entirely suitable for physical education groups to include both sexes. At these levels, it is more or less customary for the classroom teacher to provide most of the physical education instruction with the assistance of a special teacher from time to time. There is a great deal of emphasis on rhythm work, various types of circle games, and other games which do not involve complex rules or highly organized competitive team play. The same activities are enjoyed by both boys and girls. The simple, nonstrenuous nature of the activities does not require a subsequent shower to remove perspiration odors, and the handling of mixed classes by one teacher would make showering difficult to supervise. Therefore, locker and shower rooms are usually not provided for these grades.

Upper Elementary Grades

At or about the age of the average fifth-grade pupil, particularly in the case of boys, interest is developed in the basic American games. Since these are somewhat more vigorous than the activities which have been carried on in earlier grades, again especially so for boys, this appears to be a natural point for the separation of sexes for physical education. From this age onward the natural interests of boys will tend more and more to be directed toward more organized and vigorous games. Wherever it is possible, therefore, it may be expected that the physical education classes will be so organized that there will be men to direct the activities of the boys and women to direct the activities of the girls. At this time it is advisable for children to wear gymnasium uniforms and to take showers so that they may return to their classrooms free of perspiration odors.

Accordingly, if it is financially possible, elementary schools should have locker rooms and suitable shower facilities sufficient to accommodate at least the fifth- and sixth-grade pupils. Actually this is too rare in practice. Also, in too many instances where provisions have been made, they have been inadequate and have fallen into disuse. It is a fair conclusion that with a program which is well developed and with finances which permit adequacy, locker and dressing rooms and suitable shower facilities should be installed in elementary schools. Otherwise they should be omitted.

Locker Rooms in Secondary Schools

In secondary schools there can be no question of the need for locker and shower facilities. Care must be taken to make certain of initial adequacy, since installations are difficult and expensive to remodel or enlarge.

The locker rooms should provide suitable locker facilities for the storage of the ordinary clothing of pupils while they are involved in the physical education program, and there should be locker or basket facilities for individual storage of pupils' gymnasium attire from day to day.

Types of Locker Facilities

There are two principal types of locker arrangements used. One of these, which might be called the multiple-locker or box-locker system, provides enough large-sized lockers to accommodate the street clothing of the greatest number of pupils who may be scheduled for physical education at any one period of the day. In a small school this may be one section of boys and one section of girls each period, and each locker room might well provide as many as forty-five or fifty full-length lockers for this purpose. For the storage of gymnasium attire, which must include the gymnasium uniforms and shoes, this arrangement provides small box lockers immediately adjacent to the full-length lockers, generally in multiples of six, since the modal school day has six physical education periods. As each class section comes in, the boys and girls go to their respective locker rooms, undress, store their ordinary clothing in the full-length lockers, take from their own assigned box lockers their gymnasium clothes, dress in this attire, and proceed to their physical education classes. At the end of the period they reverse the procedure. It is a common practice to have a padlock for each pupil which he uses on either his box locker or a full-length locker, depending upon where he has clothing stored at the moment. Opinion generally favors a padlock having a combination and master key arrangement.

This scheme has many disadvantages. It requires that there be many banks of lockers in the locker room. These tend to obscure the vision of the instructor who is supervising the locker room and lead to problems of control. Furthermore, they are always in the way and subject to damage, and they tend inevitably to make the room dark and difficult to clean. Since the gymnasium attire is always stored in these lockers, it is necessary that there be ample, specially designed ventilation through the lockers and that it be in operation at all times.

Because of the deficiencies of the box-locker system, efforts have been made to develop a satisfactory arrangement in which the gymnasium clothing can be removed from the locker room except when it is in use. The so-called basket system is one attempt at solving this problem. This is essentially a modification of the box-locker system in which wire mesh or steel strip baskets take the place of the box lockers. Since these baskets are separate units, they can be moved and taken out of the locker room for storage elsewhere between periods of use. This arrangement usually makes it possible to place the street clothes lockers around the walls of the locker room, hence making it unnecessary to have banks of standing lockers cluttering up the floor area and interfering with supervision.

There are two general types of storage for the basket lockers. In one case, the basket is taken by the pupil to a specially ventilated area in which it is placed either in a cubicle or on a shelf. In the other case, basket trucks are provided, with all of the basket lockers necessary for one gymnasium class on one or two trucks. These trucks can, between periods of use, be kept in a specially ventilated room under lock and key and brought out by the instructor as needed. When they are wheeled into the locker room, the pupils take their respective baskets to dressing benches adjacent to their street clothing lockers and change their clothing. Here again a combination padlock is transferred as needed between the street clothing locker and the pupil's individual basket.

Of the two methods of storing basket lockers, the use of wheeled trucks is preferred because of its flexibility. The truck or trucks can be placed at any convenient point in the locker room for access by pupils, whereas the use of shelving or cubicles in a separate room to which the pupils must carry the baskets will lead to traffic congestion and difficulty of supervision.

Advantages and Disadvantages of Baskets. The advantages claimed for the basket system are, first, that the absence of standing lockers in the floor area of the locker room makes it possible for the instructor to see all of the room from any one point and to attain better supervision and control of the activities of the pupils. The absence of the banks of lockers also provides a lighter and brighter locker room, and the less obstructed floor area can be easily and thoroughly cleaned. Another advantage of the basket system is that the dressing area can be kept more free of odors, since the perspiration-laden clothing is kept elsewhere. Finally, the mechanical ventilation of a small storage room is less expensive than that of banks of lockers, and suitable equipment is therefore more likely to be provided and continuously operated.

The disadvantage of the basket system is that the baskets are essentially more fragile than box lockers. When they are used, it is important that their handling be carefully supervised and that procedures be worked out with the classes so that when the pupils are in the gymnasium, the baskets are placed either on the tops of the street-clothing lockers, in the lockers, or back on the trucks in such fashion that there is regularity of procedure and no difficulty in identification of the baskets.

SHOWER ROOMS

There are three basic types of shower facilities prevalent in schools. One is the individual shower compartment, with or without curtains and sometimes with a dressing booth for each shower, or with combinations of two such booths for each shower. A second type is sometimes called the gang shower and consists of an open space with shower heads at intervals around the walls. One of these gang showers will accommodate several students at a time, and the usual arrangement is to plan enough shower heads so that from one third to one quarter of the pupils to be served in each class period may be accommodated at once in the shower room. Another type of shower not so commonly found is a progressive or walk-through type. It has been called the "sheep dip" type. This installation consists of a relatively narrow passageway containing shower heads with temperature controls arranged so that the pupil receives progressively warmer and then colder water as he goes through the passageway. The preferred type for boys or girls appears to be the open, gang shower room. Occasionally public demand may require modification in the case of girls, but this demand is usually satisfied by the installation of a limited number of individual compartments which can be used by the pupils who prefer them.

For ease of supervision by the instructor, who generally has pupils changing clothes in the locker room and groups in the shower room at the same time, it is becoming fairly common practice to make the walls around the shower room and the body drying space only semi-partitions no higher than necessary to accommodate the shower heads at shoulder height.

The relative location of the various elements is important. There should be a body drying room or space between the locker room and the shower facilities, with a floor area which should be at least as large as that of the shower room. Located conveniently to this body drying space should be a place where towels may be handed out and where they may be returned after use. Adequate toilet rooms or spaces should be located where they will be accessible in the travel between the locker room and the drying and shower room.

FIRST-AID ROOMS

A desirable feature in every secondary school physical education suite is a first-aid or treatment room, which should be adjacent to the locker room. The customary emphasis upon the boys' program usually insures this facility for boys, but it should be emphasized that there should

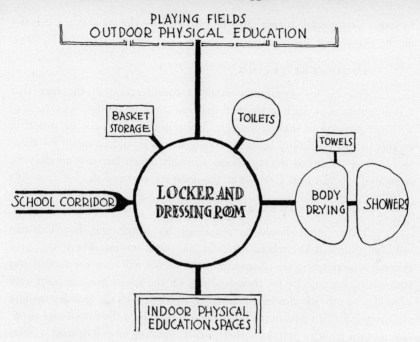

Figure 9. Space Relationships in the Locker and Shower Area.

also be adequate facilities for girls. The space provided for boys may allow for one or two rubbing tables, washbowl, whirlpool bath, heat lamp, closet for storage of crutches, stretcher, splints, etc., and a first-aid cabinet. The size of the room and the amount of equipment will vary according to the size of the school. These facilities do not replace the regular health suite of the school.

STORAGE

Storage for the gymnasium area demands careful planning. For gymnasium apparatus there should be spaces opening directly upon the gymnasium floors, usually with large or double doors. For athletic equipment there should be storage spaces convenient to the team rooms and coaches' offices. The amount and design of storage necessary will depend upon the physical education and athletic programs. In planning a gymnasium layout it is best to have the local physical education officials compile a complete list of all gymnasium apparatus and all athletic equipment to be used. From this list the storage requirements can be determined. Some margin for unforeseen needs must be allowed. It is important not to forget that special storage must be provided for the piano when it is not on the gymnasium floor.

EQUIPMENT DRYING

Storage for equipment involves consideration of the fact that certain equipment, such as football uniforms, will be brought in saturated with perspiration or soaked by rain. These items should not be stored in lockers in this condition. Suitable arrangements should be made for them to be hung in special drying rooms through which hot dry air may be circulated. Special heat controls at this location are needed.

TOWEL STORAGE AND SERVICE

Every pupil should have a clean dry towel each day. This can only be insured if the school provides the towel service. There are three general procedures in use. Sometimes the school will own the towels and contract with a laundry for their washing. Or the school may contract with a laundry to provide clean fresh towels as needed, with the laundry owning the towels. A third possibility is for the school to own the towels and maintain its own laundry system, either in each building or as a central service. The procedure to be employed is a matter for local option. Suitable storage space for towels must be located reasonably close to the shower rooms. Daily laundry deliveries require suitable closets and shelving, with good delivery access.

If the school maintains its own laundry, space must be provided in the planning for the laundry equipment. Technical advice must be sought, with space requirements and layout depending upon the equipment to be used.

OFFICES AND WORK SPACE

Proper planning of physical education and athletic facilities requires the provision of suitable staff quarters. These must include office space for the people in charge of the various phases of the program for each sex, and desk space for those who are engaged in daily instructional activities. Programs are staffed differently in various places, and the staff organization as it exists and as it may be changed or expanded should be carefully worked out by the local school authorities as a basis for planning staff quarters. Among the positions most commonly involved are the following: director of physical education (for both boys and girls, or separately for each sex), director of athletics, various coaches, physical education instructors for boys, and physical education instructors for girls. In a small school, some of these functions may overlap. For example, one person may be director of physical education and athletics, and perhaps carry a part-time load of instruction. Physical education instructors may also be coaches. In a larger school, there will be a larger staff and greater separation of functions and assignments. Where a school may be expected to increase in enrollment, it is well to provide some margin of space to cover the needs of a larger staff in the future.

An office space for a person in charge of the program or some phase of it should preferably, but not necessarily, have outside light, and be large enough to provide room for a desk, two or three chairs, a table, files, and one or more lockers. Adjacent to it should be a storage closet for items that are too valuable to be stored otherwise, as, for example, stop-watches, cameras, and starting pistols. There should also be a private toilet and shower room.

For groups of physical education instructors and for coaches there may be rooms in which several desks may be placed. This space should be large enough to accommodate one or two tables, extra chairs, and filing cabinets.

Athletic Facilities

PHYSICAL education and athletic facilities are closely related since athletics is essentially part of the physical education program. Among the more prominent indoor sports are swimming, basketball, and wrestling. Of these, there is no question that basketball has the greatest popular appeal. Consequently, basketball is the indoor sport which is most contributory to the criticism of overemphasis. Among the outdoor sports, football occupies a similar position.

THE PLACE OF BASKETBALL

Basketball is one of the great American indoor sports which has developed along with the physical education program. It has suffered many abuses at the hands of the public because of the overemphasis given to it as a spectator sport. Accordingly, there has been from time to time on the part of some of the public, and to some extent on the part of educators, a reaction against even the provision of facilities which make it possible for boys and girls to play the game. However, physical education is dull work if there is no competitive aspect to it.

Basketball affects not only the size but also the design of a gymnasium, particularly with respect to the amount of spectator space or seating which should be provided. But spectatorship is not a primary educational objective. There is good reason for saying that school games should be played for the benefit of the pupils, including not only those who actively take part but those others who are interested in the achievements of their classmates. Certainly it is desirable from every point of view that all basketball games played by public school teams take place within their own gymnasiums and that they not be played in municipal arenas or university gymnasiums merely for the purpose of attracting spectators and making money.

The emphasis upon basketball varies from place to place, and it changes in any one community from time to time. Obviously there are cases where public sentiment is so strongly in favor of providing an arena for basketball that substantial investment must be made in spectator space if any physical education facilities are to be approved by the voters. It is certain that these requirements of citizens must be met if they have sufficient support and if they are not entirely out of reason. Where thoroughly inadequate spectator space is provided and there is even reasonable interest on the part of parents and citizens in the activities of the youth of the community, a sorry situation, and one that is detrimental to the maintenance of good will toward the school, may develop. One of the most frustrating experiences for a parent is to be denied admittance to a performance in which his children or his neighbor's children are participating.

The lack of adequate seating capacity also leads to serious administrative difficulties. When some people have to be denied admittance, it is more difficult to make sure that each person who is admitted has a ticket and is eligible to enter. Those who are denied admission may be so aroused that they engage in individual antisocial actions or in undesirable or dangerous mob activities. In addition, there is the ever-present danger that hazardous situations will be created by admitting far more people than can be safely accommodated.

Despite the costs and other problems involved, there seems to be a tendency to build up participation in both intramural and interscholastc basketball for boys. The general practice is to provide a fairly generous amount of spectator space in terms of average community interest in these games. There is also some increased interest in competitive sports for girls. Whatever the local decision may be, the requirements for basketball must usually be taken into account in designing a secondary school gymnasium.

SIZES OF BASKETBALL COURTS

There are certain accepted standards for sizes of boys' basketball courts, as follows: for senior high school, 50 feet by 84 feet; for junior high school, 45 feet by 72 feet; and for elementary school, 40 feet by 60 feet.

These are the dimensions for the basketball court alone, and it is essential that sufficient floor space be left outside these lines without infringing upon the area set aside for seating. For the safety of the players, several feet of clear space are required on each side of the court and at each end.

With relation to the standard sizes, it is interesting to note that there has been a tendency to upgrade the requirements at each level. There is some tendency to build elementary school gymnasiums with basketball floors meeting the junior high school standards and to build junior high school courts of senior high school dimensions. The senior high school pupils who play basketball, particularly on varsity teams, are sometimes provided with what has generally been designated as the standard size for college basketball courts (50 feet by 94 feet). One of the reasons for this, of course, is that regional and state tournaments (presumably and ostensibly established only for the interest of the pupils, but it may be surmised, sometimes with a faint hope of accumulating funds from the sale of tickets) are usually played on college or university courts. This being the practice, it is argued that it is only common sense that a high school basketball team be able to practice and play its games on courts of this size.

TEAM ROOMS

Team rooms are required only in secondary schools, and the greatest need and most elaborate installations are at the senior high school level. The number and size of these rooms will depend upon the scope of the athletic program in existence or anticipated. It is desirable, although too often neglected, that the program for girls receive as much attention and emphasis as is given to the program for boys. Rooms are necessary for both home teams and visiting teams. It is undesirable to have a situation in which visiting boys' teams use the girls' facilities because of lack of other suitable quarters.

Team rooms used for football and cross-country in the fall can be used for basketball and wrestling in the winter, and for baseball and track in the spring. Subvarsity squads may be scheduled to use the general physical education locker and shower rooms, if separate lockers are provided for their athletic suits and equipment.

A team room area should provide a locker room with as many lockers as the maximum expected membership in the squad, with benches, rubbing tables, and first-aid cabinet. An adjacent shower room should have at least one fourth as many shower heads as the expected squad membership.

Where a field house or stadium at an athletic field is situated some distance from the school building, some of the team room and equipment storage facilities may be located there. It is important, however, that all the facilities be considered together in the planning process. Facilities installed in field houses and stadiums should have the same quality of equipment and meet the same standards of sanitation and safety as those in the main building.

SERVICES TO SPECTATORS

All physical education facilities should be on the ground floor level. This includes the gymnasium floor, the pool, and the locker and shower rooms. The gymnasium should be close to the athletic and play fields, yet it should have convenient access for the public and should have a service driveway and adequate adjacent parking space. In a large installation traffic and safety experts should be consulted on the layout of drives and parking areas. Exits from the gymnasium must be directly to school corridors or to the outside, and the number and width of exits must be adequate for the maximum seating capacity of the gymnasium. State and local code requirements must be carefully checked.

One or more ticket booths or windows should be located in the lobby of secondary school gymnasiums in such fashion that lines may form inside the lobby without interference with traffic.

Toilet rooms for public use should be conveniently located and adequate to serve the expected crowds. Under no conditions should plans provide for the public to enter the pupils' locker and shower rooms or team rooms.

FACILITIES FOR COACHES AND OFFICIALS

Home team coaches are usually members of the instructional staff and to a large extent work in the physical education department. Their needs are usually met by the offices and related facilities already described for physical education instructors. There should also be a room where officials may change their clothes before and after games. This space should be large enough to serve at least four persons at one time and should be fitted with lockers, table, and chairs. It should also have an adjacent toilet and shower room.

OUTDOOR ATHLETIC FACILITIES

Chapter 12 discusses the necessity of acquiring sufficient usable acreage to provide space for out-of-door athletic facilities. It is important that the accommodations both for day-by-day outdoor physical education activities and for athletics, whether intramural or interscholastic, be on the school site and properly located in relation to the school building.

Space does not permit the presentation of complete specifications for each type of outdoor facility, but a few observations will be made to point up situations where the planning must be thorough and in careful alignment with local needs. It is essential that even for a small secondary school there be at least one practice football field in addition to the one on which games are played. For larger schools there should be several practice fields. It is also advisable to provide suitable fields for girls to play soccer and field hockey, since reliance upon part-time use of the boys' practice fields usually results in crowding out the girls' activities. Space should be laid out for running tracks and field events in the original planning even if their installation is delayed. Full-length straightaways for the dash events should be included. The size and features of stadium facilities will vary according to the emphasis upon spectatorship and local public demand to see games. Obviously, care must be taken not to overbuild. The same factors will control the installation of facilities for night games, if they are to be permitted.

CHAPTER 17

OTHER INSTRUCTIONAL SPACES

The School Library
Study Facilities
Instructional-aids Facilities
Conference Rooms
Student Activity Spaces

THE modern school building contains many facilities with instructional values in addition to those spaces described in previous chapters. This chapter will consider the library, study facilities, instructional-aids facilities, conference rooms, spaces for the activities of student organizations, and accommodations for student social activities. This classification is somewhat arbitrary and chosen for convenience in discussion. Actually the same space in some schools may serve more than one of the above-mentioned purposes. Local school program organization is again important as a basis in planning.

The School Library

THE educational process functions in a world of books. The chief purpose of a school library is to make available to the pupil, at his easy convenience, all the books, periodicals, and other reproduced materials which are of interest and value to him but which are not provided or assigned to him as basic or supplementary textbooks.

ESSENTIAL LIBRARY FUNCTIONS

The essential functions of a school library which must be considered in the planning of a school building are:

1. To provide a suitable place for the storage of books and periodicals where they will be easily available to those who have use for them.

2. To provide a place where books and periodicals may be read and studied under quiet and comfortable conditions.

3. To provide means and convenience for lending books and periodicals, accounting for circulation, and receiving materials upon their return.

4. To provide means for display or promotion of materials in order to attract the interest of pupils and stimulate their use.

5. To provide means by which materials and information sought by pupils and teachers can be readily found.

6. To provide facilities for library administrative work, for conferences and committee work, and for such routine activities as classification and repair.

7. To provide facilities which permit the instruction of pupils in techniques of library use.

ESSENTIAL LIBRARY SPACES

A complete school library requires, as a minimum, a reading room, an office space, a work space, storage space for books, and storage for materials. In small schools all of these facilities may be arranged in one room. In larger units more elaborate accommodations will include several rooms, differentiated in use, and each serving a specific purpose. Elementary school libraries generally are relatively simple both in organization and accommodations. Secondary school libraries, however, are more complex both in facilities and functions and are more likely to have accessory spaces for allied or related activities such as conference rooms, viewing rooms, and listening booths.

SECONDARY SCHOOL LIBRARIES

On the secondary school level the variety of reference material and the necessary amount and variety of free reading require a central library for each school. Also at these levels the pupils are old enough to profit from instruction in the use of the library. It will be convenient to discuss the various library facilities in terms of a complete secondary school library and subsequently to discuss the modifications which may be applicable to elementary schools.

The Reading Room

The "rule of thumb" for the size of a secondary school library reading room is that it should seat comfortably about 10 percent of the enrollment expected in the school. Higher or lower percentages may be needed, depending upon the school program and schedule. It is generally agreed that the library reading room is not a study room, but a place to which pupils are allowed to go or to which they are referred if they need to use the materials available there. Accordingly, in any program which allows the pupil to have periods for study purposes, facilities other than the library reading room must be provided. The staffing of the library, the physical layout of the library reading room, and the rules and regulations which govern the availability of this room to the pupils must be such that the librarian does not need to be a disciplinarian over pupils who are not interested in taking full advantage of the privileges offered.

Too large a reading room is difficult to supervise and control, even when all other factors are most favorable. It is reasonable to say that no single reading room should seat more than 100 pupils. If the total needs exceed this limit, more than one reading room should be planned, or it may be advisable to use folding partitions to break up a larger area into smaller ones. Rough estimates of the amount of the reading room floor space required may be made by allowing 25 square feet per reading station. For example, if the library is to accommodate 100 pupils at one time, the reading room should contain about 2,500 square feet of floor space. It is most desirable, however, that a trial layout of the location and the size of tables and chairs be provided, since the shape of the reading room will have some effect upon the economical use of the total area.

Generally, it is considered good practice to have tables seating six or eight pupils. Chairs, of course, should be comfortable and durable. There should be some variety of sizes of tables and chairs, particularly in a junior high school.

Storage of Books. One of the major functions of the library is the storage of books and periodicals where they are available for reference or for free reading. It is usually most convenient to install bookshelving on most of the available wall space of the reading room or rooms. In secondary schools the books generally are stacked on an average of eight to a linear foot of shelving. Provision should be made for at least 5,000 books in a small high school with larger schools sometimes provided with several times that number. A minimum schedule might well be 10 books for each secondary school pupil.

In the design of the shelving, the lowest shelf may be as close to the floor level as 4 inches and the top shelf can be as high as $6\frac{1}{2}$ to 7 feet. Shelves should be easily adjustable. The various sections should be arranged so that the shelf length in any one section will be approximately 3 feet. In some installations the lower shelves are slanted downward to the rear so that the books may be easily identified from a standing position.

Equipment. In addition to the tables and chairs for reading purposes, the reading room should also include a circulation desk, a card catalog file, bulletin boards, racks for magazines and newspapers, display counters, and legal- and letter-size filing cabinets. The circulation desk should be convenient to the main entrance to the library, and the card catalog and other files should be placed near by.

Physical Environment. Because reading and studying are the primary purposes of the reading room, excellent illumination, both natural and artificial, is a must. The light should provide sufficient illumination without glare or offending shadows upon the reading. The light distribution and the design of finishes for wall and ceiling areas should be such that excessive brightness contrast will be avoided. The general atmosphere of the room should not be austere nor overornamental. The total effect ought to be one of quiet, restful, and pleasant surroundings, conducive to concentration upon the task at hand with a minimum of interruption or distraction from the physical environment or other sources.

The necessary conditions of quiet for a library reading room require careful acoustical design. It is necessary to subdue sounds originating in the reading room itself and also to control sounds arising outside. Particular attention should be paid to the quietness of the floor, the quietness of hardware, and the choice of proper glides on the furniture.

Office

The librarian's office should have an abundance of outside light or should be well lighted artificially. It should be convenient to the library reading room and large enough to accommodate a desk, desk chair, extra chair, table, filing cabinet, and a small amount of bookshelving. It is sometimes convenient to have a glass area in the partition between the office and the reading room.

Workroom

Adjacent to the library reading room and also immediately accessible to the librarian's office there should be a workroom equipped with the following items:

1. Sink with hot and cold water.
2. Work counter.
3. Table and chairs.
4. Typewriter and typewriter desk or stand.
5. Bookshelving.
6. Electrical outlets.

7. Storage cabinets located either under the counter or above it or both.

In a small library the workroom and the librarian's office may be a combined unit.

Storage Room

In small library installations a need for storage of work materials, supplies, and books temporarily off the shelves may be met by storage cabinets in the workroom or a small closet leading directly off the workroom. In larger libraries a separate room with suitable shelving and connected directly with the workroom should be provided.

Stack Room

The need for a stack space or a stack room depends upon the relationship between the amount of bookshelving which can be installed in the reading room and the anticipated amount needed in terms of the expected total number of books to be housed when the school reaches its ultimate planned size. For high school use it is not desirable that bookshelves be arranged in alcoves or arrayed in stacks because of the difficulty of supervision. Only when there is no more wall space available should stack shelving be used. Nevertheless, for a school which may increase substantially in size, or where the total number of books will outgrow the shelving which can be installed in the original reading room or rooms, it is desirable to plan space serviceable for expansion of book storage. Suitable open stacks can then be installed when necessary.

Other Library Rooms

Many secondary schools include one or more small conference rooms in the library suite for use by groups of pupils or others in connection with library activities such as preparation for a debate or committee report. These rooms should be located for ease of supervision by the library staff and, if used by pupils, should have large glass areas in the partitions facing the reading room. These rooms may serve also as the general conference rooms of the school, which are described later in the chapter, or may be solely for library use, depending upon the size of school and other factors.

As librarians add disc and tape recordings to their collections, there is need for small rooms with proper acoustics where one or two pupils can use these materials without disturbing others. These also should be in sight of the library staff and might be equipped with double glazed panels especially designed to reduce noise transmission.

ELEMENTARY SCHOOL LIBRARIES

A child in the elementary school needs to have access to many books besides those which are directly assigned as basic or supplementary textbooks. During the six years of the elementary school the child is continuously progressing in his ability to read, and the books and periodicals which are provided for him must be chosen so that the reading difficulty level of the material will not be so hard as to discourage the youngster nor so immature that it will not be interesting to him.

A major question which usually arises in the planning of an elementary school building is whether or not to include a library. There are many who advocate a separate library room and auxiliary spaces in every school, elementary or secondary. Others believe that the elementary school should rely solely upon collections of books in the classrooms—collections which are quite extensive and which are changed from time to time. Those who advocate the building library usually maintain that the classroom libraries are also necessary and that one of the functions of the building library is to service the classroom collections and keep them up to date. The differences of opinion on this matter are based on differences of concept of the role of the library at this level and in part upon concern for costs of construction and operation. Since both the educational point of view and the financial situation will vary from place to place, this issue must be resolved for each community as a basis for planning its own elementary school facilities.

The Educational Need

The persons who advocate the building library for an elementary school stress the need for making a wider selection of books available than is usually provided in classroom libraries, and they emphasize the importance of having children begin to acquire at an early age the habit of going to a library when they need information or recreational reading material. They point to the large percentage of adults who never go near a library and who might have become library users if the habit had been established before they left school. The need for learning to use the card catalog and to find materials on the library shelves is another reason advanced for the building library. The opponents take the position that adequate collections of books can be provided in all classrooms, supplemented by a reserve in the building, and that the supervision of a teacher who is well acquainted with the reading skills and interests of each child will promote better use of the books than would be possible if the selection were made with assistance of a building librarian. The library habit and the teaching of library skills can be started at the elementary school level by occasional trips to a public library or a

bookmobile, but the secondary school is early enough for intensive development along these lines.

The Economic Aspects

The economic aspects of the problem concern building costs and
supplying the services of a librarian. Both are expensive, and their cost
must be weighed against the value of this service as compared with other
facilities and services desired in the local school.

Solving the Problem

These differences in opinion can be resolved in several ways, each
calling for different library facilities, which would range from a small library room operating only infrequently to a full-scale operation not unlike
that already described for secondary schools. It is important that the local
planning activities include careful study of these divergent points of view,
and that the building plans be made according to the conclusions thus
reached.

Whether a separate library, classroom libraries, or both are provided, the
authors would urge that there be an ample and changing supply of current
books for all grades and that the services of competent library and teaching-
aids consultants be readily available to the teachers.

COMMUNITY SERVICE BY THE SCHOOL LIBRARY

In some communities, the school library serves also as the library
for the community at large, especially in smaller places where limited funds
permit no other arrangement. Also it is not uncommon to find branch public
libraries in school buildings in larger places, serving in some cases the adult
public only and in others both the adults and the pupils. Such arrangements, in the eyes of their proponents, are not only economical, but also
may make available to the school personnel and general public alike a more
extensive library collection and a more competent library staff than would
otherwise be possible. Some school officials object to the mingling of pupils
and adults in the same library, or prefer to be free of the problems of serving
the general public even when no such mingling is involved. Many public
librarians argue, with substantial facts to support them, that the circulation
of library materials among the adults of the community will be greater if the
public library is located apart from the school. They point out that a public
library should be on a busy street where many people are passing, while a

school should be in a more isolated location. They point out also that many adults are reluctant to go to a school building to obtain library service.

Again this difference of opinion is one which cannot be resolved by consulting an authority or finding out what the neighbors do. The opinions and reports of experience of others will be helpful, but a local decision must be made in the light of local conditions. Satisfactory planning of the library quarters in a school building cannot be achieved except by chance unless a sound local policy is made for the guidance of those who plan the building.

LOCATION OF LIBRARY

The location of the school library should be determined largely in terms of the convenience of the greatest number of its users. In the elementary school there is reason for a location most convenient to the rooms for the upper grades. In secondary schools preference is usually given to proximity to rooms scheduled for English and social studies. General centrality within the total layout of the school may well be preferable. The library, if it has a reading room, should be located where pupils will be least disturbed by noises arising either from within the building or without. If it is to be a public library, ease of access from the street or parking lot is desirable and the location should permit use at night and during times when school is not in session. Access to drinking fountains and toilets must be considered.

Since the space needs of the library may increase in future years, it is advisable to provide some adjacent room into which the library can readily expand.

Study Facilities

MOST secondary school programs require study accommodations each period for pupils who are not at that time scheduled for a class. To some extent these pupils may be assigned to vacant classrooms, but in order to achieve economy of staff time and ease of scheduling, larger rooms are usually provided.

The amount of study space required depends upon the number of pupils in the school and the program. Assuming no reduction in the number of subjects taken by each pupil, a schedule with longer and fewer periods each day leaves less study time and reduces the study room requirements. In fact, some schools are so organized that all in-school studying is done under the supervision of the regular classroom teachers and in their classrooms. With this kind of schedule, which is not customary, no separate study space is necessary.

When study space is needed, the average amount required per period can be calculated by the formula in Chapter 6. However, the seating capacity provided should allow for perhaps 50 percent more than the average, since some periods will have heavier than average loads.

NATURE AND LOCATION OF STUDY SPACE

The space to be used for study purposes calls for careful planning. As indicated earlier in the chapter, the use of the library is a perversion of the purposes of that facility, and is to be avoided. Nor is the answer to be found in the old-time study hall, which was a barren, prisonlike room of huge size under the supervision of one or more teachers whose principal task was to enforce silence. These evils can be reduced by providing smaller rooms, perhaps with the maximum size no greater than that of two regular classrooms. Another approach to a solution is to provide comfortable and attractive study quarters with good lighting and with acoustical treatment to reduce the noise level. It is probably desirable for the study rooms to have the quality of an attractive reading room with comfortable tables and chairs in place of fixed seating arranged in rows. Since not all studying involves writing, a substantial quota of comfortable armchairs might be included. A third approach to alleviate the ills commonly associated with study halls might be to give the pupil some choice of whether he uses his nonclass time in study or in other ways. If pupils could repair to a suitable lounge room if they did not feel in the mood for study, the study hall might become a more successful institution.

Since the study room requirements are likely to change from time to time, it would be prudent to design this space so that it could readily be converted into classrooms. This can be done and still maintain the desired study atmosphere.

A space often used for study purposes is the cafeteria dining room. If all pupils are not excused for lunch at the same time, this plan requires use of vacant classrooms for study purposes during lunch, but such rooms are available at that time. If the dining room is used for study purposes, it requires some special thought in design, as discussed in Chapter 19. The location of the study rooms should be convenient to the classrooms and to the library. The latter is particularly important because pupils may discover library needs during a study period and should be able to go to the library with a minimum of inconvenience and loss of time. Excellent arrangements may be designed with the study room adjacent to the library reading room.

Instructional-aids Facilities

AUDIO-VISUAL AIDS CENTERS

Films, film strips, slides, models, recordings, and other audio-visual aids are increasingly brought in to supplement the printed page as instructional devices. It is not unrealistic to predict that the day will come when many of these materials will be as freely available to teachers as reference and supplementary books are now. If these aids are to be used effectively, there is need in each building for a place or places to store, distribute, and service these materials. Facilities and services not provided in individual buildings should be readily available through some central agency in the school system or some conveniently located regional agency.

The minimum facilities provided in each building should probably include the following:

1. A convenient place to keep and use catalogs and references that would help teachers select the proper teaching aids.

2. A convenient place to store films, slides, recordings, and other materials which are used with sufficient frequency to justify retaining them in the building permanently.

3. A place where films can be rewound and inspected, other materials can be checked upon return, and minor repairs can be made, unless these services are furnished at a central agency.

4. A place or places where projection equipment can be stored so as to be readily available to any classroom.

A single teaching-aids room in the building might serve all these purposes, or these activities might be scattered among several rooms. In a large building or one of more than one story, the storage of heavy projectors should be decentralized so that the equipment need not be carried long distances or up and down stairs.

In addition to these minimum needs, provision must be made either within each building or at some convenient central place for the following activities:

1. The meeting of groups of teachers to select materials for purchase and to preview films and other items preparatory to classroom use.

2. The instruction of groups of teachers in the use of the available materials, and of teachers or pupils in the care and use of the equipment.

3. The ordering of teaching aids materials, supplies, and equip-

ment, and the keeping of the related accounts and records.

4. The storing of materials less commonly used, their circulation to other schools, and the keeping of the related records.

5. The inspection, cleaning, and repair of equipment.

In a large school system it would probably be more economical to provide many of these services in a central agency serving all schools and providing general supervision over the smaller centers in the individual schools.

Most of the common items of instructional-aids equipment, particularly such items as radios, record players, recording machines, film-strip projectors, and movie projectors, will be provided for each building and permanently assigned there. Less common items, such as microprojectors and working models, which are too expensive to be purchased for each school and which are used so rarely that it would be wasteful to assign one permanently to each building, should be kept in the instructional-aids center of the school system. However, for such equipment as is regularly assigned to each school building, suitable storage space must be provided.

RESOURCE CENTERS

Increasing reference is being made in school building planning, particularly for elementary schools, to a resource center. The term is used with various meanings but in general it refers to a space where teachers or pupils may find instructional materials not available in each classroom. Among these materials may be cardboard, lumber, or other construction materials for projects, science equipment and supplies, instructional-aids equipment, toys, maps, charts, and possibly reference or library materials as a reserve for classroom libraries.

A resource center space must be designed in terms of its probable use in accordance with local program planning. If lumber is to be stored in it, there should be suitable racks. Deep shelves for sheets of cardboard, cupboards for science equipment and supplies, and space for storing visual aids equipment must be provided as needs can be foreseen. If, as may be possible in an elementary school, library books are to be kept in the resource center, there must be a suitable amount of adjustable shelving. If the room is to be used for previewing or rewinding films, the dimensions should be sufficient and a work table or counter should be provided.

COMBINATION OF LIBRARY AND INSTRUCTIONAL-AIDS CENTER

It is sometimes suggested that the library expand its functions to encompass all instructional aids rather than just printed materials. Under this arrangement, the library staff would assist teachers in selecting all types of teaching aids and would be responsible for the acquisition, storage, and distribution of them. Arguments for this plan are based upon concern for offering the teachers maximum assistance.

This combination of functions, however, involves many difficulties. Librarians are generally trained to know printed and published materials, to catalog them, and to administer the distribution of these materials. As far as the cataloging and distribution of other teaching aids are concerned, the techniques and procedures are closely similar to those for books and periodicals. There are, however, great differences in the techniques of handling these different kinds of materials. Of even greater importance is the fact that the use and care of audio-visual equipment requires specialized knowledge and skills which bear no relation to the skills or learnings in the usual library training program.

In light of the uncertainty regarding the future trend of the organization of instructional-aids work and its relationship to the library function, it would be well to place the instructional-aids accommodations adjacent to the library facilities so that the two may be operated independently or as a single unit.

Conference Rooms

THE amount of committee work and the number of conferences among pupils, teachers, parents, or combinations of these groups, is not generally realized by the public at large. Provisions must be made for this need both in individual school buildings and in the school system as a whole. In large school buildings, it is desirable to have conference rooms for general use as well as a room reserved for a faculty workshop. In a system having several schools, a centrally located faculty workshop and professional library will have a great deal of use. This should be a space which will accommodate the largest expected number who will work on any staff committee or council in a conference situation. Conference tables and comfortable chairs should be provided. Bookshelving, chalkboards, bulletin boards, and mounts for displays should also be furnished. Such a room ought to be well lighted and designed acoustically to facilitate conference discussions.

Student Activity Spaces

THERE are many activities in addition to classroom instruction which are in essence a part of the instructional program because of the learning values involved. These activities begin in the elementary school, but they become more varied and more numerous as the pupil progresses through the secondary school. The activities include those of student government organizations, which exist in simple form in the elementary grades and reach a high level of development in the secondary school. Class and club organizations also present many opportunities for pupils to learn to work together, to understand forms of group action, and to develop an appreciation of many important principles of citizenship. For all of these activities, proper facilities are needed in the school plant.

There are also various groups whose activities are practical applications of classroom learnings. A common illustration is a school newspaper club, which has a continuing purpose of applying learnings in English, as well as serving a need for doing creative work for the benefit of all pupils. Activities of this nature require suitable working quarters.

In addition, there is a social aspect to school life which, with proper motivation and direction, should be given suitable means of expression. This aspect would include such activities as group parties and school or class dances, both formal and informal, highly organized or spontaneous and casual. Somewhere in the total school plant proper facilities should be available for all of these programs.

ROOMS FOR GROUP MEETINGS

Some of the building spaces described elsewhere in this book will serve many of the pupil activity purposes. Conference rooms in the library suite or elsewhere will meet some of the needs of student government groups and class and club committees. For larger groups the auditorium or little theater may be required. If the cafeteria dining room is divided into smaller areas of various sizes by folding partitions, more spaces for student activities, including club meetings and committee sessions, will be made available. For the work of the student newspaper group in a secondary school, or any similar organization having equipment and materials in more or less continuous use throughout the school year, it is well to provide a separate space, possibly about one half the size of a classroom, which can be regularly and exclusively devoted to such specialized use.

SPACE FOR DANCES AND PARTIES

For the social activities of groups of pupils, a floor suitable for dancing or large parties is often required. Under certain restrictions, the gymnasium floor can be used, and for some groups the cafeteria dining room may be suitable. For both of these spaces, it is important to recognize that for social events the pupils may wish to decorate the rooms. The provision of tacking or nailing strips around the upper portion of the walls or the

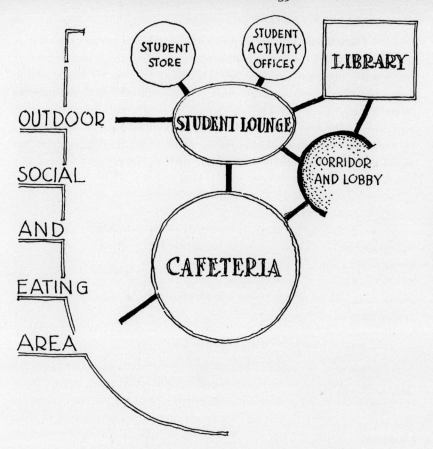

Figure 10. Student Center—Elements and Relationships.

installation of hooks or other types of fixtures for attachment of wires is a wise forethought. Provision should be made for the convenient storage of gymnasium equipment or dining room furniture during these social affairs.

LOUNGE ROOMS

There is an increasing belief that a comfortable student lounge room has value in a secondary school. This area, which could well accommodate from 5 to 10 percent of the total enrollment, should be designed and equipped for social lounging purposes with easy chairs, attractive decorations, possibly with murals done by the students, a record player, a piano, a radio, and perhaps a television set. Acoustical treatment must receive careful consideration.

STUDENT CENTERS

The student activity facilities just mentioned are an expression of the idea that the secondary school is really a miniature community where youth work, play, and live together. This being so, would it not be well to group together, insofar as reasonably possible, all of these spaces and to create a student center? The student union on the college campus is an expression of the same idea. Should it not in modified form be developed in high schools? Figure 10 indicates the elements and space relationships that would need to be considered in planning such a center.

CHAPTER 18

MISCELLANEOUS SERVICE FACILITIES

Health Service Facilities
Food Service Facilities
School Offices
Facilities for Staff Comfort and Convenience
Facilities for Building Operation and Maintenance
The Supply and Storage Problem
The Administrative Headquarters of a School System

A SCHOOL building typically includes many facilities which are necessary for the convenience and welfare of pupils and staff, for the effective administration of the school, or for the operation of the physical plant. Some of these may be used incidentally or part-time for instructional purposes, but they are included primarily for other reasons. Under this category would come the rooms and spaces for the health service program, for the preparation and serving of food, for the administration of the educational program and keeping the related records, and for the operation and maintenance of the physical plant itself. Another type of service facility includes the lounges, restrooms, and other spaces provided for the comfort and convenience of the staff and the toilet rooms for pupils. Public address and other communication systems also belong in this category. Except for pupil toilets, which are discussed in a later chapter, these various special facilities comprise the subject matter of the present chapter.

The principle discussed at many places in this book with respect to the relationship between program and plant applies as much to these service facilities as to classrooms. In fact, it may be more evident here, since the nonteaching activities vary more from school to school than does the classroom work, and this is reflected in the physical plant. The need for anticipating future change is also important at this point since many of these auxiliary services are of relatively recent origin and much subject to frequent expansion and change.

353

Health Service Facilities

GENERAL acceptance exists of the proposition that the school has some responsibility for providing a health service program for the protection of pupils, but there is great difference of opinion and practice with respect to the nature and extent of such programs. In some cases, little more than emergency first aid is provided; in others there are frequent medical and dental examinations. The school may have full responsibility for the program, or all or part of the burden may be carried by other community agencies. Likewise, the responsibility for providing the necessary physical facilities may rest with the board of education alone or may be shared with another agency. With such variations in belief and practice, it is imperative that thorough analysis be made of the local practice and future prospects before deciding what health service facilities to supply in a given school building.

For purposes of the discussion which follows, the possible health service activities are classified under five headings and the building implications of each are presented. These types of activities are: (1) making daily health inspections; (2) conducting medical or dental examinations; (3) providing medical or dental treatment; (4) administering first aid; and (5) isolating pupils who are ill or in need of rest.

DAILY HEALTH INSPECTIONS

The simplest and probably most common health service is the daily inspection of each pupil by the teacher, principal, or nurse to look for evidences of illness. This is most often done in the classroom by the teacher and involves looking for a running nose, inflamed eyes, skin rash, or other superficial clues. No special building facilities are required for these inspections themselves. The facilities required for handling the cases of illness or suspected illness revealed by the inspection are the same as those required for other aspects of the program discussed below.

MEDICAL AND DENTAL EXAMINATIONS

Medical examinations of pupils are sometimes performed by private physicians in their own offices, but in other cases are conducted at the school. The examinations at school are often quite simple and require only a room with a storage closet and with such equipment as a desk, a few chairs, a cabinet for supplies, an eye-testing chart on the wall, and scales. A clear space of 20 feet may be required for vision testing. This is sometimes provided by using a mirror or by opening a door into an adjoining room. If the examination is more thorough, there may be need for an examination table and one or more small rooms or screened off areas where pupils can undress in private. Except for the simplest of programs, a water closet in a separate room and a lavatory with hot and cold water are very desirable.

For dental examinations, a simple dental chair and a small case for instruments and supplies are all that are necessary in addition to the facilities for medical examinations. The chair need not be equipped with water and electricity if used only for dental inspections. Dental facilities do not require a separate room unless the school is quite large.

There is an increasing use of dental and chest X-rays in health examinations. These are often provided in mobile units or at some agency outside the school, but there may be cases where the school installation should include such equipment.

In addition to the examination room itself, it may be necessary to have a small waiting room where six to eight pupils may wait their turn to be admitted. This is particularly true where a summer health check-up is conducted and the exact time of arrival of parents and their children cannot be controlled. In a small school the waiting room of the general office may serve the health unit also.

In a large school with a resident nurse it may be advisable to provide her with a separate room where she can keep records and do other desk work. In small schools this facility might be provided in the examination room or in the waiting room. A desk, one or two chairs, and files are all the equipment normally required.

MEDICAL AND DENTAL TREATMENT

In general, school medical examiners refer pupils to their family physicians for treatment and confine the treatment of pupils at school to emergency cases or to minor ailments that would otherwise be neglected. They may go somewhat further in caring for indigent pupils, especially in the dental field, with some school systems providing complete dental service in such cases. School-sponsored medical or dental treatments may be provided in a nonschool clinic or a private practitioner's office, in a specially equipped trailer or other mobile unit, in a central school clinic serving an entire school system or region, or in an individual school building. If these facilities are to be provided in a school building, they can be combined with those for examination purposes, although more floor space and equipment may be required. The space requirements and equipment needs will depend upon the nature and extent of treatment given, and should be planned in cooperation with local health authorities.

FIRST AID

The administration of first aid requires little in the way of special facilities, since rooms provided for medical examinations or treatment can serve as first-aid stations. In addition, there should be first-aid equipment in places of high hazard such as gymnasiums, shops, and laboratories, especially in a large building where the medical examination room may be a considerable distance away.

ISOLATION AND REST

If a child becomes ill at school or is suspected of having any contagious disease, it is desirable that there be some place where he can be isolated for the protection of others and for his own welfare. This should not be on a chair in the office where many people come and go. The best arrangement is a room where the pupil can lie down under supervision without being disturbed. A cot space in the health suite is a good arrangement, if properly located for supervision.

There are other cases where there is need for pupils to rest who are not ill enough to be sent home. They could use the cots in the health suite or similar facilities elsewhere in the building. Where there is much use of the health suite, separate resting facilities are desirable. For older pupils, there should be separate cot rooms for boys and girls. Toilets should be convenient to each cot location. There is no way to determine how many children will be ill at one time, but a rough estimate would be that one cot should be provided for every 300 to 400 pupils.

LOCATION OF HEALTH UNIT

There are some who would place the health unit in the gymnasium area because of the relationship between health service on the one hand and health instruction and physical education on the other. There are others who would have the health unit in the administrative suite. The latter is particularly appropriate where there is no resident nurse and the principal or secretary in the office must supervise any pupils who may be resting or in isolation. With a full-time nurse in the building, this need does not exist. If the health unit is used for preschool examinations or other service at times when school is not in session, the location should be one which permits using the health unit without opening any large part of the remainder of the building.

INSTRUCTIONAL ASPECTS OF HEALTH SERVICE

While health education is a proper field of instruction in the school, it is not the primary purpose of health service. The two are separate, but there are many excellent opportunities for incidental health instruction in connection with the operation of the health service program. Questions, comments, and explanations by the nurse, doctor, or other person performing the health service may contribute significantly to the health knowledge of the child. If a parent is present at a health examination, his knowledge may also be extended by the experience. These instructional possibilities impose no new building requirements, but if many parents are involved, the provision of waiting space and a readily accessible location for the health suite are more important than might otherwise be the case.

Food Service Facilities

FOR generations children have carried lunches to school, for even in village schools there were usually some who lived too far away to go home for a noon meal. The consolidation of small schools into larger ones and the development of high schools with their larger attendance areas added to the number of children who could not go home at noon. These trends, combined with the increasing conviction of many parents and teachers that children should have a hot lunch, led to the establishment of school lunch service, often operated in its initial stages by groups of volunteer parents. In more recent years the movement has gained impetus because of the increased employment of women outside the home and the desire of mothers to have freedom for other activities without regard to the school's noon hour schedule. Increasing use of school buildings for adult community functions has added another justification for school kitchens and dining rooms.

It is necessary in the planning of a new building to raise the question of whether or not any lunch service facilities should be included. This matter is one for purely local decision, but the trend is such that it would seem wise to provide in all new buildings for the future operation of school lunch service even though space is not allotted for it in the initial construction.

GENERAL NATURE OF FOOD SERVICE PROGRAM

In planning the food service facilities of a school building, the first step is to determine what services are to be provided and in what manner. Consideration should be given to the following:

1. The serving of partial or complete noon lunches to pupils and teachers.

2. The serving of dinners or other meals to school or community groups on special occasions.

3. The serving of milk, juice, or other food in mid-morning or mid-afternoon in the classrooms, especially to younger children.

4. The serving of refreshments at athletic contests, at meetings, or in connection with other events at the school.

The serving of noon lunches is usually provided in a large dining room adjacent to a room or rooms housing the food preparation, serving, and dishwashing areas. Cafeteria service is the more common practice, but table service is sometimes the rule, especially for younger children. Under this latter arrangement, pupils may serve and clear tables and pupils or teachers may act as table hosts or hostesses. Manners and other educational and social values are emphasized. Another development is the decentralization of eating, using several small dining rooms or even classrooms for this purpose.

The serving of banquets and other meals on special occasions is usually done with the same facilities required for regular school lunch use. If any special provision is required, it is usually limited to a few extra items of kitchen equipment or dishes, some special storage spaces, or some special thought in planning the location or arrangement of the dining room.

The serving of milk or other food in the classrooms between regular mealtimes requires rather simple physical facilities, but not makeshift arrangements. Bottles of milk standing in warm corridors and cases of empty bottles outside classroom doors are evidences of inadequate planning for this service. Some means need to be evolved for distributing full bottles or cartons and collecting empties, for keeping food under refrigeration within the classrooms or at some central point in the building, and for storing supplies and doing necessary incidental cleaning.

The serving of refreshments involves such a variety of practices that generalization is difficult. The facilities for preparation and serving are usually simple, but should conform strictly to all applicable sanitary requirements. If properly located, the regular lunch facilities of the school may be used for preparing and serving these refreshments, or they may be prepared here and taken to the place of serving in insulated carts or other suitable containers. If such arrangements are made, adequate safeguards must be established to prevent damage to the equipment or interference with the regular lunch operation. If such safeguards cannot be assured or if the lunchroom location is inappropriate, special facilities might better be provided at the place of need. This might include a refreshment stand at the football field or adjoining the gymnasium, a combination sink-stove-refrigerator unit and cupboards in a conference room, or other similar facilities.

DETERMINING NUMBER TO BE SERVED

An important factor in fixing the size of the kitchen and auxiliary rooms is the total number of meals to be prepared at any one time. The size of the dining room also depends upon the number who eat there at one time. Thus, it is necessary to make a reasonably accurate estimate of the future number of patrons. The capacity for which the building is planned is a starting point, but from this must be deducted an allowance for normal absence. Moreover, pupils may or may not be allowed to go home for lunch or to eat elsewhere outside the building. Some pupils may bring their lunches to school and may or may not be required to eat in the lunchroom. If pupils are not required to eat at the building, the percentage who actually do so may vary over a wide range. Accurate information on the trend of this percentage is essential, and consideration should be given to any factors which might change its direction or rate. It is well to note that in general the trend is for a greater proportion of the pupils to eat at school because of more working mothers outside the home, greater recognition of the need for nutritious and well-balanced meals at noon, and increased emphasis upon the school lunch as a desirable social and educational experience. To the estimated number of pupils eating at school must be added the number of teachers and other staff members for whom lunches must be prepared and served. The impact of these calculations on dimensions of the kitchen, dining room, and other spaces will be discussed as each of these rooms is discussed below.

LOCATION OF LUNCHROOM[1]

If the lunchroom is to serve most effectively its intended purposes, it must be properly located with respect to the remainder of the building and the out-of-doors. The kitchen must be located so that delivery of supplies and removal of wastes can be easily handled. This demands easy access to a service drive. If the lunchroom is not on the ground level, a freight elevator becomes necessary unless the feeding operation is very small. Elevators are expensive to install and operate, and always involve some measure of inconvenience in use. Kitchens are sometimes located on a top floor presumably to avoid the spread of cooking odors throughout the

[1] Although the lunchroom in a school is usually a cafeteria, the more general term "lunchroom" may be used in this chapter to encompass both the cafeteria and table service arrangements.

building. With proper mechanical ventilation this problem can be solved without regard to location. Current thinking strongly favors a ground-floor location unless there are impelling local reasons to the contrary.

Proper location of the dining room is largely a matter of convenience to its users. Pupils using the room at noon should be able to reach it easily without undue traffic congestion on stairs or in passageways. The location should permit easy egress from the dining room to other parts of the building or to the outside without interference with incoming traffic. If the room is to be used also for public affairs, easy access from parking areas is required; it should be easy to reach from the auditorium or other meeting places in the building where people might assemble before or after eating; and the location should permit independent use of the kitchen and dining room without opening the remainder of the building. If the dining space is decentralized in the building, each dining space should be located for ease of transporting food and dishes between it and the kitchen.

KITCHEN AND RELATED FACILITIES

The school kitchen is essentially a factory for the production of meals according to a fixed time schedule. If the operation is to be efficient, there must be careful attention in planning to many details, and especially to equipment selection and layout. The assistance of a competent specialist in this field will often pay big dividends.

The basic ingredients in kitchen planning are the number of meals to be prepared, the nature of the menus, and the time schedule. From these facts it is possible to determine the kinds and quantities of different foods that must be processed, the size of staff needed, and the kinds and sizes of equipment required. For example, if the specialist knows that macaroni and cheese is at times the main dish, he can calculate for a given number of persons how many pans of a certain size are required and how much oven space they will take. In this way he can determine whether the range ovens will suffice or additional ovens are needed. In like manner, he can determine the size of mixer required to mash potatoes and whether or not a steam kettle is advisable for cooking soup. The equipment list developed in this fashion is far superior to one taken from a book or magazine or from a neighboring school.

The arrangement of the kitchen should expedite the flow of supplies from delivery truck to storage, from storage to preparation areas, from preparation areas to cooking or serving areas, and from stoves and ovens to serving areas. The movement of each item along these routes should be as direct as possible without interfering with the work of other people, and the distances should be short. It is desirable in the planning process to make trial layouts to scale, using templates cut to the same scale to represent the equipment, and to check carefully the routing of personnel as various typical kitchen operations are performed. This procedure will also produce a more satisfactory answer to the question of kitchen size than can be found in published standards.

Many times a school building will be designed with a reasonable expectation of later enlargement to accommodate more pupils. Since a school kitchen includes so much equipment with pipes and conduits buried in the floor, it is very expensive to enlarge and rearrange. It would be well, therefore, to make the initial room adequate in size, to plan the final layout at the beginning, and to have the installation of additional equipment at predetermined places as the sole or major adjustment required to increase the capacity at some future date.

The size and nature of storage rooms will depend upon the kinds of items to be stored and the quantities purchased at one time. Separate refrigerated and unrefrigerated storage spaces are usually required with good ventilation for the latter. Space for keeping frozen foods is often advisable.

Particular attention to health and safety is essential in designing the kitchen. This includes protection against accidents, fire, vermin, flies, and rodents. Floors and wall surfaces should be impervious to moisture, oils, and grease, and counter tops and other work surfaces should be corrosion resistant and easy to clean. An ample supply of hot water should be provided for cleaning. Garbage and other wastes, if not burned or discharged into sewers, should be stored in tight containers in a suitable place outside the kitchen. Ventilation should be designed to prevent kitchen odors from traveling into the dining room or other parts of the building.

Central Kitchen

In some systems where most of the schools are small, a central kitchen may be provided and the food delivered to each school ready to serve. Sometimes even the dishes and tableware are brought in, collected after use, and returned to the central kitchen for washing. In other cases, the dishwashing and possibly some of the food preparation is done locally. These arrangements greatly reduce the kitchen requirements in the individual school and may call for only a simple serving room. They have not won wide acceptance, but may have value in some situations. If there should be any doubt about the permanence of such a plan in a new building, the design should permit the later addition of a complete kitchen.

Rooms for Kitchen Staff

Two kinds of specialized space are normally provided for staff use, office space for the manager and a small room including toilet, locker, and possibly shower facilities for the kitchen help. The former may be simply a place in the kitchen for a desk, a chair, and a file, but in a larger school it is usually a separate room. In either event, it should be located to permit easy supervision of the kitchen and of deliveries. The toilet and locker room should be convenient to the kitchen and to the building entrance used by kitchen employees.

DISHWASHING

Pots and pans are normally washed in a special sink in the kitchen and dishes from the dining room in a mechanical dishwasher, unless the school is quite small. The dishwashing area requires a properly located window or door through which dirty dishes are received, a counter for scraping and possibly prerinsing dirty dishes and stacking them in racks, the dishwashing machine, a counter for removing clean dishes from the racks, and perhaps shelves for storage of clean dishes. Particular attention must be given to the means of transporting clean dishes to the places where they will be used and to the removal of garbage scraped from the dishes. Unnecessary lifting and carrying should be avoided. In small schools all of the dishwashing facilities may be in one section of the kitchen, while in large installations a separate room will be required. A location adjacent to the kitchen is desirable, but in some installations a more remote location will be warranted to provide a better traffic pattern in the serving and dining areas.

SERVING FACILITIES

The plan of operation of the dining room will determine the nature of the physical facilities for getting prepared food from the kitchen to the tables. The most common plan is the use of one or more cafeteria lines located for convenient replenishment from the kitchen and for smooth flow of pupil traffic into and out of the dining room. The number of lines depends upon the age of pupils, the variety of food from which the pupil may choose, and the arrangement of the counter facilities. As a general guide, one might assume that one counter will serve 12 to 15 persons per minute.[2]

A common error in planning is failure to provide enough cafeteria

[2] National Council on Schoolhouse Construction, *Guide for Planning School* *Plants*. Nashville, Tenn.: The Council, 1953, p. 103.

lines. One high school, for example, with a dining room capacity of almost 600, found it necessary to have a lunch period 25 minutes longer than anticipated because it took so long for the 600 pupils to pass through the two cafeteria lines. Insufficient serving facilities also lead to problems of maintaining order in long lines of pupils who are impatient to be served, and to problems of control of pupils who finish eating early and have nothing to do for the remainder of the period. The resulting boisterousness may well destroy the quiet, relaxed atmosphere which should prevail at mealtime.

Another frequent error, and a most troublesome one, is to locate the serving counters, dirty dish return windows, and dining room exits so that pupils with trays of food or dirty dishes or pupils leaving the dining room must pass through lines of pupils waiting to be served. This leads to noise, mischief, and frequently accidental spilling of trays. Such an arrangement is undeniable evidence of poor planning.

Another problem which is often overlooked in planning is the serving of partial lunches to pupils who bring food from home. If there are many of them, these pupils might well be served at a special counter stocked with the few items which they are likely to desire. This will avoid congestion and delay in the lines where full lunches are obtained. Also, where the service is cafeteria style, a special counter for teachers is advisable, thus enabling them to have quicker service without breaking into the line of pupils and allowing them time for noon-hour duties or needed relaxation.

If the plan of operation calls for table service, a pass window or serving table or counter will be satisfactory, since only a few persons will pick up food to take to the tables. These must be located with a view to easy movement of the servers without interference by other workers or by persons entering the dining room.

Should dining space be provided at several locations in the building, the kitchen equipment and layout will have to provide for the loading and unloading of carts, and each of the dining areas will require space to operate and unload the cart. A simple serving table might suffice in each dining room, or a heated serving counter may be required, depending upon the time and manner of delivery of the food from the kitchen and the manner of serving.

DINING SPACE

The atmosphere of the dining room should be conducive to leisurely eating without excessive noise or boisterousness. Perhaps this idea can best be expressed by saying that the school dining room should have the characteristics of a good restaurant with its variety of shapes and arrangements of tables, its pleasant lighting and good acoustical conditions, and its paintings, pictures, and other decorative features. Such conditions are difficult to achieve in a large, rectangular room, and this is one reason for dissatisfaction with the typical large school cafeteria. One answer to the problem is to divide a large dining room into several small ones by use of sliding or folding partitions. This has the advantage of making available a large space for banquets or other social affairs.

Smaller rooms at several locations throughout the building is another means of achieving a more favorable dining environment. These might also be used as pupil lounges, conference rooms, or for other purposes. This decentralization requires the transporting of food and dishes through the building, and may require that the gymnasium or some other large space be planned for occasional banquet use. For the latter, a caterer's counter and storage facilities would be needed.

Another type of decentralized dining is for pupils to get lunches in the cafeteria and take them to their classrooms to eat, or to have lunches delivered to the rooms in insulated carts or other containers. Such an arrangement creates what is probably the minimum practical size of group, but it involves new problems in handling food and dishes. It would be most readily adaptable to a nondepartmentalized school where each group of pupils has its own room. Before this arrangement is adopted, full consideration should be given to the psychological needs of teachers and pupils alike for a break in the school day which is provided by going elsewhere to eat and to the problems of cleaning up the classrooms after lunch and ridding them of lingering food odors.

Separate dining rooms for teachers are generally considered desirable, unless the plan of operation requires that they eat with their pupils. If separate rooms are adopted, they should be in a quiet and pleasant location, since the justification for them is that they provide opportunity for needed relaxation.

Size of Dining Room

The amount of space required for dining room purposes will depend upon the number of persons eating at any one time. The normal allotment is 10 to 12 square feet per person, but the only sound approach is to prepare trial layouts of the equipment on a scale drawing. Some margin for growth may be advisable, or the plan can provide for later addition of dining room space to accommodate a larger enrollment. Tables and chairs are the common equipment. While ruggedness is necessary, there is no reason why beauty cannot also be provided with the variety of colorful as well as durable plastics and metals now available for such purposes. A variance in size and shape, with some tables in booths and some in the open, also adds to the attractiveness of the room.

If the dining room is to be used for activities requiring the removal of all or part of the tables and chairs, folding or stackable equipment is suggested. Tables and benches folding into the wall may be used, or they may be carried or wheeled into storage rooms provided for this purpose.

For the convenience of persons using the dining room, consideration should be given to the following:

1. Handwashing facilities at or near the entrance, unless provided in the rooms from which pupils come to lunch.
2. Toilet facilities near the entrance.
3. Shelves at the entrance where pupils may leave their books while they eat.

School Offices

LITTLE question is likely to arise in planning a school building with regard to the need for some office space. There will, however, be uncertainty with respect to who should have offices, where the various offices should be located, and how they should be arranged and equipped.

LIST OF NEEDED OFFICES

The question of who should have offices should be answered in terms of the duties to be performed, but unfortunately considerations of prestige and status sometimes intrude. It seems clear that office space should be furnished for the following:

1. Any person whose duties consist primarily of desk work, telephoning, interviewing, and the like. (E.g., a principal, a guidance counselor, or a secretary.)
2. A part-time teacher who has duties such as indicated above and whose classroom is not available or suitable for these non-teaching duties. (E.g., a teacher serving part-time as a counselor or department head.)
3. A full-time teacher or other employee whose regular working space is not suitable for the keeping of records and other desk work. (E.g., a physical education teacher, a custodian, or a lunchroom manager.)
4. A full-time teacher whose classroom is not available for his use during his nonteaching periods.

Application of these principles will result in a different list of offices in each school, depending upon the size and variety of staff, policies with regard to classroom usage, and other aspects of the program.

Some of the persons in need of office space can share it with others, but some will need privacy. A separate office is justified for anyone whose telephone conversations, dictation to a stenographer, or interviews with callers are of such nature as to require privacy in order to avoid embarrassment or disclosure of confidential information. Thus, a principal or a guidance counselor would normally have a private office. Beyond this, the justification for a private office is that it increases efficiency by providing relatively greater quietness and freedom from interruption. This principle would apply to anyone entitled to office space, but usually has only limited application because of the expense involved. Teachers, for example, normally have access to desk space in a teachers' workroom, if they have any office space, and all or most secretaries are in a single, large room in most schools.

Anticipating Future Needs

The makeshift offices found in school buildings throughout the country are evidence of failure to foresee, often for only a few years, any expansion of the nonteaching staff of the school. As a general rule, schools are understaffed in the areas of administration and supervision. Many elementary schools have teaching principals. There are too few instructional supervisors at both the elementary and secondary school levels. There are too few guidance workers, and too little secretarial and clerical assistance is provided. The recognition of these needs outruns the facilities in most schools. This fact, coupled with the ever-present prospect of increasing enrollments, calls for designing the office facilities of a new school building for future expansion without crowding out other needed spaces. A spare office or two in large schools is not likely to be wasted; the smaller school as a minimum should have the office suite so located that it can be expanded in at least one direction, and preferably in more than one direction. A location next to a main entrance, a stairway, or a toilet room makes expansion impractical in that one direction.

LOCATION OF OFFICES

The location of a given office or office suite is determined only in part by the need for expansibility. Other factors that should be considered are: (1) accessibility to persons who will come to the office; (2) important functional affinities with other parts of the building; and (3) the need for use during times when the remainder of the building is closed.

Accessibility of the principal's office is generally provided by placing it on the ground floor where it can easily be found by a person coming into the building through a major entrance. Other offices, such as those of the librarian, a physical education teacher, or the lunchroom manager, are less often visited by persons from outside, and need to be accessible primarily from the major area to which they are attached.

The functional affinities that are important in office location also vary with the type of office. The principal's secretary should have office space conveniently located with respect to the office of the principal, a teachers' workroom should be near the classrooms of the teachers who use it, and the librarian's office should be readily accessible from both the reading room and the workroom, to cite a few examples.

Certain offices, particularly those in the main office suite of the building, may have to be open during vacation periods or other times when the remainder of the building is not in use. The locations of such offices should be such that as little as possible of the remainder of the building need be heated or kept open.

PRINCIPAL'S OFFICE SUITE

Every school, except one of very small size, will have its administrative center which will include at least office space for the principal. There will usually be space here also for some secretarial workers and possibly for assistant principals and other professional workers. A minimum array of offices for a school with a nonteaching principal would be:

1. An office where the principal can work without interruption and use the telephone, dictate, and conduct interviews in private.
2. An office where the secretarial staff can greet visitors, type, keep records, and do other clerical work.
3. Waiting space for visitors.

Beyond these minimum needs, consideration should be given to the following:

1. A separate workroom where the secretarial staff can operate duplicating machines, assemble duplicated materials, and perform similar tasks without interference with other office operations.
2. An office supply room, which might or might not be combined with the workroom.

3. A fireproof room or vault for records, unless fireproof files are provided in the outer office.

4. A conference room where committees and other groups may confer.

The Principal's Private Office

The private office of the principal must give him the necessary privacy and at the same time give him ready access to records. The arrangement should permit him to work in his office without interruption by persons in the outer office, and should make it possible for him to enter or leave by a private entrance as well as through the outer office. Attractive but not ornate furnishings and equipment are appropriate, and the size should be ample to accommodate the necessary office equipment and chairs for perhaps five or six visitors at one time. The provision of space for larger groups is questionable if a suitable conference room is available near by.

Other Private Offices

The larger school, especially at the secondary school level, will have need for other private offices, depending not only upon size but also upon the nature and organization of its administrative and supervisory staff. These might include offices for assistant principals, deans, guidance counselors, supervisors, treasurers, registrars, and possibly others. It is convenient to have all these persons in one suite because it permits quick access to records and facilitates easy communication. However, some decentralization may be desirable to avoid congestion, provided the offices are not too far removed from one another. Also, the counselors' offices need the privacy afforded by a separate entrance and waiting room.

Communications

The principal's office suite is the traditional communications center for the building, and as such includes the clock and program mechanism and controls, the telephone switchboard, the public address control equipment, public telephones for pupil and teacher use, and mailboxes and bulletin boards for teachers. The concentration of all of these in one place often results in unnecessary confusion that causes almost complete stoppage of normal office work several times a day. Decentralization of at least some of these items should be seriously considered. The teachers' mailboxes and bulletin board could be in a near-by teachers' lounge, public telephones could be in a booth off the lobby or a corridor, some of the clock and program mechanism (but not the controls) could be outside the office, and the public address controls could be in a studio used for the teaching of speech and dramatics. The principal should have a public address microphone in his office, but he need not have the control panel there where he may be tempted to interrupt classes by unnecessarily frequent announcements and where its use by others will interrupt the normal work of the office.

Facilities for Staff Comfort and Convenience

SCIENTIFIC studies as well as practical experience during the past few decades have convinced administrators in all lines of endeavor that greater attention should be given to working conditions and other factors affecting the comfort and convenience of employees. In addition to compelling humane considerations, there is now irrefutable evidence that such attention raises the morale of workers and increases their efficiency. Application of this enlightened point of view to school-plant design calls for places where teachers and other employees can eat in quiet and pleasant surroundings, relax and chat with others during brief rest periods, lie down to rest in a quiet place in case of need, and attend to personal toilet and grooming needs in private.

Many existing school buildings, particularly the older ones and those in smaller communities, are extremely lacking in such facilities. A locked stall in the pupils' toilet or a small, drab "restroom" with uninviting wicker furniture are frequently available for teachers, or possibly only for female teachers, and there is no provision for other employees. Teachers and other staff members crowd in at the head of the line in the cafeteria and eat at a table in one corner of the pupils' dining room or in a makeshift teachers' dining room.

TEACHERS' LOUNGE AND RESTROOMS

The activities to be housed in a teachers' restroom can be classified into three types, each requiring some separation from the other two. First are those activities appropriate in a lounge, including reading, writing, conversing with others, smoking, or just sitting. The lounge room may be shared by men and women, or separate lounges may be provided. With the increasing percentage of male teachers, their needs should not be overlooked, as they frequently are, especially in elementary school buildings. The lounge should be conveniently located, but even more important are privacy, quietness, a ventilation system that will permit smoking, and furnishings that are conducive to relaxation. Storage facilities are needed for books, magazines, and writing materials, and clothing and other personal belongings may also be kept here. If not found elsewhere, the lounge should also include facilities for making coffee, tea, sandwiches, and other snacks, and for serving them.

Figure 11. Schematic Plan for a Teachers' Lounge.

The second type of space required is a room where one or more persons may lie down in quiet and semi-darkness to rest. A separate room is needed for each sex, but the two rooms might be adjacent to a common lounge. Convenient access to toilets is needed without going through the lounge.

The toilet room itself is the third type of space required. In addition to the necessary plumbing fixtures, there should be soap, towels, mirrors, and other provisions for personal grooming. The toilet room should be readily accessible from the lounge as well as the cot space, but the entrance from a common lounge should not be direct, since this might be embarrassing. The plumbing fixtures should be of a quiet type, or be placed to minimize any noise which might disturb a person lying down in an adjacent room or which might embarrass the user, especially when there is a common lounge.

LOUNGES AND RESTROOMS FOR OTHER EMPLOYEES

Facilities similar to those described for teachers are needed by other employees, except that they will be little used for reading or writing. The extent to which separate facilities are provided for different classes of employees will depend upon the size and character of the staff. Secretaries and teachers might share the same facilities in a small school, and cooks and matrons would be another possible combination.

A facility which is very often furnished is a shower to permit custodians to clean up after a day's work. Some of these are not used as intended. This suggests installation of rough plumbing and floor drain only rather than complete omission of the facility when there is doubt about the immediate use of the shower.

Clothing storage for office workers is usually provided in the offices where they work, but may be in a lounge. Toilet rooms, too, are sometimes provided in the office suite, but are often not used in a small office because the noise of the plumbing fixtures may be embarrassing. The use of silent fixtures and proper location would reduce this objection.

Facilities for Building Operation and Maintenance

THE modern school building is a complicated structure representing a considerable investment of public funds. If this investment is to yield the maximum return and not be wasted by poor maintenance practices, the design of the building must be such that proper operation and maintenance are facilitated. This applies both to the structure itself and to the mechanical equipment in it. Attention has been directed in an earlier chapter to the importance of selecting this equipment in terms of long-range cost; the discussion here will be limited to spaces needed for operation and maintenance.

SPACES FOR MECHANICAL EQUIPMENT

There is great diversity in the types of heating plants, ventilating systems, and other mechanical installations, and each involves different provisions of space in the building. A central, coal-fired heating plant, for example, presents an entirely different design problem than small, automatic, gas-fired units scattered through the building. Not only are the spaces different, but there are differences in respect to delivery and storage of fuel and removal of wastes that are reflected in the building layout. Because of these variations, only general suggestions can be offered here.

A frequent error in designing these rooms, particularly where a central heating plant is used, is to make the rooms of such size or shape that it is difficult to operate or service the equipment. The location of the heating plant should be such that an explosion will not endanger the occupants of the building, and at the same time such that it is conveniently accessible to any employee who must work both here and elsewhere in the building. Delivery of fuel to storage and movement from storage to furnace should require a minimum of manual labor and provide a maximum of safety. There must be sufficient space around the equipment for ease of cleaning and repairing it, including particularly sufficient room for cleaning and replacing boiler tubes. Provision should be made for easy replacement of boilers and other equipment without cutting or dismantling the equipment or removing reinforced concrete walls. The nature of this problem is illustrated by the experience of one school where a new stoker had to be cut in two to get it into the boiler room and then welded together again when it was installed. In locations where drainage is a problem, special attention may be required to see that electric motors and other equipment that would be damaged by water are put in protected places.

CLEANING AND SERVICING THE BUILDING

The routine care of a building necessitates conveniently located places where custodians can keep mops, brushes, brooms, pails, cleaning compounds, wax, towels, soap, step ladders, and other tools and supplies which are frequently needed. Electrical outlets for vacuum cleaners and other machines and hot and cold running water are also essential. A custodian should not have to go to another floor, or to a distant part of the same floor in a large building, to get frequently needed items. The dimensions of the storage rooms should be carefully planned in relation to the items to be stored and used there. The door height and the depth and height of room, for example, should permit easy handling and storing of the maximum size of step ladder that will be used, and faucets should be high enough for the containers that will be filled there. These particular examples are chosen because they are based on frequent oversights in planning.

Similar facilities are required for the servicing of the grounds. Water should be provided at convenient locations, and storage should be available for coils of hose, lawn mowers and rollers, hand tools, and other equipment used out-of-doors. The frequent finding of these items in the boiler room several steps below grade is mute evidence of an oversight in planning.

REPAIR FACILITIES

There is a wide variety of practice with respect to maintenance and repair. Some school systems have most of this work done by local craftsmen, others have itinerant maintenance crews on the board of education payroll, and some leave all or most of the work to the building custodian until a major repair is needed. Local craftsmen and itinerant school maintenance crews usually travel in trucks that are in essence mobile shops, and there is little provision that need be made for them except convenient sources of electricity and possibly water and a suitable parking area while working. Where the building custodian or an itinerant craftsman does any repair work in the building, suitable shop space should be provided. The extent and nature of this space must be based upon local decisions as to what repairs will be made there. This facility might or might not be combined with a storage room or other space in the building, depending upon the size of building, the amount of shop space needed, and other factors.

ELEVATORS

In a large multistory building there are many supplies and pieces of equipment to move from one floor to another, and an elevator is a great convenience. This facility is also a blessing to pupils and teachers whose health makes it inadvisable to climb stairs. Since elevators are quite expensive to install and maintain, an objective in planning the building should be to make them unnecessary.

The Supply and Storage Problem

UNBELIEVABLE quantities of supplies of great variety come into a large school building in the course of a year. If these are to be handled effectively, there must be a planned system for handling each type of item, and the building must be designed accordingly.

CENTRAL STORAGE VERSUS BUILDING STORAGE

In a school system where there is more than one building, it is necessary to make a decision regarding central storage before the storage facilities of a particular building can be planned. If most items are stored in a central warehouse and delivered to schools as needed, the storage facilities in each building can be relatively small. Some school systems, however, have most items delivered directly to schools by jobbers, and this requires larger storage rooms in the individual buildings. A choice between central warehousing and building storage is also required with respect to unused school furniture and other equipment.

STORAGE FACILITIES IN THE BUILDING

Two general principles are suggested for designing the supply and storage facilities in the individual building: (1) there should be a minimum of handling; and (2) there should be adequate precautions against pilfering, spoilage, and other losses.

For convenience in handling and checking, a central receiving and storage room in the building has many advantages. A suitable drive and loading dock can be provided, the custodian or other person in charge can have close at hand a desk and other facilities for checking the items delivered against the requisitions or purchase orders, and one person can control the distribution of supplies throughout the building. Exception is usually made for lunchroom supplies, which are delivered directly to the kitchen; for industrial arts supplies, which are usually delivered directly to the shop; and for fuel for the heating plant, which is delivered directly to the coal bin or oil storage tank.

Once the supplies have been received and checked at the central storage and receiving room, they may be taken to smaller storage rooms throughout the building. For example, mimeograph paper can be transferred to an office storage room and paper towels to storage closets near toilet rooms.

These various storage rooms should be equipped with counters, shelving, bins, etc., designed for the particular items to be stored in them, with proper attention to sizes as well as quantities. Economy of floor space as well as efficient handling of supplies requires planning each storage room in detail before construction rather than after the building is occupied.

The Administrative Headquarters of a School System

As soon as a school system reaches the size where it has more than one building, the problem of housing the central administration should be raised. Often a policy of drift is pursued with the superintendent remaining in the school building where he formerly served as principal. This arrangement frequently has unfortunate effects on the educational program because the superintendent is likely to give an undue share of his attention to the needs of the school where he is housed, to the neglect of the other schools. This arrangement also has the effect in many cases of depriving the school principal of his proper leadership role because it is so easy for him and others to turn to the superintendent with the problems as they arise. This impoverishes him professionally and creates divided loyalties which in some communities have led to devastating controversy.

For these reasons, the authors strongly urge that the superintendent and other central office personnel be housed outside of any building occupied by pupils. If the headquarters must be in a school building, they should be as effectively isolated as possible from the school and preferably with complete separation. Rented quarters, offices in a remodeled school building no longer used by pupils, or offices in a specially designed headquarters building are all to be preferred over sharing a building with one of the schools.

NATURE OF THE FACILITIES

The central administrative quarters in most school systems are not, and should not be, ornate monuments. They should, however, be reasonably attractive, dignified in appointments, comfortable, and efficiently planned. Since the staff and functions to be housed vary greatly from one school system to another, it is difficult to generalize with respect to the facilities needed. An early step in the planning should be a listing of all the persons likely to be housed in the building, initially and in the foreseeable future. The nature of the duties of each needs to be analyzed with respect to the types of spaces required, and attention must be directed to the groupings of offices implied in these activities and in the pattern of administrative organization.

In addition to offices for the administrative and supervisory officials of the school system and their secretarial and clerical assistants, the central headquarters will probably require some or all of the following facilities:

1. A board of education meeting room with space for visitors and representatives of the press.
2. Conference and meeting rooms of various sizes.
3. A professional library and curriculum center for the school system.
4. A center for administering and servicing the audio-visual aids or teaching aids program of the school system.
5. Central clinic facilities for pupils in all schools.
6. Central warehousing for supplies.
7. Central maintenance shops.
8. Facilities for storage and repair of buses and other board-owned motor vehicles.
9. Workrooms, storage rooms, lounges, restrooms, lunch facilities, and other features similar to those provided for use by the staffs of the individual school buildings.

CHAPTER 19

COMBINATION FACILITIES

Criteria for Judging Combinations
Gymnasium Combinations
Cafeteria Combinations
Auditorium Combinations
Corridor Combinations
Other Combinations

P<small>RACTICALLY</small> anyone who has ever helped to plan a school building has had to face the issue of what combinations of rooms, if any, would be advisable. And certainly almost everyone who has ever taught at the elementary or secondary level has had some experience with combination facilities. Combinations are brought about by the desire of school authorities to have every type of room needed for the program, accompanied by financial inability to provide separate facilities or by a realization that separate facilities would not be sufficiently utilized to justify them. Sometimes some combinations work well, but frequently the opposite is true. Too often combinations are decided upon hastily for budgetary or other reasons without careful thought as to the demands of the program and as to what is the best solution. Sometimes when combinations are necessary, they are designed without full consideration of the requirements of each type of activity to be housed in them.

It might be argued that school people are too much concerned with complete utilization of some spaces. They are certainly more concerned about this than are other public bodies. Everyone agrees that a council chamber should be provided in a city hall and that it should be designed for its principal function and that alone. Yet the typical council chamber is in use one evening per week, or less. Much the same might be said of the court room, the town hall, the city auditorium, or the armory. Yet the public does not consider these spaces to be an extravagance. Of course, school planners should strive for efficient utilization, but sometimes attempts at this may go too far, especially if they cause compromises which result in unsuitable space.

Criteria for Judging Combinations

THE authors believe in sound economy. They believe that it is achieved by the kind of planning which results in a building that fits the program rather than restricts it. The authors also believe in reasonable utilization of space and that combinations are sometimes justified and can be planned so that they are workable.

There are two basic criteria for judging any proposed combination— the needs of the program and economy.

THE NEEDS OF THE PROGRAM

In studying the feasibility of a proposed combination, the first consideration should be whether the use of the combination causes problems of scheduling to the extent that the program will be harmed. For example, if cafeteria dining space is to be considered for use as a study hall, will it be needed as a study hall at the very time when it is needed for dining? Or, if the gymnasium is used for dining space, will it be needed for noon-hour recreation while it is fulfilling its dining space function? Not only the regular daily program needs, but also the so-called extracurricular needs and community-use needs should be considered when thinking about problems of scheduling.

The second consideration in connection with the needs of the program is the matter of suitability of a given space. Will the gymnasium make a usable auditorium? Will the cafeteria dining space provide appropriate music facilities? Will the labor of changing every day from one use to another be such as to hurt either use and to consume time which might better be used for instruction?

ECONOMY

The second criterion is economy. Square feet of building area cost money, both to construct and to operate. For the sake of economy all space in a school building should be utilized to the maximum reasonably possible. If a study of the program indicates that a certain space is to be used only a comparatively short time per day, it then becomes questionable whether the space should be provided unless dual use can be made of it.

Sometimes, in the name of economy, unsatisfactory combinations have been accepted where more careful planning would have revealed their unworkability and might even have found a way of providing separate facilities within the budget. For example, the square footage of the stage of a large gymnasium-auditorium, plus a comparatively few more square feet, might provide a good, small or medium-sized auditorium. Careful planning might result in finding this additional square footage by reducing slightly the spectator space in the gymnasium, by reducing unneeded corridor space, by reducing the size of the study hall, or by other means or combination of means without hampering the school program. The careful planner will search diligently for a better solution before accepting an undesirable combination.

A wide variety of combinations, both good and bad, have been tried in school buildings. Some are workable in one situation but not in another, depending upon the educational program and other variable factors. Special names have even been coined, such as gymnatorium, cafetorium, and gymnateria. It will not be practicable to try to list here all possible combinations or to discuss them. A few of the more common ones will be listed and discussed in terms of the criteria mentioned earlier.

Gymnasium Combinations

THE GYMNASIUM AS AN AUDITORIUM

The gymnasium-auditorium combination is probably the most common of all. It developed naturally from the desire of the school and community to have both a gymnasium and an auditorium and a feeling that separate facilities, both rather large and expensive, could not be afforded or justified.

Problems of Scheduling

The scheduling difficulties will depend, of course, upon the frequency of the different kinds of activities which are to be conducted in the gymnasium-auditorium. First, the needs of the physical education program should be determined. In addition to the physical education classes, the space will be used for practice by the interscholastic athletic teams and the home games of these teams. There are also the various intramural games to be scheduled. It will also be needed for noon-hour and after-school recreation groups. Beyond these uses by in-school groups, the demands upon the space for use as a gymnasium by various community groups must not be overlooked.

Second, there will be frequent occasions for use of the facility as an auditorium. Some will be regularly scheduled, others not. If dramatics classes are part of the curriculum, they will use the stage as their classroom for many of their activities, such as rehearsals and the arrangement and construction of scenery and properties. There will be regularly scheduled school assembly programs. Also, school "pep" meetings will be held and groups such as classes or clubs may meet or give programs. In many schools a senior class play is a yearly event. There may also be other all-school dramatic presentations. These require the use of the stage for rehearsals during and after school, as well as the use of the entire auditorium for performances. School parties and dances may be frequent, and sponsors may wish to install decorations in advance. The space will also be in demand for use as an auditorium by community dramatic and social groups, and parent-teacher association meetings will also be held here. If there is a community concert or lyceum series, it may need the facility five or six evenings during the school year.

It is evident that there will be many difficulties in scheduling these many and varied activities in the gymnasium-auditorium. Whenever two or more activities need the space at the same time, friction between sponsors of the activities is engendered and the program of the group which is denied the use of the facility will suffer.

Suitability of Space

As a gymnasium the combination may be fairly adequate, since these facilities are usually designed so that the gymnasium function will be well served. The basketball playing court will be of standard size and, if the stage is placed at one end, there can be folding bleachers on each side and a folding door can divide the floor space into two adequate physical education spaces. Often, however, especially in the smaller facilities, the stage is placed at the side of the room, and is used for seating space during athletic contests. Unless bleachers are placed on the stage, the number of persons who can sit there and have a good view of the game is very limited. Even with bleachers set up on the stage, some people at the ends of the bleachers cannot see the entire court. Also, with the stage at the side, the use of folding doors to divide the playing floor is more difficult. In some designs the stage is a hazard for physical education classes and basketball teams, because the edge of the stage projects beyond the line of the wall onto the playing floor. Because of the use of the room as an auditorium, some difficulties are experienced in the placement of basketball goals and other gymnasium apparatus.

It is as an auditorium that the combined facility has the greatest short-comings. The flat floor provides very poor sight lines for persons watching a production on the stage. Considerable space at the front corners of the room is unusable for auditorium seating, due to inability to see part of the stage. Due to the use of the space as a gymnasium, its character is somewhat barnlike and unattractive for auditorium purposes. The basketball goals on the walls and up against the ceiling hardly lend attractiveness to the room. Because of the size and shape of the room and because of its hard finishes, the acoustical properties are not good for auditorium purposes. Many of the dramatic and musical productions will be by children with immature voices. They will not be heard by a large part of the audience. Even with mechanical amplification, the reverberation time may be such that hearing is difficult. Other difficulties will be experienced. When the room functions as a gymnasium, there is great likelihood of damage to stage draperies, scenery, and properties. The heating and ventilating system if adjusted for comfort for one type of activity may be quite unsatisfactory for the other type of activity.

One of the principal difficulties, and certainly one of the most annoying, is the handling of the folding chairs for auditorium seating. Much labor and time are involved in taking the chairs out of storage and arranging them properly in rows. Likewise, it is no small task to put them away again. Even with sturdy chairs, breakage is frequent. The best of them are less comfortable than fixed auditorium seating. So great are the labor, inconvenience, and delay that, even with well-designed handling and storage facilities, the use of the space as an auditorium is restricted, and desirable educational activities are omitted.

Some of the criticisms of the combination auditorium-gymnasium apply mostly to its use in secondary schools, and to a lesser degree to its use in an elementary school. In the latter the facility can be much smaller, and it can serve well as a children's playroom. When used as an auditorium, it is small enough that the acoustics can be quite good and is quite suitable for smaller meetings. The activities for the space will be much fewer and less varied, and scheduling difficulties will not be great, at least for a small school. But if the elementary school is large, or if a departmentalized program involving physical education classes and auditorium classes is operated, the same difficulties of scheduling and operation mentioned earlier will be experienced.

Economy

There is no question that there is less total square footage in a combined gymnasium-auditorium than in separate facilities of the same capacity and that the cost of construction will be less. But perhaps two facilities of this size are not needed, and perhaps careful planning can discover ways of saving space throughout the building without hurting the program so that the space saved, plus the extra space and expense of making the gymnasium into an auditorium, would be enough to build a satisfactory auditorium.

A careful study of all aspects of the problem should be made before deciding upon the combination, and economy should be viewed not only from the standpoint of possible savings in first cost, but also from possible losses due to inadequacy of the facility for the program needs, scheduling difficulties, and the time and labor required for frequent conversion from one use to the other.

Design Suggestions

It is certainly evident that this combination should be avoided, especially for secondary schools. However, if it must be used, the following suggestions may prove helpful:

1. Provide adequate and safe storage space for stage properties.

2. Provide a substantial folding door across the stage opening.

3. Try to use folding chairs which are comfortable, quiet, easily handled, and durable. Provide convenient and adequate storage space for them. The dimensions of such space must be carefully computed for efficient storage of the numbers of chairs to be used. The storage space must be easily accessible.

4. For a large gymnasium-auditorium it may be best to place the stage at one end. Then, for smaller audiences the folding door which divides the floor space for physical education purposes can be closed to reduce the size of the auditorium. This will also tie up only one half of the floor space.

5. In a secondary school, it is essential that another space be provided somewhere in the school for smaller meetings. This will reduce somewhat the scheduling difficulties for the larger room. If possible, there should be a small auditorium with a good stage. This would be large enough to accommodate all except a few of the auditorium activities. For the two or three occasions per year, such as commencement, when a large crowd is expected, the gymnasium could be used with a temporary or folding stage.

THE GYMNASIUM AS A CAFETERIA

Another combination found rather frequently is one whereby the playing floor of the gymnasium is used as dining space for school lunches.

Sometimes the room has to serve not only as a gymnasium-auditorium, but also for this third function. It the latter is the case, the addition of the dining function adds one more difficulty to the scheduling problem. Assuming only two uses of the space, namely as a gymnasium and as dining space, there may still be scheduling conflicts. It is often desirable to use the gymnasium floor for recreation during the noon hour. Also, the length of time during which the gymnasium will be used for dining, for placing tables and chairs before lunch, and for clearing them away and cleaning up litter after lunch may seriously restrict the use of the space for physical education classes.

Inasmuch as the space is usually designed primarily as a gymnasium and its use as a dining space is rather incidental, the adequacy of the space as a gymnasium is little affected by the dual use. The food preparation and serving areas are generally arranged so that they can be completely separated from the gymnasium floor. Perhaps the presence of food odors is not desirable and the litter left from lunches may be a problem, but this need not be serious. Adequacy for dining purposes is certainly questionable. A dining space should be designed for friendliness, relaxation, and sociability. The size, appearance, and acoustical properties of the gymnasium hardly meet these objectives. In many gymnasiums there is a typical gymnasium odor, perhaps due to inadequate ventilation in the adjacent locker rooms. This odor is not what one would wish to have or expect to find in a restaurant dining room. It is just as out of place in a school dining room.

Many multipurpose rooms in the elementary schools serve gymnasium, auditorium, and school lunch purposes. Scheduling difficulties may not be as severe as in a high school and some of the other objections may not be present to the same degree, but the space is still far from ideal for dining purposes. Also, in the elementary school, the space may be needed for noon-hour recreation at the very time it is in use for dining. Labor may also not be as plentiful to set up the space for dining and to clear it away and clean up for other uses. The labor of doing this each day may be enough to cause the tables and chairs to be left permanently in position, thereby eliminating the use of the space for children's games and physical education. Various types of tables and benches which fold into the wall or can be rolled out of the way have been devised. These help solve the problems of labor and time, but not those of schedule conflicts and other objections.

It would seem that, although space may be saved by this combination, the disadvantages are so great, especially in the secondary school, that other more feasible combinations should be sought.

Cafeteria Combinations

THE desire to arrange for some use of the cafeteria dining space for other purposes than dining is understandable. Unless this is done, this space will stand idle about three quarters of the school day. It then becomes a question of examining possible combinations to decide which ones are most feasible. The following paragraphs will discuss the cafeteria as a study hall, as a library, as a music room, as an auditorium, and as social space. These combinations will be examined from the standpoint of how well they suit the educational program.

THE CAFETERIA AS A STUDY HALL

The use of cafeteria dining space for study hall purposes has been a natural one. The cafeteria furniture can serve fairly well for study purposes, and little or no rearrangement is necessary for its use at lunch time. The size, shape, and acoustics of the room can be favorable, and the natural and electric lighting can be made suitable for either purpose.

There may be some difficulties in scheduling. If the space is used for dining for a double lunch-hour period, this will be about one quarter of the school day and the school will have to operate without a study hall for that length of time. This difficulty is alleviated by the fact that some of the pupils are at lunch, and some classrooms are vacant and available for study purposes, if needed.

If this combination is used, the following should be considered:

1. The furniture should be suitable for both uses. Comfort, durability, ease of handling and cleaning, light finishes, and resistance to stains should be carefully checked.
2. Shelf space should be provided for reference books.
3. The food preparation and serving areas should be completely separated to keep kitchen noises from the study area, and the ventilation should be designed to keep out food odors.
4. Location may be a problem. A study hall should be close to the library and both should be centrally located in the building. Such a location may not be best for a cafeteria. The factors on which cafeteria location should be based have have been stated in Chapter 18. They are somewhat contrary to those for location of a study hall.

On the whole, it would appear that, if the school program is such as to require a study hall, the use of the cafeteria dining space for this purpose, while perhaps not ideal, is economically justifiable and represents one of the more desirable combinations.

THE CAFETERIA AS A LIBRARY

The use of the dining space as a library is another possible combination, which is perhaps less desirable than the use of the space as a study hall. It is suggested that, at this point, the reader review parts of Chapter 17, in which the purposes of the library and the nature of the space to be provided are discussed, and then do the same with the material on lunch facilities in Chapter 18. The authors believe he will come to the same conclusions that they have, namely, that the two functions are so different and the kinds of spaces which will best house these functions are so different that an attempt to combine them in one space is inadvisable. The general atmosphere of the room is not suitable for a library, and there are problems of damage to library equipment and loss of books when the room is used for dining. The library and cafeteria require different locations within the building. The library is needed all during the school day, after school hours, and perhaps in the evening. During the noon hour it should be available for voluntary reading and study. Because of these objections, it is believed that such a combination would in most cases be harmful to the program and poor economy.

THE CAFETERIA AS A MUSIC ROOM

Another use which is sometimes suggested for the cafeteria dining space is for music instruction. Insofar as scheduling is concerned, such an arrangement might be fairly workable if the number of music groups meeting regularly is small enough so that the space is not needed for music when in use for dining. When planning the daily schedule for use of a dining space, the planner should remember to allow for the time needed daily for preparing the space for dining and for cleaning it after each meal.

The space itself is not wholly suitable for music instruction. It is desirable to locate music facilities near the auditorium stage. Such a location may be quite unsuitable for a cafeteria. The shape of the space may or may not be such as to permit the arrangement of a group of performers in an arc in front of the director. Music activities require pianos, record players, sheet music, band and orchestra instruments, band uniforms, choir robes, music stands, and other items that must be safeguarded, and it would be inconvenient to have to put them away each day. Dining room furniture, also, will have to be put out of the way each time the space is used for music and replaced again before the space is used for dining. The acoustical requirements of a music room are somewhat different than for a dining space.

Practice rooms and an instructor's office are commonly considered to be desirable in a music suite, and there may be difficulty in providing them with the dual use.

These difficulties are not insurmountable, especially if music groups meet only occasionally, but other possible combinations should be explored before this one is accepted. If music is placed in the dining room, particular attention should be given to adequacy and convenience of storage of the music supplies and equipment, to ease of removing the dining room furniture, and to acoustics.

THE CAFETERIA AS AN ASSEMBLY SPACE

Use of the cafeteria dining space for assembly purposes is another solution to the problem of obtaining increased utilization of this space. Within limitations, this may be a desirable plan. Of course, no flat floor is ideal for auditorium seating, and the dining room is certainly not an acceptable substitute for a full-fledged auditorium as described in Chapter 15. However, there are many meetings of groups for which the auditorium may be too large. A smaller group, nearly filling a smaller assembly space, can develop much better group feeling and a better meeting can generally be conducted than would be possible in a large auditorium. For the smaller groups, a flat floor will not be a handicap. The stage need not be pretentious and can be, perhaps, a folding or portable stage divided temporarily from the rest of the room by draperies hung from the ceiling. This will be satisfactory for a very simple dramatic production, for speakers, recitals, and the sort of activity not requiring extensive properties, lighting, and scenery.

Scheduling difficulties should not be serious, as it will not usually be desired to hold a meeting or an assembly at mealtime. There is, of course, the problem of what to do with the dining tables. If they are not removed, the audience capacity is materially reduced. Space must be provided for easy and quick storage of them. The tables themselves must be designed for compact storage, durability, and stability, and with surfaces which can be easily cleaned. Other suggestions which should be considered if the dining space is planned for assembly purposes are:

1. Provide exits to care for the maximum capacity of the room.
2. Design carefully to prevent sound transmission between the food preparation and serving spaces and the dining space.
3. Provide an adequate ventilating system for capacity occupancy, and make sure that ventilation from the kitchen is designed to prevent food odors from reaching the dining space.

4. Provide adequate means for darkening the space for those assembly activities which require it.

5. Provide an electrical outlet for a projector and conduits so that the speaker cable does not have to be run on the floor.

THE CAFETERIA AS SOCIAL SPACE

An extension of the idea of utilizing the cafeteria dining space for assembly purposes is its use for general school and community social activities. If used for this purpose, it will be necessary to provide space for storing cafeteria tables and, at times, some of the chairs, so that the labor of conversion is not too great. Such a dual use would appear highly desirable and economically and educationally sound. There should be almost no scheduling conflicts between the daily use for dining and the use for social affairs. Many of the social affairs will be held in the late afternoon, in the evening, and particularly on Friday and Saturday evenings.

The location of the cafeteria to serve its primary function should not be much different from the location needed for social affairs. But attention should be paid to accessibility to parking areas, zoned heating and ventilating, and provision for using this space without opening the rest of the plant.

The same provisions for storage, darkening, exits, ventilation, noise control, electrical outlets, and stage, mentioned earlier in connection with use of the space as an assembly space, apply to the more generalized social use.

Especially in warmer climates, some dining spaces are designed so that indoor dining space can be merged with an outdoor dining area, perhaps in an open court. Likewise there could be a design and location to permit the dining room to be merged with an indoor lobby-social area. The proximity of the kitchen is ideal for preparing and serving light lunches, or if the cafeteria has a snack bar, this can be used for this purpose.

It would appear that the use of the cafeteria dining space for social activities is one of the most desirable examples of dual use. However, the space does not become useful social space automatically. Careful thought must be given to this dual use during the planning of the building. Such planning will pay dividends in sound economy and in the provision of a very attractive social area for youth and adults.

Auditorium Combinations

WHEN fairly complete auditoriums are provided in school buildings, it is sometimes apparent to those in authority that the space will not be completely utilized, at least to the extent that regular classrooms are utilized. Consequently, attempts are made to find some dual use to justify the expense. Such an objective is commendable, yet it sometimes results in combinations which are unwise. Not only do they force undesirable compromises in the design of the auditorium, but they sometimes provide unsuitable housing for the other function.

First, perhaps, the possibility should be investigated of more complete use of the auditorium as an auditorium. The principal justification for a school auditorium is its use for instruction in auditorium-type activities, just as the principal justification for a gymnasium is instruction in physical education. A school which has not had a good separate auditorium in the past and which is moving into a new building where one is provided, may not realize fully at first the opportunity which it now has to broaden its program and to give wider experiences to more children.

THE AUDITORIUM AS A STUDY HALL

The use of an auditorium as a study hall is probably an inheritance from the old plan of secondary school organization under which each child had a desk in a general assembly room. This large assembly room housed the entire student body, and each pupil kept his school materials here. He reported to this desk every morning for the attendance check and went back to it during the day whenever he was not in a class or some other group activity. This was the study hall, and it also served as the auditorium. Commonly, morning exercises were held in it. There was at first only a platform at the front of the room for the teacher in charge, but later stages came to be installed and the room became a school and community auditorium.

It is only natural, then, that someone might suggest that the audience space of a new auditorium might also be used as a study hall. This is usually accomplished by placing a hinged tablet arm on the right side of every other one of the auditorium seats, or at least enough to provide for the maximum expected study hall load.

With respect to scheduling and suitability of space, this combination must be given a low rating. In the traditional high school program a study hall is needed every hour of the school day. When the space is in use as an auditorium, the study hall use must be suspended. Some may argue that the use of the auditorium will involve the entire student body, thereby cancelling the need for a study hall at that time. But if a good functional auditorium is used only for student assemblies and for out-of-school hour community functions, the justification for having it at all is questionable, important as the two uses mentioned may be. If there is good utilization of the auditorium as an instructional room, the use of the audience space for study hall purposes will conflict with such use.

Furthermore, the audience space of an auditorium is not suitable for study hall purposes. The student needs more than a seat and a small tablet arm for real study. He may wish to use several references and have them all spread out in front of him. The tablet arms must be of small size if they are to fold out of the way to permit passage between rows of seats. Some of them are hardly large enough to hold an $8\frac{1}{2}''$ x $11''$ sheet of paper. At best, they are noisy, awkward, and inadequate. Also, the lighting of the audience space in a well-designed auditorium is designed for purposes other than study. It may be partially decorative, designed to provide safe movement of crowds and to focus attention on the stage. An attempt to provide light of adequate quality and quantity for study purpose conflicts with the objectives of auditorium lighting.

Since most pupils do not usually view a study period as the most interesting part of the school day, the architecture of the study hall should not emphasize the confinement idea. A broad view of the outdoors and other ways of creating a feeling of openness are desirable, but the well-designed auditorium may have no windows.

The daily use of the auditorium seating by active and fidgety youth is bound to bring about excessive wear, marking, and other damage to the seating. This presents a continual maintenance problem. Frequently it will not be possible to make repairs in time for public use. Because of this problem, the quality and type of furniture is compromised.

THE AUDITORIUM AS A MUSIC FACILITY

A common recommendation of school planners is that the music instruction rooms be located near the auditorium stage because music groups will wish to use the stage frequently. Consequently, it is sometimes suggested that the stage be used regularly as a music instruction room. In some cases it is thought that the first few rows of auditorium seating might accommodate regular vocal classes. These proposals should be examined carefully in terms of the program needs and the suitability of the space.

How many groups, large and small, vocal and instrumental, will meet daily? How many teaching stations are needed? Obviously, the auditorium, whether the stage or the seating space, will provide but one station because of sound interference. What are the needs for the use of the stage by other groups? Are there regularly scheduled classes in dramatic arts? Will not stagecraft groups need to tie up the stage for several weeks in preparation for a production? How frequent will be the use of the auditorium for assemblies and other purposes? The answers to such questions will show whether there will be scheduling difficulties serious enough to impair not only the music program but other programs of equal importance. The usual school experience is that there are many scheduling difficulties in connection with the normal use of the auditorium without housing music classes there.

There are other questions that should be raised. Will the stage be an adequate facility for music instruction? Or will the auditorium seating, front and center, provide a proper place for vocal music classes? Are practice rooms needed? Where will uniforms, instruments, music, and music stands be stored? Will there be difficulty in preventing damage to stage scenery and properties by the music group, as well as damage to music equipment by other school and community groups using the stage? Will natural lighting, electric lighting, heating and ventilation, and acoustics be satisfactory for both regular auditorium use and for music classes? Answers to these questions are likely to raise serious doubts about the use of stage or audience space for regular music classes.

THE AUDITORIUM STAGE AS A GYMNASIUM

In the 1920's the idea of using the stage as a gymnasium and the auditorium audience space as seating for spectators gained considerable popularity. It is not seriously considered today. Usually the stage was not adequate as a gymnasium, and those using the seating space could not see parts of the gymnasium playing court. Also, the use of the stage as a gymnasium practically prevented the space from being used, except occasionally, as a stage. The same scheduling difficulties were experienced with this scheme as were described earlier for the gymnasium-auditorium.

Corridor Combinations

CORRIDORS in most school buildings represent noninstructional space. During the planning process careful study should be made to see whether, without obstructing the operation of the school or impairing its safety, the amount of corridor space can be reduced or more constructive use made of it by modification of design.

THE CORRIDOR FOR CLOTHES STORAGE

Use of the walls of the corridor for storage of pupils' clothing has been discussed in Chapter 13. In that chapter is also mentioned the storage of clothing in alcoves off the corridor. In spite of unfavorable experiences with alcoves in the past, due to difficulty of supervision, designs with this feature in somewhat modified form have been appearing. Sometimes this space is placed at one end of a wide enclosed area between two parts of the building. The rest of the space is used not only as a passageway but also for lounging and social purposes. The clothing may be hung in the open on hangers. Above this are lockable boxes of proper size for storage of books and other personal effects. It is claimed that the openness of the plan and the proximity to the social space will remove the difficulties of supervision.

The use of this scheme is, perhaps, an expression of a feeling of dissatisfaction with the traditional corridor having lockers along the walls, and is an attempt to find a better scheme. No doubt other and better solutions will evolve.

THE CORRIDOR AS A STAGE

A modification of the gymnasium-auditorium has been to use the corridor as a stage. Provisions are made for hanging drapes to close off part of the corridor for stage purposes. When not in use, a folding or roll-down door is used to divide the corridor from the gymnasium which is the audience space. There is little about this scheme to commend it. About all it provides is a speaking platform or seating space for a basketball game. It is not, nor can it be, an adequate stage.

THE CORRIDOR AS DINING SPACE

Attempts to make constructive use of the corridor have sometimes resulted in the use of the space for dining. If this is done in a corridor of regular width and design, it has two serious defects. First, the placing of tables, chairs and people in the corridor creates a hazard. The corridor probably would not have been built unless it were needed for interior circulation and for safe and rapid egress. Any blocking of the corridor could cause a tragedy. The second defect is that such space is not attractive or comfortable dining space. But the corridor design can be such that fairly good dining space can be provided. This is done by widening the corridor in a certain area and providing a view of the outdoors. The space must be wide enough so that tables and chairs will not block the regular use of the corridor. Also, the kitchen and serving area must be conveniently located. Often such space, without a dividing wall between it and the corridor, can be provided quite economically. The plan has worked well in some small elementary schools. Before its adoption, however, it should be given careful study as to adequacy of space to accommodate the number to be served, as to suitability of the space for dining purposes, and as to safety and non-interference with other school activities.

THE CORRIDOR AS SOCIAL SPACE

One of the desirable characteristics of any school building is that it be an attractive and pleasant place for the occupants. Much progress has been made in designing elementary schools which are noninstitutional in character, and increased attention is being paid to this feature in secondary school designs. One of the methods of doing this has been to widen the corridor into a sort of lobby. Sometimes there will be several of these spaces, with each one used as a planning and social area for a group of rooms, or there may be reading alcoves across the corridor from the library on an outside wall. In other cases there may also be one larger space for the school as a whole to use as a sort of student center. It may be that the cafeteria opens into this space, so that both can be used as a social center and dining space. It can be a place for free reading, for visiting, and for school parties and other social functions.

But simply widening the corridor into an open lobby space will not be enough. Like any other feature of the school building, there must be careful planning of the space in terms of the kinds of activities which may occur there. Such questions as the following should be considered:

1. How many will wish to use this space at one time during the school day?
2. If used for student parties after school and in the evening, how large will the group be and what facilities and equipment will they need?
3. What storage space will be needed?
4. What refreshment facilities, if any, will be needed?
8. How can the space be arranged for ease of supervision?
6. What are the possible groupings of other facilities near or connected with this corridor lobby?
7. Will the activities and arrangement of this space interfere at times with the use of the corridor for circulation and for safe egress from the building?

Other Combinations

Only a few of the more common combinations have been discussed. The authors have been more concerned with emphasizing a method of evaluating proposed combinations than with discussing completely any one combination or with making a complete listing of all possible combinations. No doubt other and better combinations than any mentioned here exist. It is to be hoped that the creativity of educators and architects will produce others. Each one should be investigated carefully in terms of scheduling difficulties, ease of conversion when use is changed, adequacy of the space for all assigned functions, and economy. Should a proposed combination rate high in the evaluation and seem to be feasible, every effort should then be made to plan it carefully so that it can best serve in its several roles.

CHAPTER 20

DESIGNING FOR SAFETY

Safety of Structure
Safety of Egress and Circulation
Safety Against Fire
Safety Against Accidents Inside the Building
Safety of Site and Playground

THE safety of school children is a serious public responsibility. No community should rest easy as long as some of its buildings fall short of meeting reasonable safety standards, and any compromise with good safety and health practices in designing new structures should be firmly resisted. It may be possible to do without an auditorium, a swimming pool or a gymnasium for a while, justifiable and necessary as these may be; it should never be permissible to compromise with the safety of children.

Safety of Structure

OBVIOUSLY, a building and all its parts must be designed so that it will stand. The design must be adequate to withstand the conditions to be expected in the location in which it is built. In some states, earthquake shocks of some severity are to be expected during the life of the building. In others, a heavy snow load may be anticipated. It is the function of the architect and his engineering staff to study the local conditions and to design the structure with an adequate margin of safety. The function of the local school authorities, then, is to employ a competent architect who will not compromise with safety of structural design.

Safety of Egress and Circulation

ONE of the first considerations in examining any proposed school building plan is to ask: How can the occupants get out? Can they leave rapidly and safely? Is there possibility of their being trapped in the building? Are there cul-de-sacs or areas or rooms where a fire or smoke condition in a certain location might prevent occupants from getting out?

LOCATION OF EXITS AND STAIRWAYS

For maximum safety of egress, every building should be of one-story design, and every room should have two ways out at opposite sides of the room, with one of these ways being directly to the outdoors. Notice that in Figure 12 each room has two means of egress, one through the cor-

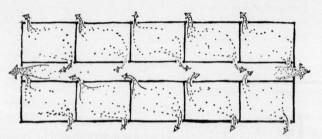

Figure 12. Classrooms with Direct Exits to Outdoors.

ridor and the other directly to the outdoors. Notice also that the corridor doors of the classrooms are not directly across from each other, and that congestion is thereby reduced. Also observe that the corridor door from each classroom is as far as possible from the other exit.

It is possible, however, to design buildings of more than one story with each classroom having only an exit through the corridor and to do this in such a way that the possibility of being trapped in the building is remote. Note that in Figure 13 the exits from the building are at opposite ends,

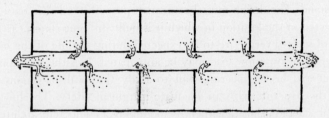

Figure 13. Classrooms with Exits to Corridor Only.

thereby reducing the possibility of both being blocked at the same time. The same plan might be used for the second floor, with stairways at the ends.

Figure 14 depicts a typical two-room school plan of a few years ago. A fire in the vestibule could block egress from both rooms. This building could be made safer by placing an exit from each room to the outdoors at *a* and *c*, or by extending the vestibule to make it a corridor as long as the building and with an exit at each end, as illustrated in Figure 15. When the latter is done, the possibility that egress will be completely blocked is reduced greatly.

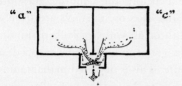

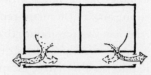

Figure 14. Exits Concentrated at One Point.

Figure 15. Exits Widely Separated.

Every occupant, on leaving a classroom, should have two ways of turning. If he finds one way blocked he should be able to turn in the opposite direction and reach another exit or stairway, independent of and remote from the first. He should never have to pass by one exit or open stairway to reach another exit or stairway. Dead-end corridors are poor safety design. Yet many building codes permit limited dead-end pockets, and many of the building plans described and illustrated in current periodicals on school administration violate this basic principle.

In Figure 16, showing a typical second-floor plan of not too long ago, occupants of rooms 1 to 7 inclusive have a choice of ways of leaving. If

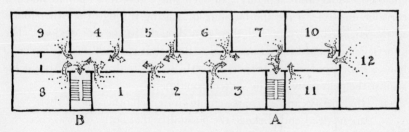

Figure 16. Dead-End Pockets in Corridors.

stairway A is blocked, they can turn in the opposite direction and leave by stairway B or vice versa. But the occupants of rooms 8, 9, 10, 11, and 12 are not so fortunate. If stairway A is blocked and if the heat and smoke block the corridor, the occupants of rooms 10, 11, and 12 are trapped. Likewise, a blocking of the corridor by smoke from stairway B would trap the occupants of rooms 8 and 9. A partial correction of this condition, especially in an existing building, is to enclose the stairways, or at least to place a fire stop across the top of each stairwell so that it will not act as a flue to convey smoke and fire into the corridor. This would allow a person safely to pass one stairway to reach the other.

In any arrangement which requires children to enter a corridor from a classroom in order to leave a building, there is always the possibility that the corridor will be filled with smoke before the children get out. As pointed out above, the more remote the exits or stairways are from each other, the less the possibility that both or all will be blocked simultaneously. In order to reduce further the danger of children being trapped, some codes require an alternative escape route. This is depicted in diagrammatic form in Figure 17, an assumed second floor. Note that each classroom has

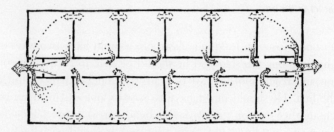

Figure 17. Exits Through Adjoining Classrooms.

the usual door to the corridor and also connects with the ones next to it. Each of the end classrooms has a third door leading directly into a fully enclosed, smokeproof stairway. An occupant could, if he should find the corridor unusable, leave the building by passing through the other rooms to the enclosed stairway and then pass directly to the out-of-doors. The same scheme could be used on the first floor, but it would seem simpler to have a door from each classroom directly to the out-of-doors. Arguments against the plan shown in the sketch would be:

1. If stairways and exits are remote from each other and if there are no dead-end pockets, the possibility that both stairways or exits will be blocked at once or that the corridor will be unusable before the building could be emptied is greatly reduced.

2. The extra doors cut down usable and valuable wall space in the classrooms.

3. As a building is used throughout the years, the occupants become careless and furniture is placed in front of connecting doors, making them unusable when really needed in time of crisis—an argument which would have no merit if the oc-

cupants used these doors for frequent fire drills or other purposes.

It may be argued that with fire-resistive construction there is no danger
from fire. This is not so. As soon as a building is occupied it contains materials which will burn. A comparatively small fire will create a tremendous
volume of heat, noxious fumes, and smoke. People have died in fire-resistive
buildings not by burning, but by suffocation. All firemen know that it is
common to find occupants dead from suffocation a great distance from a
fire. Dangerous fires can and do happen in "fireproof" buildings. All buildings, fire-resistive or not, should be designed for easy and safe egress; outside fire escapes are a confession that the original design was faulty.

DESIGN OF CORRIDORS

Corridors have the double purpose of providing for convenient
and easy movement of occupants from one part of the school building to
another and of providing for fast and safe egress from the building. In designing a building, decisions must be made as to what corridors, if any, are
essential, and as to how wide they shall be. With the self-contained classroom concept it has been found that even in cold climates it is possible to
provide a functional and safe building for elementary school purposes without much, if any, corridor space. But with the type of program which
required frequent movement of occupants from one room to another, as is
usually the case in secondary schools, corridors are still considered to be
essential in cold climates, although there has been some experimentation in
northern locations with campus plans which demand few or no corridors.

Corridor Width

The width of a corridor will depend upon these considerations:

1. *The number of rooms to be served.* Obviously, more rooms
mean more occupants. If all the rooms empty at once and all occupants wish to move from one part of the building to another, the
corridor should be wider.

2. *Single or double loading.* If classrooms are located only on one
side rather than on both sides of a corridor, the number of occupants
wishing to use a given corridor space at one time will be less, and
therefore the required width will be less.

3. *Other means of egress.* If every classroom has a door leading
directly to the outdoors, the width of the corridor becomes less
important from the standpoint of safety of egress; the use of the corridor for interior circulation is the prime concern, and this can be
determined only on the basis of the program.

4. *Location of clothes storage.* In a program calling for frequent movement of pupils from room to room it is commonly desired to provide storage for pupils' personal belongings outside the classrooms. If stored in corridor lockers this presents a problem of congestion. Accordingly, it is necessary to give careful attention to traffic load in corridors and the space required for pupils standing in front of open lockers on either or both sides of the corridor.

5. *The type of program.* If the self-contained classroom idea gains greater acceptance in secondary schools, it will affect the amount of traffic in corridors and could reduce the corridor space.

Other Aspects of Corridor Design

Other points are also to be observed in corridor design, as follows:

1. *Constancy of width.* Any constriction actually reduces the effective width of the entire corridor to the width of the narrowest part, thereby causing traffic bottlenecks, which may be dangerous.

2. *Avoidance of projecting obstructions.* Doors are best fully recessed and should not project into the corridor at any point in their swing. Some codes require that doors shall not project more than 6 or 8 inches. No columns or other parts of the structure should project into corridors. Such items as drinking fountains, fire extinguishers, and standpipe hose should be fully recessed. Sharp corners should be avoided by cutting back the corner or using rounded block or tile.

3. *Exits and stairways.* Locations should be visible from the corridor.

4. *Well-lighted corridors.* In one-story buildings, it is common practice to admit much daylight into corridors. Electric lighting should be of adequate intensity to provide for safe travel, to dispel gloom, and to enable the child to see into his locker. For safety's sake, lighting should be instantaneous when the switch is operated. In order to prevent pupils from playing with light switches and to promote economy, it has been common practice to use only key-operated switches in corridors. This is not good safety practice. There may easily be a time when safety requires immediate light. When no one with a key is available, the results could be serious and tragic.

5. *Safe and durable corridor floor finishes.* This seems obvious, yet some corridors are dangerously slippery. Although this may be partly due to faulty maintenance, it is well to choose floor materials which will stand the heavy traffic and yet be safe for travel.

DESIGN OF STAIRWAYS

The stairways are, in a sense, an extension of the corridors. They, like corridors, must provide for quick and safe egress from the building and for safe and convenient circulation. Since vertical travel is more hazardous than horizontal travel, every effort must be made to make stairways safe.

Number of Stairways

Every school building of more than one story should have at least two stairways, remote from each other and accessible from the corridor door of every room used by pupils. Additional stairways, properly placed, will be needed according to the square footage of area in the upper stories or according to the number of occupants an upper story is designed to accommodate. The number of stairways, or at least the number of units of stairway width, is usually provided for in a local or state building code. Most of these codes are based on the recommendations of the National Fire Protection Association.[1] Where the code leaves room for choice, it is well, for ease of circulation as well as for safety, to have more stairways of standard width rather than fewer of multiple-lane type.

Location of Stairways

Previously mentioned has been the principle of avoiding dead-end pockets and providing opportunity for each occupant, on leaving a classroom, to have a choice of ways of reaching an exit or stairway. This indicates that stairways should be at the ends of corridors, but does not necessarily mean that the stairway ought to be in the corridor itself. About the only advantage in putting a stairway in the corridor is that it is readily visible. This arrangement has the disadvantage of reducing expansibility of the building (the stairway has to be removed to extend the corridor) and of cutting in half the exit width at the end of the corridor on the first floor. The preferred practice is to turn the stairway at right angles to the corridor, and place it between the corridor and outside wall.

Stairways should be as far removed from each other as possible in order to reduce the possibility that all will be blocked at the same time. The old practice of having a grand, wide stairway at the center of the building may have produced desired architectural effects, but it also reduced the possibility of safe egress in event of fire.

[1] *Building Exits Code*. New York: 1952, pp. 71–72. National Fire Protection Association,

Width of Stairways

The *Building Exits Code* specifies the number of units of stair width needed for safe and rapid egress under various conditions. Two-lane stairways are accepted for most school situations. The code provides that each lane have access to a handrail. If stairways of more than two lanes must be used, they should be divided into two-lane widths by handrails.

Handrails should be of proper height for the age of the occupants. Usual heights above the edge of the nosing are 26 inches for elementary schools and 30 inches for secondary schools. Handrail ends should be curved into the wall. A frequent source of maintenance trouble is loose handrails, and particular attention should be paid to this detail to insure that they will not come loose after a few months' use. Balustrades should be at least 42 inches high.

Steepness of Stairways

A frequent fault of older buildings is that stairways are too steep. The *Building Exits Code* states that "Treads and risers shall be so proportioned that the sum of two risers and a tread, exclusive of its projection, is not less than 24 nor more than 25 inches. No riser shall be more than seven inches and no tread less than 10 inches exclusive of its projection." [2] This standard is for all places of public assembly. For schools even more gradual dimensions are advisable, with risers of $6\frac{1}{2}$ inches for elementary schools and 7 inches for high schools and with treads no less than 11 inches in either case.

Dimensions of treads and risers should be consistent throughout the stairway. Many accidents have been caused by one riser in a stair run being slightly greater than the others. Also, all stairways in the building, at least those to be constantly used by pupils, should be of the same dimensions. Lack of consistency in this regard can cause accidents. No winding stairways, obtained by gradually narrowing the tread from one end to the other, should be permitted. Treads should be equipped with nosings, flush with the tread, of nonslip materials, and of appearance contrasting with the rest of the tread.

Construction of Stairways

All stairways should be of incombustible materials except for handrails. Many codes, to prevent stairways from acting as flues in case of fire and to provide for safe egress, require that stairways be fully enclosed; others require this only in buildings of three or more stories. Such en-

[2] *Ibid.*, p. 12.

closures should have fire-resistive walls and ceilings, and doors should be of light weight metal with wired glass. An enclosed stairway should be designed so that occupants can go directly from it to the outdoors without passing through any open corridor or hall space.

Runs and Landings

Any stairway between two stories should have two runs of risers broken by a landing. The two runs should not be continuous in the same direction. Landings should be at least as wide as the stairway. No door should open immediately at the top or bottom of a flight of stairs. Rather, a landing at least as wide as the swing of the door should be provided between the door and the stairway. There should be no stair run of less than three risers.

No storage closets should be permitted to open into a stairwell. These are frequent sources of fires, and such a fire would block the use of the stairway. If a storage closet is located under a stairway but opening into an entirely separate space, it should be of fire-resistive construction so that a fire within that closet could not possibly make the stair unusable.

No stairway should have unprotected open wells between runs, which would make it possible for someone to fall through the opening or to drop objects on those below.

Lighting of Stairways

Obviously, all stairways, for safety's sake alone if for no other, should be provided with adequate lighting, both natural and electrical. Switches for stairway lighting should be located in the walls at the top and bottom of the stairway where one would naturally expect to find them.

NUMBER, LOCATION, AND DESIGN OF EXITS

Under the section on "Safety of Egress and Circulation," principles were given for the location of exits. It remains to discuss other aspects of location and the number of general exits and their design. Again, the *Building Exits Code*[3] will provide information regarding the number of units of exit width to be provided.

General Exits from the Building

People in a panic will use the exits to which they have become accustomed, and will ignore other means of egress to which they are not accustomed. Little-used exits may be obstructed by storage of materials, especially if properly designed and located storage space is not provided.

[3] *Ibid.*, pp. 70–73.

Therefore, exits should be located not only for safety of egress, but also for convenience of egress.

If a school has to be situated on an inadequate site so that part of the building is along a busy street or highway, exits should be placed so that pupils will not be rushing headlong out of an exit into vehicular traffic.

All exit doors should swing in the direction of egress. General exit doors should be equipped with good quality panic bars, that is, horizontal bars which unlatch the door when pushed. If doors do not lock securely, bars or chains are frequently placed across them to keep the building secure against unauthorized entrance. Such practice is extremely dangerous, since these devices are often left in place when the building is occupied. Use of top quality hardware, plus sturdy door design and proper maintenance, can reduce this source of danger. Generally, double doors which butt against each other are more difficult to keep in alignment and are easier to "jimmy" than are single doors. Consequently, multiple doors of the single-leaf variety, with mullions between them, are recommended. Or double doors butting against a center mullion can be used. In order to provide for bringing bulky objects into the building, the center mullion should be removable.

Exit doors should be equipped with safety glass. It is well to have no glass at the level of the panic bar. Severe injuries have resulted from a child's missing the panic bar or push plate and running an arm through the glass panel.

Whenever possible, steps in a corridor should be avoided, especially near an exit. One or two isolated steps are particularly hazardous, because they are not easily seen. Also, steps should be avoided just outside an exit. In all cases, there should be sufficient inside and outside lighting to provide for safety.

Exits from Classrooms

Many codes wisely require that no classroom door shall be more than 100 feet from an exit or stairway. Usually, classrooms of average size need only one door to the corridor. Extra doors are costly and take up valuable wall space. Only in special cases does safety demand extra doors. Among the rooms needing a second door are:

1. Classrooms designed to accommodate more than 40 pupils, including music rooms and study halls.
2. Chemistry laboratories.
3. Homemaking rooms, especially cooking rooms.
4. Shops.

Where two exits are required, they should be remote from each other. If both open into the corridor, they should be at opposite ends of the room. If one opens to the outdoors—and this is especially recommended in shops —it should be at the opposite corner of the room from the other exit.

Doors in a classroom, like all doors in a school building, should be equipped with the kind of hardware that permits the door to be opened from the inside by turning the knob, even though it may be locked from the outside. This principle should apply even to closet doors, so that it will be impossible for any person to be locked inside the building or in any space within the building.

Exits from the Auditorium

The auditorium presents the problem of moving a large number of people safely and quickly, both in normal usage and in times of stress. The commonly used exits should be adequate. Each aisle should terminate in an exit to the lobby. Multiple exits to the outdoors should be clearly visible, and one should not have to traverse a long corridor to reach them. In addition to the main or commonly used means of egress, others should be provided which lead directly to the outdoors, or at least to the outdoors by a short passage enclosed against fire and smoke. In the traditionally shaped auditorium there should be, in addition to the main exits at the rear, other exits at the right front and left front of the room. Other exits may be necessary and desirable in the side walls, depending upon the capacity and shape of the room. Any place of public assembly should have its main floor at ground level. It should not be necessary to move large numbers of people up or down stairs to get in or out. Balconies, if provided, should have at least two means of egress remote from each other.

All exits should be equipped with illuminated signs, with current provided by separate circuits originating ahead of the main line switch. Stand-by emergency lighting is often provided for such areas so that a failure in the regular source of power will not darken the exit lights. Such lighting should also be extended to hallways and stairways through which it is necessary to travel to leave the building.

In spaces used for other purposes as well as auditorium seating, such as multipurpose rooms, gymnasium-auditoriums, or cafeterias, it is common practice to use folding chairs. The fact that these are movable can create a serious hazard in time of panic, when people will shove them out of the way in order to reach the exit doors as quickly as possible. Some local and state regulations require three or more of these single units to be clamped together side by side so that rows and aisles can be better maintained.

Gymnasium Exits

Exits should be located in relation to the public seating space in the gymnasium. Folding bleachers are often provided along the sides of the long axis of the playing court. Sometimes a second level of folding or fixed bleachers is provided on one or both sides of the gymnasium. Such an arrangement practically dictates adequate exits at the four corners of the gymnasium. Again, it should be possible for the audience to reach the outdoors from the main floor quite directly without passing up or down stairs. With two levels of seating, this is hardly possible, at least on a level site, but stairways or passageways down long hallways should be reduced to a minimum.

Cafeteria Exits

Cafeterias are finding increased use for school social affairs and as small auditoriums, as well as for dining purposes. Consequently, it is necessary to study the exit situation carefully, especially since the adjacent kitchen is a place of high fire hazard. Adequate exits to the corridor and to the outdoors should be provided at places in the room farthest removed from the kitchen.

Safety Against Fire

PREVIOUSLY discussed in this chapter are features of planning in regard to location and design of exits, stairways, and corridors. These in themselves should furnish protection against loss of life due to fire. In the following sections other features will be examined which should be included in a building to prevent loss of life from fire and also to prevent property damage due to fire.

TYPE OF CONSTRUCTION

Fire-resistive construction provides the maximum protection against destruction of property.

In general, state school building codes do not require fire-resistive construction in one-story buildings, although some local building codes do. Some state building codes require fireproof construction in buildings of more than one story, with a basement being defined as one story. Others require fire-resistive stairways and corridors only in two-story buildings, but fireproof construction for three or more stories. From the standpoint of safety to life, adequate, well-placed, and well-separated exits are more important than the type of construction.

To prevent the spread of fire, many codes require self-closing fire doors and fire walls between parts of buildings having different fire ratings. This is often the case when an addition to an existing building is to be constructed. The law governing the addition may require it to be fire-resistive, while the law at the time the original building was constructed did not. It is common sense to protect the new building from being damaged by fire originating in the older and less protected portion.

In one town, a fire-resistive gymnasium, shop, and home economics room were added to an old high school building of wood interior. One night the old building burned completely. Because no fire door was provided between the old and new sections the newer section was seriously damaged by the intense heat, smoke, and water. It was only after several weeks of work and the expenditure of thousands of dollars on repairs that the newer section could again be used. In another town, where a similar situation existed, automatic fire doors were installed to protect the new section from the old. Here, also, a completely destructive fire occurred in the old building. The fire doors operated, and school was carried on in the newer building on the next day. Expenditures for repairs in the new building were practically zero.

Many buildings of a fire-resistive type have wood paneling in lobbies and at similar locations. This does not present a serious fire problem if the paneling is installed directly on masonry, even though wood grounds embedded in masonry are used. If wood furring with open space in back of the paneling is used, a serious fire hazard can result. Certain kinds of finishes used on wood paneling or for other purposes are also fire hazardous and should be avoided.

Structural steel, if exposed to fire, will actually collapse more quickly than a solid or laminated wood beam. For acceptance as fire-resistive construction, protection of the steel by fire-resistive materials such as plaster, concrete, or masonry is needed. Mineral acoustical tile alone, although not combustible, is usually not accepted as adequate protection for steel.

PROTECTION OF HEATING AND VENTILATING DUCTS AND SPACES

A duct or flue, especially if vertical or if connected to a ventilating fan, can serve to spread fire and smoke quickly through an entire building. It is therefore good practice to include in each supply duct on the discharge side of the fan a fire damper controlled by a fusible link. Also, the fan should stop automatically when the damper closes.

If exhaust air ducts are to discharge into a combustible space, they also should be equipped with self-closing fire dampers. Many fires, originally quite small and easily controllable, have ignited a whole building quickly because the exhaust ventilating ducts acted as chimneys for the fire and conducted it quickly into a combustible attic space. Other vertical spaces in a building, such as wastepaper chutes and dumb-waiter shafts, also need to be protected against acting as flues in a fire.

To reduce duct work and to provide simplicity and economy of construction, it has been fairly common practice to supply tempered air to classrooms by means of metal ducts, but to return it through the corridors to the fan chamber for recirculation. Air leaves the classrooms by louvers in the doors or by ports in the corridor walls. This may be dangerous, since fire in one classroom would result in the smoke and fumes from that fire immediately reaching the corridor and perhaps filling with smoke the very space needed to evacuate children from the building.

THE HEATING PLANT

Fires in buildings frequently start in heating plant rooms. Also, there is always the danger of an explosion of a steam boiler, a hot-water heater, or a hot-water tank. It is, therefore, good practice to segregate the heating plant from the rest of the building. The safest location is in an entirely separate building. This is a common practice with large buildings or where several buildings are to be heated from one plant. The next safest location is adjoining the building, but not under any part of it. Walls should be fire-resistive, and the ceiling, which is also the roof of the heating plant room, should be noncombustible and of light construction. Any opening between this room and the rest of the building should be protected by a fire door with a self-closing device. The poorest location is under any portion of the building. Completely fire-resistive walls, ceiling, and doors may prevent the spread of fire from this location, but there is no protection against an explosion.

A frequent fault with heating plant installations is that sufficient amounts of air for combustion are not provided. This causes poor combustion and excessive fuel bills, and may result in a serious explosion. To correct this condition the door of the heating plant room may be wedged open, thereby defeating the purpose of a protecting fire door.

Another common defect is that relief and safety valves of the proper size are not supplied. An inadequate relief valve on a closed-type hot-water heating system or on a "domestic" hot-water supply system can permit a violent explosion. It is well to have the entire heating plant installation checked by a licensed boiler inspector before it is placed in operation, and then to provide for frequent periodic rechecks of all safety and relief valves as well as other controls.

HOT SPOTS

Certain rooms or spaces in a school building are more fire hazardous than others. The heating plant room has already been mentioned. Other locations are the stage, the shops, the cafeteria kitchen, the homemaking kitchen, the chemistry laboratory, and storage rooms.

Stage fires usually occur because of use of flimsy flammable materials, with fires starting from smoking, bad electrical connections, or stage properties such as candles, hot floodlights, etc. The stage itself should have fire-resistive walls and ceiling. Draperies should be flameproof. An automatic sprinkler system is advisable, and fire extinguishers should be readily at hand.

Activities such as painting, varnishing, welding, and gluing in the school shops make this area prone to fires. Automotive shops, because of gasoline, are especially hazardous. Isolation of shops in one-story wings will reduce the possibility of fire spread. Adequate and well-located exits are essential, as are fire extinguishers of the proper kind.

Chemistry laboratories, home economics rooms, and cafeteria kitchens should have exits so located that no one can be trapped in any part of the room by fire. Wool blankets for extinguishing clothing fires should be readily available. Fire extinguishers should be close by.

Storage rooms should be studied for their hazards, and some should be of fire-resistive construction and equipped with fire doors. Flammable liquids should be stored in the building only in small quantities and in safe containers according to local code regulations. The gasoline-driven power lawn mower should be stored either in a separate building or in a fire-resistive room opening only to the outdoors. No storage should be permitted in the heating plant room or in a fan room.

The practice of baling wastepaper is a questionable one from the standpoint of fire hazard. A properly designed incinerator for burning of waste is desirable and safe. This avoids the hazardous and unsatisfactory practice of burning waste in the school yard.

FIRE EXTINGUISHERS

Fire extinguishers should be provided at hazardous locations and at convenient places throughout the building. A good location is near each fire-alarm sounding station. Extinguishers should be housed in special cabinets or on suitable racks on the wall.

The correct type of extinguisher should be available for the kind of fire most likely to occur at each location. This is important because in an emergency a person is likely to grab the nearest extinguisher without regard to its effectiveness or to the hazard to himself that might result from its use. The following suggestions may be helpful:

1. For general use throughout the building, standpipes and hose racks, soda-acid extinguishers, or water pumps may be used. However, they are not effective on flammable liquid fires, and they are not safe to use on electrical fires because of the shock hazard.

2. Carbon tetrachloride is good for electrical fires because it is a nonconductor. It is appropriate to have available near electrical panels. Because of the fumes created, it should not be used on hot metal or in a confined space.

3. Carbon dioxide and dry chemical extinguishers are also suitable for placement near electrical panels and equipment. They are effective and safe for general use and for flammable liquid fires, as well as for electrical ones, but are not good for deep-seated or smoldering fires.

4. Foam extinguishers are good for flammable liquid fires and for general use, but not for electrical fires. Appropriate locations are near flammable liquid storage, in garages, and in automotive shops.

Standpipe and fire hose, although considered satisfactory by some fire-fighting authorities, have not been completely practical for school use. They are subject to tampering and to causing excessive water damage in case of mischief or vandalism. Consequently, to prevent trouble, valve handles are likely to be removed and lost, thereby rendering the equipment practically useless. Of course, practically any device is subject to abuse and no extinguisher is any better than its maintenance.

It is also excellent practice for the protection of property to provide an automatic sprinkler system for places of high fire hazard, such as auditorium stages, stage scenery storage, paper storage, lumber storage, and flammable liquid storage.

Another important consideration is the adequacy of a water supply for fire fighting. In a city it should be determined whether the water main for fire fighting is of adequate size to supply the apparatus which would assemble to fight a major school fire. Where the school must provide its own water supply, the design should provide for this need. Many schools which could have been saved have burned completely because of lack of adequate water for fire fighting.

FIRE ALARM SYSTEMS

Fire alarm systems should be so designed that an alarm can be sounded from at least one location in the corridor of each floor. Horns or gongs should be so situated that they can be heard throughout the building. The alarm system should be used for no other purpose than for giving an alarm for a fire drill or an actual fire. It should be distinct in tone from all other signal systems. It is good practice to have alarm-sounding stations near points of fire hazard. There ought to be a sounding station and an alarm signal station in the janitors' quarters and in the heating plant room. When it is so located, the custodian can quickly give an alarm, if necessary, and will also be notified by signal if an alarm is given elsewhere. In some cities it is the practice to connect the fire alarm system to the local fire department, with provisions for breaking the connection when the system is used only for a fire drill.

There are systems which will give an alarm when the temperature of any space rises unduly rapidly or reaches a certain point. This is not to take the place of the regular fire alarm system. Rather, the value lies in setting off an alarm both in and outside the building when a fire may start in a part of the building where it will not be discovered or when the building is unoccupied, thereby making it possible to discover and attack a fire in its early stages. In some installations it is arranged to connect the system electrically to the local fire department.

ELECTRIC WIRING

Many fires are caused by defective electrical wiring. It is therefore important to make sure that the wiring is adequate and that it is done in conformity with the best practices. An attempt to economize on this feature of the building is the height of false economy. In the first place, the electrical contract will represent only a small percent of the total building cost. A saving, then, of 10 or 20 percent on this contract will represent only a small amount when compared to the total cost of the building. Yet the cheapening of the electrical installation may not only impair the usefulness of the building and make impossible adequate lighting, but it may also be the cause of a destructive fire costing many times the amount saved by a cheap electric system. Rewiring to make up for deficiencies is expensive. The difference in first cost between an adequate system and an inadequate one is quite minor.

There should be enough circuits to do the job without overloading. There should also be provision for the addition of circuits when needed. Wiring should be of adequate size to carry the load without voltage drop. The system should be controlled by adequate circuit breakers or fuses, and fuses of higher amperage than that for which the circuit was designed should never be used. One frequent deficiency is a lack of convenience outlets. Such a lack will result in the use of unsafe and extra long extension cords, which is an invitation to trouble.

A good safety and fire prevention provision is to install pilot lights for all electric heat outlets and for remote or infrequently seen lights and motors.

All electrical panels in the building should be of the dead-front panel type. With them there is no possibility of shock from touching the panel. Any other electrical equipment or appliance should be so designed and connected that no shock can result from touching any normally exposed part.

GAS

Gas is used in many school buildings. To prevent explosions or fires, certain precautions should be observed. All gas should have a distinctive and readily detectable odor. Gas supply lines should not be run long distances under buildings and through pipe tunnels. Each room which has multiple gas outlets, such as home economics laboratory, a chemistry laboratory, or a shop, should be equipped with a master valve conveniently located and readily distinguishable. The use of such a valve by the instructor will prevent dangerous accumulation of gas in an unused room as a result of leakage in individual fixtures or failure to turn them off completely. A master valve should be provided outside the building for the use of the local fire department.

Safety Against Accidents Inside the Building

WITH hundreds of children moving about in a school building, accidents are bound to occur. However, the number of them, and perhaps their seriousness, can be reduced by careful attention to certain features of design. Some of these have already been mentioned in discussions of stairways, corridors, and exits. These included, among others, elimination of projections in corridors, the use of special block or tile on corners, safety glass in exit doors, and nonslip nosings on stair treads.

A few other features need examination. Ramps are usually considered preferable to stairways if the stairway is to have fewer than four risers; however, a ramp which is too steep is a hazard. A one-foot rise in 10 feet of run should be the maximum pitch allowed. The floor of the ramp should be of permanent nonslip finish.

Accidents are frequent in locker and shower rooms. Some of them occur because of natural "horse play" in these areas. No building design will prevent this. A frequent cause, however, is slipping on wet floors. Floor finishes in locker and shower rooms, besides being of a type which is sanitary and easily cleaned, should include abrasive aggregate or be of nonslip tile. Adequate floor drains should be provided. Panel heating in the floor would appear to be particularly advantageous in this area in that it, plus adequate ventilation and floor drains, will help to keep the floor dry. It is also well established that damp floors allow certain fungi to live and that dry floors and feet are a good preventative. Provisions should be made for regulation of the temperature of hot water supply to shower fixtures to prevent scalding. If radiators are used for heating locker rooms, they should be located at such a height that pupils will not bump or fall against them.

Accidents are frequently caused by people coming unexpectedly upon a step or obstruction on leaving a school building in darkness. Much of this can be prevented by provision of proper entrance and yard lights. Devices are available which permit a light to remain on for a time after the switch is set in the "off" position.

Although the maintenance of buildings is beyond the scope of this book, it can be pointed out here that many accidents in schools occur because of slippery floors. Floor materials, especially for corridors, should be of a type which does not require a high polish wax for maintenance. Asphalt tile is quite satisfactory for corridors and classroom floors, but it should be maintained by other methods than the use of a slippery wax.

Safety of Site and Playground

In a preceding chapter there is a rather complete treatment of the many problems involved in site selection and development. Here will be discussed only such aspects of the site and playground problem as related to safety.

LOCATION OF SITE

A site should be located with the safety of those who are going to use it in mind. To locate a building so that children have to walk considerable distances along a dangerous highway is certainly not good practice. Or to locate it so that many children have to cross an arterial highway or a railroad crossing or to walk along an unprotected canal would also be questionable. It is also undesirable for children to have to pass through an industrial area in order to reach the school. As the area to be served by a school increases, increasing difficulty is experienced in finding a site which will not violate one or more of the above principles. Close cooperation with city and regional planning agencies and co-ordination with the master plan for the area, together with good long-term planning and site acquisition well in advance of need, will help solve this problem.

It is also preferable not to locate school buildings on busy highways. Not only is the noise and dirt of the highway a nuisance, but the location will increase dangers to children. It is much better for a school bus to turn off from a highway onto a side road or street and thence to the school site than for it to turn directly off from the main highway into the school driveway. Likewise, the traffic danger to a bus or other vehicle leaving the school site and passing directly onto the highway is greater than that of a vehicle which travels a side road first. If a school playground has to be next to a busy street or highway, it should be separated from the street by a high, substantial, and safe fence.

The site should be located in an environment which does not pose moral or physical dangers to children. Of course, some areas of cities have a high crime incidence and are unattractive physically. Adults and children live in these areas, and children have to have a school within reasonable distance of where they live. However, effort should be made to locate the site so dangers are reduced. From the physical danger standpoint it would be unwise to locate near a gravel pit, an abandoned mine shaft or open well, an oil storage depot, a busy railroad, or a dangerous industry, for example.

SITE LAYOUT FOR SAFETY

The first consideration in providing for safety of layout is adequate size. It is obvious that as the site becomes smaller, more and more people and activities are going to have to be pushed together into a smaller and smaller space, thereby increasing the danger of accidents. There is no substitute for sufficient land area. The building should be set back an adequate distance from the street. This will reduce the danger of children rushing impulsively out of the building into the street. It will also make possible more attractive landscaping, a better view of the building from the street, and a safer layout of sidewalks and driveways. Sidewalks should be laid out so that they will be used. Attempts to force foot traffic onto walks which require a considerable increase in travel distance for the walker will not serve. Service driveways and access driveways to the site should be planned so that there will be a minimum of intersection of foot traffic lanes, including traffic from the building to the playground. Well-planned space and sheltered facilities should be provided so that unloading from buses or cars can take place without children having to cross any vehicular traffic lane to get into the building. The bus garage and bus maintenance shop, if located on the site at all, should be planned so that there will be no maneuvering of buses, especially in reverse, in areas where children may be playing or passing. An off-street parking area for cars should be provided remote from any area where children will be moving.

Many children will ride bicycles to school. If they ride them on the sidewalks, it is a hazard to pedestrians. On the other hand, if they ride them in the driveways when motor vehicles are passing, it is hazardous to the cyclist. On some sites a separate lane for bicyclists, running from the street to the bicycle parking area, has proved to be a satisfactory method of solving this problem.

It is well to plan and provide a separate play area for younger children on an elementary school site, and for elementary school children if elementary and secondary children are housed on the same site. Otherwise, the older children will be likely to usurp areas and engage in games dangerous to smaller children. On a roomy site it will be possible to lay out game areas and courts so that they do not overlap. When the site is smaller, this will be more difficult.

PLAYGROUND EQUIPMENT

Playground equipment should be located so that moving equipment such as swings will be well separated from normal routes of children passing from the playground. This section should also be separated from other play activity areas. There should be room enough so that items of playground equipment will not be crowded into a small area. It is obvious that such crowding will bring about interference of one group of children using one piece or bank of equipment with other groups, with the result that serious accidents may occur.

The question of how much playground equipment to purchase and which pieces are the least dangerous is a difficult one. If there has to be a choice between spending money for land and spending it for equipment, the choice should go to the former. Children need level land free from holes, obstructions, and other hazards where they can run and romp without being in such a crowded situation that collisions are frequent. Trees with their shade and beauty can add much to a school site, but improperly located on a playground, they can be a serious hazard. Children can have fun and exercise if playground balls of various sizes and courts are provided, together with the necessary nets and standards. Most elementary schools will want to have some equipment beyond this. It then becomes a problem of confining the equipment to that which is most useful and safe. Swings, slides, and horizontal bar towers are probably the most commonly used items of equipment on playgrounds. Yet when swings are used by large numbers of children on playgrounds, there will be some accidents. Probably the most frequent one is that of a child's being struck in the head by a swing seat. The use of soft rubber molding for the seat, or of a flexible seat, can reduce the severity of such accidents. Reduction of playground hazards is achieved by a combination of adequate space, wise selection and placement of equipment, good maintenance, and good administration and supervision.

PLAYGROUND SURFACING

An important part of providing a safe playground is proper surfacing. Ideally, the best surface is a good turf on well-drained land, but maintenance of such a surface is practically impossible where there is a concentration of play on a small site and where apparatus is used. There is no one surface which will be satisfactory for all conditions. It therefore becomes a problem of choosing a surface on the basis of the probable use. The following considerations are pertinent:

1. Site development plans should provide for grading and drainage to facilitate quick drying.
2. Cost of a surface under consideration should be considered not only from the standpoint of initial cost, but also from that of future maintenance cost and the total welfare of the children involved.
3. The ease of keeping a surface clean is important.
4. In certain areas, the surface should have good traction or non-slipping qualities whether wet or dry.
5. The surface should be tough, weather resistant, and such that it can readily be patched or resurfaced. Apparatus areas should have surface materials of good resiliency. Experimentation is constantly taking place in the search for a stable, durable and yet resilient and non-abrasive surface.

CHAPTER 21

DESIGNING FOR VISUAL AND AUDITORY COMFORT AND EFFICIENCY

Importance of Good Visual Conditions
Amount or Intensity of Light
Brightness
Brightness Goals
Types and Patterns of Light Fixtures
Daylight Control and Use
Auditory Conditions

———————

REGARDLESS of the type of program offered in any school, normal children must see and hear to do their work. This chapter will discuss the principles or goals for a good visual environment and methods of reaching these goals. Accomplishment of good auditory conditions, also of primary importance, will then be considered.

Importance of Good Visual Conditions

CHILDREN during the school day will engage in numerous and varied visual tasks including reading, writing, drawing, painting, modeling, working with tools and machines, manipulating scientific apparatus, watching demonstrations, and many others. Reading will be done from books and other materials at desks and tables, as well as from charts, chalkboards, and bulletin boards. Maps, globes, graphs, models, charts, and other audio-visual devices will be used, with and without projection.

These tasks will involve critical seeing, that is, seeing which involves focusing the eyes upon a visual task as contrasted with relaxed vision occurring in viewing a landscape. It is important, then, that the schoolroom environment of the child be such as to make it possible for him to see comfortably and efficiently. Poor visual conditions, if not actually harmful to the eyes, cause undue expenditure of energy and undue tension and straining to see, thereby bringing about fatigue, irritation, and behavior problems.

The careful school planner will recognize the importance of this matter and will incorporate good visual conditions as a basic feature of his design rather than as something to be added to a building after it has been completed. His objective will be to design the classroom so that a child may sit at any place in it and in any position without sacrificing visual comfort and efficiency. At the same time the other features of classroom design, such as friendliness, informality, flexibility, and a feeling of closeness to the outdoors must not be sacrificed. Children must be able to see out and must not feel walled in.

The meeting of these objectives is a large order, and there is no one perfect or standard solution. Rather, the problem must be studied in terms of orientation, outside environment, climate, and other factors, as will be explained below. It involves the co-ordination of all elements, such as roof design, fenestration, interior finishes, and electric lighting. Certain basic understandings are necessary for a successful approach to the problem of providing good visual conditions.

Amount or Intensity of Light

One of the basic factors in providing a good visual environment is intensity of light. This is the amount of light falling on a given surface and is measured in foot-candles. An increase in intensity does not, in and of itself, guarantee better vision. Until recent years the contrary has been regarded as true, and the knowledge that it is not true is apparently far from widespread today, judging by lighting installations seen in many new school buildings or from the thoughtless use of some designs for daylighting.

It is true, of course, that some light is necessary for seeing and that visual acuity increases as the amount of light increases. However, such increases in visual acuity are not proportional to increases in intensity, especially as high foot-candle levels are reached. But the amount of light is not the whole story by far. The human eye can, by expansion or contraction of the pupil, adjust itself to a wide range of light intensity, but it cannot adjust to two or more brightness levels existing at one time within the visual field. The eye will tend to accommodate itself to the brightest level within the visual field. When driving an automobile into the sun, for example, one may have an abundance of light, yet one does not see the highway comfortably or well. This is true even if the sun is well to one side of the direct line of sight. The pupil of the eye contracts to accommodate itself to the bright spot, thus making it possible to see everything else less well.

Brightness

THE second basic factor is brightness, which is related to but different from intensity. Brightness is the amount of light emitted by or reflected from a surface, and is measured in foot-lamberts. An object is visible because of the light it emits, because of the light reflected from it, or because of a difference in brightness between it and other objects. When light strikes a surface, a portion of it is absorbed and the remainder reflected. A black surface absorbs practically all the light striking it and has a very low reflection factor, but a white surface may reflect more than 85 percent of the light falling upon it.

MEASUREMENT OF BRIGHTNESS

The relationship between intensity and brightness may be expressed as a simple mathematical formula, as follows:

$$\text{Foot-candles} \times \text{Reflection factor} = \text{Foot-lamberts}$$

Thus, 50 foot-candles striking a surface with a reflection factor of 80 percent produces a brightness of 40 foot-lamberts.

Brightness is also produced by direct transmission. A light fixture in operation is producing light and has brightness. The usual measure of direct or emitted brightness from a light source is candles per square inch. This, however, is easily transposed into foot-lamberts, as one candle per square inch equals 452 foot-lamberts.

Rough measurements of brightness and rough computation of reflection factors may be obtained by proper use of a foot-candle meter. However, good results in obtaining measurements of brightness of the sky, light fixtures, and room surfaces require the use of special brightness measuring equipment. Formerly such equipment was elaborate and expensive, required a technician to operate, and involved some subjective judgment. With increased demand for brightness measurements, improved and simpler equipment has been developed with direct brightness readings easily made.

THE VISUAL TASK

The conditioning of the environment for visual comfort and efficiency involves control of brightness as related to the visual task. The visual task may be defined as the object upon which the child's eyes are focused at a particular time. For comfortable and efficient seeing, the task must not only have light upon it, but must also have within its parts maximum brightness contrast. Black print on white paper is an illustration of maximum brightness contrast within the task, making it easy to see the print. Faded blue print on white paper, such as may be found from some duplication processes, is more difficult to see. Sewing on dark cloth with thread of the same color represents a very difficult visual task because of lack of contrast within the task.

THE TOTAL VISUAL FIELD

But the child's eyes see more than the task itself, even though he may be concentrating earnestly upon it. In the more technical literature the total view encompassed by the eyes is divided into various fields, called successively the focal field, the central field, the surrounding field, and the peripheral field. The brightness conditions within these fields have a great effect on ability to see a task well. For optimum seeing conditions, the brightness differences in the surrounding and peripheral fields of vision, namely, all the view encompassed by the eye except the task, should be as small as reasonably possible. Definite limits will be discussed below. It should be realized that, whereas the total visual field of one child while working on one task may take in only a part of the classroom, the visual fields of all the children in the room working on all their varied tasks really include during the course of the day the entire classroom. It is necessary, then, to keep brightness differences at a minimum in the entire classroom including walls, ceiling, fixtures, trim, floor, furniture, windows and what-ever is seen through them—in short, everything in sight.

Various authorities have set standards of acceptable brightness differences. All of them agree that as brightness differences outside the task are reduced and approach uniformity, visual conditions are improved. All of them also agree that a uniform brightness is practically impossible to obtain and that even if obtainable it would not be psychologically good.

Brightness Goals

THE National Council on Schoolhouse Construction has adopted the following goals for the total visual environment where critical seeing tasks are being performed:

Goal A—The foot-lambert brightness of any surface viewed from any normal standing or sitting position in the schoolroom should not exceed ten times the foot-lambert brightness of the poorest lighted task in the room.

Goal B—The foot-lambert brightness of any surface viewed from any normal standing or sitting position in the schoolroom should not be less than one-third the foot-lambert brightness of the poorest lighted task in the room.

Goal C—The foot-lambert brightness of any surface immediately adjacent to the task should not exceed three times the task brightness.

Goal D—Brightness-difference between adjacent surfaces should be reduced to a minimum.

Goal E—The brightness goals stated above assume a lighting system that provides from twenty to forty foot-candles on the poorest lighted task. As foot-candle levels are increased, sources of high brightness should be controlled to approach more nearly the brightness of the task. The extent of the area of the surface producing brightness has a measurable effect upon visual comfort. Generally, small areas of either extremes of brightness are less noticeable than are large areas of the same brightness.[1]

INCREASING LOW BRIGHTNESS

For the reduction or control of brightness differences in accordance with these goals, it is necessary to increase the brightness of commonly darker areas, and to reduce or control the brightness of high brightness sources. Common areas of low brightness are ceilings, walls, floors, furniture, and chalkboard.

Ceilings

Light which is absorbed in the ceiling is lost and of no use to the child in the classroom. Therefore, ceilings should be of as high a reflection factor as possible. A flat white finish will give an initial reflection factor of 85 percent. Experience has proved that in a classroom with windows on one side only, the application of flat white paint to a dark ceiling will double the amount of light on the inside row of desks. To avoid excessive

[1] National Council on Schoolhouse Construction, *Guide for Planning School Plants.* Nashville, Tenn.: The Council, 1953, pp. 156–157. Two additional goals were adopted at the September 1955 meeting of the National Council on Schoolhouse Construction, but are not yet included in any publication. They will read as follows:

Goal F—Light distribution from any source should be of such a nature that direct and specular glare are eliminated for the observer to the greatest possible degree.

Goal G—These objectives or goals should be achieved without the loss of a cheerful, friendly and aesthetically pleasing classroom environment and with the need in mind for a balanced and acceptable thermal and auditory environment.

specular reflections, flat paint should be used. Window design, to be discussed more fully under daylighting techniques, should be such that the top of the glass in the windows is as close to the ceiling as possible, thereby making better use of the ceiling as a reflecting and light diffusing agent. Likewise, light fixtures, also to be discussed later, should be selected and installed to illuminate the ceiling evenly rather than spottily and thus to increase the evenness of light distribution throughout the room.

Side Walls

For the minimum difference in brightness, side walls also should be white. However, since lack of color and variety in the room would be psychologically objectionable, it is recommended that side walls, at least down to wainscot height, be painted in light pastel shades having a reflection factor of not less than 60 percent. There would be nothing wrong with painting the entire wall, ceiling to floor, in the light color. However, for maintenance reasons, some may wish to finish the lower wall slightly darker. But the lower wall, including the baseboard, should have not less than a 40-percent reflection factor and only flat finishes should be used. Trim should have a reflection factor approximately equal to that of the wall, but it may be of a different color. It should have a dull finish.

Floors

Floor finishes should have a reflection factor of from 30 to 40 percent. Natural finished maple, well maintained, will provide this. A plastic or asphalt tile or linoleum in a solid light color selected from the "C" or "D" group, and without a checkerboard pattern of contrasting brightness or a dark border, will also be satisfactory.

Furniture

Desks, cabinets, and other furniture should have a finish with a 30- to 40-percent reflection factor. This should include not only the surface, but also the sides, framework, and seats. Durable plastic finishes in light colors for desk tops are in common use, but some of them are rather glossy, making possible excessive specular reflection and glare.

Chalkboards

A properly maintained black slate chalkboard provides an excellent writing surface and provides good brightness contrast between white chalk and the black surface. However, large amounts of black surface soak up a great deal of light. Also, with light walls and with a high level of illumination, there is objectionable and uncomfortable brightness difference between the blackboard and the area surrounding it. For these reasons, lighter colored boards of various materials are now commonly found in schools. These boards, very often of green color, give a reflection factor of 20 to 25 percent when chalked in. However, there is less contrast between the board and the chalk so that a high level of illumination on the board is necessary if markings on the board are to be readily distinguishable. Supplementary lighting on the chalkboard may be indicated.

CONTROLLING HIGH BRIGHTNESS

The second, and more difficult, part of providing acceptable brightness ratios within the visual environment is the control of high brightness. Goal A stated above furnishes a desirable limit. Common sources of high brightness are direct sunlight, a bright sky vault, sunlight on adjacent light colored buildings, banks of snow or bare ground, and electric light fixtures. If the task viewed by the child has a brightness of 30 foot-lamberts, the brightest area visible in the room or through the windows should not be more than 300 foot-lamberts, according to Goal A. Yet a clear blue sky may have a brightness of 1,000 foot-lamberts, and a hazy sky will be even brighter and may go as high as 2,000 foot-lamberts. White clouds will vary from 3,000 to 5,000 foot-lamberts. Sunlight on a white building will give a brightness of 3,000 to 8,000 foot-lamberts. When these are compared with a task brightness of 30 foot lamberts; it will be seen that brightness ratios may vary from 33 to 1 to more than 250 to 1. These high brightnesses are not limited to any one orientation. A north sky can be just as bright as other parts of the sky vault and sometimes even brighter.

Many light fixtures in common use violate the limits prescribed in Goal A. Even today many classrooms are illuminated by bare incandescent lamps. A bare 200-watt filament lamp has a brightness of 65,000 foot-lamberts. Again assuming a task brightness of 30 foot-lamberts the ratio is over 2,000 to 1. The enclosing globe commonly used over incandescent bulbs will have a brightness of from 800 to 1,200 foot-lamberts, about 10 times as bright as allowed by the prescribed 10 to 1 ratio. Nor are fluorescent lamps, in and of themselves, an acceptable answer. A bare fluorescent lamp has a brightness of from 1,400 to 1,900 foot-lamberts. Even the larger diameter fluorescent tubes have brightness far beyond acceptable limits. Shielded fluorescent fixtures vary greatly in brightness. Some are as low as 300 to 350 foot-lamberts; others as bright as 1,200 foot-lamberts. Some of these, then, at the lower range may with proper installation, come within the 10 to 1 limit. Luminous indirect (either incandescent or fluorescent) or concentric ring, silver bowl incandescent fixtures, depending as they do upon the white ceiling for light reflection, are of the lowest brightness of all.

Obviously, then, the problem of controlling high brightness, whether from artificial or natural sources, is a major one and a challenge to the designer. In comparatively few cases is it given the consideration it deserves. It involves more than buying a new light fixture or shielding a bare window by the use of a window shade. It is a major problem of design, involving co-ordination of all the elements bearing upon the particular problem. Furthermore, it is not probable that any one solution which will apply everywhere will ever be found. No one bilateral lighting scheme, no one fenestration pattern or material, and no one light fixture, incandescent or fluorescent, will give the answer. Each building presents a different problem in this respect. Climate, budget, site, program, size of building, orientation, environment—some or all will differ with each building, requiring unique, creative, and sound solutions. But the principles behind the provision of a good visual environment are the same for all buildings, and each solution should be evaluated as a whole in terms of these principles.

Types and Patterns of Light Fixtures

THE design of an appropriate system of electric lighting is one of the principal elements in providing for visual comfort and efficiency. Such a system should be designed and fixtures carefully selected so that the goals mentioned above will not be violated. In general the lighting system which is the least noticeable and which at the same time provides adequate intensity will be the best from the standpoint of comfort. This practically indicates some sort of indirect or semi-indirect system, with the light source itself concealed or of low brightness, and with full advantage taken of the reflecting and diffusing value of a white ceiling and light side walls and finishes. Attention should also be given to the probable use of the room. For example, most elementary schoolrooms are used only in the daytime. The lighting system for such a room should be designed primarily to supplement daylight, especially in the interior of the room when daylighting from one side only is used. If some of the newer daylight designs are used so that the room is well supplied with natural light during daylight hours, the electric lighting system can be even less extensive and expensive, but adequate wiring to allow for future changes should be provided. Many high school rooms such as shops, homemaking rooms, library, gymnasium, music rooms, and others will receive extensive night use.

Here the problem is to provide a system which will take the place of daylight and provide good intensity with visual comfort.

Considerations to be observed, in addition to those based on brightness difference principles in the selection of a lighting system, fall roughly into the categories of economics, safety, and performance. In appraising a proposed system from the standpoint of economics, one should consider original installation cost, ease and expense of maintenance, light output per watt of current consumed, utility rates, and hours of burning per year. From a safety standpoint, instant starting may be required and stroboscopic effects must be avoided where there are turning wheels. Under performance should be considered such things as need for dimming, effect of spectral quality on color discrimination, possibility of focusing, pattern of output, and appearance of the room.

INCANDESCENT PATTERNS AND SYSTEMS

Incandescent fixtures can be arranged in two or three rows of two or three fixtures each, depending upon the width and length of the classroom. Spacing and height of suspension should be such as to give a uniform pattern of light at the level of the working surfaces in the room and to avoid spots of relatively high brightness on the ceiling. They should be of low surface brightness or of semi-indirect type. Fixtures using the silver bowl bulb, shielded by concentric rings or other means, and plastic bowl fixtures are commonly used.

Sometimes fixtures are recessed flush with the ceiling or a drum type fixture is mounted against the ceiling. With such schemes the brightness ratio of the fixture to the ceiling is excessive, and the brightness ratio between the fixture and the task is outside the 10 to 1 ratio recommended in Goal A.

Another incandescent system which has sometimes been used in schools is floodlights beamed on the ceiling, with the lamps aimed to give the ceiling an even brightness. The light sources are concealed from view. This, then, is a totally indirect system which is pleasing and comfortable. Its effectiveness depends upon keeping the ceiling white and the room finishes of light color. It is particularly useful where only enough light to supplement daylight is desired. For nighttime use, there might be some difficulty in providing adequate intensity by this method.

FLUORESCENT PATTERNS AND SYSTEMS

Fluorescent fixtures in two or three continuous rows parallel to the windows can produce excellent illumination. Intensity can be increased by increasing the number of tubes per fixture. Fixtures should be suspended and a major part of the light output should be on the ceiling, with suspension low enough to allow the troughs of light to overlap. All visible surfaces of the fixtures should be of low brightness and tubes should be shielded.

If egg-crate louvers are used for shielding, they should be deep enough and set close enough together so that the tubes will not be visible at normal viewing angles. When egg-crate louvers are used and much of the light is cast downward, other patterns than those indicated above may need to be employed if distribution of light at desk level is to be uniform throughout the room. When the tube is visible from any viewing angle, there is always the possibility of the tube being seen by reflection on a glossy surface. A complete shield of low brightness will avoid this effect.

Sometimes the fluorescent fixtures are recessed in the ceiling. This is called troffer lighting. Objections to it are the same as for recessed incandescent fixtures.

Fluorescent lighting lends itself well to a development commonly known as the "ceiling of light." In this plan the fluorescent tubes are placed in a regular pattern above a suspended ceiling of transluscent plastic, or egg-crate louvers of light metal or plastic. This system can provide a high intensity without spots of high brightness. Drawbacks have been:

1. Such a system is expensive in initial cost.
2. If a sheet of plastic is used, the problem of keeping it clean may be burdensome.
3. If egg-crate louvers are used, the usefulness of the ceiling as a surface for reflecting and diffusing daylight is practically destroyed, and reflection from desk tops and other glossy surfaces may be a problem.

Many other variations of systems mentioned above can be worked out. Others, different and better, will surely be developed. No one system is perfect for use everywhere. Illumination of each space is a separate technical problem. Each demands its own solution, making use of all the resources available. Each proposed solution should be evaluated in terms of basic principles for visual comfort and efficiency.

FLUORESCENT OR INCANDESCENT?

Since the advent of fluorescence as a practical method of producing light energy, there has been a great deal of controversy regarding the comparative merits of incandescent and fluorescent systems for general use in schools. In a commendable desire to increase intensity of illumination in classrooms, many school systems change to fluorescent installations. Such a change might be of great benefit if made in accordance with the principles stated earlier in this discussion. In too many cases, however, these principles are overlooked, and unshielded fixtures are used. In many such installations there is no accompanying program of redecoration and refinishing, with the result that, even though the level of light intensity is materially increased, the visual conditions are less comfortable than before. The results being unsatisfactory, blame is placed on fluorescent lighting rather than on the design of the installation.

Fluorescent lighting is just another tool which can be used by the designer to produce a satisfactory visual environment. Like other tools or techniques, it can be well used or misused and is not a panacea. Nor should it be adopted because it is new, modern, or different. Complete engineering analysis in terms of the goals previously outlined is desirable to determine the proper light source to be used for any given school installation.

Daylight Control and Use

THE problem of bringing sufficient daylight into the classroom has long been of concern to school building planners and the writers of state codes. With the widespread use of the double-loaded corridor in a multi-story building, rather strict rules were developed to control the glass area and location. For example, it became the custom, and sometimes the law, to require that a classroom be about half as high as it was wide in order to bring the tops of the windows high enough to get some light across to the corridor side of the room. While the resulting 11- to 12-foot ceilings are lower than those in many buildings of the previous century, the room still has an undesirable excess of cubage. Along with this requirement was often coupled the stipulation that the area of the window glass should be at least 20 percent (sometimes 25 percent) of the area of the classroom floor. Other regulations prescribed that the top of the glass surface had to be within a certain number of inches of the ceiling line. All of these requirements had some reason for being made and considerable merit in requiring well-designed fenestration for unilateral lighting. However, they also had the effect of restricting experimentation and flexibility in design. In some cases the codes rule out bilateral lighting and permit wider classrooms with clerestory lighting only as exceptions to the regulations.

Efforts to design a school building in which all classrooms have sufficient daylight under ordinary sky conditions, with a relatively even distribution in all parts of the room, have led to many innovations in building design. The admission of daylight in large quantities into schoolrooms has now become quite common in practically all parts of the country. This trend, however, has brought its own problems. In too many cases thought has apparently been given only to the admission of daylight with little or no study of the problem of its control. There has been, perhaps, too much blind acceptance of certain clerestory or monitor window arrangements to provide bilateral lighting or too ready acceptance and indiscriminate use of new forms and types of glass. Some architects, once having developed a certain method of daylighting a room and having used it fairly successfully in one situation have continued to use it everywhere, regardless of orientation or environment.

This is a complex problem, with several elements, some of which seem to be conflicting. Among the elements to be considered are:

1. It is desired to let daylight into the room.
2. High brightness in the visual fields must be avoided, and therefore there must be control of one's view of the sky, the sun, or any high brightness area as seen through the window openings.
3. Children must be able to see out and not feel walled in.
4. Children must be able to work in any part of the room and face in any direction with visual comfort.
5. A fairly even distribution of light in all parts of the room is desired.
6. In some climates avoidance of excessive heat loss is important, while in other climates, and in the late spring and early fall in most climates, avoidance of heat gain is just as important.
7. Since most authorities agree that the place to use the projected audio-visual materials is in the classroom and not in a special room if they are to be of the most educational value, the problem of darkening becomes more difficult as more window area is used. At least partial darkening is still considered necessary for some kinds of projection.

HOW MUCH DAYLIGHT?

The complexity of the problem, plus climatic factors, has led some school planners to the conclusion that little reliance should be placed on daylight. They state that with modern ways of producing electric light economically it is possible to produce a steadily good visual environment without major reliance on daylight. Also, they say that any room depth or shape is then possible. They believe that only enough window area need be provided to give a view of the outdoors and prevent a feeling of claustrophobia. It is also sometimes stated in support of this position that in some parts of the United States a large portion of the daylight hours is cloudy and that most teachers leave electric lights on even in well day-lighted rooms whether they are needed or not.

These arguments have weight, but do not tell the whole story. In stating that the sun shines only a small portion of the time in some localities, these school planners ignore the fact that there is much daylight whether the sun shines or not. Actually, in one state which does have frequent cloudy days, measurements of light intensity taken out of doors during a steady rain revealed an intensity of 250 foot-candles.

Furthermore, in placing dependence upon electric lighting alone, it is assumed that the fixtures will be maintained at a high level of efficiency. But even in many fairly large school systems, lighting systems are not main-tained well. One has but to go into schoolrooms to find light bulbs that are burned out and not replaced, or fluorescent tubes that do not light, or are so near the end of their lives that they have lost much of their efficiency, or are flickering. In times of financial stringency, maintenance is even worse. Daylight is free and there is just as much of it during a financial depression as during prosperous times.

It is further believed by those who argue for daylight design that there is something psychologically better about a schoolroom flooded with day-light. It seems more natural and pleasant and less artificial and institutional. It just looks like a better place for children and children's reactions to their environment confirm this. The lack of research data to prove this last statement is admitted.

Those who advocate major dependence upon electric lighting state that whereas a consistently steady intensity of illumination can be provided by electric lighting, the amount of daylight varies from one moment to the next as clouds pass over the sun or as other external conditions cause such variance. Actually, this is an advantage since a variation in intensity is natural, pleasant, relaxing, and psychologically desirable. An absolutely steady intensity may be just the opposite. The human eye can adapt itself to a wide range of intensities without discomfort, strain, or appreciable loss of visual efficiency as long as the total visual environment follows the principles of brightness balance.

How, then, shall the daylighting problem be solved? Several commonly practical solutions will be examined·and discussed.

SINGLE-LOADED CORRIDOR WITH A CLERESTORY

Figure 18 portrays two early bilateral designs. They involve a corridor with classrooms on one side only and with orientation of the main windows commonly to the north and with the clerestory to the south. They have been used to a limited extent in two-story buildings, as shown

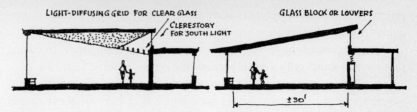

Figure 18. Bilateral Lighting with Clerestory.

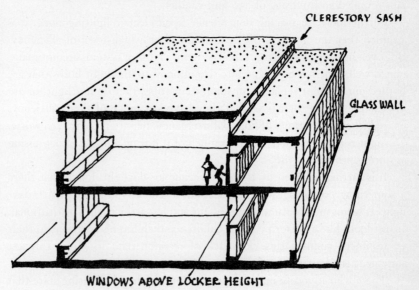

Figure 19. Bilateral Lighting in a Two-Story Building.

in Figure 19, by letting much daylight into the corridor and placing high level windows in the inside wall of the classroom above the locker or door height, thereby "borrowing" light from the corridor. This design does provide adequate daylight and a fairly even intensity in all parts of the room. Either a sloping or level ceiling may be used, but ceilings must be white and other room finishes of a light color. The fenestration should be continuous to avoid alternate bright windows and relatively dark piers between them. The clerestory windows should be large enough to let in enough daylight to make it worth while. Experience has shown that at least two and one half feet of glass height is necessary in the clerestory.

This design in actual use has had several common deficiencies. First, there is often a failure to shield the south windows satisfactorily. Some architects have used a diffusing glass in the clerestory on the theory that it will break up the sunlight. They neglect to consider that this type of glass, when the sun strikes it, is excessively bright and within the visual fields of the room occupants. Others have used directional glass block in the clerestory. This is a better solution, provided enough block is used. Brightness is reduced and light is directed by the block to the white ceiling from whence it is reflected and diffused. The block panel may, however, be somewhat beyond the brightness limits of 10 to 1 at certain sun angles. Some have justifiably wished to use the clerestory windows for ventilation. This cannot be done with a solid glass block panel. The mistake has then been made of placing one or two ventilating panel windows in the clerestory, thereby creating panels of high brightness and defeating the purpose of using the glass block. Panels of adjustable metal louvers for ventilating have been successfully used to solve the problem. Another method of shielding the clerestory has been the use of fixed louvers of wood or light-weight metal, either inside or outside the room. These are set at an angle to catch sunlight or daylight and reflect it onto the ceiling of the room, but are close enough together so that the horizontal bands of bright and dark appearance commonly found with venetian blinds are avoided. Translucent, light-colored traverse drapes have also been used for shielding, but their brightness may also exceed acceptable limits when the sun strikes them.

A second common fault is failure to shield the north windows. It is commonly assumed that inasmuch as there is no sun in the north, no shielding is necessary. This is not true, for a north sky frequently will have a brightness of 2,500 or more foot-lamberts. Previous discussion indicated an upper limit of 300 foot-lamberts if the task has a brightness of 30. In deciding upon the shielding for the north windows, or any other windows, the environment of the school must not be neglected. For example, if one looks out and sees a bank of evergreens rather than a bright sky, the shielding problem is reduced. On the other hand, a sand dune, a snow bank, or an adjacent white building can be objectionally bright.

Finally, some architects use the single-loaded corridor and clerestory design for all orientations. Some have even turned the main windows to the south without shielding and at the same time have used a glass block clerestory on the north for no good reason except possible reduction of heat loss.

BILATERAL LIGHTING WITH A DOUBLE-LOADED CORRIDOR

Locale of site, size of building, and a desire to get more use of corridors have influenced some to adapt the clerestory section to double loading of the corridor. This is sometimes done by depressing the corridor roof, as shown by Scheme A in Figure 20. This is subject to the same advantages and deficiencies as mentioned above. Usually, but not always, the orientation has been east and west rather than north and south. Directional glass block is commonly used in the main windows, with a vision strip below, and the same type of glass block is used in the clerestory. Interestingly enough, the most common question about this design in areas where there is snow is, "Won't the trough fill up with snow?" Admittedly, this appears likely, but it rarely happens in practice. There have been several

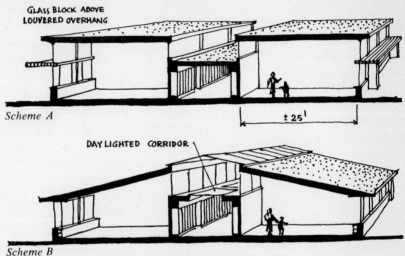

Figure 20. Bilateral Lighting with Double-Loaded Corridor.

variations of this design. One is shown in Scheme B of Figure 20. This design provides a light well above the corridor by means of the skylight. Glass panels along the upper inside wall of the classroom admit daylight into the room and glass strips or ports let daylight into the corridor.

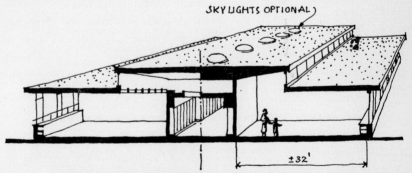

Figure 21. Daylighting Through a Monitor Window. (Note: *A different scheme is illustrated in each half of the section.*)

A somewhat similar design with a double-loaded corridor makes use of a monitor, as shown in Figure 21. This, it will be observed, is really unilateral lighting with the upper part of the windows moved back toward the inside classroom wall. Advantages and disadvantages of this and other cross sections could be given. Each one may have been, in the place where it was originally used, a sound solution to a problem. But no one will work well everywhere, and every one ought to be evaluated in terms not only of whether daylight is admitted, but how well it is controlled. No solution can be used thoughtlessly as a standard answer.

GLASS BLOCK

No discussion of daylight design or high brightness control would be complete without mentioning some advantages and disadvantages of the use of glass block. This material is a useful tool which can be used and misused. It should be used intelligently and discriminately after careful consideration of its characteristics and of its usefulness in solving the particular problem at hand.

Advantages of the light directional block would appear to be:

1. The block shields the bright sky from view.
2. Light striking the block is refracted by built-in prisms and directed to the ceiling, thereby throwing more light to the interior of the room and giving a better distribution of intensity throughout the room than would be the case with clear glass and unilateral fenestration.
3. The double surface with dead air space between has some advantage over a single pane in reducing heat loss.
4. While the block may be broken by stones it does not break as easily as ordinary glass and both faces are seldom broken at once.

Disadvantages are:

1. Some feel that the wall of block, even with a clear glass vision strip below, is too confining, heavy, formal, and institutional.
2. At some sun angles and viewing angles the block has a brightness such that the ratio between it and some of the tasks in the room will materially exceed 10 to 1.
3. The brightness of the vision strip may be excessive when compared to the brightness of the block panel above it, although in some installations this has been corrected by using a special glass of low light transmission in the vision strip.
4. In the warmer months there is an objectionable solar heat

gain, and the block being a solid panel the problem of cooling by natural ventilation is increased, especially if there is no opportunity for cross ventilation in the room.

5. Some critics have felt that on a cloudy day the use of this material gives the classroom a dismal cast.

6. The block, in shielding the sky, does permanently block out a large part of the view. Except for very special uses, such as a swimming pool, the entire wall should never be closed in, and the block should be above the eye level of the average person when standing.

EXTERNAL CONTROL DEVICES

In an effort to control sunlight and to shield the bright sky from the view of the room occupants, several external control devices have been used. Among them are overhangs, horizontal louvers, vertical louvers, and "jib" walls. An overhang is an extension of the roof beyond the wall of the building. Horizontal louvers might be said to be a permanent, non-adjustable venetian blind, mounted outside the window. Sometimes, to add to their effectiveness and to avoid a "walled in" feeling, they are suspended from an overhang. Vertical louvers have been used to a somewhat lesser extent. They are mounted so that the room occupant, when looking out at a certain angle, will not see the sky. This assumes a fixed furniture arrangement within the classroom. Jib walls are really extensions of the end walls of the classroom through the outside walls. They furnish a sort of vertical louver on the outside between classrooms which tends to fix permanently the position of the classroom wall and thereby restrict flexibility.

All of these devices have merit when properly used. Too often they appear to have been used only for architectural effect without much thought as to their worth in controlling brightness. Sometimes their dimensions seem to have been arrived at by chance or by aesthetic considerations rather than by a careful study of the problem of brightness control. If used, they should accomplish a purpose and be designed according to the principles or goals previously mentioned, with the visual task of the child in the schoolroom as the starting point.

INTERNAL CONTROL DEVICES

Several light control devices and designs have already been mentioned or discussed in connection with shielding from sunlight and other high brightness from the outside. Another purpose of controls is to darken the room for projection. As more daylight is admitted into the classroom, the problem of room darkening increases. Improved methods of daylight projection would, of course, reduce or eliminate this problem.

With the traditional school window design the common practice is to provide translucent fabric shades on spring rollers, of which the best are center hung, double-roller shades. For darkening purposes, separate shades of opaque material are hung over the regular shades, sometimes with special side channels to insure complete darkening. These installations usually cause some trouble and are not usable with a continuous window design that has the venting type sash instead of the traditional double-hung type. A similar situation prevails with respect to venetian blinds. These are fairly effective with traditional windows, although they have the disadvantage of being hard to clean and of getting out of order. Also, they are seldom adjusted properly and when raised shut off light from the top foot or so of the windows, thereby defeating the purpose of having the window heads close to the ceiling. They do not meet the need with continuous fenestration.

With the use of continuous fenestration has come the adaptation of an old device, namely drapes which may be drawn to and fro horizontally. The disadvantages which formerly worked against the common use of this arrangement were: (1) the weight of the fabric; (2) the fading and rotting of the drapes in the sunlight; (3) the high cost; (4) the bulk of the drapes when drawn back; (5) the difficulty of cleaning; and (6) the inefficiency of tracks and hangers.

Recent developments which have brought drapes back into favor include the manufacture of varieties of synthetic and plastic fabrics which are light in weight, color fast, durable, easily cleaned, of little bulk, and flame resistant; and the design of tracks and hangers which operate very easily and are almost foolproof. These drapery materials are available in translucent and opaque form. They are particularly adaptable for use with clerestory window strips and all designs of continuous fenestration.

The relatively small expense of these installations makes it possible to install double sets, one translucent and one opaque, for use where excessive brightness makes necessary a full degree of control. On windows where brightness is controlled by other means, only the opaque drape may be used. Translucent drapes for brightness control may be satisfactory in some instances and unsatisfactory in others. When exposed to direct sunlight, they may be excessively bright. In a sunless orientation, they will shield well, but will cut off the view. They will also be a handicap to the use of the windows for natural ventilation.

WINDOW SILL HEIGHTS

A question which the architect has to answer and in which the educator should have more than a casual interest is the height of the classroom window sills. There may be a conflict between two different objectives. One is to design a school which is not walled off from the world about it, but which has a sense of continuity with the out-of-doors. Certainly, lowering the window sill is one way of obtaining this feeling. But when the sill is lowered, additional high brightness areas, such as bare or snow-covered ground may enter the visual fields of the occupants of the room and this violates the second objective, which is to provide visual comfort. It is a question, then, of what the conditions are outside the window. If they are such that there is a probability of high brightness, then some method of shielding must be provided. Possibly an arrangement whereby the lower sash could be covered independently and easily could be devised. This could be used as the occasion demanded. Or perhaps low transmission glass could be used to control this external brightness. At any rate, the ancient rule of thumb that the window sill should be at the approximate eye level of a seated child is not a suitable guide for all situations. This will not be the same for all children in a classroom and certainly will vary greatly between children of different age or grade levels. The answer will have to be found in each building in terms of its environment and in terms of the atmosphere which the designer is attempting to create. Whatever he decides, however, he should not do it without attention to conditions affecting the visual environment.

TOP LIGHTING AND LOW CEILINGS

In the school buildings of several decades ago, skylights were frequently employed. In many cases, they were not satisfactory and were soon covered and sealed. There were several things wrong, including:

1. The skylights leaked, and the glass became dirty.
2. There were objectional shafts of sunlight entering the room and causing heat gain, especially for those who had to sit in the sunlight.
3. There was heat loss and condensation during the heating season.

In recent years, with the emphasis on daylight design, the idea of top lighting has been revived. Some architects have resisted bilateral lighting with its broken roof line because of resulting complications in design. They have felt that if light could be introduced from the top it would be possible to have a simple flat roof, to lower the ceiling, and still to get good results. This would save cubage and thus reduce the cost of construction as well as of heating. It is claimed that the new skylights are of better design than the old ones and that the type of glass used has been greatly improved. There are still present, however, the problems of control of sunlight, heat gain, and heat loss. The lessons of experience should not be ignored.

Plastics were developed during World War II for use in "bubbles" in fighter planes and bombers. From this has grown the use of these materials for top lighting in school buildings. Some condensation difficulties were originally reported, but these have been corrected by providing an air space between a double layer. This also reduces heat loss and gain.

Research has developed prismatic glass block for weather-tight ceiling installations. Certain types are designed so that at the high sun angles experienced during the warmer months in the temperate zone, the sunlight is so refracted that it does not enter the room, while light from other angles can enter and is diffused. It is important that these blocks be installed with proper orientation to compass directions. It is claimed that these installations reduce heat loss and solar heat gain.

All of these designs are attempts to capture the advantages of the old skylight without its disadvantages. All should be scrutinized with respect to the following questions:

1. Will the installation stand up during the life of the building and maintain its efficiency without excessive maintenance?
2. Is the heat gain and heat loss problem solved?
3. Will there be good distribution of daylight throughout the room, or will there be a relatively bright area under the installation?
4. What will be the brightness of the skylight as compared to task brightness and as compared to the brightness of the ceiling around the installation? Are Goals A and D as stated earlier in this chapter violated? Will this vary with the time of day and season of the year?

The lowered ceiling height, which often accompanies top lighting, also must be critically examined with respect to its effect on visual environment. A lower ceiling means lower window heads, and this makes it more difficult for light from the side windows to penetrate to the far side of the room. A uniform spread of either daylight or artificial light from the ceiling is also harder to achieve with a low ceiling. Finally, the low ceiling makes it difficult to suspend the light fixtures low enough to obtain fairly even brightness on the ceiling itself.

Incidentally, the low ceiling reduces the amount of air per pupil in the room, and this must be taken into account in designing the ventilation.

In many ways low ceilings and top lighting are desirable, but each suggested design must be evaluated in terms of many factors. Not the least of these is the provision of visual comfort and efficiency for the occupants. The goals mentioned earlier in the chapter provide a basis for evaluation.

Auditory Conditions

JUST as a large part of the activities of the occupants of a school building involves seeing and therefore makes important the provision of conditions for visual comfort and efficiency, so does another large part of the activities involve hearing. Children not only have to hear clearly, but they also have to be shielded from unwanted and nerve-jangling, extraneous noises. The school is inhabited by live, active, human beings and should be so designed that they can act normally in relaxed fashion without being unduly disturbing to or disturbed by other normal activities.

Sound conditioning is especially important in today's schools, where many noisy activities such as music, games, and shop work are common. In the classroom several activities may be going on simultaneously, none of them particularly noisy, but together creating enough noise to be objectionable. When there is lack of sound conditioning, children will expend undue amounts of energy straining to hear. As the day wears on, voices rise in pitch, tension increases, and the stage is set for behavior problems. Tired people, both adults and children, are irritable. Proper noise control can prevent at least some of this.

EXTERNAL NOISE

Part of the noise problem in school buildings comes from outside. In buildings located close to a railroad, practically all activity involving hearing has to cease whenever a train passes. In some schools there is the continual roar of traffic from a near-by highway. In other cases, children on the playground are just outside the windows of classrooms where others are trying to study. Although acoustical treatment within the building may deaden the noise by preventing it from bouncing around within the room, the main answer to the problem has to be found elsewhere. Obviously, the prevention of railroad, street traffic, and industrial noise lies in the proper location of the school site and the proper location of the building on the site. At least it can be far enough back from the street to reduce traffic noise, and the windows of classrooms need not face the highway or be close to it. A large site will also make possible a site layout which can place playground activities remote from classroom windows.

NOISE TRANSMISSION WITHIN THE BUILDING

The building should be designed to reduce noise transmission from one part to another. Proper arrangement of rooms is one way of accomplishing this. It would be unwise, to say the least, to locate a library over a band room or shop, or to place a classroom so that the door opens directly into a gymnasium. The music room or suite of rooms should be isolated, with nothing above or below it. The same can be said of the shops. The gymnasium certainly should not be in the center of things where its noise can be transmitted to rooms all around it. Other similar examples could be mentioned.

It is apparent that the spread-out, one-story building has definite advantages when it comes to isolation of noisy elements. Such isolation becomes more and more difficult as the building is pushed together and piled floor on floor. However, even in a one-story, spread-out type of building there still will be a problem of preventing sound transmission. For example, the drafting room in a shop suite may need to be isolated from the shop noise, or the choral music room may need to be isolated from practice rooms or the adjacent instrumental rooms.

Proper structural design is one means of reducing noise transmission. A resilient wall, such as one of lath and plaster, will vibrate and transmit sound, and noise will be carried through floors and other parts of the structure. The application of acoustical tile or acoustical plaster does not solve these problems, although it may be of some value. The control of structure-borne noises is a technical matter requiring competent engineering services.

The ventilating system is a common offender in transmitting sounds. Rooms which are unusually noisy should be served by separate ducts, or adequate baffles and sound-absorbing materials should be installed in the ducts. Any acoustical materials used for this purpose should be capable of maintaining efficiency in spite of accumulated grime and dust. Frequently much benefit can be achieved by the mounting of fans and motors on blocks of rubber or other resilient material, and by the use of flexible connections between fans and ducts.

REDUCTION OF REVERBERATION TIME

Proper hearing depends in part upon echoes or reverberation from surrounding surfaces. If the reverberation time is too great or too small, speech will be hard to understand, voices will be unpleasant, or other hearing difficulties will be encountered. Difficulty in hearing often causes a raising of voices or turning up the volume control on a radio or other mechanical device. This often merely adds to the difficulty and leads to irritation and fatigue.

Classrooms

There is no disagreement as to the need for control of reverberation time in classrooms. However, some acoustical engineers believe that the common practice of placing acoustical treatment on the entire ceiling produces an overcorrection. There is no particular reason why the acoustical material has to be on the ceiling. As a matter of fact, the light reflecting qualities of the ceiling would be improved if it could be of a smooth white material. Some classrooms have been treated successfully by the use of sound-absorbing materials on upper walls only, and in some cases the shape and dimensions of the room are such that no applied materials are needed.

Corridors and Stairways

The smooth nature of corridor finishes with tile or terrazzo floors and glazed tile walls, all highly sound reflective, make corridors into giant sound tunnels. Add to this the opening and closing of steel lockers and the normal sounds of youthful conversation and traffic movements, and a tremendous volume of confusing noise results. The time between classes should be a time for relaxation. Excessive noise prevents this. Corridors, then, should be designed or treated to reduce sharply the noise level. Probably the ceiling is the best location for acoustical materials here. With low ceilings in corridors, there is always the temptation for the tall youngster to jump up and touch the ceiling or to stick a pencil into the soft material. Therefore, the acoustical material in a corridor should be located with this in mind and should be of a type that will stand up under such treatment. Stairways present similar problems of noise control.

Gymnasiums

Noise control is often neglected in gymnasiums, probably on the theory that a lot of noise is going to be created here anyway. This is a mistake. A gymnasium is constructed primarily for instruction in physical education. The instructor ought to be able to make himself heard. Even during basketball games with the organized cheering, all can be more comfortable if the noise level is reduced. Lack of acoustical correction is especially serious if the space is also to be used for assembly or auditorium purposes. In selecting and installing acoustical materials in a gymnasium, it must be anticipated that it will often be struck by basketballs, indoor baseballs, and other objects.

Dining Rooms

The lunch hour ought to be a period of relaxation, of free and happy conversation; it should not be a hubbub. Proper acoustical conditions are essential. These can be achieved in part by use of smaller dining rooms, but other design solutions will also have to be considered.

Auditoriums

How silly it is to build a room where people are expected to sit and listen and then not design it so they can hear comfortably. Yet, this mistake has been made often. The problem is increased when it is realized that many of the speakers and performers are children who are shy and have immature voices. The proper design of an auditorium and its stage is a technical engineering problem involving the shape of the room as well as the use of sound-absorbing materials in the right places. It requires the advice of an acoustical engineer more often than has usually been recognized in practice.

Swimming Pools

Swimming pools by their very nature abound in highly reflective surfaces, not the least being the surface of the water. In some indoor pools it is practically impossible to be heard while a group of children is in the water, even when some acoustical materials have been provided. This may be serious, since the ability to make oneself heard and the ability to distinguish between sounds may make a difference between living and drowning. Safety demands adequate acoustical treatment here. The materials and methods of installation used should be capable of withstanding high humidity.

Music Rooms

The acoustical design of a music room is especially difficult because the correct reverberation time is essential for a satisfactory musical performance. Too short a reverberation time can be just as unsatisfactory as one that is too long, that is, a room can be too "dead" as well as too "lively" acoustically. As in the case of an auditorium, the services of an acoustical engineer may be advisable here.

Shops

Perhaps for the same reasons as in gymnasiums, acoustical treatment is often omitted from shops. But noise can be just as nerve-wracking and tiring here as anywhere else, and the safety aspect cannot be ignored

Proper acoustical design of shop areas is not a luxury, but a real necessity. Durable, easily cleaned materials should be used.

MATERIALS FOR ACOUSTICAL TREATMENT

In the selection of acoustical materials, consideration should be given to the following questions:

1. How efficient is the material in absorbing sound? Can enough correction be secured by using it on the available surfaces?
2. How can the material be cleaned? Will it lose its acoustical properties if painted with oil paint? With nonbridging paint? Can it be spray painted many times without losing its acoustical properties?
3. What are the light reflecting qualities of the material? If acoustical plaster is used, will it dry into a dull gray or into nearly a pure white?
4. Is the material fire-resistive? If not, is it fire-retardant or slow-burning? If not, can it be securely mounted directly on fire-resistive materials so that there is no space between the material and the surface on which it is mounted?
5. Does it, in order to be acoustically efficient, depend upon expert workmanship and careful supervision of application? (Some acoustical plasters, unless mixed to exactly the right consistency and applied without too much pressure, lose their acoustical properties. On the other hand, they do furnish, or can furnish if properly applied, protection for structural steel in buildings required to be fire-resistive.)
6. If the material is where it can be reached, will it stand the hazards of use of the building by youth or will it damage easily?

All of the above again emphasize the need for careful consideration of the problem, for competence on the part of the architect, and for willingness on his part to employ expert assistance for the solution of the more technical aspects of the problem.

CHAPTER 22

HEATING, VENTILATING, AND SANITARY FACILITIES

Heating and Ventilating Objectives
The Heating System
Methods of Ventilating
Sanitary Facilities

THE importance of proper heating and ventilating of school buildings goes without challenge. Certainly in all parts of the United States, except perhaps in the extreme south, it will be necessary to increase the indoor temperature over that of the outdoors on some days. The problems of heating increase in seriousness as one moves north, but some provision must be made practically everywhere. Likewise with ventilation. There will be need for positive ventilation of some spaces in all school buildings. In the milder climates, the general ventilation problem may be one of cooling during much of the year, and buildings will be designed and oriented to make maximum use of prevailing winds.

Heating and Ventilating Objectives

CERTAINLY children and teachers cannot be expected to do their best work in buildings which are uncomfortably cold or hot, where the humidity is excessively high, or where the air is stagnant. There are too many schools at present in the United States where children sometimes wear galoshes all day because of cold floors or cold drafts. There are others where lack of controls causes classrooms to be overheated, with the result that children are listless and sleepy. It is the purpose of the heating and ventilating systems to provide the thermal and atmospheric conditions, including air movement, necessary for bodily comfort and health.

441

TEMPERATURE

The body itself is somewhat of a furnace and the food consumed, through chemical reactions in the body, is burned and converted into heat. If the body loses its heat too rapidly by transfer to colder surroundings, the person feels cold. If surrounding objects are so warm that the body cannot lose its heat rapidly enough, the person feels warm. In winter, heavier clothing is worn not to keep the cold out but to furnish insulation to keep the body from losing its heat too rapidly.

Different individuals have different metabolic rates and differ in their reactions to heat or lack of it. Different people dress differently. One person may feel that a room is very comfortable, while another feels chilly. Also, in general, older people like warmer rooms. Thus there is a difference between a teacher's opinion as to a comfortable temperature and the needs of the children. As far as children are concerned, it is probably true that most classrooms are overheated.

The temperature to be maintained in a space will also depend upon the kinds of activities conducted there. Usually building codes recommend a temperature of 68° to 72° for spaces used for sedentary activity. For spaces devoted to moderate activity, such as corridors, temperatures two to four degrees lower are recommended, while in areas of vigorous activity, such as a gymnasium, a temperature of 65° or less may be satisfactory. For obvious reasons, locker and shower rooms are kept much warmer, and air temperatures of 80° to 86° are commonly recommended for swimming pool rooms.

AIR MOVEMENT

It is generally agreed among heating and ventilating authorities that some air movement is necessary. The human body will not be comfortable in a pool of stagnant air. Air movement will prevent pockets of excessive humidity, equalize temperature throughout a given space, and remove odors and vitiated or stale air. During the heating season, for reasons of comfort, the velocity of air movement should not exceed 25 lineal feet per minute. In warm weather comfort will be increased if air velocity is somewhat greater.

HEALTHFUL CONDITIONS

The relationship of heating and ventilating to health is perhaps harder to prove than the relationship to comfort. Whether extreme and rapid fluctuation of temperatures is injurious to health and encourages respiratory infections is debatable. Certainly popular opinion contends that such variations are harmful, but this opinion is supported by some medical authorities and denied by others.

One of the functions of a ventilating system which is related to health is to remove injurious fumes and dust created in laboratories, shops, and other places in the building. In some cases, there is also need to wash or filter the air brought in from outside because of some source of pollution in the neighborhood.

Another health objective of the ventilating system might be to reduce spread of airborne diseases. The purification of air by germicidal lamps or aerosols has been tried in some schools, but its value in school situations has not been established.

MEETING THE OBJECTIVES

The above objectives may be reached by various devices ranging from the simple space heater to complicated systems of heating and ventilating. The system to be adopted for a given building will depend upon many factors, among which are climate, size and type of building, cost, ease of maintenance, continuous availability of trained operating and maintenance staff, and safety. There may be as much objection to overelaboration as to oversimplification. Too many elaborate and expensive systems of ventilation have remained unused in school buildings after a short time, partly because of expense of operation and poor design, but also because of lack of trained personnel to keep them operating properly. Having shut off the ventilating system, the school relies on window ventilation for which the building was not designed. Oversimplification, too, can be a mistake. Dependence on the busy teacher rather than on automatic controls may result in neglect because of the teacher's concern for other things.

The Heating System

TYPES OF SYSTEMS

Unless the heating unit is a device in the room, there must be some means of transporting the heat from the heater to the space to be heated. This is commonly done by forcing steam through pipes, by circulating hot water through pipes, or by moving hot air through ducts by natural or mechanical means. Each of the principal types of heating systems will be discussed briefly.

Direct Radiation

In a direct radiation system, steam or hot water radiators are located in the classrooms, usually under the windows. These may be the conventional cast-iron type or the newer types using finned tubes and other finned radiation surfaces. The radiators should be wall hung for ease of cleaning and should be shielded to promote air circulation around them, to protect those closest to them from too much heat, and to guard against pupils being burned by bumping against them.

Unit Ventilation

The unit ventilator is a combined heating and ventilating unit in the form of a room radiator containing a motor-driven fan, automatic controls, and automatic dampers to regulate the amount of outside air to be admitted and the amount of recirculation. Supplementary wall radiators are usually provided. Continuous fenestration has increased the window area of classrooms and increased the loss of body heat to the colder glass. Newer designs of unit ventilation have, by one means or another, arranged to reduce this discomfort by providing a blanket of warm air over this wall. The unit ventilator has the advantage of providing an independently controlled ventilating system for each classroom without duct work. Disadvantages are that for first-floor rooms the wall ports through which fresh air is admitted are often close to the ground and considerable dust and dirt may be pulled in by the fan. Efficient filters are provided, but they need regular cleaning if trouble is to be avoided. Also, while each unit has the advantage of being independent, there is the disadvantage that each has a motor, controls, a filter, and a damper which need regular servicing and may get out of order. Older models often became noisy after a few years of use, but this objection has largely been overcome in newer models.

The unit ventilator, as it pulls in outside air, creates a slight increase in atmospheric pressure in the room, thereby reducing infiltration of cold air through cracks around the windows. It is usually considered best, however, to relieve this pressure somewhat by providing a small port for its release into the corridor or by using an exhaust shaft discharging into an exhaust plenum and thence through the roof. Often this exhaust port is placed in the wardrobe so that air will be forced through the space and ventilate the pupils' clothing. An alternative, if the pupils' toilet room is located off the classroom, is to exhaust the air through the toilet room, thereby assuring the proper direction of air to prevent toilet room odors from entering the classroom. Similar internal pressure conditions can be created by other systems of ventilation.

The unit ventilator should not be confused with the unit heater, which is simply a heating unit with a fan to blow air across it. The unit heater provides no fresh air supply, may be noisy, and is not recommended for classroom use or for use where fresh air supply and quiet operation are requirements.

Gravity Warm-air Systems

Warm-air systems were prevalent in older school buildings. These buildings were likely to be square in shape or at least very compact and two and a half stories or more in height. Warm air could rise naturally without a fan from the basement location of the furnace up through the building. The use of gravity warm-air furnace systems has largely been discontinued.

Forced Warm-air Systems

Forced warm-air systems are similar in principle to the gravity warm-air furnace except that air is heated, usually at a central point or points, by forcing it to pass over heated steam coils or other heat sources and thence to the rooms. Commonly the central coil does only part of the heating job, and the final boost in air temperature is given by a small steam coil located in the duct just before it opens into the classroom. The smaller coil is controlled by a thermostat in the classroom.

A more recent development of the forced-air system is perimeter heating. This involves forcing warm air under the floor and introducing it into the space to be heated through several openings around the perimeter of the room. Air is exhausted from the room through one or two larger registers high on the inside wall. This is a reversal of the natural convection currents which the gravity system uses. The system has gained popularity for home heating and is being used in some small school buildings.

The Split System

The split system is a combination of the forced warm-air system and direct radiation in the room. The air supply is warmed to a predetermined temperature by a thermostatically controlled steam coil and forced into the room by one or more central fans. Air exhausted from the room is returned to the fan room and recirculated with some fresh air added. Air washers, filters, etc., may be included in the air circulatory system, if needed. The radiators in the room supply additional heat and are thermostatically controlled to regulate room temperature. Such a system can be very satisfactory if properly designed, operated, and maintained. It does involve rather complicated and elaborate controls, and for successful long-term operation requires the continuous availability of a well-trained maintenance staff. There have been other objections to this system, partly due to faulty design. Among these are:

1. Because air is recirculated, odors from science laboratories or from homemaking or cafeteria kitchens have been circulated throughout the building in some cases.

2. Successful and efficient operation, depending on proper balancing of air supply, is hard to achieve.

3. With one central fan and heating coil for a fairly large building, long duct runs from the fan to the end rooms are necessary. There is a considerable drop in air temperature between the time the air leaves the fan room and the time it is delivered in a distant room. Theoretically, the wall radiation controlled by the room thermostat should make up this difference. Actually, it may not, and occupants of some rooms may complain about cold drafts. Such complaints may result in increasing the air temperature, thereby overheating the rooms closer to the fan. This could be corrected by booster coils in the duct as described above, or it could be corrected by providing several fan rooms and coils, perhaps with each fan supplying four to six classrooms.

It has been customary in some split systems to use the corridor as a return air space, thereby eliminating about half of the duct work. This is not recommended, since it may result in greater fire hazards as explained in an earlier chapter.

Radiant Panel Heating

The radiant panel system heats a space by raising the temperature of one or more of its interior surfaces. Most installations have been in floors, although there is no theoretical reason why the ceiling or side walls (or all of them) could not be used. This system has recently been finding increased use in schools, especially for kindergarten rooms, automotive shops, locker rooms, and other rooms where it is particularly desired not to have cold floors. This is really a direct radiation system, except that instead of having a small radiation surface at a high temperature, there is a larger radiation surface, the whole floor or ceiling, at a lower temperature. Usually hot water is used as the transfer medium, although hot air has been used in a few installations.

The panel heating system requires careful and expert engineering. Properly designed and installed, it appears to have several advantages, such as:

1. Increased comfort of the occupants, together with a lack of consciousness that there is any heating system.

2. Steady temperature.

3. Reduction of temperature differential between floor and ceiling.

4. Warm floors.
5. Lack of violent drafts if windows are opened, especially in one-story buildings.
6. Increase in flexibility resulting from the fact that the system is built into the floor or ceiling structure and does not dictate placement of dividing walls.
7. It is claimed that comfort can be attained at lower temperatures and that operating economies will be obtained.

There are also certain disadvantages, including:

1. The system depends upon a radiating surface, usually a concrete floor slab, attaining a certain temperature and by radiation warming other surfaces. This takes considerable time. It has been found best to keep a building at a steady heat over weekends because of the time lag in bringing it up to a comfortable temperature on Monday morning. Also, the building will cool off as slowly as it heats, and a sudden increase in outdoor temperature may leave the building too warm. The use of outdoor thermostats responsive to changes in outdoor temperature is only a partial correction.
2. In cold climates, unless there is very careful engineering, including an adequate and properly adjusted system of controls, it has been found that floors become too warm for comfort. Actually, if the system is working as intended, the room should be comfortable, and even on a very cold day the floor should not feel warm to the touch. If the floor temperature exceeds the skin temperature of the feet, about 85°, the feet become uncomfortably warm. Some people now believe that in cold climates, reliance should not be placed on floor panel heating alone.
3. If the heating pipes are buried in the concrete floor slab, any leakage will be difficult to repair.
4. If mechanical ventilation is necessary, the cost of the radiant system, plus the cost of the tempered air system, may be excessive.

Probably a better system for a severe climate would be to rely on the warm panel for only part of the heat and to use tempered air to make up the difference, thereby providing for quicker adjustment to outdoor temperature changes. This would also provide ventilation and, if the floor panel is supplying only part of the heat, the floor would not need to be too warm.

Another form of heating which seems to have promise and to answer some of the objections to floor panels is using the ceiling as a radiation surface. It is believed that the ceiling can be kept at a higher temperature than the floor with no discomfort to the occupants, and that the heating or cooling time lag can also be reduced. It is also claimed that the floor is heated somewhat by absorbing radiant heat from the ceiling. Ventilation can be provided through a perforated ceiling or by other means.

Further progress in the field of school heating is needed and will no doubt occur. There should be constant endeavor by engineers to provide systems which will be economical of operation, simple to maintain, and adequate to the job for the situation in which they are installed.

TEMPERATURE CONTROLS

Each room in a school building should have its individual thermostat controlling the temperature of that room. This may seem unduly expensive, and it may be argued that four or five rooms with the same exposure on the same floor and in the same wing could be controlled by one thermostat. This neglects the fact that there will be different numbers of people in each room, thereby changing the heating need. There may also be activities in one room different from those in another, or one room may have more heat loss than another, especially if it is an end room. If all are on the same thermostat, these varying conditions cannot be met. Thermostats should be securely mounted and covered to prevent tampering. In gymnasiums or similar places, they should be protected by substantial shields.

THE HEATING PLANT

Previous chapters have discussed heating plant location and its separation from the rest of the building by fireproofing. A few other matters need consideration. First, there is the question of whether, for a given building, there should be one heating plant or several. A few years ago, the opinion would have been practically unanimous in favor of one plant. To-day, opinions would vary. In former days, coal was universally used as a fuel, usually hand fired. This tied the plant to a central coal pile and dictated one plant. Today, automatic firing with oil or gas is much more prevalent. Also, buildings today are likely to be spread out into several fingers or wings. There is considerable heat loss in moving heat long distances. It may be wise in some cases, especially where a building is to be expanded wing by wing as the population grows, for each wing to have its own small, automatically fired plant. If a central plant is to be constructed in such a case it must, in order to allow for future expansion, be built much larger than it originally needs to be, thereby tying up scarce dollars in space and equipment which may not be used for some years.

On the other hand, there may be operating economies in having one plant rather than several, even with automatic firing. Also, having several plants necessitates several sets of boiler controls to service and maintain, a multiplication of things to get out of order. In any heating plant there is also the potential of fire and explosion. Several plants certainly multiply this danger. The question should receive careful consideration, and the advice of the architect's engineers will be of great value. One solution may be wise in one case and unwise in another, depending upon climate, size and type of building, and other factors.

ZONING

Whether there is one heating plant or several, provision should be made for zoning the building so that the parts likely to be used outside of regular school hours can be heated independently. Although it is probably unwise to let the temperature of any part of the building fall too far during the night, it is also unnecessary to have to heat all rooms to a comfortable temperature when only a part of the building is used. "Day-night" thermostats can be used effectively with the night temperature set 8° to 10° below the day temperature and with provision for maintaining the day temperature during evening hours in any particular room if desired.

Space which should be zoned for independent heating should certainly include the auditorium and music room, the gymnasium and related facilities, the cafeteria, the shops, and the administrative suite. Local study may indicate others, such as the library, a few classrooms, the homemaking suite, etc., depending on anticipated usage.

Methods of Ventilating

IN FORMER years, it was believed that there was something unhealthful, if not poisonous, about air in a room occupied by a number of people. This earlier belief was reflected in state ventilating codes requiring 30 cubic feet of fresh air per occupant per minute. Although the necessity for such a fresh air supply has been disproved, some state codes still require it. The authors know of school buildings of considerable size in severe northern climates where this much air is taken into the building at a temperature of zero or below, heated to a comfortable temperature, pushed through the rooms, and immediately discharged to the outdoors without recirculation. The fuel cost is tremendous, yet it is not evident that children in such buildings are any more healthy than others in buildings where the ventilation system is much more moderate.

However, one has but to enter a classroom full of children during the heating season in a building where there is no ventilation and where classroom windows are closed to realize that some sort of ventilation is necessary. The room is usually too warm, the humidity is high, children are listless, and the odor is unpleasant. Just how much air movement and how much fresh air are needed are questions upon which there is no firm agreement, although 10 to 15 cubic feet of air per minute per person, or two to three air changes per hour, are commonly recommended.

Ventilating methods in general may be roughly classified as window ventilation, mechanical exhaust, mechanical supply, and various combinations of two or more of these methods. For selection of the kind or kinds of ventilating to be provided, the planner must consider such things as climate, activities to be carried on in a space, safety, cost of installation and operation, simplicity and ease of maintenance, co-ordination with the heating system, and size, shape, and type of building.

WINDOW VENTILATION

Window ventilation has the advantage of being the least expensive. There are no ducts, coils, dampers, motors, or fans. All one has to do is open a window and natural air currents will provide some air change. It can be successful in some types of buildings, if the building is specifically designed for it. This type of ventilation finds widest acceptance in the warmer climates and in one-story buildings.

With the increase of one-story construction and bilaterally lighted buildings throughout the country, this method of ventilating, once almost abandoned in northern climates, has gained favor again. It has been found that it can work fairly well when windows are carefully designed to prevent drafts and when openings are provided in the opposite wall to make possible a gentle cross ventilation. This seems especially true in radiant-heated buildings.

Twice in the above paragraphs it has been stated that window ventilation can work well. It can, but it seldom does because it depends upon the human element. Teachers are busy people. Working with children takes all their attention. Furthermore, the nature of the senses of human beings is such that they become accustomed easily to an odor or to stuffiness in the room, especially if it comes on gradually. So, although conditions may seem bad to a person coming in from outside, the occupants of the room have not realized it, and the windows are not opened. In some rooms, where teachers understand the need and systematically include proper ventilation as part of their room procedure, conditions will be fairly good. In other cases in the same building, the result will be just the opposite.

MECHANICAL EXHAUST

With mechanical exhaust systems fans are used to pull air from the classroom to the outdoors. Infiltration through cracks around windows or through open windows is relied upon for air supply. Exhaust from the classroom may be through the wardrobe, thence by duct to a plenum, and thence to the out-of-doors. In some instances, air passes from the classroom to the corridor and then out by a corridor ceiling exhaust fan.

Such a system may be an improvement over straight window ventilation in that positive exhaust is provided. But there are objections, including:

1. There is no planned fresh air supply. With the powerful exhaust fan operating, there must be a supply from somewhere to replace the exhaust air. Cases have been known where the exhaust fan, when turned on, reversed the draft in the boiler room chimney.

2. There is little provision for equal ventilation of all rooms. If the total capacity of the fan is a given number of cubic feet per minute, and if windows are opened in one or two rooms, the fan will get all of its supply from those rooms and there will be little or no exhaust from the other rooms.

This method of ventilation is, however, a proper way to ventilate a toilet room, a locker room, a laboratory, or a kitchen, where the intent is to pull objectionable odors from these rooms and to make sure that the direction of air is from the building through the room to the outside, rather than the reverse.

MECHANICAL SUPPLY

With mechanical supply systems tempered air is supplied to the rooms and stale air pushed from the rooms by incoming air. Recirculation may be varied from 100 percent to none, depending upon temperature and needs. Air may be supplied through ducts by a central fan, or it may be supplied to each room individually by a supply fan in the room. The unit ventilator system, the split system, and the forced warm-air system, described earlier in this chapter, are examples.

SPECIAL VENTILATING PROBLEMS

Certain parts of the school building have special ventilating problems. Auditoriums and other places where people assemble need ample ventilation. Here the problem may be largely one of cooling. If the room is heated when empty to a comfortable temperature and then is filled with hundreds of people, the combined heat generated from their bodies will raise the temperature to an uncomfortable level unless provisions are made for lowering temperatures by ventilation. Prime considerations in the ventilation of such spaces are quietness of operation and avoidance of drafts. In the best installations, tempered air enters at low velocity at many points in the room rather than at high velocity at a few points. Also, deflectors are used to prevent the air from blowing directly upon the occupants. For quietness, fans should be remote and there should be flexible sound-breaking connections between the fan and the duct work. Fans should be of a quiet type.

Special ventilation will be needed in the shops to remove dust and welding and paint fumes. In the automotive and certain other shops special attention should be given to a positive means of removing exhaust gases from internal combustion engines. Carbon monoxide poisoning is a real hazard here.

Locker rooms are usually less effectively ventilated than any other part of a school building. The high humidity and the storage of gym clothing combine to create a difficult problem. Its solution is a technical engineering problem beyond the scope of this book. However, a few comments of a nontechnical nature can be made, as follows:

1. The system should be just as continuously operated as any other part of the system and as much longer as necessary to keep undesirable odors to a minimum.

2. Air from the locker rooms should be exhausted directly to the outdoors and should never enter the recirculating system.

3. Supply openings should be so located that air does not blow upon the occupants. Air blowing upon a wet body will cause rapid evaporation and chilling.

4. The lockers and baskets in a locker room should be so designed and located that air can circulate around them.

Other spaces which require special and separate exhaust ventilation are toilet rooms, teachers' lounges, science laboratories, homemaking rooms, and cafeteria kitchens.

Sanitary Facilities

CHILDREN learn during every waking moment. Much of their learning comes from their environment. The kinds of sanitary facilities provided in a school building have a relationship to what children are learning. For example, if toilet rooms are in dark, damp, basement areas, or if they are odorous and cannot be kept clean, they are certainly not teaching children cleanliness and proper mental attitudes toward the human body and its functions. Realization of this principle has had a marked effect on location and design of sanitary facilities for schools. Good sanitary facilities are of primary importance from this as well as from the health and safety standpoint.

WATER SUPPLY

An adequate and safe water supply is a first step in providing proper sanitary facilities. When schools are built in villages or cities with public water systems, the difficulty of the problem is reduced. If there is no public water system, the provision of an adequate and safe supply is a first consideration in selecting a school site. Usually a local health department can advise regarding the kind of water which can be obtained in a given location. The design of the well, its capacity, and its location are all important. Sanitary engineering services should be utilized.

With a private supply, the water should be tested frequently for safety. With either a public or private supply, the water analysis should be known so that steps can be taken, if necessary, to soften the water and thus to eliminate stains on fixtures and provide for better soap utilization in cleaning. Such water analysis will also indicate what kind of treatment, if any, for use of the water in steam or hot water boilers.

Assuming that an adequate and safe supply can be delivered to the school grounds, there are still a few other considerations. What will be the water demand by the school at any one time? This will determine the size of the main line entering the school building. If the main line is too small, and it often is, water pressure will be inadequate to operate drinking fountains properly and to operate flush valves on toilet fixtures. Water demands in a school are spasmodic, especially in a secondary school where classes move periodically. Good engineering design will specify oversized water lines.

Hot Water Supply

Every school building should have a hot water supply. It should, of course, be available in all lavatories and wherever else it is needed. The hot or warm water should be immediately available upon opening the tap. This can be accomplished by insulating the supply line and by providing a hot water loop around the building with hot water circulated by a pump. It will then be necessary to run the water only out of the riser before it becomes hot. Adequate thermostatic controls should be provided to prevent obtaining scalding water at a general use tap. For special high temperature needs, such as for dishwashing in the cafeteria, a special booster heater can be provided.

Drinking Fountains

Many schools have too few drinking fountains. The National Council on Schoolhouse Construction recommends a minimum of one on each floor with a ratio of one to 75 children.[1] Some state codes call for one per 100 pupils. These standards are often violated.

Recently, with the development of the self-contained classroom, it has become common practice to have a drinking fountain in each classroom, which is a decided improvement. Besides having one in each classroom, there should be at least one in the corridor of each wing of the building. For economy of plumbing it is common practice to locate those in the corridor close to the toilet rooms. Fountains should never be located in the toilet room itself or in combination with a faucet. It is better to have several individual fountains, widely separated, than to have one location with multiple nozzles. When fountains are located in classrooms it is common practice, for economy reasons, to place a drinking fountain nozzle at one end of a work sink, separate from the regular faucets, but using the same drain. This is probably fairly satisfactory, if the height and location are such that the smallest children can reach it. A separate fixture is better.

Additional drinking fountains should be located in locker rooms, the gymnasium, the shop, and the music room. There should also be one or more of a frost proof type convenient to the playground. When there is a lobby at the entrance to the building or in connection with an auditorium or gymnasium, one or more fountains should be located in each lobby.

When situated in corridors, fountains should be as completely recessed

[1] National Council on Schoolhouse Construction, *Guide for Planning School Plants*. Nashville, Tenn.: The Council, 1953, p. 135.

as practically possible. Electric water cooler fountains are now coming into use in school buildings. Space should be provided for recessing them, leaving adequate space on all sides of the cooler for air circulation.

Drinking fountains should be of a smooth, easily cleaned material. The nozzle should be designed to prevent the mouth of the user from coming into contact with it or the water from falling back upon the nozzle. To prevent possible back siphonage, the outlet of the nozzle should be located above the rim. Practically all drinking fountains which anyone would consider using in schools are now designed this way. But in practice many of them do not work well. Usually this is not due to any flaw in the fountain, although adjustment of valves may be needed, but rather to insufficient water pressure. The fountains are commonly used most between class periods. At the same time, flush valves in toilet rooms are being operated, the water pressure at the drinking fountain is inadequate, and all that is obtained is a dribble. People, attempting to get a drink, will place their mouths so that they touch the nozzle, thereby defeating the purpose of the fountain design. Either the fountains should have a separate supply line from the water main or the total supply to that area of the building should be more adequate.

Hose Bibs

If custodians are to be expected to work efficiently, there must be conveniently located hose bibs. One with a lockable handle is necessary in each general toilet room. There should also be frequent hose bibs outside the building so that long runs of hose for lawn watering will not be needed.

SEWAGE DISPOSAL

The ability to have adequate, safe, and trouble-free sewage disposal facilities should be investigated whenever a school site is being selected. Whenever possible, connection should be made to a public sewer. If the school has to provide its own disposal facilities, the design will depend upon contour of the site, soil conditions, and other factors. Care should be exercised not to locate septic tanks and tile fields where future building extensions and driveways are likely to be placed. This again argues for a well-conceived total plan for any site, with possible future developments receiving adequate consideration.

The design of such facilities is a technical problem, and expert services should be utilized by the architect. There should be a careful checking of local and state codes and close cooperation with the health department having jurisdiction. The school should certainly not be guilty of violating good health, conservation, and stream purification practices in this or any other respect.

TOILET ROOMS

The location, adequacy, and design of toilet rooms is an important part of the planning of any school building. With good planning, embarrassment can be avoided and constructive mental and sex hygiene attitudes can be fostered. Improperly done, the results can be just the opposite.

Location

It has been common practice for many years to place toilet facilities next to kindergarten rooms and, to a somewhat lesser extent, first-grade rooms for use by the children of those rooms only. Recently, there has developed a practice of placing toilet facilities adjacent to every elementary school classroom. Small toilet rooms off the corridor are provided for adult use and for emergency use by children.

The trend toward classroom toilets appears to be sound. It is certainly more in keeping with the way children have been brought up in the home. It is a known fact that some children cannot use a general toilet room in the presence of others. Having a toilet off each room can be as natural a situation as it would be in a home. There need be no waiting until a recess period, requesting permission, or lining up in the corridor to wait for facilities to be available. Furthermore, the room toilet is convenient for supervision by the teacher.

Different designs have developed for room toilets. One practice, where a number of classrooms are lined up in a row, is to have at either end of the classroom a toilet for each sex, with two classrooms sharing each toilet except for the end ones. This has worked out quite well in some cases and is certainly an improvement over the general toilets. The principal objection is that when two classrooms share the toilet, there is shared responsibility for its management, with some possibility of embarrassment and friction. An alternative to this scheme is to provide a separate, one-fixture toilet room for each sex off each classroom. This meets the objection to the shared toilet but requires more fixtures. Another alternative is simply to provide one single-fixture toilet room off each classroom, to be used by both sexes. This at first may seem radical until it is remembered that this is the normal situation in every home. With sensible treatment, this scheme can work very well. It will actually result in a need for fewer fixtures than any other scheme, including the general toilet plan. Often the toilet room has no wash bowl, as the work sink in the classroom can be used for handwashing.

When classroom toilets are not used, it is certainly desirable to have separate general toilet rooms for the younger children, especially if secondary school and elementary age children are to be housed in the same building. General toilets should be located close to where the children are, and there should be a toilet room for each sex on each floor or in each major division of the building. Boys' and girls' toilets are commonly located next to each other with pipe space between. A janitor's closet is placed between the two entrance doors with pipe space accessible from the janitor's closet. The janitor's closet will include a low rim service sink of nonabsorptive material and with high faucets so that pails can be filled with hot or cold water as needed. Such an arrangement is economical of plumbing. It is common practice to place one toilet room above another in a multistory building, another economical practice in regard to plumbing lines and ventilating ducts. However, with the growing practice of having a sink in each classroom, it is desirable to run plumbing lines through the building, and there can be more freedom in locating toilet rooms.

Toilets for public use should be located adjacent to the auditorium and to the gymnasium. In some small schools this has not been done, with the result that sports fans invade the locker rooms between halves of a basketball game to use toilets there and to hear what the coach says to the players. This is hardly a desirable situation. One solution is to locate general toilet rooms for pupils so that they can be used by those attending functions in the auditorium or gymnasium. Other locations where toilets are sometimes provided are the administrative suite, the guidance offices, the health suite or clinic, the teachers' room, the custodians' quarters, and the cafeteria help's quarters. Other locations may also be necessary and desirable, such as in or near the shops, the homemaking suite, the auditorium stage, and the music suite.

School playgrounds are, and should be, used for evening, week-end, and summer recreation purposes. It is good practice to plan the school building to facilitate this and to provide general toilet rooms so located and arranged that they can be used by the school when the school program is in operation and be available for use from the playgrounds at other times without opening the rest of the building. Sometimes this is done by placing these rooms at the end of a corridor, with a corridor gate separating them from the rest of the school. Another arrangement is to have doors directly to the outdoors from these toilet rooms as well as doors directly to the corridor. Either set of doors can be locked as the occasion demands.

Number of Fixtures

The number of toilet fixtures to be provided in relation to the pupil capacity of the building has long been a question. The literature on school-plant planning and most state or local codes establish standards or regulations. Each, however, is somewhat of a compromise. Some studies have indicated that commonly accepted standards are in excess of need.[1] Actually, the number required depends greatly upon the policies concerning use. With free and informal use, fewer fixtures are necessary. If regimentation exists or if the program is departmentalized, use will be spasmodic. There will not be enough fixtures at the time of peak load, but during the other times there will be very low utilization. In the elementary school, the classroom toilet provides a sensible answer.

Toilet Room Finishes and Arrangement

Sanitary finishes should be used throughout a toilet room. Floors should be of smooth, nonslip, and nonabsorptive materials. A floor drain should be provided in each general toilet room, although with stall type urinals and with the floor pitched toward them, a drain may not be necessary in the boys' room. A drain will prevent the floor and adjacent areas from being flooded if a toilet fixture becomes clogged, and will also make thorough cleaning easier. Walls of toilet rooms should also be built of smooth nonabsorptive material such as glazed tile. Joints between floor and wall should be rounded to facilitate cleaning. Separate and positive exhaust ventilation should be provided.

Doors to toilet rooms should be arranged to prevent any view of the interior of the room from the corridor, or some sort of fixed screen should be provided. Stalls should be provided for water closets and partitions should be of hard, smooth, easily cleaned material.

To suggest use, it is good practice to locate the handwashing facilities between the toilet fixtures and the door. Adequate daylight should be provided, either by obscure glass windows or by means of top lighting. In the case of classroom toilets, daylight is sometimes provided by installing several glass blocks in the wall between the classroom and the toilet room.

In general toilets, mirrors, and shelves for books should be provided. Although a mirror over the lavatory may be desirable, it is also good practice to place one on another wall, perhaps over the bookshelf, thereby reducing congestion around the wash bowls.

[1] American Council on Education, Committee on School Plant Research, *The Utilization of School Sanitary Fa-cilities*. Series 7, School Plant Research, Vol. 6, No. 3. Washington, D. C.: The Council, 1942. (Out of print.)

Water Closets and Urinals

Water closets should be of vitreous china with elongated bowls and open-front seats. Pressure type flush valves should be used if sufficient water pressure is available, otherwise the common tank is indicated. In some locations the quiet type should be used to avoid embarrassment. The scheme of an automatic flushing arrangement connected with a toilet seat is not favored. Water closets are now available in the 10-, 13-, 14-, and 15-inch heights from floor to rim. The 13-inch size is recommended for elementary schools and the 14-inch size for secondary schools.

Either the stall type or the wall hung type of urinal appears to be satisfactory. Flushing may be by individual fixture, or automatically timed for the battery of urinals.

Handwashing Facilities

A totally acceptable solution to the problem of providing handwashing facilities in pupil toilet rooms in public schools has yet to be found. Various designs have been tried. All have more or less serious drawbacks. The following characteristics are desired:

1. Tempered water should be available through a mixing faucet upon the operation of the valve. There must be no danger of scalding and one should not have to wait a considerable period for the warm water.

2. The valve-operating mechanism should be such that both hands can be free while water is running. One cannot soap and scrub his hands by rubbing them together if one hand is used to hold a faucet open. Yet unless there is automatic closing, the water may carelessly be left running.

3. Water should flow over the hands and down the drain. It should not be possible to close the drain. At home a stopper for the drain or a closing valve may be practical; in a pupils' general toilet room in a school it is not.

4. The handwashing station should preferably be an individual one. When two or more children are using one station, mischief is invited.

5. The mechanism should be trouble free even with hard usage. Hard water deposits should not impair its functioning. Finishes should be smooth, and cleaning should be easy.

6. The total arrangement should be of a size to fit the age ranges of children using it.

7. The arrangement should be economical of space.

CHAPTER 23

ECONOMY

Achieving Economy Through a Building Survey
Achieving Economy Through Good Educational Specifications
Achieving Economy Through Good Architectural Work
Achieving Economy Through Sound Financing
Fallacies in Cost Comparisons

T HROUGHOUT this volume the authors have advocated good planning and have written about a host of desirable features and attributes of good school buildings. In so doing they may have created the impression in the minds of some readers that good planning is expensive—that perhaps the best thing for a board of education of modest means to do is to employ an architect who is known to be able to design substantial, low-cost buildings, and to forget all the falderal of surveys, educational specifications, and planning committees which will only pile up additional building costs.

The authors are not insensitive to building costs, but they do not believe that the road to economy lies in lack of planning. On the contrary, they believe that the need for thorough planning is even greater when funds are limited because a community of little resources cannot afford to spend its money for the wrong things. They believe this because in their experience they have witnessed so many times the unfortunate results of lack of planning, of opportunistic construction, and of the search for cheapness. They know that lack of planning has resulted in the waste of public funds for low-cost buildings that are expensive to maintain and operate, that are unsafe and unhealthful, that are a hindrance rather than an aid to the educational program, and that are in the wrong places.

There is today a vast backlog of school building needs resulting from a long period of very little schoolhouse construction, high postwar building prices, shifts in population, and high birth rates. The ability of school districts to raise funds for construction purposes has lagged far behind the increasing needs. Tax valuations have not kept pace with rising costs, and state legislatures have been slow to recognize and close the gap. It is this situation which tempts so many boards of education to accept the gold brick of cheapness instead of the true gold of real economy.

Real economy in a school building may be defined as the most value for every dollar spent. It is compounded of many elements, the most important of which is the extent to which the building will meet the needs of the school program throughout its useful life. Also, the truly economical building will safeguard the thousands of children who will use it throughout the years—it will provide a safe, healthful, and emotionally satisfying environment for young people. Finally, the truly economical building is one which makes the community a better place in which to live and thus attracts new families and creates new employment opportunities.

It is the purpose of this chapter to point out the major opportunities for achieving economy in each of the principal phases of planning and conducting a school building program.

Achieving Economy Through a Building Survey

THE school building survey has been discussed at length in the early chapters of this book as the first step in the planning of a school building, and it is here that the first opportunities for economy arise. To discuss completely these opportunities would require repetition of much of what has been written in these earlier chapters. For this reason, attention will be centered here on only a few of the ways in which the survey can contribute to the wise expenditure of building needs.

DETERMINING NATURE AND EXTENT OF PROGRAM

One of the first steps in a school building survey is to determine the nature and extent of the school program for which housing must be provided. If building funds are scarce and are committed to a particular building project without such review of the entire school program, the risk is great that the money will be wasted to some extent by spending it for the wrong things, that so much money will be spent for one purpose that other needed facilities cannot be provided, or that the money will be spread over so many projects that none can be of satisfactory quality.

One decision which must be made with respect to program is the age range to be served. Should the school district operate nursery schools and kindergartens? Should it offer a community college program and adult education classes? In fact, one might ask whether it is able to support a high school, because there are thousands of school districts throughout the country which operate high schools so small that they cannot provide a good program at reasonable cost. When the educational program is extended beyond the resources of the community, the taxpayer is not likely to get his money's worth because neither the building facilities nor the funds for current operation will permit a suitable quality of education for the dollars spent. It would be far better in such cases to restrict the program to those activities which the community can support reasonably well, or to join with another district to provide a sufficient tax base for the more complete program.

The building survey will direct attention to similar questions in regard to the services to be provided for whatever age groups are encompassed. It will, for example, raise questions regarding the nature and extent of the health service program, guidance, recreation, and other noninstructional activities, as well as about the instructional program itself. Again, these various services must be examined in order to avoid overcommitment of funds to one at the expense of others and to avoid a program that is spread so thin that no part of it can be adequately financed. It is better to do well what is done, and to leave the rest until later, rather than to do a lot of things so inadequately that the program suffers throughout the lifetime of the building.

Finally, the same questions should be raised with respect to various community services of the schools, and there are the same risks involved in proceeding without surveying the total problem. In all these questions of program it is essential that a long-range view be taken so that there is a better chance of having building facilities adaptable to future changes in program.

DETERMINING SIZES AND LOCATIONS OF BUILDINGS

While there has been a considerable public awakening to the problem of increasing enrollments, there is no easy way to predict the magnitude of the increase or the shifts of population that will affect the future sizes and locations of school buildings. The building survey, while far from infallible in this respect, provides the best available guide to the number and distribution of pupils in future years. If building funds are spent without such study, several major risks are incurred: (1) more building capacity may be provided than will be needed for many years to come; (2) a building may grow by small additions to the point where it has so large an enrollment that the quality of education suffers; (3) opportunities to buy needed sites at reasonable prices may be overlooked until it is too late; and (4) buildings may be erected in the wrong places and then not fully utilized. Surely none of these is the way to economy.

DETERMINING USE OF EXISTING FACILITIES

A third major way in which a school building survey promotes economy is by promoting the most efficient use of existing buildings worthy of continued service. It is often possible through careful study to increase the utilization of existing space by shifting the attendance district boundaries or changing the grades assigned to it. Also, it is frequently possible to get more educational value from an existing building by changing its use, or the use of some part of it, to a purpose for which it is better adapted. Careful study may result in inexpensive remodeling that will pay big dividends in improved educational opportunities, or that will make it unnecessary to erect new facilities.

There are many cases where the taxpayers can get more for their money if the school and other community agencies cooperate in providing certain facilities, and thus avoid needless duplication. Common examples are playgrounds and auditoriums. The school building survey should call attention to these opportunities for economy in the use of public funds.

Achieving Economy Through Good Educational Specifications

It is in the preparation of educational specifications for the individual building, perhaps, that there is most fear that thorough planning will lead to a higher priced building. The cooperative planning approach advocated earlier in this book will bring into the process many persons whose wishes may exceed the community's financial resources, or, more frequently, outrun the community's seeming willingness to spend money for school purposes. If the wishes of all these participants are merely added together, the cost is very likely to be quite high. But, even more serious, the building that would thus be secured would not necessarily be educationally efficient over a period of years. In the educational planning process, as indicated in Chapter 7, full opportunity should be given for the wishes and hopes of all participants to emerge and receive full consideration, but as the planning proceeds the attention should shift from wishes to needs and from present needs to probable future needs. Only when there is a thorough understanding of the building facilities needed now and in the foreseeable future will it be possible to design a building that will provide the most educational value for every dollar spent—in other words, that will be truly economical and not merely cheap.

The development of educational specifications per se will not assure economy, but good educational planning will avoid, on the one hand, the holding down of costs without regard to the effect on education and, on the other hand, the inflation of costs or unwise use of funds to satisfy the whims and impulses of inexperienced participants in the planning process. Above all, good educational planning will lead to the use of limited resources for the facilities most likely to promote the desired educational program in the foreseeable future and avoid wasting money to build for an unwanted educational program.

Achieving Economy Through Good Architectural Work

THE wise board of education will insist upon the best architectural service because it will realize that the costs of initial construction and of operation and maintenance over the years will be largely determined by the architect's competence, honesty, and application to the problem at hand. When costs are high and funds are scarce, there will be a great temptation to listen to the practitioner who tries to sell his services on the basis that he can build cheaper or that he will work for a smaller fee than other architects. But it is the truly creative and capable architect who will produce the most economical building, for he will strive not only to keep within the budget but also to provide the building that best satisfies the educational requirements and is economical to operate and maintain. When the good architect is forced to compromise to keep costs down, he will choose wisely his methods of achieving lower costs and will frankly tell his client what he has done. He will accept the challenge and do his utmost to solve the problems in his client's interest. He will save many times over the small difference between his fee and that of a less capable architect. Excellent architectural service is an excellent means to true economy.

SPECIFIC ARCHITECTURAL APPROACHES TO ECONOMY

The specific ways in which an architect can economize in the use of his client's money are legion, and no attempt will be made to discuss them here except in general terms. Six broad avenues of approach are suggested and explained briefly in the numbered paragraphs that follow: [1]

1. *Shape and Perimeter of Building.* The amount of wall construction required to enclose a given amount of floor space will vary with

[1] For a detailed discussion of ways of reducing costs of construction, see: Caudill, William W., *Toward Better* *School Design.* New York: F. W. Dodge Corporation, 1954, Chap. 4.

the shape of the structure. It follows, then, that the architect must consider the length of the perimeter of the building, if he seeks to avoid high costs. This does not mean, of course, that he seeks only to achieve a short perimeter, for there may be instances where the economy of a short perimeter is lost because of structural problems it creates. Also there are objectives other than low cost that must be satisfied. For example, the architect will seek to provide good natural lighting and ventilation, and he will strive for certain groupings of facilities in the interest of safety, noise control, efficient functioning of the program, etc. In general, irregular shapes, extra corners, bay windows, and other irregularities of building outline add to the cost, but something more than a rectangular box may be justified for aesthetic or other reasons.

2. *Economical Use of Floor Space.* The amount of floor space is largely determined by the educational specifications, and thus is often beyond the control of the architect. However, the architect can often suggest ways of eliminating little used spaces, and still leave the decision to be made by the educational planners. This is particularly true if the architect participates in the preparation of the educational specifications, as he should do. Once the educational specifications are established, the architect can still achieve substantial economies by his arrangement of the spaces within the building and on the site. He can, for example, reduce corridor areas in various ways, or he can design them to serve other functions in addition to circulation.

3. *Choice of Materials.* The cost of construction can easily be reduced by cheapening the hundreds of items that go into the building. The architect can, for example, use a lighter roof, a cheaper floor covering, or less expensive hardware. In choosing the materials the architect must always keep in mind the effect upon the efficiency and cost of operation and maintenance throughout the life of the building, as well as upon the cost of construction. He must also consider the objectives with respect to aesthetics, safety, etc.

4. *Methods of Construction.* The building industry is constantly developing new methods of construction that reduce the amount of labor or material required. The good architect can save money for his client by keeping fully abreast of these developments and designing buildings to make use of the most economical construction techniques that satisfy the other objectives.

5. *Complete Drawings and Specifications.* The bid which a contractor makes on a school building project is based chiefly upon his estimate of the cost of materials and labor required to erect it. If the drawings and specifications are incomplete or vague with respect to what is required, or if the architect has a reputation among contractors for annoying and delaying practices during construction, the better contractors will either not bid or will submit higher bids in self-protection.

6. *Bidding Procedures.* The good architect can often save his client money by advising him well on the time of bidding, since the best prices will be obtained when contractors are not busy with other work. However, if the building planning has started too late, as is so often true, delay in asking for bids may be inadvisable, and this door to economy is closed to the architect. The architect can also be of service by inviting reputable contractors to bid, thus securing more competition and possibly more competent workmanship as well.

TEMPORARY BUILDINGS

In a search for the maximum value for building dollars, boards of education are often urged to erect temporary structures. Those who advocate them usually have good intentions. They feel that a temporary building can meet a critical need more quickly and more cheaply, and that it can be replaced in "a few years when things are better." These arguments sometimes seem quite plausible, but experience has been that the time never seems quite appropriate to abandon the temporary building. There are in use today "temporary" frame buildings erected shortly after World War I.

In judging the economic aspects of these buildings, primary attention must be placed on whether the school district is getting full value for every dollar spent. If a temporary building is used for only a few years, its cost per year may be quite high in comparison with a permanent building, unless the temporary building can be sold or used for another purpose to advantage. If the temporary structure is used for a long period of time, the cost per year must include the additional costs for operation and maintenance. Above all, these costs must be considered in relation to health and safety standards and the impact upon the educational program. In all too many cases these structures have been drab and uninspiring and have seriously violated minimum standards of health and safety.

There are, to be sure, some situations where the need for a permanent building is uncertain. If the children involved cannot be satisfactorily housed elsewhere until the uncertainty can be resolved, temporary buildings may be the answer. However, often a better solution would be the erection of a more permanent structure that could be readily converted to some other use.

STOCK PLANS

The stock plan idea also has appeal to the financially hard-pressed community. The uninformed layman feels that there must be some standard answer to what a good school building is and that, once determined, it can just as well be repeated everywhere at considerable saving. He has seen the savings made through mass production of other commodities and does not see why they cannot be achieved in school buildings. But each school must fit the community and the neighborhood it is to serve. Each building must be designed to fit a program. It must fit the site on which it is to be located. And each school should be an improvement over every other school.

There may be cases where a large school system may build two or three identical buildings. If the sites are about the same, if the program is the same, and if the capacities are to be the same, there may be some justification for use of the same plans. There may be some savings, especially if the buildings are to be constructed at the same time by the same contractor.

But this does not mean that it would be wise to adopt one or more stock plans to be used on a state, regional, or national basis, or, in most cases, on a local basis. Such a scheme would violate practically all of the principles of school building planning which have evolved through years of experience. It would tend to mechanize education, freeze a program, and stop progress.

It does not follow that every time a building is planned, all that has previously been learned should be thrown away. Of course, good solutions can be repeated, if they fit the new situations. Much has been learned, for example, about what constitutes a good elementary school classroom. This learning should be utilized while improvements are sought. This does not imply a complete stock plan or standard building.

There is a lag between scientific progress and its application to the construction industry. This lag should be decreased. Code requirements sometimes prevent this. There would appear to be nothing wrong with the development of standard interchangeable building units which can be prefabricated in mass and assembled completely on the job. They should be such that the units can be put together in great variety of arrangements. It may be practical to have a standard building module, but not a standard building. Such a development might make use of mass production techniques and produce savings.

Achieving Economy Through Sound Financing

THE interest on a bond issue is as much a part of the cost of a school building as the money paid to a contractor. On a large, long-term issue, a small difference in the rate of interest may make a difference of many thousands of dollars in the ultimate cost of the project. Low interest rates are achieved by offering the bonds for sale when market conditions are right, by selling the bonds in attractive denominations, by securing competition in bidding, and by meeting fully all technical requirements that affect the safety of the purchaser's money. Legal requirements with respect to bond issues vary considerably from state to state, and in general must be strictly followed. The wise board of education and superintendent will engage expert legal and financial consultants to guide them from the first resolution leading to the bond issue to the completion of the sale.

Again, it should be pointed out that a complete long-range program includes a sound plan for financing. If building construction is systematically scheduled and needs are anticipated in advance, it may be possible to finance construction from the proceeds of an annual special tax levy deposited in a building fund. Such pay-as-you-go financing will obviously reduce the total building costs by the amount which otherwise would be paid as interest on a bond issue.

Although in some cases careful planning may make "pay-as-you-go" possible, it cannot work in a district where population increases are sharp or where, for some reason that could not be foreseen, a major portion of the total plant of the district must be replaced at one time. In very small districts and in districts faced with major needs and with low assessed valuations per child, such pay-as-you-go financing will be impractical.

Fallacies in Cost Comparisons

IN THEIR search for low-cost buildings, many boards of education, school administrators, and citizens fall into the error of assuming that the various unit costs reported to them are directly comparable and that the building with the lowest cost per square foot or per cubic foot is the most economical. The conclusion is unsound for several reasons. In the first place, the unit cost depends upon the character of the structure. A gymnasium, for example, requires far less dense construction than a classroom wing and will normally cost less per square foot or cubic foot. Secondly, an uneconomical use of space may result in a misleadingly low unit cost. For example, a building with a lot of unnecessary basement or attic area would have a relatively low cost per cubic foot, but might not be cheap in terms of usable area. Finally, the methods of computing area and cubage are not the same in all architectural offices, and two architects with the same set of drawings and cost figures might come out with different unit prices.

This whole problem of unit costs is so involved and lacking in standardization that the layman would do well to give little attention to such figures. Such comparisons as he makes between schools should be made with expert assistance and should center attention on such factors as educational suitability of the buildings and general quality of construction.

BIBLIOGRAPHICAL NOTES

THE AUTHORS of this volume have written from their experience as practitioners in the school-plant field. They have made no systematic canvass of the literature, nor have they prepared any formal bibliography in the course of their writing. At the few places where major dependence was placed upon the work of others, appropriate footnotes have been used.

The literature in the school-plant field is extensive. Bibliographies published by Indiana University list approximately 7,000 titles prior to 1937. The current rate of publication is several hundred items per year. Thus, it would appear that a complete school-plant bibliography as of today would be well in excess of 10,000 items. Many of these publications describe existing conditions or procedures in certain limited geographical areas, often only one building, or a single school district. Others consist in considerable measure of pleadings or exhortations with respect to a certain problem or procedure. Standards of various kinds are proposed, often in terms of specific dimensions or sizes. Only a few of the writings are based upon fundamental research.

Considerable sophistication is required of one who is to make effective use of this vast array of literature. The need for careful selection is evident from the number of titles available, and it is reinforced by the wide range of quality as well as kind of published material. Even with the best of selection, caution must be used in generalizing from what is read. Throughout this volume, the authors have stressed the principle that a school building should be planned in terms of the program that is most likely to be housed in it. This means that there must be no "ready-to-wear" educational specifications or plans. The answer to a planning problem in a given situation must be found through analysis of the program to be housed in that particular school, rather than by reference to what is reported or advocated in the literature.

Obviously, this does not mean that the literature is of no value. Quite the contrary, familiarity with what has been written is necessary for effective school-plant work. The competent worker in this field should be familiar with the findings of research, and he should know well the literature with respect to pertinent principles and procedures which might apply in any situation. Beyond this, his reading should serve primarily to stimulate his thinking and feed his imagination so that he can devise solutions to his own problems.

There are several types of literature which might be helpful to the school-plant worker. The major research studies, and some materials which may not be research, are summarized in the *Encyclopedia of Educational Research* [1] which is supplemented periodically by the *Review of Educational Research*. The *Guide for Planning School Plants* [2] and other publications of the National Council on Schoolhouse Construction express the judgments of the principal school-plant persons in the country and are consistent with the point of view expressed here with respect to the need for hand-tailoring in the planning of each building. The 1948 yearbook of the American Association of School Administrators [3] provides a good overview of the whole field of school plant from the point of view of the school administrator. Helpful articles also appear in the annual proceedings of the Association of School Business Officials.

These general publications include some consideration of the planning processes discussed in Part One of this volume. Other helpful references dealing with process, not including those mentioned in footnotes in Part One, are:

Caudill, William, *Toward Better School Design*. New York: F. W. Dodge Corp., 1954.

Clapp, Wilfred F., "Cooperative Planning of School Plants," *American School and University*, 24:161–164, 1952–53.

Engelhardt, N. L., Sr., "Flow Charts of School Building Planning," *American School and University*, 26:117–120, 1954–55.

Guenther, Carl F., "Educational Consultants—Their Function and Work," *American School and University*, 26:113–116, 1954–55.

Handler, A. Benjamin, "School and Municipal Relationships in Overall Community Planning," *American School and University*, 27:117–122, 1955–56.

Leggett, Stanton, "Educational Specifications for New School Buildings," *American School and University*, 22:81–84, 1950–51.

Van Nuys, Jay C., "The Architect and the Tailor-Made School," *American School and University*, 23:139–142, 1951–52.

Whitehead, Willis A., "The Architect and School Planning," *School Executive*, 66:11–14, April, 1947.

There has been much more written about the nature of the physical facilities than about the planning process. Some of these references deal with the entire

[1] Holy, T. C. and Herrick, John H., "School Plant." In Monroe, Walter S., ed., *Encyclopedia of Educational Research,* rev. ed. New York: Macmillan Co., 1950, pp. 1099–1121.

[2] National Council on Schoolhouse Construction, *Guide for Planning School Plants*. Nashville, Tenn.: The Council, 1953.

[3] American Association of School Administrators, *American School Buildings*. Washington, D. C.: The Association, 1949.

school plant and others with some one type of room or facility. Among the former are the publications of the American Association of School Administrators and the National Council on Schoolhouse Construction previously mentioned. Other helpful publications are:

Caudill, William W., and Pena, William M., "What Characterizes a Good School Building?" *School Executive*, 70:19–22, June, 1951.

Engelhardt, N. L., Engelhardt, N. L., Jr., and Leggett, Stanton, *Planning Elementary School Buildings*. New York: F. W. Dodge Corp., 1953.

———, *Planning Secondary School Buildings*. New York: Reinhold Publishing Corp., 1949.

Perkins, Lawrence B., and Cocking, Walter D., *Schools*. New York: Reinhold Publishing Corp., 1949.

The special treatises on some one aspect of a school building are very numerous and cover a wide range of quality. Some of them are prone to urge acceptance of specific standards or design details which may not be applicable in all situations, but this is not universally true. Among the more helpful special treatises are the following:

Jones, Sarah, and McJenkin, Virginia, "So You Are Building a Library," *School Executive*, 71:51–53, May, 1952.

Lee, Ata, *Space and Equipment for Homemaking Programs*. Miscellaneous No. 9, Division of Vocational Education, Office of Education, Federal Security Agency. Washington: Government Printing Office, 1950.

Leu, Donald J., "Selecting the School Site," *American School Board Journal*, 128:54, January, 1954.

Luehring, F. W., *Swimming Pool Standards*. New York: A. S. Barnes and Co., 1939.

Michigan Department of Public Instruction, *Community School Camps—A Guide for Development*. Lansing: The Department, 1951. (Mimeo.)

Music Educators National Conference, *Music Buildings, Rooms and Equipment*. Chicago: The Conference, 1955.

National Facilities Conference, *A Guide for Planning Facilities for Athletics, Recreation, Physical and Health Education*. Chicago: The Athletic Institute, 1947.

National Science Teachers Association, *School Facilities for Science Instruction*. Washington: The Association, 1954.

Neilson, Donald W., and Nixon, J. E., *Swimming Pools for Schools*. Stanford: Stanford University Press, 1954.

Reed, John Lyon, *et al.*, "Symposium: The Secondary School Plant of the Future," *American School and University*, 24:127–142, 1952–53.

Robinson, Horace W., "Auditorium and Stage Facilities," *Bulletin of the National Association of Secondary School Principals*, 33:159–172, December, 1949.

Wilson, Russell E., "*Flexible Classrooms—Practical Ideas for Modern Schoolrooms*. Detroit: Carter Co., 1953.

A helpful type of literature is the current magazines, and particularly the *American School Board Journal*, *Architectural Forum*, *Architectural Record*, *Nation's Schools*, *Progressive Architecture*, and *School Executive*. Closely akin to these is the *American School and University*, a yearbook published by the American School Publishing Corporation of New York. Many of the articles in these publications are of the kind that should be used as food for the imagination rather than as definitive answers to the reader's particular building problems.

Useful bibliographies of recent school plant literature are to be found in the *Review of Educational Research*, the *Encyclopedia of Educational Research*,[4] *American School Buildings*,[5] and *American School and University*.[6] In 1953 the Association of School Business Officials published an extensive bibliography by Levin.[7] The most extensive bibliographies are those by Henry Lester Smith and others at Indiana University, but these do not cover the literature beyond 1936.[8]

[4] Holy and Herrick, *op. cit.,* pp. 1119–1121.

[5] American Association of School Administrators, *op. cit.,* pp. 325–341.

[6] Hayes, Dale K., "School Plant Bibliography—Selected Sources and References for School Plant Planners," *American School and University*, 27: 453–472, 1955–56. (This reference also contains a list of other bibliographies.)

[7] Levin, Sol, *A Selected Bibliography of Business and Plant References for the School Administrator*. Kalamazoo: The Association of School Business Officials of the United States and Canada, 1953.

[8] Smith, Henry Lester, and Chamberlain, Leo Martin, *A Bibliography of School Buildings, Grounds, and Equipment*. Indiana University, Bulletin of the School of Education, Vol. 4, No. 3, January, 1928.

———, and Noffsinger, Forest Ruby, *Bibliography of School Buildings, Grounds, and Equipment, Part II*. Indiana University, Bulletin of the School of Education, Vol. 9, No. 2. March, 1933.

———, and Noffsinger, Forest Ruby, *Bibliography of School Buildings, Grounds, and Equipment, Part III*. Indiana University, Bulletin of the School of Education, Vol. 9, No. 3. June, 1933.

———, and Noffsinger, Forest Ruby, *Bibliography of School Buildings, Grounds, and Equipment, Part IV*. Indiana University, Bulletin of the School of Education, Vol. 11, No. 2. March, 1935.

———, and Moore, Harold E., *Bibliography of School Buildings, Grounds, and Equipment, Part V*. Indiana University, Bulletin of the School of Education, Vol. 21, No. 2. March, 1945.

———, and Moore, Harold E., *Bibliography of School Buildings, Grounds, and Equipment, Part VI*. Indiana University, Bulletin of the School of Education, Vol. 21, No. 5. September, 1945.

INDEX